STUDY GUIDE

for

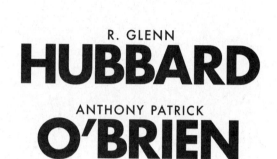

R. GLENN
HUBBARD

ANTHONY PATRICK
O'BRIEN

Kelly Blanchard
Perdue University

Jim Lee
Texas A&M University
Corpus Christi

Pearson Prentice Hall

Boston San Francisco New York
London Toronto Sydney Tokyo Singapore Madrid
Mexico City Munich Paris Cape Town Hong Kong Montreal

Executive Editor: David Alexander
Senior Developmental Editor: Lena Buonanno
Production Editor: Alison Eusden
Manufacturing Buyer: Linda Cox

Pearson Prentice Hall™ is a trademark of Pearson Education, Inc.

Prentice Hall
is an imprint of

www.pearsonhighered.com

1 2 3 4 5 6 BB 12 11 10 09

ISBN-13: 978-0-13-602201-5
ISBN-10: 0-13-602201-4

CONTENTS |

PREFACE|

Why Should You Use the Study Guide?

This Study Guide has been written for use with *Microeconomics, Third Edition,* by R. Glenn Hubbard and Anthony Patrick O'Brien. The textbook and Study Guide both apply economic principles to real-world business and policy examples. The Study Guide summarizes the material covered in the main text and provides you with additional exercises to help you practice interpreting graphs, analyzing problems, and applying the economic concepts you learn to real-life situations. The Study Guide will be especially helpful to you if this is your first course in economics. You can use many of the key concepts you will learn here in other economics and business courses you take. Please see **pages vi–ix** for a list of other resources, including MyEconLab, that you can use to help you with the course.

Study Guide Contents

Each of the 18 chapters of the Study Guide contains the following components:

1. Chapter Summary and Learning Objectives
Each chapter begins with a list of the learning objectives that appear at the beginning of each textbook chapter. Each learning objective is accompanied by a brief summary of the material in the textbook that covers that learning objective.

2. Chapter Review
This offers you a synopsis of each of the sections in each chapter. Reading the Chapter Reviews is a great way to reinforce your understanding of the material in the textbook and prepare for examinations.

3. Study Hints
Study Hints, located in the Chapter Review, will help you understand economic principles and their application through the use of examples that are different from those in the textbook. Select Study Hints also refer you to features in the textbook—for example, *Solved Problems*, *Making the Connection*, and end-of-chapter *Problems and Applications*—that relate to the topics covered in the Chapter Review.

4. Solved Problems
The textbook includes worked-out problems, usually two or three per chapter, each of which is tied to one of the learning objectives. Each of the Study Guide chapters includes one or more additional Solved Problems.

5. Key Terms
Each of the corresponding textbook chapter's bold key terms are defined.

6. Self-Test
This section of the Guide will help you prepare for quizzes and exams. There are approximately 40 multiple-choice questions, five short answer questions, and 15 true/false questions for each chapter. The answers to all questions appear at the end of the Self-Test, along with comments that help explain each answer.

Study Tips

1. *Read the textbook chapter – but don't just read the chapter*. To do well in your economics course, you must be able to apply what you learn and not just memorize definitions and read graphs. Both the textbook and the Study Guide have a number of features that allow you to apply and understand what you learn. Take advantage of these learning aids. Economics is a participant sport, not a spectator sport. Use your pencil. Draw graphs, don't just look at them. Try the calculations. Use your calculator.

2. *Attend class and ask questions*. Take this course as seriously as your instructor does. Taking days off will not help you do well in any course and is poor preparation for your life after graduation. Many students are hesitant to ask questions during or outside of classroom meetings because they feel they are the only ones who do not understand a topic (this is almost never true) or that their instructors feel they have better things to do (this is almost never true as well). Your instructor will appreciate the effort you make to learn what can be a challenging subject.

3. *Don't leave the subject in the classroom.* The key to doing well in your course is to understand how to apply economic concepts in real-world situations. Learning economics is similar to learning a new language. You will become fluent in the economic way of thinking only after you learn to recognize and apply concepts found in newspaper articles, magazines, and everyday conversation.

4. *Organize a study group*. If possible, study with other students in your class. Participating in a study group can help you learn economics—students will bring different insights to the group—and make learning more enjoyable. Explaining a topic to a friend will help you discover areas where you need to spend more study time.

More Study Resources for You

MyEconLab puts you in control of your learning through a collection of testing, practice, and study tools tied to the online, interactive version of the textbook and other media resources.

Here is a snapshot of what students are saying about MyEconLab:

"It was very useful because it had EVERYTHING, from practice exams to exercises to reading. Very helpful." —student, Northern Illinois University

"I would recommend taking the quizzes on MyEconLab because it gives you a true account of whether or not you understand the material." —student, Montana Tech

"It made me look through the book to find answers, so I did more reading." —student, Northern Illinois University

4.3 Government Intervention in the Market

◁◁ ◁ ① ② ③ ④ ⑤ ⑥ ⑦ ⑧ ⑨ ⑩ ▷ ▷▷   End of Chapter 3.7

0 correct | 0 of 27 complete

Problem 3.7. Suppose that the government sets a
price floor for milk that is above the competitive equilibrium
price.

1) In the figure to the right, identify the quantity that is sold
with the price floor using the point drawing tool. Attach the
provided label.

2) Compare the economic surplus in this market when there
is no price floor and when there is a price floor. Do this by
shading the change in economic surplus as a result of the
price floor using the triangle drawing tool. Attach the
appropriate lab[...] in[...] b[...] c[...]
(new economi[...]
(deadweight lo[...]

*If you are no[...]
the wrong dra[...]*

Price

22—
20—
18—
16—
14—
12—
10—
8—

Supply

Price floor

Quantity sold
Deadweight loss

Demand

32 36 40

⊗ **Sorry, that's not correct.**

Consumers are willing to purchase a quantity indicated where the price floor
intersects the demand curve. This quantity is less than the equilibrium amount.

(Done)

Click a line or point to select it.

? Reset

All parts showing

(Clear All)   (Check Answer) | (Close)

You can study on your own, or you can complete assignments created by your instructor. Within
MyEconLab's structured environment, you practice what you learn, test your understanding, and pursue a
personalized study plan generated from your performance on sample tests and from quizzes created by
your instructor. In Homework or Study Plan mode, you have access to a wealth of tutorial features,
including:

- Instant feedback on exercises that helps you understand and apply the concepts
- Links to the eText to promote reading of the text just when you need to revisit a concept or
  explanation
- Step-by-step guided solutions that help you to break down a problem in much the same way an
  instructor would do during office hours
- Pop-up summaries of the appropriate learning objective to remind you of key ideas while
  studying
- Pop-up key term definitions from the eText to help you master the vocabulary of economics
- Links to the important features of the eText, such as *Solved Problems*, *Making the Connection*,
  An Inside Look, and *Don't Let This Happen to YOU!*
- A graphing tool that is integrated into the various exercises to enable you to build and manipulate
  graphs so that you better understand how concepts, numbers, and graphs connect

Home | Help | Support | Inst

myeconlab

My Courses

Student
Course Home
Economic News
Quizzes & Tests
Study Plan
Homework
Results
Calendar
Textbook Resources
Student Center

Instructor
Course Manager
Homework Manager

Hide Navigation Buttons

Study Plan

Le

Click a chapter below to start practicing, or follow these steps to create a personalized study plan.

① Take a sample test or an assigned test or quiz. Then return to this page.

② Practice the topics you need to study (◄).

③ To prove mastery(✴), take another sample test or an assigned test or quiz.   ► L

[Show All] ◄ Show What I Need to Study   ➡ Jump to where I

Book Contents for All Topics	Correct	Worked	Available Exercises
⊕ Ch 1: Economics: Foundations and Models			60
⊕ Ch 2: Trade-Offs, Comparative Advantage, and the Market System			26
⊕ Ch 3: Where Prices Come From: The Interaction of Demand and Supply			49
⊕ Ch 4: Economic Efficiency, Government Price Setting, and Taxes			49
⊕ Ch 5: Externalities, Environmental Policy, and Public Goods			37

⏮ ◀ ① ② ③ ④ ⑤ ⑥ ⑦ ⑧ ▶ ⏭   End of Chapter 4.4

0 correct | 0 of 8 complete

Problem 4.4. In the graph on the right, the demand for hamburger buns has changed because the price of hamburgers has risen from $2.50 to $2.60 per package.

Hamburger buns
Price (dollars per package of buns)
4.00

Guided Solution

Cross-price elasticities measure the change in quantity demanded of one product when the price of a *related* good changes. For example, hamburger buns are related to hamburger meat. The two goods complement each other. When consumption of one good increases, the amount consumed of the related good increases, also.

We calculate the cross-price elasticity of demand using the formula below.

$$\text{Cross-price elasticity of demand} = \frac{\text{Percentage change in quantity demanded of one good}}{\text{Percentage change in price of another good}} = \frac{(Q_2 - Q_1)}{\left(\frac{Q_1 + Q_2}{2}\right)} \div \frac{(P_2 - P_1)}{\left(\frac{P_1 + P_2}{2}\right)}$$

As when computing the price elasticity of demand, we use the midpoint formula. The only difference is instead of computing the percentage change in the good's own price, we use the percentage change in the price of the related good.

Press Continue to see more.   ?

5 parts remaining   [Continue]   [Close]

MyEconLab includes the following additional features:

- **eText**—In addition to the portions of eText available as pop-ups or links, a fully searchable eText is available if you want to read and study in a fully electronic environment.
- **Print upgrade**—If you want to complete assignments in MyEconLab but read in print, Pearson offers registered MyEconLab users a loose-leaf version of the print text at a significant discount.
- **Glossary flashcards**—Every key term is available as a flashcard, allowing you to quiz yourself on vocabulary from one or more chapters at a time.
- **Research Navigator (CourseCompass version only)**—Research Navigator provides extensive help on the research process and four exclusive databases of credible and reliable source material, including *The New York Times*, the *Financial Times*, and peer-reviewed journals.

PowerPoint® Slides

Download PowerPoint® slides from **www.pearsonhighered.com/hubbard**, and use them as a study aide or bring them to class to take notes during the lecture. The slides include:

- All graphs, tables, and equations in the text
- Figures in step-by-step, automated mode, using a single click per graph curve
- End-of-chapter key terms with hyperlinks to relevant slides

eTextbook

CourseSmart goes beyond traditional expectations providing instant, online access to the textbooks and course materials you need at lower cost. You can also search, highlight, and take notes anywhere at anytime. See all the benefits to you at **www.coursesmart.com/students**.

CHAPTER 1 | Economics: Foundations and Models

Chapter Summary and Learning Objectives

1.1 Three Key Economic Ideas (pages 4–7)

Explain these three key economic ideas: People are rational. People respond to incentives. Optimal decisions are made at the margin. **Economics** is the study of the choices consumers, business managers, and government officials make to attain their goals, given their scarce resources. We must make choices because of **scarcity**, which means that although our wants are unlimited, the resources available to fulfill those wants are limited. Economists assume that people are rational in the sense that consumers and firms use all available information as they take actions intended to achieve their goals. Rational individuals weigh the benefits and costs of each action and choose an action only if the benefits outweigh the costs. Although people act from a variety of motives, ample evidence indicates that they respond to economic incentives. Economists use the word **marginal** to mean extra or additional. The optimal decision is to continue any activity up to the point where the marginal benefit equals the marginal cost.

1.2 The Economic Problem That Every Society Must Solve (pages 7–11)

Discuss how an economy answers these questions: What goods and services will be produced? How will the goods and services be produced? Who will receive the goods and services produced? Society faces **trade-offs**: Producing more of one good or service means producing less of another good or service. The **opportunity cost** of any activity—such as producing a good or service—is the highest-valued alternative that must be given up to engage in that activity. The choices of consumers, firms, and governments determine what goods and services will be produced. Firms choose how to produce the goods and services they sell. In the United States, who receives the goods and services produced depends largely on how income is distributed in the marketplace. In a **centrally planned economy**, most economic decisions are made by the government. In a **market economy**, most economic decisions are made by consumers and firms. Most economies, including that of the United States, are **mixed economies** in which most economic decisions are made by consumers and firms but in which the government also plays a significant role. There are two types of efficiency: **Productive efficiency** occurs when a good or service is produced at the lowest possible cost. **Allocative efficiency** occurs when production is in accordance with consumer preferences. **Voluntary exchange** is a situation that occurs in markets when both the buyer and seller of a product are made better off by the transaction. Equity is more difficult to define than efficiency, but it usually involves a fair distribution of economic benefits. Government policymakers often face a trade-off between equity and efficiency.

1.3 Economic Models (pages 11–14)

Understand the role of models in economic analysis. Economists rely on **economic models**, which are simplified versions of reality used to analyze real-world economic situations. Economists accept and use an economic model if it leads to hypotheses that are confirmed by statistical analysis. In many cases, the acceptance is tentative, however, pending the gathering of new data or further statistical analysis. Economics is a *social science* because it applies the scientific method to the study of the interactions among individuals. Economics is concerned with **positive analysis**—what is—rather than **normative analysis**—what ought to be. As a social science, economics considers human behavior in every context of decision making, not just in business.

1.4   Microeconomics and Macroeconomics (pages 14–15)
Distinguish between microeconomics and macroeconomics. **Microeconomics** is the study of how households and firms make choices, how they interact in markets, and how the government attempts to influence their choices. **Macroeconomics** is the study of the economy as a whole, including topics such as inflation, unemployment, and economic growth.

1.5   A Preview of Important Economic Terms (pages 15–16)
Become familiar with important economic terms. A necessary step in learning economics is to become familiar with important economic terms, including *entrepreneur, innovation, technology, firm, goods, services, revenue, profit, household, factors of production, capital,* and *human capital.*

Appendix: Using Graphs and Formulas (pages 24–35)
Review the use of graphs and formulas.

Chapter Review

Chapter Opener: Microsoft Versus the U.S. Congress on Worker Visas (page 3)
Information technology firms, like Microsoft, often have difficulty filling positions with U.S. citizens. While foreign workers could fill some of these vacancies, worker visas for foreign workers are limited in the United States. Tighter controls on worker visas continue to restrict the ability of U.S. firms to hire foreign workers.

The textbook describes how economics is used to answer many important questions, including the economic effect of the immigration of skilled workers. All of these questions represent a basic economic fact of life: people must make choices as they try to attain their goals. These choices occur because of scarcity, which is the most fundamental economic concept. The resources available to any society—for example, land and labor—to produce the goods and services its citizens want are limited. Society must choose which goods and services will be produced and who will receive them.

1.1   **Three Key Economic Ideas (pages 4–7)**
Learning Objective: Explain these three key economic ideas: People are rational. People respond to incentives. Optimal decisions are made at the margin.

Economics examines how people interact in markets. A **market** refers to a group of buyers and sellers of a good or service and the institution or arrangement by which they come together to trade. Economists make three important assumptions about the way people interact in markets. First, people are rational. This means that buyers and sellers use all available information to achieve their goals. Second, people act in response to economic incentives. Third, optimal decisions are made at the margin. The terms *marginal benefit* and *marginal cost* refer to the additional benefits and costs of a decision. Economists reason that the best, or optimal, decision is to continue any activity up to the point where the marginal benefit (or MB) equals the marginal cost (MC). In symbols, we can write $MB = MC$.

 Study Hint
You should not assume that the phrase "people respond to economic incentives" means that people are greedy. This phrase is an objective statement or a statement shown to be true rather than a belief or an opinion. Economists do not believe people are motivated solely by monetary incentives. Many people voluntarily devote their time and financial resources to friends, family members, and charities.

The first *Solved Problem* is at the end of this section of the textbook. Each *Solved Problem* helps you understand one of the chapter's learning objectives. The authors use a step-by-step process to show how you can solve the problem. Additional Solved Problems, different from those that appear in the textbook, are included in each chapter of this Study Guide. Work through each of these to improve your understanding of the material presented in each chapter.

1.2 The Economic Problem That Every Society Must Solve (pages 7–11)

Learning Objective: Discuss how an economy answers these questions: What goods and services will be produced? How will the goods and services be produced? Who will receive the goods and services produced?

The basic economic problem any society faces is that it has only a limited amount of economic resources and so can produce only a limited amount of goods and services. Societies face **trade-offs** when answering the three fundamental economic questions:

1. *What* goods and services will be produced?
2. *How* will the goods and services be produced?
3. *Who* will receive the goods and services produced?

The **opportunity cost** of any activity is the highest-valued alternative that must be given up to engage in that activity.

Societies organize their economies in two main ways. A **centrally planned economy** is an economy in which the government decides how economic resources will be allocated. From 1917 to 1991, the Soviet Union was the most important centrally planned economy. Today Cuba and North Korea are among the few remaining centrally planned economies. A **market economy** is an economy in which the decisions of households and firms interacting in markets allocate economic resources. The United States, Canada, Western Europe, and Japan all have market economies. Privately owned firms must produce and sell goods and services that consumers want to stay in business. An individual's income is determined by the payments he receives for what he has to sell.

📖 Study Hint

In a centrally planned economy, government officials or "planners" are responsible for determining how much of each good to produce, who should produce it, and where it should be produced. In contrast, in a market economy no government official determines how much corn, wheat, or potatoes should be produced. Individual producers and consumers interact in markets for these goods to determine the answers to *What? How?* and *Who?* The role of government in a market economy is similar to that of an umpire in a baseball game. Government officials can pass and enforce laws that allow people to act in certain ways, but they do not participate directly in markets as consumers or producers.

The high rates of unemployment and business bankruptcies of the Great Depression caused a dramatic increase in government intervention in the economy in the United States and other market economies. Some government intervention is designed to raise the incomes of the elderly, the sick, and people with limited skills. In recent years, government intervention has expanded to meet social goals such as the protection of the environment and the promotion of civil rights. The expanded role of government in market economies has led most economists to argue that the United States and other nations have **mixed economies** rather than market economies.

Market economies tend to be more efficient than planned economies because market economies promote competition and **voluntary exchange**. There are two types of efficiency. **Productive efficiency** occurs when a good or service is produced at the lowest possible cost. **Allocative efficiency** is a state of the economy in which production represents consumer preferences. Specifically, every good or service is produced up to the point where the marginal benefit that the last unit produced provides to consumers is equal to the marginal cost of producing it. Inefficiencies do occur in markets for three main reasons. First, it may take time for firms to achieve productive efficiency. Second, governments may reduce efficiency by interfering with voluntary exchanges in markets. Third, production of some goods may harm the environment when firms ignore the costs of environmental damage.

Society may not find efficient economic outcomes to be the most desirable outcomes. Many people prefer economic outcomes that they consider fair or equitable even if these outcomes are less efficient. **Equity** is the fair distribution of economic benefits.

Extra Solved Problem 1-2
Advising New Government Leaders
Supports Learning Objective 1.2: Discuss how an economy answers these questions: What goods and services will be produced? How will the goods and services be produced? Who will receive the goods and services?

Suppose that a poor nation experienced a change in government leadership. Prior to this change the nation employed a centrally planned economy to allocate its resources. The new leaders are willing to try a different system if someone can convince them that it will yield better results. They hire an economist from a nation with a market economy to advise them and will order their citizens to follow the advisor's recommendations for change. The economist suggests that a market economy replace central planning to answer the nation's economic questions (*what, how,* and *who*?).

a. What will the economist suggest the leaders order their citizens to do?

b. Do you believe the leaders and citizens will accept the economist's suggestions?

SOLVING THE PROBLEM:
Step 1:   Review the chapter material.
The problem concerns which economic system a nation must select, so you may wish to review the section "Centrally Planned Economies versus Market Economies" on page 9 of the textbook.

Step 2:   What will the economist suggest the leaders order their citizens to do?
Market economies allow members of households to select occupations and purchase goods and services based on self-interest and allow privately-owned firms to produce goods and services based on their self-interests. Therefore, the economist would advise the leaders of the poor country to not issue any orders.

Step 3:   Do you believe the leaders and citizens will accept the economist's suggestions?
Even democratically elected leaders, especially those with significant government involvement in the nation's resource allocation, will find it difficult to accept the new system. They may wonder how self-interested individuals will produce and distribute goods and services to promote the welfare of the entire nation. This new system requires a significant reduction in government influence in people's lives; history has shown that government officials are often reluctant to give up this influence. Acceptance is most likely when the leaders have some knowledge and experience with the successful operation of a market economy in other

countries. Ordinary citizens are more likely to accept the economist's suggestions because they will have more freedom to pursue their own economic goals.

1.3 Economic Models (pages 11–14)
Learning Objective: Understand the role of models in economic analysis.

Models are simplified versions of reality used to analyze real-world situations. To develop a model, economists generally follow five steps.

1. Decide on the assumptions to use in developing the model.
2. Formulate a testable hypothesis.
3. Use economic data to test the hypothesis.
4. Revise the model if it fails to explain well the economic data.
5. Retain the revised model to help answer similar economic questions in the future.

Models rely on assumptions because models must be simplified to be useful. For example, models make behavioral assumptions about the motives of consumers and firms. Economists assume that consumers will buy the goods and services that will maximize their satisfaction and that firms will produce the goods and services that will maximize their profits.

An **economic variable** is something measurable that can have different values, such as the wages of software programmers. A *hypothesis* is a statement that may be correct or incorrect about an economic variable. An economic hypothesis usually states a causal relationship where a change in one variable causes a change in another variable. For example, "outsourcing leads to lower wages for software programmers" means that an increase in the amount of outsourcing will reduce the wages of software programmers. **Positive analysis** is analysis concerned with what is and involves questions that can be estimated. **Normative analysis** is analysis concerned with what ought to be and involves questions of values and basic assumptions.

 Study Hint
The feature *Don't Let This Happen to YOU!* appears in each chapter to alert you to mistakes often made by economics students. To reinforce the difference between positive and normative statements, review *Don't Let This Happen To YOU!* "Don't Confuse Positive Analysis with Normative Analysis," in which the minimum wage law is discussed. Positive analysis can show us the effects of the minimum wage law on the economy, but it cannot tell us whether the policy is good or bad. Nor can positive analysis tell us whether we should increase or decrease the minimum wage. The discussion of whether a policy is good or bad will depend on an individual's values and experiences and falls under the realm of normative analysis.

Positive economic analysis deals with statements that can be proved correct or incorrect by examining facts. If your instructor stated, "It is snowing outside," it would be easy to determine whether this statement is true or false by looking out a window. Normative analysis concerns statements of belief or opinion. If your instructor wants to go skiing that evening and states, "It *should* be snowing outside today," you could not prove the statement wrong because it is a statement of *opinion*. It is important to recognize the difference between these two types of statements.

Extra Solved Problem 1-3

Sunspot Activity and Economic Growth

Supports Learning Objective 1.3: Understand the role of models in economic analysis.

Sunspots are sites of strong magnetic fields that appear as dark regions on the surface of the sun. The number of sunspots varies over an 11-year cycle. British economist William Stanley Jevons (1835–1882) advanced a theory, or model, of economic growth based on the occurrence of sunspots. Changes in the number of sunspots cause variations in the earth's temperature and, according to this theory, changes in agricultural output. Agriculture accounted for a much greater share of total output of the economies of Great Britain and other nations in Jevons' time than in modern times.

Source: *History of Economic Theory and Thought. Jevons Sunspot and Commercial Activity*
http://www.economictheories.org/2008/08/jevons-sunspots-and-commercial-activity.html

How can we develop and test a sunspot model of economic growth?

SOLVING THE PROBLEM:

Step 1:   **Review the chapter material.**

The problem concerns how models are used to analyze economic issues, so you may wish to review the section "Economic Models," which begins on page 11 of the textbook.

Step 2:   **To develop and test a sunspot model of economic growth, we follow these steps:**

1. *Decide on the assumptions to use in developing the model.* Two assumptions of Jevons' model are: (a) Changes in the earth's temperature are related to the amount of sunspot activity. (b) Changes in the earth's temperature cause variations in the value of a nation's output of goods and services.

2. *Formulate a testable hypothesis.* The value of a nation's output of goods and services is greater in years of greater than average sunspot activity than in years of lower than average sunspot activity.

3. *Use economic data to test the hypothesis.* Compare changes in sunspot activity with changes in a standard measure of the value of a nation's output of goods and services; the most common measure is Gross Domestic Product or GDP. Because sunspot activity varies in 11-year cycles, data should cover at least one of these cycles. If data for the United States are used, years of greater than average sunspot activity should be associated with years of above average economic growth, while years of lower than average sunspot activity should be associated with years of below average economic growth.

4. *Revise the model if it fails to explain well the economic data.* The model could fail if factors other than sunspot activity have a significant impact on economic growth. These factors include variations in the price of energy, investments in new technologies, and changes in tax rates and other government policies. A revised model would examine the separate influence of sunspots and these other factors.

5. *Retain the revised model to help answer similar economic questions in the future.* Although the sunspot model is based on a plausible relationship between climate changes and changes in agricultural production, agriculture accounts for a much smaller percentage of the output produced in the United States, Great Britain, and other western nations in the 21st century than it did in the 19th century. In turn, other factors have been shown to be important in affecting economic growth.

1.4 Microeconomics and Macroeconomics (pages 14–15)

Learning Objective: Distinguish between microeconomics and macroeconomics.

Microeconomics is the study of how households and firms make choices, how they interact in markets, and how the government attempts to influence their choices. **Macroeconomics** is the study of the economy as a whole, including topics such as inflation, unemployment, and economic growth.

Extra Solved Problem 1-4

Watching From On High—and Low

Supports Learning Objective 1.4: Distinguish between microeconomics and macroeconomics.

Sports fans are accustomed to seeing game action on television from different camera angles. For popular events such as the Olympics, World Series, and Super Bowl, network coverage captures action from ground level as well as from higher locations. At many events there is a camera located in a blimp that circles above the venue where the event is held. The aerial view of the blimp's camera is often visually appealing but is never broadcast for very long; the athletes can be seen only from a great distance, if they can be seen at all. Coverage of the events often includes a view from a mobile or "sideline" camera that can zoom in on individual players or fans sitting in the stands, a degree of detail in stark contrast to that provided by the aerial view. How do the different camera angles help to explain the difference between microeconomics and macroeconomics?

SOLVING THE PROBLEM:

Step 1:   **Review the chapter material.**

The problem concerns the differences between microeconomics and macroeconomics, so you may want to review the section "Microeconomics and Macroeconomics" on page 14 in the textbook.

Step 2:   **Compare the focus of microeconomics with the television coverage of a sports event.**

Microeconomics focuses on how individual households and firms make choices, how they interact in markets, and how the government attempts to influence their choices. This focus is similar to that of a sideline camera at a football game. The camera can focus in on an individual player or fan.

Step 3:   **Compare the focus of macroeconomics with the television coverage of a sports event.**

Macroeconomics is the study of the economy as a whole, including topics such as inflation, unemployment, and economic growth. Macroeconomics does not study the decisions made by individuals but the consequences of the actions of all decision makers in an economy. This is similar to the blimp's aerial view of the venue where a sports event occurs. You can see the entire venue, but the blimp's point of view is too far away to see any individual player or fan.

1.5 A Preview of Important Economic Terms (pages 15–16)

Learning Objective: Become familiar with important economic terms.

This chapter introduces twelve economic terms that will each be covered in depth in future chapters. Those terms are: *entrepreneur, innovation, technology, firm, goods, services, revenue, profit, household, factors of production, capital, and human capital.*

Appendix
Using Graphs and Formulas (pages 24–35)
Learning Objective: Review the use of graphs and formulas.

Graphs of One Variable

Bar charts, pie charts, and time-series graphs are alternative ways to display data visually. Figures 1A-1 and 1A-2 illustrate how relationships are often easier to understand with graphs than with words or tables alone.

Graphs of Two Variables

Both microeconomics and macroeconomics use two-variable graphs extensively to show the relationship between two variables.

You need to understand how to measure the slope of a straight line drawn in a graph. The slope of a straight line can be measured between any two points on a line because the slope of a straight line has a constant value, so we don't need to worry about the value of the slope changing as we move up and down the line. Slope can be measured as the change in the value measured on the vertical axis divided by the change in the value measured on the horizontal axis. In symbols, the slope formula is written as $\Delta y/\Delta x$. The formula is also described as "rise over run." The usual custom is to place the variable y on the graph's vertical axis and the variable x the horizontal axis. If the slope is negative, then the two variables are inversely (or negatively) related. If the slope is positive, then the two variables are directly (or positively) related. Keep in mind that a relationship between any two variables does not necessarily imply a cause and effect relationship between those two variables.

We can show the effect of more than two variables in a graph by shifting the line representing the relationship between the first two variables. For example, we can draw a graph showing the effect of a change in the price of pizza on the quantity of pizza demanded during a given week. We can then shift this line to show the effect of a change in the price of hamburgers on the quantity of pizza demanded.

If the relationship between two variables is nonlinear, you can still calculate the slope. The slope of a nonlinear curve at a given point is measured by the slope of the line that is tangent to that point.

Formulas

The formula for a percentage change of a variable over time (or growth rate) is:

$$\frac{\text{Value in the second period} - \text{Value in the first period}}{\text{Value in the first period}} \times 100$$

The formula for the area of a rectangle is Base × Height. The formula for the area of a triangle is ½ × Base × Height.

Key Terms

Allocative efficiency A state of the economy in which production is in accordance with consumer preferences; in particular, every good or service is produced up to the point where the last unit provides a marginal benefit to society equal to the marginal cost of producing it.

Centrally planned economy An economy in which the government decides how economic resources will be allocated.

Economic model A simplified version of reality used to analyze real-world economic situations.

Economic variable Something measurable that can have different values, such as the wages of software programmers.

Economics The study of the choices people make to attain their goals, given their scarce resources.

Equity The fair distribution of economic benefits.

Macroeconomics The study of the economy as a whole, including topics such as inflation, unemployment, and economic growth.

Marginal analysis Analysis that involves comparing marginal benefits and marginal costs.

Market A group of buyers and sellers of a good or service and the institution or arrangement by which they come together to trade.

Market economy An economy in which the decisions of households and firms interacting in markets allocate economic resources.

Microeconomics The study of how households and firms make choices, how they interact in markets, and how the government attempts to influence their choices.

Mixed economy An economy in which most economic decisions result from the interaction of buyers and sellers in markets but in which the government plays a significant role in the allocation of resources.

Normative analysis Analysis concerned with what ought to be.

Opportunity cost The highest-valued alternative that must be given up to engage in an activity.

Positive analysis Analysis concerned with what is.

Productive efficiency A situation in which a good or service is produced at the lowest possible cost.

Scarcity A situation in which unlimited wants exceed the limited resources available to fulfill those wants.

Trade-off The idea that because of scarcity, producing more of one good or service means producing less of another good or service.

Voluntary exchange A situation that occurs in markets when both the buyer and seller of a product are made better off by the transaction.

Self-Test

(Answers are provided at the end of the Self-Test.)

Multiple-Choice Questions

1. Which of the following questions could be answered using economics?
    a. "How are the prices of goods and services determined?"
    b. "How does pollution affect the economy, and how should government policy deal with these effects?"
    c. "Why do firms engage in international trade, and how do government policies affect international trade?"
    d. All of the above are economic questions.

2. Which of the following statements best defines scarcity?
    a. Scarcity studies the choices people make to attain their goals.
    b. Scarcity is a situation in which unlimited wants exceed the limited resources available to fulfill those wants.
    c. Scarcity is an imbalance between buyers and sellers in a specific market.
    d. Scarcity refers to a lack of trade-offs.

3. When you think of an arrangement or institution that brings buyers and sellers of a good or service together, what are you thinking of?
    a. marginal analysis
    b. a market
    c. scarcity
    d. rational behavior

4. Fill in the blanks. In economics, as well as in life, optimal decisions are made _____.
    a. once all costs have been considered
    b. only when all benefits have been considered
    c. in their totality
    d. at the margin

5. In Solved Problem 1-1: "Apple Computer Makes a Decision at the Margin" which of the concepts below is most applicable in solving the problem?
    a. the concept of what a market is
    b. rational behavior and how people respond to economic incentives
    c. marginal analysis
    d. the concept of scarcity and trade-offs

6. Which of the following is not among the fundamental economic questions that every society must solve?
    a. What goods and services will be produced?
    b. How will the goods and services be produced?
    c. What goods and services will be exchanged?
    d. Who will receive the goods and services produced?

7. What types of economies require that answers be given to the following questions: what goods and services will be produced, how will the goods and services be produced, and who will receive the goods and services produced?
    a. market economies
    b. centrally planned economies
    c. mixed economies
    d. all of the above

8. In what type of economy does the government decide how economic resources will be allocated?
    a. a market economy
    b. a mixed economy
    c. a centrally planned economy
    d. none of the above

9. Which of the following is the best classification for the economies of the United States, Canada, Japan, and Western Europe?
    a. market economies
    b. mixed economies
    c. centrally planned economies
    d. none of the above

10. Which of the following terms best refers to a fair distribution of economic benefits?
    a. productive efficiency
    b. allocative efficiency
    c. voluntary exchange
    d. equity

11. Which of the following is achieved when a good or service is produced up to the point where the marginal benefit to consumers is equal to the marginal cost of producing it?
    a. productive efficiency
    b. allocative efficiency
    c. equality
    d. equity

12. Which of the following terms summarizes the situation in which a buyer and a seller exchange a product in a market and, as a result, both are made better off by the transaction?
    a. productive efficiency
    b. allocative efficiency
    c. voluntary exchange
    d. equity

13. What does an economy achieve by producing a good or service at the least possible cost?
    a. productive efficiency
    b. allocative efficiency
    c. voluntary exchange
    d. equity

14. Which of the following best describes the characteristics of models used in economics?
    a. Models are approximations to reality that capture as many details as possible.
    b. Models are usually complex abstractions of reality that simulate practical problems.
    c. Models are concerned with what economic policies ought to be.
    d. Models are simplifications of reality that include only essential elements and exclude less relevant details.

15. Which of the following is not an essential component of an economic model?
    a. assumptions
    b. hypotheses
    c. variables
    d. normative statements

16. What is the purpose of an economic hypothesis?
    a. to establish a behavioral assumption
    b. to establish a causal relationship
    c. to make a statement based on fact
    d. to determine the validity of statistical analyses used in testing a model

17. What type of economic analysis is concerned with the way things ought to be?
    a. positive analysis
    b. marginal analysis
    c. normative analysis
    d. rational behavior

18. What type of statement would "A minimum wage actually reduces employment" be considered?
    a. a positive statement
    b. a marginal statement
    c. a normative statement
    d. an irrational conclusion

19. Which of the following is an example of a positive question?
    a. Should the university offer free parking to students?
    b. Should the university provide more financial aid assistance to students?
    c. If the college increased tuition, would class sizes decline?
    d. Should the college cut tuition to increase enrollments?

20. Which of the following questions can be answered using normative economic reasoning?
    a. If a college offers free parking, will more students drive to campus?
    b. If a college provided more financial aid, would more students go to college?
    c. If a college hires better qualified instructors, will more students attend?
    d. Should a college cut tuition to stimulate enrollments?

21. Which of the following involves an estimation of the benefits and costs of a particular action?
    a. positive analysis
    b. normative analysis
    c. the market mechanism
    d. an irrational conclusion

22. What type of assessment is one in which a person's values and political views form part of that assessment?
    a. a positive assessment
    b. a normative assessment
    c. a microeconomic assessment
    d. a macroeconomic assessment

23. Fill in the blank: _____ is the study of how households and businesses make choices, how they interact in markets, and how the government influences their choices.
    a. Microeconomics
    b. Macroeconomics
    c. A market mechanism
    d. Marginal analysis

24. Which of the following covers the study of topics such as inflation and unemployment?
    a. microeconomics
    b. macroeconomics
    c. Both microeconomics and macroeconomics give equal emphasis to these problems.
    d. none of the above

25. What is the name given to the development of a new good or a new process for making a good?
    a. an invention
    b. an innovation
    c. entrepreneurship
    d. capital

26. What is the name given to the practical application of an invention?
    a. a model
    b. an innovation
    c. voluntary exchange
    d. capital

27. What is the stock of computers, factory buildings, and machine tools used to produce goods better known as?
    a. physical capital
    b. technology
    c. innovation
    d. goods and services

28. Human capital is
    a. physical capital produced by human resources.
    b. stocks and bonds that are owned by humans rather than corporations.
    c. the accumulated training and skills that workers possess.
    d. physical capital owned by humans rather than corporations.

29. Which of the following graphs shown below is the graph of a single variable?

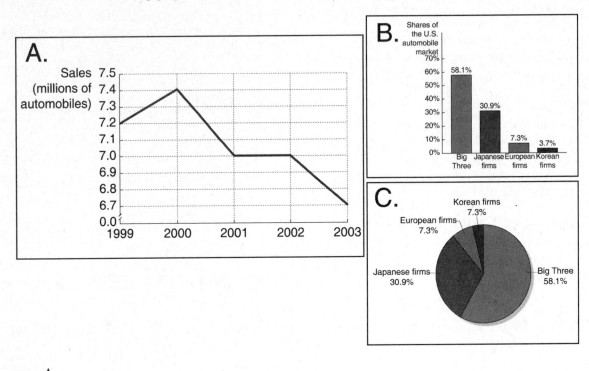

a. A
b. B
c. C
d. all of the above

30. Which of the following is a graph of the relationship between two variables?

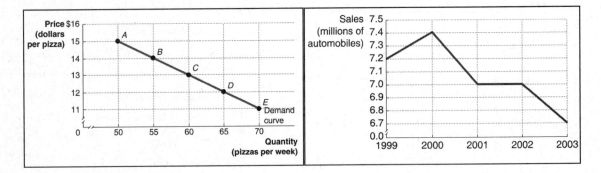

a. the graph on the left
b. the graph on the right
c. both graphs
d. neither graph

31. Fill in the blanks. The slope of a straight line equals the change in value on the _____ axis _____ by the change in the value on the other axis between any two points on the line.
a. horizontal; multiplied
b. horizontal; divided
c. vertical; multiplied
d. vertical; divided

32. Refer to the graph below. What is the value of the slope of this line?

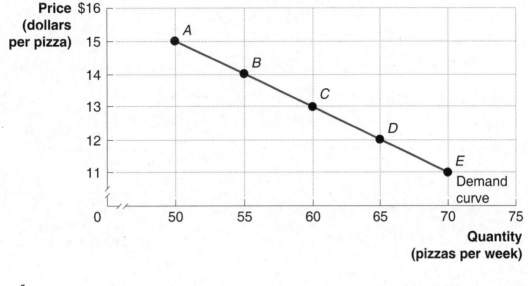

a. −5
b. −1/5
c. −1
d. There is insufficient information to compute the slope of this line.

33. Refer to the graph below. Which of the following explains why the line shifts to the right?

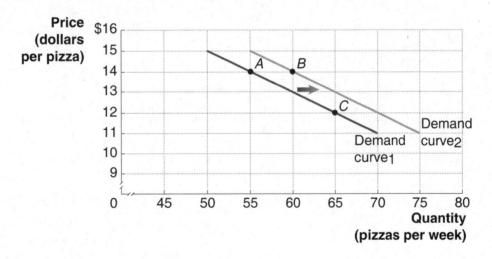

a. There was a change in the price of pizza.
b. There was a change in the quantity of pizza demanded.
c. There was a change in a third variable other than the price or quantity of pizza demanded.
d. all of the above

34. Refer to the graph below. How many variables are involved in explaining the move from point *A* to point *C* on this graph?

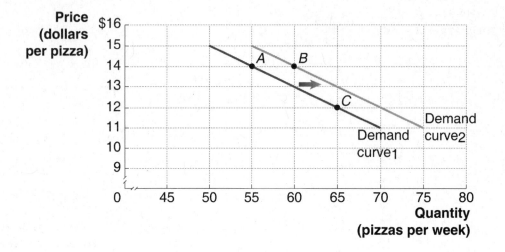

a.   one
b.   two
c.   three
d.   more than three, at least four

35. Suppose that there are three variables involved in the graph below: (1) quantity, (2) price, and (3) a third variable. Which of those variables causes the move from point *C* to point *D* in the graph?

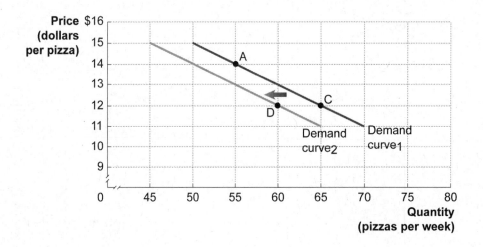

a.   the first variable, quantity
b.   the second variable, price
c.   the third variable
d.   either a. or b.

36. Refer to the graph below. What is the best descriptor of the relationship between disposable personal income and consumption spending?

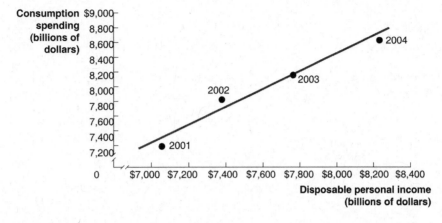

a. a positive relationship
b. a negative relationship
c. a relationship that is sometimes positive and sometimes negative
d. a relationship that may be positive and negative, but sometimes neither positive nor negative

37. Refer to the graph below. What can be said about the value of the slope of this curve?

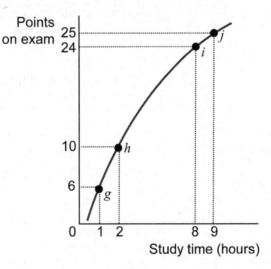

a. The value of the slope is greater between points i and j than between points g and h.
b. The value of the slope is greater between points g and h than between points i and j.
c. The value of the slope is the same between any two points along the curve.
d. We cannot determine whether the slope is greater between g and h or i and j because the relationship between "Points on exam' and "Study time" is not linear.

38. Let V_1 equal the value of a variable in period 1, and V_2 equal the value of the same variable in period 2. What is the rate of growth between periods 1 and 2?
    a. $[(V_1 + V_2)/2] \times 100$
    b. $[(V_2 - V_1)/V_1] \times 100$
    c. $(V_2 - V_1)/(V_1 + V_2)$
    d. $V_2 - V_1$

39. Refer to the graph below. Which of the formulas below must you apply to compute the shaded area shown on the graph?

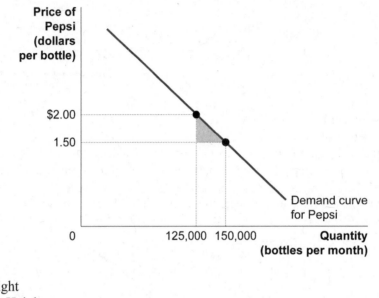

    a. Base × Height
    b. ½ × Base × Height
    c. 2 × Base × Height
    d. none of the above

40. Refer to the graph below. What is the name of the area contained in rectangle A?

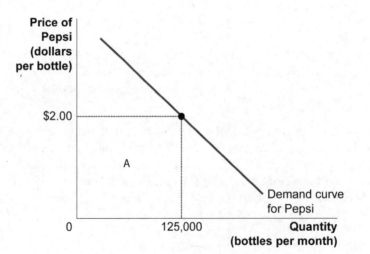

 a. total cost
 b. total revenue
 c. price
 d. average cost

41. Refer to the graph below. What is the value of the shaded area shown on the graph?

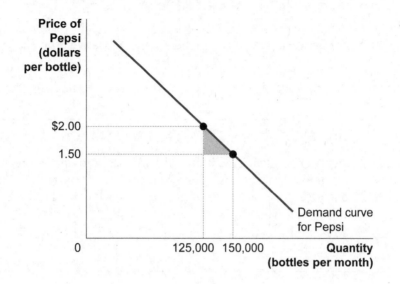

 a. $300,000
 b. $225,000
 c. $62,500
 d. $6,250

42. Refer to the graph below. What is the value of the area contained in rectangle A?

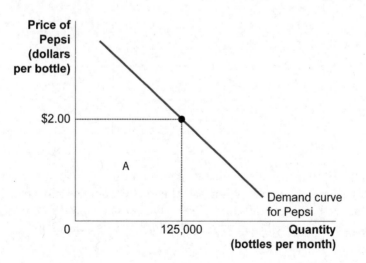

 a. $2.00
 b. $125,000
 c. $250,000
 d. There is not enough information to determine the area.

Short Answer Questions

1. Why do economists distinguish between financial capital and physical capital?

   _____

   _____

2. Explain the difference between productive efficiency and allocative efficiency.

   _____

   _____

3. Economists rely on economic models and tests of hypotheses to analyze real-world issues. The use of models and hypothesis testing is common in the natural sciences such as physics and chemistry. Yet, economics is considered a social science, not a natural science. Why?

   _____

   _____

   _____

   _____

4. Write an example of a positive statement and an example of a normative statement.

   _____

   _____

   _____

   _____

5. Duncan Grant, a freshman economics student at John Borts University, claimed that fresh water is a necessity for all human beings. When asked by his economics instructor if he would be willing to buy a 16 ounce bottle of water for $5.00, Duncan declined. What economic principle would explain Duncan's refusal to buy something that he insists is a necessity?

   _____

   _____

True/False Questions

T F 1.   Stating a hypothesis in an economic model is an example of normative analysis.

T F 2.   An entrepreneur is someone who works for a government agency.

T F 3.   Economists assume that human beings respond only to monetary incentives.

T F 4.   In a centrally planned economy the goods and services produced are always distributed equally to all citizens.

T F 5.   Equity is achieved when economic benefits are equally distributed.

T F 6.   A mixed economy is an economy in which the three fundamental questions (*What? How? Who?*) are answered by a mixture of consumers and producers.

T F 7.   Both market economies and centrally planned economies face trade-offs when producing goods and services.

T F 8.   When economists assume people are rational, this means that consumers and firms use available information to achieve their goals.

T F 9.   Government intervention in the U.S. economy increased dramatically as a result of the Great Depression.

T F 10. Economists use normative analysis to show that the minimum wage law causes unemployment.

T F 11. Microeconomics is the study of how households and firms make choices, how they interact in markets, and how the government attempts to influence their choices.

T F 12. The slope of a straight line is the same at any point.

T F 13. To measure the slope of a nonlinear curve at a particular point one must draw a straight line from the origin to the point. The slope of this line is equal to the slope of the curve at that point.

T F 14. All societies face the economic problem of having a limited amount of economic resources.

T F 15. Economic models can help analyze simple real-world economic situations but are of little value in analyzing complicated economic situations.

Answers to the Self-Test

Multiple-Choice Questions

Question	Answer	Comment
1	d	In this textbook, we use economics to answer questions such as those found in all of the choices given.
2	b	This is the textbook definition of scarcity.
3	b	This is the definition of a market.
4	d	The textbook presents three important ideas: People are rational; people respond to economic incentives; optimal decisions are made at the margin.
5	c	In solving the problem, the most applicable concept is that optimal decisions are made at the margin. An activity should be continued to the point where the marginal benefit is equal to the marginal cost.
6	c	The three questions are: What goods and services will be produced? How will the goods and services be produced? Who will receive the goods and services produced?
7	d	These questions refer to the economic problem *every* society must solve.
8	c	A centrally planned economy is an economy in which the government decides how economic resources will be allocated.
9	b	A mixed economy is an economy in which most economic decisions result from

		the interaction of buyers and sellers in markets, but where the government plays a significant role in the allocation of resources.
10	d	Equity, or fairness, refers to the fair distribution of economic benefits.
11	b	This is a state of the economy in which production reflects consumer preferences; in particular, every good or service is produced up to the point where the last unit produced provides a marginal benefit to consumers equal to the marginal cost of producing it.
12	c	This occurs in markets when both the buyer and the seller of a product are made better off by the transaction.
13	a	Productive efficiency occurs when a good or service is produced at the lowest possible cost.
14	d	Economic models are simplified versions of some aspects of economic life used to analyze economic issues.
15	d	Normative statements, statements concerned with what ought to be, are not components of an economic model.
16	b	An economic hypothesis is usually about a causal relationship, or how one thing affects another.
17	c	Normative analysis is analysis concerned with "what ought to be."
18	a	Positive statements describe "what is." A positive analysis of the minimum wage law would use a model to estimate how many workers lost their jobs because of the law, its impact on firms, and the gains to workers who received the minimum wage.
19	c	This question objectively examines a relationship between tuition and class sizes, or "what is."
20	d	This is a question of "what ought to be."
21	a	Positive analysis uses economic models to estimate the benefit and cost of a particular action. Positive questions are questions that can be tested.
22	b	A normative assessment would concern what a person believed "ought to be," not "what is." The assessment would be influenced by the person's values and political beliefs.
23	a	This is the definition of microeconomics.
24	b	Macroeconomics is the study of the economy as a whole, including topics such as inflation, unemployment, and economic growth.
25	a	An invention is the development of a new good or a new process for making a good.
26	b	An innovation is the application of an invention.
27	a	In economics, capital refers to physical capital, which includes manufactured goods that are used to produce other goods and services.
28	c	This is the definition of human capital. For example, college-educated workers generally have more skills and are more productive than workers who have only high school degrees.
29	d	The bar chart, pie chart, and time series graph are all graphs of a single variable.
30	a	The graph on the left shows the relationship between two variables: price and quantity demanded.
31	d	The slope of a line equals the change in the value on the vertical axis divided by the change in the value on the horizontal axis. The slope is sometimes referred to as "the rise over the run".
32	b	Along this line, the value of the slope is the same between any two points. As an example, as we move from B (55, 14) to C (60, 13), the value of rise is $(13 - 14) = -1$ and the value of the run is $(55 - 60) = -5$. Therefore, the value of the slope is $-1/5$.

33	c	Shifting a line involves taking into account more than two variables on a graph. In this case, something other than the price of pizza has changed, causing the demand curve to shift to the right. As a result, the quantity of pizza demanded is greater for each of the prices shown.
34	a	The movement from A to C is explained by one and only one thing: a change in price. The (quantity demanded, price) combination at A is different from that at C, but the movement from A to C is explained by a change in only one variable: price.
35	c	A shift of the demand curve is caused by a change in something other than price, such as a change in income. For each price, the quantity of pizza demanded is less than it was before.
36	a	An upward sloping line shows that the relationship between two variables is positive, that is, the variables change in the same direction.
37	b	As you move upward along the curve, the value of the slope decreases. The slope between g and h is greater than the slope between i and j.
38	b	This is the formula for computing a percentage change or a growth rate.
39	b	You are computing the area of a triangle, which is ½ × Base × Height.
40	b	Total revenue equals price × quantity, which is the area of the rectangle (Base × Height).
41	d	The area of the triangle is ½ × (150,000 – 125,000) × ($2.00 – $1.50) = $6,250.
42	c	The area of the rectangle is equal to $2.00/bottle × 125,000 bottles = $250,000, which is $250,000 in total revenue.

Short Answer Responses

1. Economists distinguish financial capital and physical capital because only physical capital (for example, machinery, tools, and buildings) is a productive resource. Financial capital includes stocks, bonds, and holdings of money. Financial capital is not part of a country's capital stock, because financial capital does not produce output.

2. Productive efficiency is the situation in which a good or service is produced at the lowest possible cost. Allocative efficiency is a state of the economy in which production reflects consumer preferences: every good or service is produced to the point at which the last unit provides a marginal benefit to consumers equal to the marginal cost of producing it.

3. Economics, unlike physics and chemistry, is a social science because it applies the use of models and hypothesis testing to the study of the interactions of people.

4. Positive statements are statements of facts, or statements that can be proven to be correct or incorrect. For example: "Abraham Lincoln was the 15th president of the United States." (This is a false statement—Lincoln was the 16th president—but it is still a positive statement.) A normative statement is an opinion or a statement of what should or ought to be. For example: "The United States should elect a female as president of the United States."

5. The principle that best describes Duncan's refusal to pay for the bottle of water is marginal analysis. The total benefit to people from fresh water is very high but the marginal benefit of water—the benefit to Duncan from an additional 16 ounces of water—is very low. Duncan probably is not very thirsty. If Duncan had not had anything to drink for two days, the benefit to him of the next 16 ounces of water he drinks would be much higher, and he might have been willing to pay the $5, or more, for a bottle of water.

True/False Answers

1. F A hypothesis is a testable statement about how the world is.
2. F An entrepreneur is someone who operates a business.
3. F Economists believe people respond to incentives, but incentives may be monetary or nonmonetary.
4. F The distribution of goods and services is determined by the government, so goods and services may or may not be distributed equally.
5. F People differ on what they believe is equitable or fair.
6. F A mixed economy is one in which government influence on the choices of buyers and sellers is greater than in a market economy.
7. T All economies face trade-offs due to scarce resources.
8. T See page 5 in the textbook.
9. T The high number of bankruptcies and high level of unemployment resulted in greater government intervention. See the section titled "The Modern 'Mixed' Economy" on page 9 in the textbook.
10. F Economists would use positive economic analysis to address this issue.
11. T This is the definition of microeconomics.
12. T A straight line has a constant slope.
13. F The slope of a point on a nonlinear curve is measured by the slope of a tangent to the curve at that point.
14. T That all societies must make choices about how to use their scarce resources is a fundamental assumption of economics.
15. F Economic models provide a foundation to analyze both simplistic and complicated economic situations.

CHAPTER 2 | Trade-offs, Comparative Advantage, and the Market System

Chapter Summary and Learning Objectives

2.1 Production Possibilities Frontiers and Opportunity Costs (pages 38–44)

Use a production possibilities frontier to analyze opportunity costs and trade-offs. The **production possibilities frontier (*PPF*)** is a curve that shows the maximum attainable combinations of two products that may be produced with available resources. The *PPF* is used to illustrate the trade-offs that arise from **scarcity**. Points on the frontier are technically efficient. Points inside the frontier are inefficient, and points outside the frontier are unattainable. The **opportunity cost** of any activity is the highest-valued alternative that must be given up to engage in that activity. Because of increasing marginal opportunity costs, *PPF*s are usually bowed out rather than straight lines. This illustrates the important economic concept that the more resources that are already devoted to any activity, the smaller the payoff from devoting additional resources to that activity is likely to be. **Economic growth** is illustrated by shifting a *PPF* outward.

2.2 Comparative Advantage and Trade (pages 44–49)

Understand comparative advantage and explain how it is the basis for trade. Fundamentally, markets are about **trade**, which is the act of buying or selling. People trade on the basis of comparative advantage. An individual, a firm, or a country has a **comparative advantage** in producing a good or service if it can produce the good or service at the lowest opportunity cost. People are usually better off specializing in the activity for which they have a comparative advantage and trading for the other goods and services they need. It is important not to confuse comparative advantage with absolute advantage. An individual, a firm, or a country has an **absolute advantage** in producing a good or service if it can produce more of that good or service from the same amount of resources. It is possible to have an absolute advantage in producing a good or service without having a comparative advantage.

2.3 The Market System (pages 49–55)

Explain the basic idea of how a market system works. A **market** is a group of buyers and sellers of a good or service and the institution or arrangement by which they come together to trade. **Product markets** are markets for goods and services, such as computers and medical treatment. **Factor markets** are markets for the **factors of production**, such as labor, capital, natural resources, and entrepreneurial ability. A **circular-flow diagram** shows how participants in product markets and factor markets are linked. Adam Smith argued in his 1776 book *The Wealth of Nations* that in a **free market**, where the government does not control the production of goods and services, changes in prices lead firms to produce the goods and services most desired by consumers. If consumers demand more of a good, its price will rise. Firms respond to rising prices by increasing production. If consumers demand less of a good, its price will fall. Firms respond to falling prices by producing less of a good. An **entrepreneur** is someone who operates a business. In the market system, entrepreneurs are responsible for organizing the production of goods and services. The market system will work well only if there is protection for **property rights**, which are the rights of individuals and firms to use their property.

Chapter Review

Chapter Opener: Managers Making Choices at BMW (page 37)

The managers at firms such as BMW (Bavarian Motor Works) must make decisions regarding the production and marketing of their products. These decisions include the location of manufacturing plants and the production methods used at these plants. Because BMW is a German firm, there are good reasons to locate factories in Germany. However, locating factories in other countries can reduce manufacturing costs (for example, by paying lower wages). Locating in countries where the automobiles are sold also reduces the risk that foreign governments will impose import restrictions.

2.1 Production Possibilities Frontiers and Opportunity Costs (pages 38–44)

Learning Objective: Use a production possibilities frontier to analyze opportunity costs and trade-offs.

Scarcity exists because we have unlimited wants but only limited resources available to fulfill those wants. This scarcity requires that we make decisions about how to use our resources. In other words, we face trade-offs. A **production possibilities frontier** (*PPF*) is a curve showing the maximum alternative combinations of two products that may be produced with available resources. A *PPF* is a graphical representation of the trade-offs and opportunity costs a producer faces. As shown in Figure 2-1, points on a *PPF* are efficient, while points under the *PPF* are inefficient. Points beyond the *PPF* are unattainable with current resources. A *PPF* will always have a negative slope because increasing production requires shifting resources away from one activity toward the second activity.

The slope of a *PPF* is used to measure the opportunity cost of increasing the production of one good along the frontier relative to the other good. The slope of a linear frontier and the opportunity cost of moving along the frontier are constant. But convex or "bowed out" production possibilities frontiers represent a more likely outcome. A convex *PPF* means marginal opportunity costs rise as more and more of one good is produced. For example, starting from point *A* in Figure 2-2 and moving downward to points *B* and *C*, the slope of the frontier becomes steeper and steeper. This means that the cost of producing one more automobile (the number of tanks that must be given up as resources are transferred to automobile production) is greater at each point.

Along a production possibilities frontier, resources and technology are fixed. If there is an increase in the available resources or an improvement in the technology used to produce goods and services, then the *PPF* will shift outward. The economy will be able to produce more goods and services, which means the economy has experienced economic growth. **Economic growth** is the ability of the economy to increase the production of goods and services. Growth may lead to greater increases in production of one good than another.

📖 Study Hint

Solved Problem 2-1 will help you draw a *PPF* and understand how a linear *PPF* illustrates opportunity costs incurred in production. Be sure you understand how slope is measured along the frontier and that the magnitude of this slope represents the opportunity cost of substituting the production of one good for the production of another.

    Making the Connection "Facing the Trade-offs in Health Care Spending" describes the choice households must make regarding how they use their limited incomes. As health care prices rise, some households choose not to purchase health insurance. As a provider of public insurance in Medicare and

Medicaid, the government also must decide where to use resources within those public insurance programs.

 2.2

Comparative Advantage and Trade (pages 44–49)

Learning Objective: Understand comparative advantage and explain how it is the basis for trade.

By specializing in production and engaging in trade, individuals can enjoy a higher standard of living than would be possible if these individuals produced everything they consumed. Specialization in production is so common that most people take for granted that they must trade income earned from their own labor to buy the services of plumbers, carpenters, medical doctors, and stock brokers. Specialization makes trade necessary. **Trade** is the act of buying or selling.

Absolute advantage is the ability of an individual, firm, or country to produce more of a good or service than competitors using the same amount of resources. **Comparative advantage** is the ability of an individual, firm, or country to produce a good or service at a lower opportunity cost than other producers. An individual country should specialize in the production of the good or services in which it has a comparative advantage, and then trade this good to other countries for goods in which it does not have a comparative advantage.

📖 Study Hint

Don't Let This Happen to YOU! clarifies the differences between absolute and comparative advantage. An individual, firm, or a country has the absolute advantage in the production of a good if that individual, firm, or country can produce more of the good. Comparative advantage in the production of a good goes to the individual, firm, or country that can produce the good at a lower opportunity cost. It is possible for an individual, firm, or country to have absolute advantage in the production of both goods, but the country will have a comparative advantage in the production of only one of the two goods.

Solved Problem 2-2 describes the benefits realized when a nation specializes in the production of a good for which it has a comparative advantage. In the problem, the United States has a comparative advantage in producing honey, while Canada has a comparative advantage in producing maple syrup. Each country should specialize in producing the good for which it has a comparative advantage and trade some of that good for the other good. With trade, the United States and Canada can consume outside of their *PPFs*.

Most examples of absolute and comparative advantage are similar to the hypothetical examples in section 2.2 of the textbook. This is due, in part, to the difficulty of identifying people who have an absolute advantage in two different areas. But the career of Babe Ruth offers a good example of someone with an absolute advantage in two activities who was still ultimately better off specializing in the activity in which he had a comparative advantage. Before he achieved his greatest fame as a home run hitter and outfielder with the New York Yankees, Ruth was a star pitcher with the Boston Red Sox. Ruth may have been the best left-handed pitcher in the American League during his years with Boston (1914–1919), but he was used more and more as a fielder in his last two years with the team. In fact, he established a record for home runs in a season (29) in 1919 when he was still pitching. The Yankees acquired Ruth in 1920 and made him a full-time outfielder. The opportunity cost of this decision for the Yankees was the wins Ruth could have earned as a pitcher. But because New York already had skilled pitchers, the opportunity cost of replacing Ruth as a pitcher was lower than the cost of replacing him as a hitter. No one else on the Yankees could have hit 54 home runs, Ruth's total in 1920; the next highest Yankee total was 11. It can be argued that Ruth had an absolute advantage as both a hitter and pitcher in 1920 but a comparative advantage only as a hitter.

2.3 **The Market System (pages 49–55)**
2.3 The Market System (pages 49–55)
Learning Objective: Explain the basic idea of how a market system works.

A **market** is a group of buyers and sellers of a good or service and the institution or arrangement by which they come together to trade. **Product markets** are markets for goods, such as computers, and services, such as medical treatment. **Factor markets** are markets for the factors of production, such as labor, capital, natural resources, and entrepreneurial ability. A **circular-flow diagram** is a model that illustrates how participants in markets are linked. The diagram demonstrates the interaction between firms and households in both product and factor markets. Households buy goods and services in the product market and provide resources for sale in the factor market, while firms provide goods and services in the product market and buy resources in the factor market. A **free market** is a market with few government restrictions on how a good or service can be produced or sold, or on how a factor of production can be employed.

Entrepreneurs are an essential part of a market economy. An **entrepreneur** is someone who operates a business, bringing together the factors of production—labor, capital, and natural resources—to produce goods and services. Entrepreneurs often risk their own funds to start businesses and organize factors of production to produce those goods and services consumers want.

The role of government in a market system is limited but essential. Although government in a market economy imposes few restrictions on the choices made by consumers, resource owners, and firms, government protection of private property rights is necessary for markets to operate efficiently.

Property rights are the rights individuals or firms have to the exclusive use of their physical and intellectual property, including the right to buy or sell it. New technology has created challenges to the protection of property rights. Unauthorized copying of music and other intellectual property in cyberspace reduces the rewards of creativity and may reduce the amount of such activity in the future.

📖 Study Hint
Consumers seldom know the identity of the people who produce the products they buy. The impersonal and decentralized character of markets is illustrated very well by the discussion of the production of Apple's iPod found in *Making the Connection* "A Story of the Market System in Action: How Do You Make an iPod?" The iPod contains 451 parts. Many of the manufacturers of the components of the iPod do not know what the final product will be. No one person at Apple knows how to produce all of these components, so Apple relies heavily on its suppliers.

The role of government in a free market economy can be compared to that of an umpire or referee in a sporting event. The most vocal critics of these officials would not argue they are not needed. It would not take long for a professional football or baseball game to turn into a shouting match (or worse!) if players were allowed to enforce the rules of their own games. However, the quality of sporting events suffers when officials bar players, coaches, or managers from participating in contests for frivolous reasons. *Making the Connection* "Property Rights in Cyberspace: YouTube, Facebook, and MySpace" reinforces the need for government protection of property rights and the difficulties associated with enforcing intellectual property rights. Material can easily be uploaded to and posted on the Internet. Once on the Internet, the material can easily be downloaded, reproduced, and reposted, so these intellectual property rights are nearly impossible to protect.

The stories of successful businesses such as Microsoft and Google can give a misleading impression about the risks of business ownership. Many businesses fail. The National Restaurant Association estimates an 80 percent failure rate for independently owned restaurants within their first two years of operation. The average work week for many small business owners is much longer than that of the average employee—80 hours is not uncommon—and owners often borrow heavily to start and maintain their businesses.

Extra Solved Problem 2-3
Adam Smith's "Invisible Hand"
Supports Learning Objective 2.3: Explain the basic idea of how a market system works.

Alan Krueger, an economist at Princeton University, has argued that Adam Smith "…worried that if merchants and manufacturers pursued their self-interest by seeking government regulation and privilege, the invisible hand would not work its magic…"

Source: Alan B. Krueger, "Rediscovering the Wealth of Nations," *New York Times*, August 16, 2001.

a. What types of regulation and privilege might merchants and manufacturers seek from the government?

b. How might these regulations and privileges keep the invisible hand from working?

SOLVING THE PROBLEM:
Step 1:   Review the chapter material.
This problem concerns how goods and services are produced and sold and how factors of production are employed in a free market economic system as described by Adam Smith in *An Inquiry into the Nature and Causes of the Wealth of Nations*. You may want to review the section "The Gains from Free Markets," which begins on page 50.

Step 2:   Answer question (a) by noting the economic system in place in Europe in 1776.
At the time, governments gave guilds—associations of producers—the authority to control production. The production controls limited the amount of output of goods such as shoes and clothing, as well as the number of producers of these items. Limiting production and competition led to higher prices and fewer choices for consumers. Instead of catering to the wants of consumers, producers sought the favor of government officials.

Step 3:   Answer question (b) by contrasting the behavior of merchants and manufacturers under a guild system and a market system.
Because governments gave producers the power to control production, producers did not have to respond to consumers' demands for better quality, variety, and lower prices. Under a market system, producers who sell poor quality goods at high prices suffer economic losses; producers who provide better quality goods at low prices are rewarded with profits. Therefore, it is in the self-interest of producers to address consumer wants. This is how the invisible hand works in a free market economy, but not in Europe in the 18th century.

Key Terms

Absolute advantage The ability of an individual, a firm, or a country to produce more of a good or service than competitors, using the same amount of resources.

Circular-flow diagram A model that illustrates how participants in markets are linked.

Comparative advantage The ability of an individual, a firm, or a country to produce a good or service at a lower opportunity cost than competitors.

Economic growth The ability of the economy to increase the production of goods and services.

Entrepreneur Someone who operates a business, bringing together the factors of production—labor, capital, and natural resources—to produce goods and services.

Factor markets Markets for the factors of production, such as labor, capital, natural resources, and entrepreneurial ability.

Factors of production The inputs used to make goods and services.

Free market A market with few government restrictions on how a good or service can be produced or sold or on how a factor of production can be employed.

Market A group of buyers and sellers of a good or service and the institution or arrangement by which they come together to trade.

Opportunity cost The highest-valued alternative that must be given up to engage in an activity.

Product markets Markets for goods—such as computers—and services—such as medical treatment.

Production possibilities frontier (*PPF*) A curve showing the maximum attainable combinations of two products that may be produced with available resources and current technology.

Property rights The rights individuals or firms have to the exclusive use of their property, including the right to buy or sell it.

Scarcity A situation in which unlimited wants exceed the limited resources available to fulfill those wants.

Trade The act of buying and selling.

Self-Test

(Answers are provided at the end of the Self-Test.)

Multiple-Choice Questions

1. What is the name given to the highest-valued alternative that must be given up to engage in any activity?
   a. scarcity
   b. the production possibilities frontier
   c. opportunity cost
   d. a trade-off

2. What happens if a country produces a combination of goods that uses all of the resources available in the economy?
   a. The country is operating on its production possibilities frontier.
   b. The country is maximizing its opportunity cost.
   c. The country has eliminated scarcity.
   d. All of the above occur if a country uses all available resources.

3. Refer to the graph below. Which of the following combinations is unattainable with the current resources available in this economy?

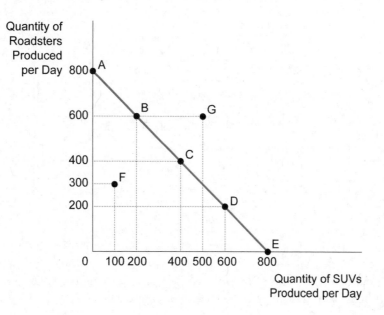

   a. combination G
   b. combination F
   c. combinations A or E
   d. All of the above. None of the combinations above can be attained with current resources.

4. Refer to the graph below. Which of the following combinations is inefficient?

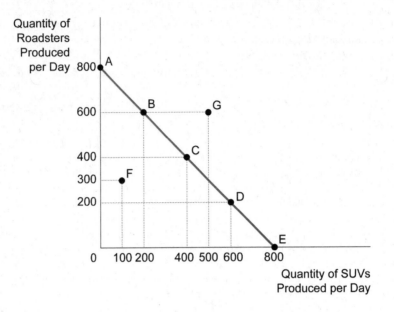

a. combination G
b. combination F
c. combinations A or E
d. both F and G

5. Refer to the graph below. Which of the following best represents the situation in which BMW *must* face a trade-off between producing SUVs and producing roadsters?

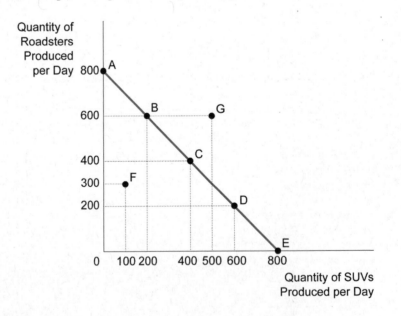

a. any point on the graph represents that trade-off
b. moving from B to C
c. moving from F to B
d. moving from C to G

6.   Refer to the graph below. How many roadsters are produced at the point where BMW produces 800 SUVs?

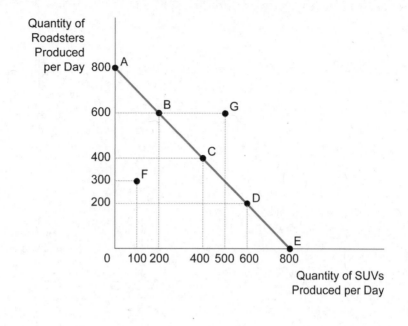

a.   0
b.   any amount up to 800
c.   exactly 800
d.   400

7.   Refer to the graph below. What is the opportunity cost of moving from point B to point C?

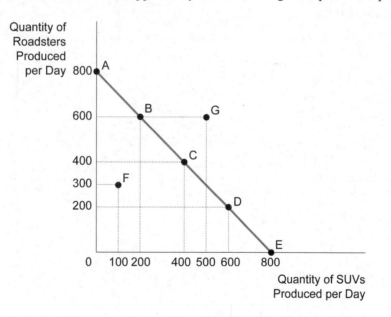

a.   200 SUVs
b.   400 SUVs
c.   200 roadsters
d.   400 roadsters

8. Refer to the graph below. The graph shows the data from Solved Problem 2-1. What is the opportunity cost of switching from Choice D to Choice E?

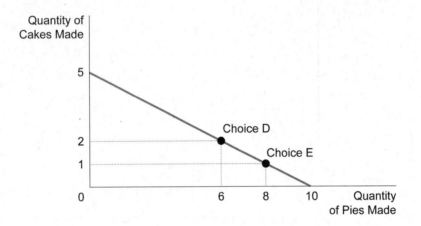

a. two pies
b. eight pies
c. two cakes
d. one cake

9. Refer to the graph below. The graph is a representation of the data in Solved Problem 2-1. In this problem, what is the opportunity cost of producing five cakes?

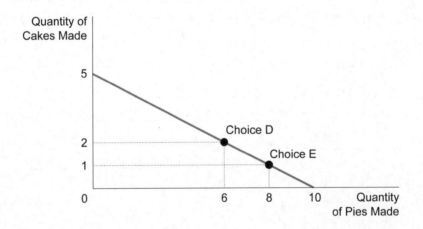

a. zero cakes
b. zero pies
c. ten pies
d. There is insufficient information to answer the question.

10. Refer to the graph below. Which of the following combinations of pies and cakes is unattainable given existing resources?

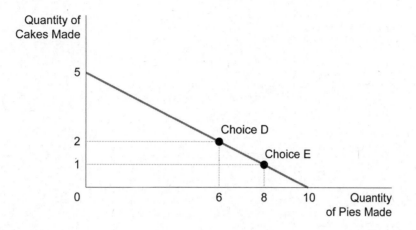

   a.   2 cakes and 6 pies
   b.   1 cake and 7 pies
   c.   0 cakes and 10 pies
   d.   4 cakes and 7 pies

11. Refer to the graph below. As you move from point A to point B and then to point C on this graph, what happens to the marginal opportunity cost?

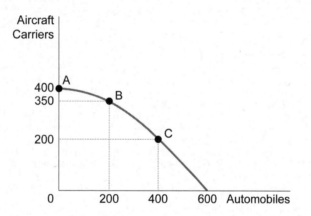

   a.   It increases.
   b.   It decreases.
   c.   It remains constant.
   d.   It equals zero.

12. Refer to the graph below. What is the opportunity cost of producing 400 aircraft carriers?

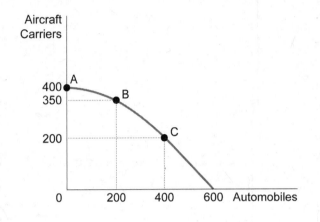

a. 200 automobiles
b. 50 aircraft carriers
c. 200 automobiles
d. 600 automobiles

13. Refer to the graph below. What is the opportunity cost of moving from point B to point C?

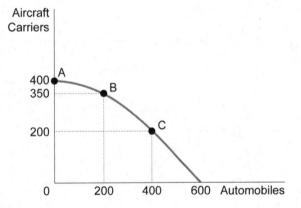

a. 200 automobiles
b. 400 automobiles
c. 50 aircraft carriers
d. 150 aircraft carriers

14. Refer to the graph below. What does the term "increasing marginal opportunity cost" mean in this graph?

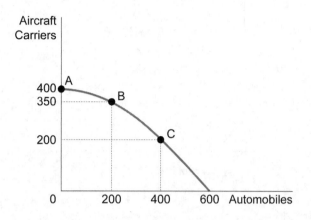

a. There is a higher opportunity cost of producing either aircraft carriers or automobiles, so long as the quantity produced of that good is decreasing.
b. There is a higher opportunity cost of producing either aircraft carriers or automobiles, so long as the quantity produced of that good is increasing.
c. Increasing the production of aircraft carriers results in higher automobile production costs, such as the costs of labor and capital to build automobiles.
d. Increasing the production of either aircraft carriers or automobiles creates more opportunities in the economy.

15. A production possibilities frontier will be linear instead of bowed out if
a. the opportunity cost of producing more of either of the two goods is constant.
b. the opportunity cost of producing more of either of the two goods is zero.
c. the opportunity cost of producing either of the two goods always increases.
d. resources are employed efficiently.

16. The principle of increasing marginal opportunity cost states that the more resources devoted to any activity, the _____ the payoff to devoting additional resources to that activity.
a. smaller
b. greater
c. proportional
d. more instant

17. Refer to the graphs below. Which graph better represents an improvement only in the technology used to make automobiles?

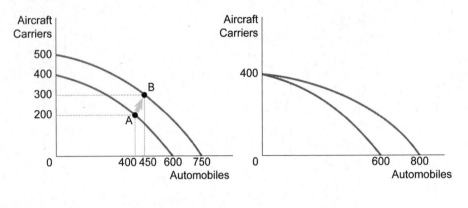

    a. the graph on the left
    b. the graph on the right
    c. both graphs
    d. neither graph

18. Refer to the graphs below. Which graph represents the concept of economic growth?

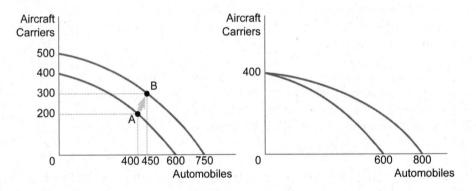

    a. the graph on the left
    b. the graph on the right
    c. both graphs
    d. neither graph

19. Refer to the graphs below. Which graph best represents the concept of economic growth?

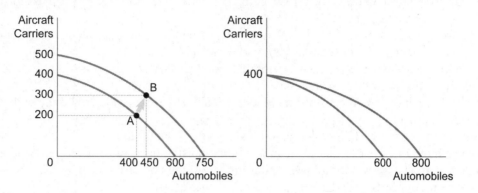

    a. the graph on the left
    b. the graph on the right
    c. both graphs
    d. neither graph

20. Refer to the graphs below. Which of the following could have caused the outward shift of the curve in the graph on the left side?

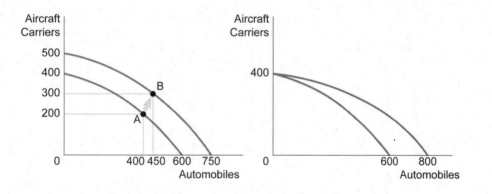

    a. an increase in technology that affects the production of both aircraft carriers and automobiles
    b. technological change that affects only the aircraft carrier industry
    c. unemployment in the economy
    d. a change in the cost of producing automobiles

21. Which of the following would create economic growth; that is, shift the production possibilities frontier outward?
    a. an increase in the available labor
    b. an increase in technology that affects the production of both goods
    c. an increase in the available natural resources
    d. all of the above

22. Which of the following statements is most consistent with positive economic analysis?
    a. The United States would be better off being self-sufficient, so it wouldn't need to rely on other nations for certain goods.
    b. The United States would be better off if it specialized in the production of some goods, and then traded some of them to other countries.
    c. The United States should produce at home the goods that it now imports—that way the nation can generate additional jobs here at home.
    d. The United States should establish trade with friendly countries and avoid trade with its enemies.

23. Absolute advantage is the ability of an individual, firm, or country to
    a. produce more of a good or service than competitors using the same amount of resources.
    b. produce a good or service at a lower opportunity cost than other producers.
    c. consume more goods or services than others at lower costs.
    d. reach a higher production possibilities frontier by lowering opportunity costs.

24. If a country has a comparative advantage in the production of a good, then that country
    a. also has an absolute advantage in producing that good.
    b. should allow another country to specialize in the production of that good.
    c. has a lower opportunity cost in the production of that good.
    d. all of the above

25. Refer to the graphs below. Each graph represents one country. Which country has a comparative advantage in the production of shirts?

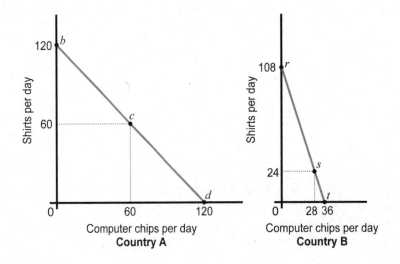

    a. Country A
    b. Country B
    c. neither country
    d. both countries

26. Refer to the graphs below. Each graph represents one country. Which country should specialize in the production of chips?

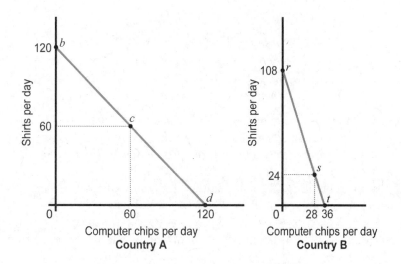

a. Country A
b. Country B
c. Neither country; they both should produce some chips and some shirts.
d. Both countries should specialize in the production of chips.

27. The table below shows the quantity of two goods that a worker in Country A and a worker in Country B can produce per day. Which country has an absolute advantage in the production of each good?

	Output per day of work	
	Food	Clothing
Country A	6	3
Country B	1	2

a. Country A has an absolute advantage in the production of each good.
b. Country B has an absolute advantage in the production of each good.
c. Both countries have an absolute advantage in the production of each good.
d. Neither country has an absolute advantage in the production of each good.

28. Consider the table below. Which country has a comparative advantage in the production of each good?

	Output per day of work	
	Food	Clothing
Country A	6	3
Country B	1	2

a. Country A has a comparative advantage in the production of both goods.
b. Country B has a comparative advantage in the production of both goods.
c. Country A has a comparative advantage in the production of food; Country B has a comparative advantage in the production of clothing.
d. Country B has a comparative advantage in the production of food; Country A has a comparative advantage in the production of clothing.

29. Consider the table below. What is country A's opportunity cost of producing 1 unit of clothing?

	Output per day of work	
	Food	Clothing
Country A	6	3
Country B	1	2

a. 2 units of food
b. ½ a unit of food
c. 6 units of food
d. 2 units of clothing

30. Refer to the graphs below. If you have a comparative advantage in the production of apples, what point would best represent your production with trade?

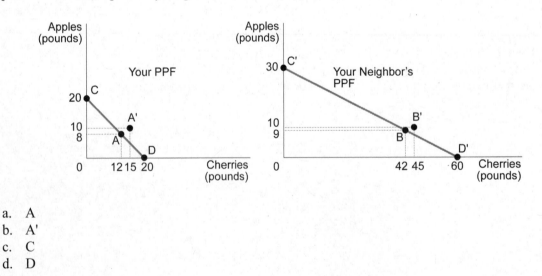

a. A
b. A'
c. C
d. D

31. Refer to the graphs below. What is point B' on your neighbor's *PPF* curve?

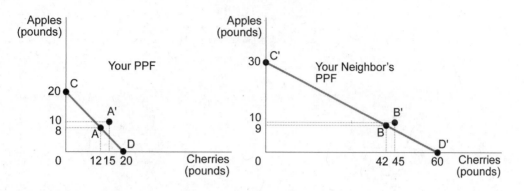

    a.   Point B' is your neighbor's production before trade.
    b.   Point B' is your neighbor's consumption before trade.
    c.   Point B' is your neighbor's production after trade.
    d.   Point B' is your neighbor's consumption after trade.

32. Which of the following refers to markets where goods such as computers or services such as medical treatment are offered?
    a.   product markets
    b.   essential markets
    c.   factor markets
    d.   competitive markets

33. In which markets are factors of production, such as labor, capital, natural resources, and entrepreneurial ability traded?
    a.   product markets
    b.   essential markets
    c.   factor markets
    d.   competitive markets

34. Which of the following comprises the two key groups of participants in the circular flow of income?
    a.   product markets and factor markets
    b.   government and the financial sector
    c.   households and firms
    d.   buyers and sellers

35. Fill in the blanks. In a simple circular-flow model, there are flows of _____ and flows of _____.
    a.   factors of production; goods and services
    b.   funds received from the sale of factors of production; spending on final goods and services
    c.   Both (a) and (b) are correct.
    d.   None of the above. Actually, there are no flows in the circular flow of income.

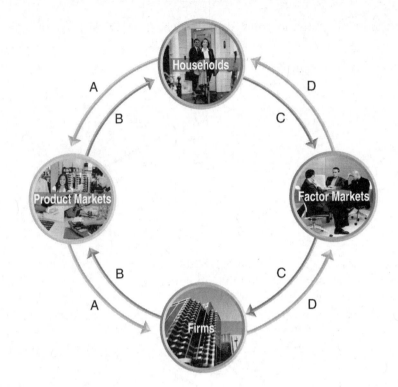

36. In the circular-flow diagram above, which arrow shows the flow of goods and services?
    a. A
    b. B
    c. C
    d. D

37. In the circular-flow diagram above, which arrow shows the flow of spending by households?
    a. A
    b. B
    c. C
    d. D

38. In the circular-flow diagram above, which arrow shows the flow of factors of production?
    a. A
    b. B
    c. C
    d. D

39. In the circular-flow diagram above, which arrow shows the flow of income paid to the factors of production?
    a. A
    b. B
    c. C
    d. D

40. According to Adam Smith, which of the following is true?
    a. Markets work because producers, aided by government, ensure that neither too many nor too few goods are produced.
    b. Market prices can come to reflect the prices desired by all consumers.
    c. Individuals usually act in a rational, self-interested way.
    d. All of the above.

41. According to Adam Smith, which of the following is the instrument the invisible hand uses to direct economic activity?
    a. price
    b. government regulation
    c. financial markets
    d. cost

42. According to Adam Smith, which of the following is necessary for the proper functioning of the market system?
    a. For markets to work, people should take into account how their decisions affect society as a whole.
    b. For markets to work, government should help citizens make the right decisions.
    c. For markets to work, people must be free to pursue their self-interest.
    d. For markets to work, people and government need to coordinate their decisions.

43. What is the role of an entrepreneur?
    a. to operate a business that produces a good or service
    b. to bring together the factors of production—labor, capital, and natural resources
    c. to take risks
    d. all of the above

44. In a free market system, which of the following groups brings together the factors of production—labor, capital, and natural resources—in order to produce goods and services?
    a. the government
    b. entrepreneurs
    c. lobbyists
    d. politicians

45. Which of the following is critical to the success of a market system?
    a. to allow individuals or firms to have exclusive use of their property
    b. to prevent individuals from buying or selling their property depending on the circumstances
    c. Both (a) and (b) are critical to the success of a market system.
    d. to allow the government to determine the optimal use of private property.

46. Generally speaking, for a market system to work, individuals must
    a. be very cautious in their approach to saving and investment.
    b. take risks and act in rational, self-interested ways.
    c. be able to evaluate and understand all available options.
    d. consult people who have experience.

47. What are patents and copyrights designed to do?
    a. prevent entrepreneurs from earning excessive profits
    b. eliminate unnecessary duplication whenever it arises
    c. protect intellectual property rights
    d. all of the above

48. What is the outcome of enforcing contracts and property rights in a market system?
    a. increased economic activity
    b. decreased economic activity
    c. no effect on economic activity
    d. an unpredictable but definite effect on economic activity

49. If a market system functions well, which of the following is necessary for the enforcement of contracts and property rights?
    a. powerful political connections
    b. an independent court system
    c. action by government to prevent the exercise of certain property rights
    d. all of the above

Short Answer Questions

1. Does the story about Apple's production of the iPod on page 52 in the textbook imply that people must cooperate with one another in order for specialization in production and trade to occur? Explain.

_____

_____

_____

_____

_____

2. Comment briefly on the following statement: "The circular-flow diagram implies that the income household members receive is directly related to the market value of the resources they own."

_____

_____

_____

3. Could a production possibilities frontier ever slope upward?

_____

_____

4. Create an example showing that absolute advantage in an activity does not necessarily imply comparative advantage in an activity.

_____

_____

_____

5. In the explanation of Adam Smith's argument in favor of replacing the guild system with a market system, the textbook states that "*a key to understanding Smith's argument is the assumption that individuals usually act in a rational, self-interested way.*" Did Smith believe that the success of a market system requires that people act selfishly?

_____

_____

_____

True/False Questions

T F 1. In his book *An Inquiry into the Nature and Causes of the Wealth of Nations*, Adam Smith argued that a guild system was the most efficient way for a nation to coordinate the decisions of buyers and sellers.

T F 2. The story about Apple's production of the iPod shows how production requires the coordinated activities of many people, spread around the world.

T F 3. A nation with an absolute advantage in the production of two goods will usually have a comparative advantage in only one of the goods.

T F 4. A production possibilities frontier that is bowed outward illustrates increasing marginal opportunity costs.

T F 5. Technological advances always increase the production of all goods and services equally.

T F 6. It is possible to have an absolute advantage in producing a good without having a comparative advantage.

T F 7. Households are suppliers of the factors of production that are used by firms to produce goods and services.

T F 8. The circular-flow diagram is used to explain why the opportunity cost of increasing the production of one good is the decrease in production of another good.

T F 9. The 5th and 14th amendments to the U.S. Constitution guarantee property rights.

T F 10. Opportunity cost refers to the all of the alternatives that must be given up to engage in an activity.

T F 11. An individual who has comparative advantage in producing a good must also have absolute advantage in producing that good.

T F 12. The Congressional Budget Office has estimated that annual federal government spending on Medicare should remain at a constant level through 2020.

T F 13. Because the governments of Hong Kong, Estonia, and Singapore impose few restrictions on economic activity, the economies of these countries approximate free market economies.

T F 14. The Bavarian Motor Works Company has always produced its automobiles in Germany to supervise production and employ German workers, who have high levels of technical skills.

T F 15. The marginal opportunity cost along a linear (straight-line) production possibilities frontier is constant.

Answers to the Self-Test

Multiple-Choice Questions

Question	Answer	Comment
1	c	Opportunity cost is the highest-valued alternative that must be given up to engage in an activity. Refer to page 39 in the textbook.
2	a	The production possibilities frontier is a curve showing all the attainable combinations of two products that may be produced with available resources.
3	a	To produce the combination G, the economy needs more machines, more workers, or more of both. If the economy were to produce 600 roadsters with existing resources, then it could produce, at most, 200 SUVs.
4	b	This combination is attainable but inefficient because not all resources are being used.
5	b	A move along the curve shows the sacrifice associated with increasing the quantity of SUVs produced, which is the amount by which production of roadsters will have to be reduced.
6	a	Point E describes this choice. Point E shows that 800 SUVs are produced when zero roadsters are produced.
7	c	As you move from point B to point C, the production of SUVs increases by 200. The opportunity cost of the increased production of SUVs is a decrease in the quantity of roadsters produced.
8	d	As you move from D to E, the production of pies increases by 2 and the production of cakes decreases by 1. Refer to pages 40–41 in the textbook.
9	c	Opportunity cost is what you sacrifice. If Rosie produced zero cakes, then Rosie could make 10 pies.
10	d	Four cakes could be produced, but only with fewer than 6 pies. Choice D on the graph shows that a maximum of 2 cakes can be made with 6 pies.
11	a	The opportunity cost associated with producing automobiles increases as more are produced. Refer to Figure 2-2 on page 42 in the textbook.
12	d	Either the economy produces 400 aircraft carriers or it produces 600 automobiles with the same amount of resources.
13	d	The economy now produces 400 automobiles instead of 200. To produce the additional 200 automobiles, the economy must decrease production of aircraft carriers by 150 (an opportunity cost 350 − 200 = 150 aircraft carriers).
14	b	As the economy moves along the production possibilities frontier, it experiences increasing marginal opportunity costs because increasing the production of one good by a given amount requires larger and larger decreases in the production of the other good.
15	a	A linear production possibilities frontier has a constant slope and, therefore, a constant opportunity cost.
16	a	This is the principle of increasing marginal opportunity cost.
17	b	An improvement in the technology used to make automobiles causes a shift of the production possibilities frontier only along the horizontal axis.
18	a	This graph shows that something affects both the production of automobiles and

		the production of aircraft carriers, such as an increase in resources or better technologies.
19	c	These graphs show an increase in the production of one or both goods. This increase in the productive capacity of the economy is referred to as economic growth.
20	a	Economic growth is the ability of the economy to increase the production of goods and services.
21	d	All of these factors create economic growth.
22	b	If a nation produced everything it consumed, then it would not depend on any other nation for its livelihood. Countries are better off if they specialize in the production of some products and trade some of them to other countries. Refer to the section entitled "Comparative Advantage and the Gains From Trade" on page 47 in the textbook.
23	a	Absolute advantage is the ability of an individual, firm, or country to produce more of a good or service than competitors using the same amount of resources.
24	c	The country with a lower opportunity cost of production has a comparative advantage in the production of that good.
25	b	The opportunity costs are as follows: The opportunity cost of shirts is: 1 chip for Country A and 1/3 chip for Country B. The opportunity cost of chips is: 1 shirt for Country A and 3 shirts for Country B. Country B has a comparative advantage in the production of shirts because it sacrifices fewer chips to produce one shirt.
26	a	The opportunity costs are as follows: The opportunity cost of shirts is: 1 chip for Country A and 1/3 chip for Country B. The opportunity cost of chips is: 1 shirt for Country A and 3 shirts for Country B. Therefore, Country A has a comparative advantage (or lower opportunity cost) in the production of chips because it sacrifices fewer shirts to produce one chip. Country A should produce chips.
27	a	A worker in Country A can produce more food and more clothing in one day than a worker in Country B.
28	c	A worker in Country A can produce 6 times as many units of food in one day as a worker in Country B, but only 1.5 as many units of clothing. Country A has a lower opportunity cost than Country B in the production of food, and Country B has a lower opportunity cost than Country A in the production of clothing.
29	a	For Country A, the production of 3 units of clothing requires a sacrifice of 6 units of food. Therefore, each unit of clothing has an opportunity cost of 2 units of food.
30	c	If you have a comparative advantage in the production of apples, then you would specialize entirely in the production of apples.
31	d	After trade, you and your neighbor can consume more than you can produce.
32	a	Goods and services are exchanged in product markets.
33	c	Labor, capital, natural resources, and entrepreneurial ability are factors of production that are traded in factor markets.
34	c	A household includes all the individuals in a home. Firms are suppliers of goods and services.
35	c	In the circular flow of income there are flows of funds and spending, and also flows of factors of production and goods and services.
36	b	Goods and services flow from firms to the households through the product market.
37	a	Spending on goods and services flows from households to firms through the product market.
38	c	Factors of production flow from households to the firms through the factor market.
39	d	Income flows from firms to the households through the factor market.
40	c	Individuals usually act in a rational, self-interested way. Adam Smith understood that people's motives can be complex.

41	a	Price represents both the value of the good to consumers and the cost (to producers) of making those goods.
42	c	Individuals usually act in a rational, self-interested way. When people act in their own self-interest, the right quantity of goods will be produced.
43	d	The role of an entrepreneur is to operate a business and take risks in bringing together the factors of production—labor, capital, and natural resources—to produce goods and services.
44	b	In a market system, entrepreneurs bring together the factors of production—labor, capital, and natural resources—to produce goods and services.
45	a	The legal basis for a successful market is property rights. Property rights are the rights individuals or firms have to the exclusive use of their property, including the right to buy or sell it.
46	b	Risk taking is an essential ingredient of entrepreneurship, and this risk taking is essential for the market system to function well.
47	c	Property rights are very important in any modern economy. See page 53 in the textbook.
48	a	Much business activity involves someone agreeing to carry out some action in the future. For a market to work, there must be property rights and enforceable contracts.
49	b	Independence and impartiality on the part of judges are very important.

Short Answer Responses

1. Cooperation is essential for specialization and trade, but it is an impersonal cooperation. It is not necessary for business owners, workers, suppliers and consumers to know or see one another. In fact, many of these individuals can be located thousands of miles away from each other, live in different countries, and speak different languages. Their cooperation is due to their self-interest, not their regard for one another's welfare.

2. This is true. For household members to earn income to buy the goods and services they want, they must first sell their resource services to firms who purchase these services in factor markets. The market value of factor services determines the income resource owners receive.

3. No, production possibilities frontiers will always slope downward. Resources used in production are scarce, and increasing production of one good will always require a decrease in the production of another good along a production possibilities frontier. This means that production possibilities frontiers are always negative sloped, or downward sloping.

4. Consider the following example: Student 1 can read 10 pages of psychology per day or 8 pages of economics per day, while Student 2 can read 5 pages of psychology per day or 5 pages of economics per day. Student 1 has an absolute advantage in reading both psychology and economics; however, Student 1's cost of reading 1 page of economics is 1.25 pages of psychology, and Student 2's cost of reading 1 page of economics is only 1 page of psychology.

5. Smith did not believe that self-interest was the sole motive nor did he believe that self-interest was synonymous with selfishness. People are motivated by a broad range of factors, but when they buy and sell in markets, monetary rewards usually provide the most important motivation.

True/False Answers

1. F Adam Smith explained the inefficiencies of the guild system and explained how markets were more efficient.
2. T See Making the Connection "A Story of the Market System in Action: How Do You Make an iPod?" on page 52 in the textbook.
3. T A nation can have the comparative advantage in the production of only one of the two goods.
4. T As the slope of the frontier becomes steeper, the opportunity cost of obtaining one more unit of one good increases.
5. F Technological advances often affect the production of some goods (those that use the advances most) more than others.
6. T Absolute advantage is about who produces more, while comparative advantage is about who produces the good at a lower opportunity cost.
7. T See the section titled "The Circular Flow of Income" on page 50 in the textbook.
8. F A production possibilities frontier, not the circular flow diagram, illustrates opportunity cost in production.
9. T Refer to page 53 in the textbook for a discussion of the U.S. Constitution and property rights.
10. F See the definition of opportunity cost on page 39 of the textbook.
11. F Comparative advantage involves production at the lowest cost, not necessarily the highest level of production overall.
12. F The Congressional Budget Office estimated that federal spending on Medicare will more than double over the next 10 years. See Making the Connection on page 41 in the textbook.
13. T See page 51 in the textbook.
14. F The Chapter Opener discusses the BMW plant in Spartanburg, South Carolina.
15. T The change in the opportunity cost per each additional unit of the good being produced—the marginal opportunity cost—is constant along a linear *PPF*.

Chapter Summary and Learning Objectives

3.1   The Demand Side of the Market (pages 66–74)
Discuss the variables that influence demand. The model of demand and supply is the most powerful in economics. The model applies exactly only to **perfectly competitive markets**, where there are many buyers and sellers, all the products sold are identical, and there are no barriers to new sellers entering the market. But the model can also be useful in analyzing markets that don't meet all these requirements. The **quantity demanded** is the amount of a good or service that a consumer is willing and able to purchase at a given price. A **demand schedule** is a table that shows the relationship between the price of a product and the quantity of the product demanded. A **demand curve** is a graph that shows the relationship between the price of a good and the quantity of the good consumers are willing and able to buy over a period of time. **Market demand** is the demand by all consumers of a given good or service. The **law of demand** states that *ceteris paribus*—holding everything else constant—the quantity of a product demanded increases when the price falls and decreases when the price rises. Demand curves slope downward because of the **substitution effect**, which is the change in quantity demanded that results from a price change making one good more or less expensive relative to another good, and the **income effect**, which is the change in quantity demanded of a good that results from the effect of a change in the good's price on consumer purchasing power. Changes in income, the prices of related goods, tastes, population and demographics, and expected future prices all cause the demand curve to shift. **Substitutes** are goods that can be used for the same purpose. **Complements** are goods that are used together. A **normal good** is a good for which demand increases as income increases. An **inferior good** is a good for which demand decreases as income increases. **Demographics** are the characteristics of a population with respect to age, race, and gender. A change in demand refers to a shift of the demand curve. A change in quantity demanded refers to a movement along the demand curve as a result of a change in the product's price.

3.2   The Supply Side of the Market (pages 74–78)
Discuss the variables that influence supply. The **quantity supplied** is the amount of a good that a firm is willing and able to supply at a given price. A **supply schedule** is a table that shows the relationship between the price of a product and the quantity of the product supplied. A **supply curve** shows on a graph the relationship between the price of a product and the quantity of the product supplied. When the price of a product rises, producing the product is more profitable, and a greater amount will be supplied. The **law of supply** states that, holding everything else constant, the quantity of a product supplied increases when the price rises and decreases when the price falls. Changes in the prices of inputs, technology, the prices of substitutes in production, expected future prices, and the number of firms in a market all cause the supply curve to shift. **Technological change** is a positive or negative change in the ability of a firm to produce a given level of output with a given quantity of inputs. A change in supply refers to a shift of the supply curve. A change in quantity supplied refers to a movement along the supply curve as a result of a change in the product's price.

3.3   Market Equilibrium: Putting Demand and Supply Together (pages 78–81)
Use a graph to illustrate market equilibrium. **Market equilibrium** occurs where the demand curve intersects the supply curve. A **competitive market equilibrium** has a market equilibrium with many

buyers and many sellers. Only at this point is the quantity demanded equal to the quantity supplied. Prices above equilibrium result in **surpluses**, with the quantity supplied being greater than the quantity demanded. Surpluses cause the market price to fall. Prices below equilibrium result in **shortages**, with the quantity demanded being greater than the quantity supplied. Shortages cause the market price to rise.

3.4   The Effect of Demand and Supply Shifts on Equilibrium (pages 81–87)
Use demand and supply graphs to predict changes in prices and quantities. In most markets, demand and supply curves shift frequently, causing changes in equilibrium prices and quantities. Over time, if demand increases more than supply, equilibrium price will rise. If supply increases more than demand, equilibrium price will fall.

Chapter Review

Chapter Opener: Red Bull and the Market for Energy Drinks (page 65)
The market for energy drinks has grown dramatically over the last decade or so. While Red Bull led the charge, competitors like Monster and Rockstar have also joined the market. The increased competition has expanded the choices available to customers, but it has also intensified the rivalry among these firms.

 The Demand Side of the Market (pages 66–74)
Learning Objective: Discuss the variables that influence demand.

Although many factors influence the willingness and ability of consumers to buy a particular product, the main influence on consumer decisions is the product's price. The **quantity demanded** of a good or service is the amount that a consumer is willing and able to purchase at a given price. A **demand schedule** is a table showing the relationship between the price of a product and the quantity of the product demanded. A **demand curve** shows this same relationship in a graph. Because quantity demanded always increases in response to a decrease in price, this relationship is called the **law of demand**. The law of demand is explained by the substitution and income effects. The **substitution effect** is the change in the quantity demanded of a good that results from a change in price, making the good more or less expensive relative to other goods that are substitutes. The **income effect** is the change in the quantity demanded of a good that results from the effect of a change in the good's price on consumer purchasing power.

Ceteris paribus ("all else equal") is the requirement that when analyzing the relationship between two variables—such as price and quantity demanded—other variables must be held constant. When one of the non-price factors that influence demand changes, the result is a shift in the demand curve—an increase or decrease in demand. The most important non-price factors that influence demand are prices of related goods (substitutes and complements), income, tastes, population and demographics, and expected future prices.

The income that consumers have available to spend affects their willingness to buy a good. A **normal good** is a good for which demand increases as income rises and decreases as income falls. An **inferior good** is a good for which demand increases as income falls and decreases as income rises. When consumers' tastes for a product increase, the demand curve for the product will shift to the right, and when consumers' tastes for a product decrease, the demand curve for the product will shift to the left. *Making the Connection* "Are Big Macs an Inferior Good?" points out that demand at many restaurants fell during the 2007–2009 recession, indicating that the products and services supplied by these restaurants is a normal good. However, McDonald's continued to have strong demand, and its sales actually increased in 2008 and 2009. This indicates that McDonald's is viewed by its consumers as an inferior good.

Substitutes are goods and services that can be used for the same purpose, while **complements** are goods that are used together. A decrease in the price of a substitute for a good, such as Red Bull, causes the quantity demanded of the substitute, such as coffee, to increase (a move along the demand curve for coffee), which causes the demand for Red Bull to fall. A fall in demand means that the demand curve for Red Bull will shift to the left. An increase in the price of coffee causes the quantity of coffee demanded to decrease, shifting the demand curve for Red Bull to the right. Changes in prices of complements have the opposite effect. A decrease in the price of a complement for Red Bull causes the quantity demanded of the complement, say a gym membership, to increase, shifting the demand curve for Red Bull to the right. An increase in the price of a gym membership causes the quantity of gym memberships demanded to decrease, shifting the demand curve for Red Bull to the left.

As population increases, the demand for most products increases. **Demographics** are the characteristics of a population with respect to age, race, and gender. As demographics change, the demand for particular goods will increase or decrease because as different demographic groups become more prevalent in the population their unique preferences will become more prevalent in the market. If enough consumers become convinced that a good will be selling for a lower price in the near future, then the demand for the good will decrease in the present. If enough consumers become convinced that the price of a good will be higher in the near future, then the demand for the good will increase in the present. ***Making the Connection*** "The Aging of the Baby Boom Generation" discusses the effects the baby boom generation is likely to have on our economy. As that generation of Americans ages, their demand for healthcare is likely to rise, while their demand for large homes is likely to decrease. These changes in demand are a result of changes in the demographics of the U.S. population.

📖 Study Hint

People often confuse a change in quantity demanded with a change in demand. When the price of a good or service changes, it can cause changes in the quantity demanded of that good or service. This change is described as a movement along a demand curve. Notice that the price of the good or service is on the vertical axis. Changes in demand result in shifts of the demand curve and are caused by changes in factors other than the price of the good itself. Be careful about how these terms are used. When demand increases (shifts to the right), we do not say that there has been an increase in the quantity demanded. Rather, we say there has been an increase in demand. If there is an increase in the quantity demanded, the cause of that would be a decrease in the price, and the increase in quantity demanded would be shown as a movement along the demand curve, not a shift.

Take time to study Figure 3-3, which shows the difference between a change in demand and a change in quantity demanded. Also take time to study Table 3-1, which lists all the variables that shift market demand curves.

Extra Solved Problem 3-1
Supports Learning Objective 3.1: Discuss the variables that influence demand.

Suppose that Bob needs to buy an automobile. Bob has decided to purchase a new Mazda Miata convertible. Bob's neighbor tells him that Mazda will be offering a $3,500 rebate on all its automobiles starting next month.

a.   Assuming that Bob can wait until next month to buy an automobile, what effect will the rebate have on Bob's demand for the Miata?

b. Which of the variables that influence demand would explain Bob's change in demand?

SOLVING THE PROBLEM

Step 1: **Review the chapter material.**

This problem is about variables that shift market demand, so you may want to review the section "Variables That Shift Market Demand," which begins on page 68 in the textbook.

Step 2: **Answer question (a) by considering how a rebate that begins next month will affect Bob's current demand for Miatas.**

Bob's demand for the Miata will decrease now and increase next month as he will wait to make his purchase in order to take advantage of the rebate.

Step 3: **Answer question (b) by determining which variable has affected Bob's demand for Miatas.**

Other things being equal, as the expected future price of the Miata falls, the demand for Miatas will fall in the present time period.

The Supply Side of the Market (pages 74–78)

Learning Objective: Discuss the variables that influence supply.

Many variables influence the willingness and ability of firms to sell a good or service. The most important of these variables is the price of the good or service. **Quantity supplied** is the amount of a good or service that a firm is willing to sell at a given price. A **supply schedule** is a table that shows the relationship between the price of a product and the quantity of the product supplied. A **supply curve** shows this same relationship in a graph. The **law of supply** states that, holding everything else constant, increases in the price of the good or service cause increases in the quantity supplied, and decreases in the price of the good or service cause decreases in the quantity supplied.

Variables other than the price of the product affect supply. When any of these variables change, a shift in supply— an increase or a decrease in supply—results. The following are the most important variables that shift supply: prices of inputs used in production, technological change, prices of substitutes in production, expected future prices, and the number of firms in the market.

If the price of an input (for example, labor or energy) used to produce a good rises, the supply of the good will decrease, and the supply curve will shift to the left. If the price of an input decreases, the supply of the good will increase, and the supply curve will shift to the right. **Technological change** is a positive or negative change in the ability of a firm to produce a given level of output with a given amount of inputs. A positive technological change will shift a firm's supply curve to the right, while a negative technological change will shift a firm's supply curve to the left.

An increase in the price of an alternative good (B) that a firm could produce instead of producing good A will shift the firm's supply curve for good A to the left. If a firm expects the price of its product will rise in the future, then the firm has an incentive to decrease supply in the present and increase supply in the future. When firms enter a market, the market supply curve shifts to the right. When firms exit a market, the market supply curve shifts to the left.

📖 Study Hint

The law of supply may seem logical because producers earn more profit when the price they sell their product for rises. But consider Figure 3-4 and the following question: If Red Bull can earn a profit from selling 90 million cans of energy drink per month at a price of $2.50, why not increase quantity supplied to 100 million and make even more profit? The upward slope of the supply curve is due not only to the profit motive but to the increasing marginal cost of cans of Red Bull. (Increasing marginal costs were discussed in Chapter 2.) Red Bull will increase its quantity supplied from 90 to 100 million in Figure 3-4 only if the price it will receive is $3, because the cost of producing 10 million more cans is greater than the cost of the last 10 million cans.

As with demand and quantity demanded, be careful not to confuse a change in quantity supplied (due only to a change in the price of a product) and a change in supply (a shift of the supply curve in response to one of the non-price factors). Constant reinforcement of this is necessary. Be careful not to refer to an increase in supply as "a downward shift" or a decrease in supply as "an upward shift." Because demand curves are downward-sloping, an increase in demand appears in a graph as an "upward shift." But because supply curves are upward-sloping, a *decrease* in supply appears in a graph as an "upward shift." You should always refer to both changes in demand and supply as being "shifts to the right" for an increase and "shifts to the left" for a decrease to avoid confusion.

Take time to study Figure 3.6, which shows the difference between a change in supply and a change in quantity supplied. Also take time to study Table 3.2, which lists all the variables that shift market supply curves.

Extra Solved Problem 3-2

To (Soy)bean or not to (Soy)bean?
Supports Learning Objective 3.2: Discuss the variables that influence supply.

Iowa, Illinois, Nebraska, Minnesota, and Indiana are the top five producers of corn in the United States. While climate and soil conditions in these states make them well-suited for growing corn, these five states are also the top soybean producers in the United States. Each year, farmers in these states must decide how many acres of land to plant with corn and how many acres to plant with soybeans.

a. If both crops can be grown on the same land, why would a farmer choose to produce corn rather than soybeans?

b. Which of the variables that influence supply would explain a farmer's choice to produce soybeans or corn?

SOLVING THE PROBLEM

Step 1:   Review the chapter material.
This problem is about variables that shift supply, so you may want to refer to the section "Variables That Shift Market Supply," which begins on page 75 of the textbook.

Step 2:   Answer question (a) by discussing the factors that would influence a farmer's choice.
Among the factors that would influence a farmer's choice is the expected profitability of the two crops. A farmer will grow corn rather than soybeans if he expects the profits from growing corn will be greater than those earned from growing soybeans.

Step 3:   Answer question (b) by evaluating which variables are most likely to affect supply in the markets for corn and soybeans.
Other things being equal, as the price of soybeans falls relative to the price of corn, the supply of corn would rise. Because corn and soybeans are alternate products a farmer could use in

production, the variable "prices of substitutes in production" would most likely explain the farmer's choice.

 ### Market Equilibrium: Putting Demand and Supply Together (pages 79–81)

Learning Objective: Use a graph to illustrate market equilibrium.

The purpose of markets is to bring buyers and sellers together. The interaction of buyers and sellers in markets results in firms producing goods and services consumers both want and can afford. At **market equilibrium,** the price of the product makes quantity demanded equal quantity supplied. A **competitive market equilibrium** is a market equilibrium with many buyers and many sellers. The market price (the actual price you would pay for the product) will not always be the equilibrium price. A **surplus** is a situation in which the quantity supplied is greater than the quantity demanded, which occurs when the market price is above the equilibrium price. Firms have an incentive to increase sales by lowering price. As the market price is lowered, quantity demanded will rise and quantity supplied will fall until the market reaches equilibrium.

A **shortage** is a situation in which quantity demanded is greater than the quantity supplied, which occurs when the market price is below the equilibrium price. Some consumers will want to buy the product at a higher price to make sure they get what they want. As the market price rises, the quantity demanded will fall—not everyone will want to buy at a higher price—and quantity supplied will rise until the market reaches equilibrium. At the competitive market equilibrium, there is no reason for the price to change unless either the demand curve or the supply curve shifts.

📖 Study Hint

It's very important to understand how demand and supply interact to reach equilibrium. Remember that adjustments to a shortage or a surplus represent changes in quantity demanded (not demand) and quantity supplied (not supply). *Solved Problem 3-3* and problems 3.4 and 3.5 in the Problems and Applications at the end of the chapter address this topic. In *Solved Problem 3-3*, we see how the demand and supply for the letters written by Lincoln and Booth determine the price for the letters written by each author. Because the supply is low relative to the demand for Booth's letters, his letters sell for a high equilibrium price. Similarly, because the supply of Lincoln's letters is large relative to the demand, his letters sell for a lower equilibrium price. Market or actual prices are easy to understand because these are the prices consumers are charged. You know the price you paid for a CD because it is printed on the receipt, but no receipt has "equilibrium price" written on it.

3.4 The Effect of Demand and Supply Shifts on Equilibrium (pages 81–87)

Learning Objective: Use demand and supply graphs to predict changes in prices and quantities.

Increases in supply result from: a decrease in an input price, positive technological change, a decrease in the price of a substitute in production, a lower expected future product price, and an increase in the number of firms in the market. A decrease in supply results in a higher equilibrium price and a lower equilibrium quantity. Decreases in supply result from the following non-price factor changes: an increase in an input price, negative technological change, an increase in the price of a substitute in production, a higher expected future product price, and a decrease in the number of firms in the market.

Increases in demand can be caused by any change in a variable that affects demand *except price*. For example, demand will increase if the price of a substitute increases, the price of a complement decreases, income increases (for a normal good), income decreases (for an inferior good), population increases, or the expected future price of the product increases. A decrease in demand results in a lower equilibrium price and lower equilibrium quantity. Decreases in demand can be caused by any change in a variable that affects demand *except the price of the product itself*. For example, demand will decrease if the price of a substitute decreases, the price of a complement increases, income decreases (for a normal good), income increases (for an inferior good), population decreases, or the expected future price of the product decreases.

📖 **Study Hint**

When demand shifts, the equilibrium price and quantity both change in the same direction as the shift. For example, an increase in demand (graphed as a shift to the right of demand) results in an increase in both the price and the equilibrium quantity. However, when supply shifts, the equilibrium quantity changes in the same direction as the shift, but the equilibrium price changes in the opposite direction. For example, an increase in supply (graphed as a shift to the right of supply) results in an increase in the equilibrium quantity, but a decrease in the equilibrium price. For additional practice be sure to review *Solved Problem 3-4* on lobsters and problem 4.5 on watermelons in the Problems and Applications section.

Key Terms

Ceteris paribus **("all else equal") condition** The requirement that when analyzing the relationship between two variables—such as price and quantity demanded—other variables must be held constant.

Competitive market equilibrium A market equilibrium with many buyers and many sellers.

Complements Goods and services that are used together.

Demand curve A curve that shows the relationship between the price of a product and the quantity of the product demanded.

Demand schedule A table showing the relationship between the price of a product and the quantity of the product demanded.

Demographics The characteristics of a population with respect to age, race, and gender.

Income effect The change in the quantity demanded of a good that results from the effect of a change in the good's price on consumers' purchasing power.

Inferior good A good for which the demand increases as income falls and decreases as income rises.

Law of demand The rule that, holding everything else constant, when the price of a product falls, the quantity demanded of the product will increase, and when the price of a product rises, the quantity demanded of the product will decrease.

Law of supply The rule that, holding everything else constant, increases in price cause increases in the quantity supplied, and decreases in price cause decreases in the quantity supplied.

Market demand The demand by all the consumers of a given good or service.

Market equilibrium A situation in which quantity demanded equals quantity supplied.

Normal good A good for which the demand increases as income rises and decreases as income falls.

Perfectly competitive market A market that meets the conditions of (1) many buyers and sellers, (2) all firms selling identical products, and (3) no barriers to new firms entering the market.

Quantity demanded The amount of a good or service that a consumer is willing and able to purchase at a given price.

Quantity supplied The amount of a good or service that a firm is willing and able to supply at a given price.

Shortage A situation in which the quantity demanded is greater than the quantity supplied.

Substitutes Goods and services that can be used for the same purpose.

Substitution effect The change in the quantity demanded of a good that results from a change in price, making the good more or less expensive relative to other goods that are substitutes.

Supply curve A curve that shows the relationship between the price of a product and the quantity of the product supplied.

Supply schedule A table that shows the relationship between the price of a product and the quantity of the product supplied.

Surplus A situation in which the quantity supplied is greater than the quantity demanded.

Technological change A positive or negative change in the ability of a firm to produce a given level of output with a given quantity of inputs.

Self-Test

(Answers are provided at the end of the Self-Test.)

Multiple-Choice Questions

1. Refer to the graph below. In the market for digital music players, price is $250 and quantity demanded is 35 million players. Which of the following interpretations of this point on the graph is correct?

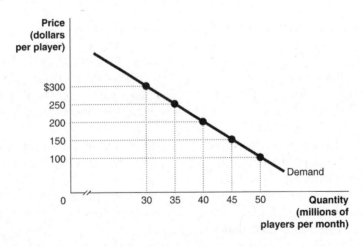

  a. This point shows that consumers spend a total of $250 on 35 million players each month.
  b. When one player costs $250, consumers buy 35 million of them per month.
  c. When one player costs $250, suppliers sell 35 million of them per month.
  d. At $250, quantity demanded equals quantity supplied.

2. What does the term quantity demanded refer to?
    a. the total amount of a good or service that a consumer is willing to buy per month
    b. the quantity of a good or service demanded that corresponds to the quantity supplied
    c. the quantity of a good or service that a consumer is willing and able to purchase at a given price
    d. none of the above

3. Which of the following is the correct definition of demand schedule?
    a. the quantity of a good or service that a consumer is willing to purchase at a given price
    b. a table showing the relationship between the price of a product and the quantity of the product demanded
    c. a curve that shows the relationship between the price of a product and the quantity of the product demanded
    d. the demand for a product by all the consumers in a given geographical area

4. Which of the following is the correct definition of demand curve?
    a. the quantity of a good or service that a consumer is willing to purchase at a given price
    b. a table showing the relationship between the price of a product and the quantity of the product demanded
    c. a curve that shows the relationship between the price of a product and the quantity of the product demanded
    d. the demand for a product by all the consumers in a given geographical area

5. Which of the following is the correct definition of market demand?
    a. the quantity of a good or service that a consumer is willing to purchase at a given price
    b. a table showing the relationship between the price of a product and the quantity of the product demanded
    c. a curve that shows the relationship between the price of a product and the quantity of the product demanded
    d. the demand by all the consumers for a given good or service

6. Refer to the graph below. What happens to quantity demanded along this demand curve?

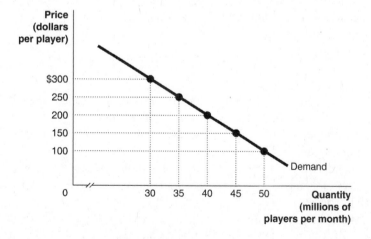

    a. Quantity demanded increases as the price increases.
    b. Quantity demanded increases as the price decreases.
    c. Quantity demanded may increase or decrease as the price increases.
    d. Quantity demanded is not related to price.

7. Refer to the graph below. Along the demand curve, what happens to the quantity demanded as the price falls from $250 to $200 per player?

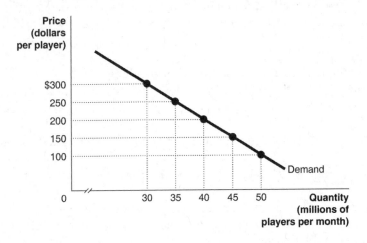

   a.   The quantity demanded increases from 35 million to 40 million players per month.
   b.   The quantity demanded decreases from 40 million to 35 million players per month.
   c.   We cannot predict the change in the quantity demanded without the supply curve.
   d.   The change in the quantity demanded is not related to a change in price.

8. When the price of a digital music player rises, the quantity of digital music players demanded by consumers falls. Therefore, the demand curve for digital music players is
   a.   unpredictable.
   b.   upward sloping.
   c.   downward sloping.
   d.   an exception to the law of demand.

9. Which of the following explains why there is an inverse relationship between the price of a product and the quantity of the product demanded?
   a.   Markets have many buyers and sellers, and all firms sell identical products.
   b.   There are no barriers to new firms entering markets.
   c.   the *ceteris paribus* condition
   d.   the substitution effect

10. What is the *law of demand*?
   a.   The law of demand states that a change in the quantity demanded, caused by changes in price, makes the good more or less expensive relative to other goods.
   b.   The law of demand states that a change in the quantity demanded, caused by changes in price, affects a consumer's purchasing power.
   c.   The law of demand is the rule that, holding everything else constant, when the price of a good falls, the quantity demanded will increase, and when the price of a good rises, the quantity demanded will decrease.
   d.   The law of demand is the requirement that when analyzing the relationship between price and quantity demanded, other variables must be held constant.

11. Which of the following is used to describe how changes in price affect a consumer's purchasing power?
    a. the law of demand
    b. the substitution effect
    c. the income effect
    d. the *ceteris paribus* condition

12. Which of the following is used to explain why consumers buy other goods when the price of a good rises?
    a. the law of demand
    b. the substitution effect
    c. the income effect
    d. the *ceteris paribus* condition

13. Economists refer to the necessity of holding all variables other than price constant in constructing a demand curve as the
    a. law of demand.
    b. substitution effect.
    c. income effect.
    d. *ceteris paribus* condition.

14. Refer to the graphs below. Each graph refers to the demand for digital music players. Which of the graphs illustrates the impact of an increase in the price of a substitute good?

    a. the graph on the left
    b. the graph on the right
    c. both graphs
    d. neither graph

15. Refer to the graphs below. Each graph refers to the demand for digital music players. Which of the graphs illustrates the impact of an increase in the price of a complementary good?

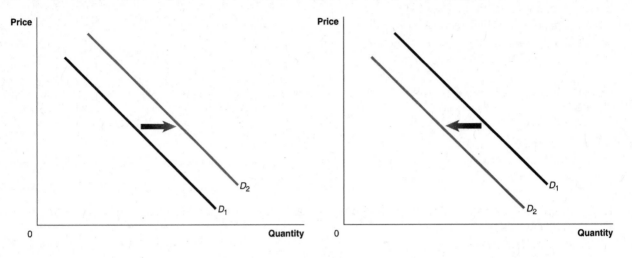

    a.   the graph on the left
    b.   the graph on the right
    c.   both graphs
    d.   neither graph

16. Refer to the graphs below. Each graph refers to the demand for digital music players. Which of the graphs illustrates the impact of an increase in income, assuming that digital music players are a normal good?

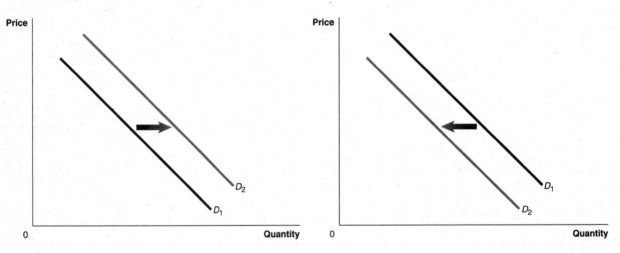

    a.   the graph on the left
    b.   the graph on the right
    c.   both graphs
    d.   neither graph

17. Refer to the graphs below. Each graph refers to the demand for digital music players. Which of the graphs illustrates the impact of an increase in consumers' tastes for digital music players?

    a.   the graph on the left
    b.   the graph on the right
    c.   both graphs
    d.   neither graph

18. Refer to the graphs below. Each graph refers to the demand for digital music players. Which of the graphs illustrates the impact of an increase in population?

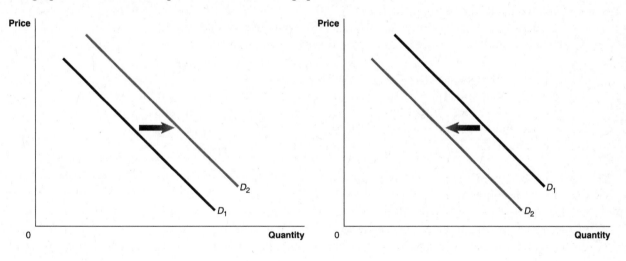

    a.   the graph on the left
    b.   the graph on the right
    c.   both graphs
    d.   neither graph

19. Refer to the graphs below. Each graph refers to the demand for digital music players. Which of the graphs illustrates the impact of an increase in the expected price of digital music players in the future?

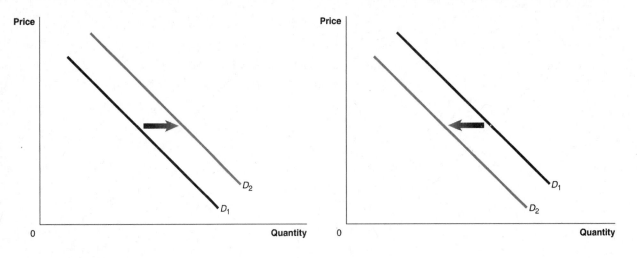

   a.   the graph on the left
   b.   the graph on the right
   c.   both graphs
   d.   neither graph

20. When two goods are complements, which of the following is true?
   a.   The two goods can be used for the same purpose.
   b.   The two goods are used together.
   c.   The demand for each of these goods increases when income rises.
   d.   The demand for each of these goods increases as income falls.

21. Which of the following describes two goods that are substitutes?
   a.   As the price of one of the goods increases, the demand for the other good increases.
   b.   The more consumers buy of one good, the more they will buy of the other good.
   c.   The demand for each of these goods increases when income increases.
   d.   The demand for each of these goods increases as income decreases.

22. If peanut butter and jelly are complements, how will an increase in the price of jelly affect the demand for peanut butter?
   a.   Demand for peanut butter will increase.
   b.   Demand for peanut butter will decrease.
   c.   Demand for peanut butter will not change, but the quantity of peanut butter demanded will increase.
   d.   Demand for peanut butter will not change, but the quantity of peanut butter demanded will decrease.

23. Which of the following would result in a decrease in the demand for Red Bull?
   a.   an increase in the price of Red Bull
   b.   an increase in the price of Monster Energy, a substitute for Red Bull
   c.   an increase in income, assuming Red Bull is a normal good
   d.   an increase in the price of pizza, a complement of Red Bull

24. What is an inferior good?
    a. a good for which demand increases as income rises
    b. a good for which demand decreases as income rises
    c. a good that cannot be used together with another good
    d. a good that does not serve any real purpose

25. What is a normal good?
    a. a good for which demand increases as income rises
    b. a good for which demand decreases as income rises
    c. a good that can be used together with another good
    d. a good that serves more than one purpose

26. Refer to the graph below. Which of the following moves illustrates a change in demand?

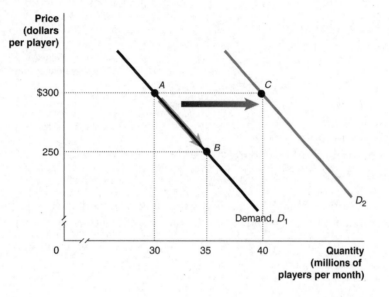

    a. the move from *A* to *B*
    b. the move from *A* to *C*
    c. either the move from *A* to *B* or from *A* to *C*
    d. the move from *B* to *A*

27. Refer to the graph below. Which of the following moves illustrates a change in quantity demanded?

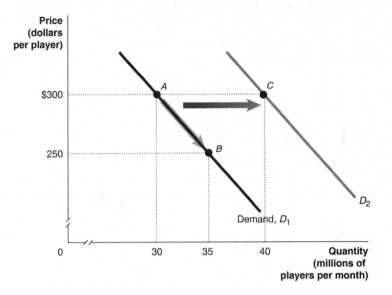

    a.   the move from *A* to *B*
    b.   the move from *A* to *C*
    c.   either the move from *A* to *B* or from *A* to *C*
    d.   the move from *B* to *C*

28. Refer to the graph below. Which of the following moves illustrates what happens when there is a change in a determinant of the demand for digital music players other than the price of players?

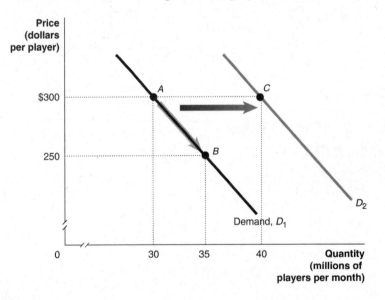

    a.   the move from *A* to *B*
    b.   the move from *A* to *C*
    c.   either the move from *A* to *B* or from *A* to *C*
    d.   none of the above

29. Refer to the graph below. Which of the following moves illustrates what happens when a change in the price of digital music players affects the market demand for players?

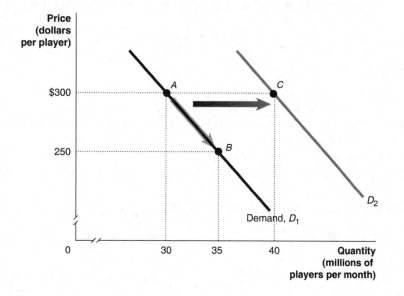

a. the move from *A* to *B*
b. the move from *A* to *C*
c. either the move from *A* to *B* or from *A* to *C*
d. none of the above

30. Which of the following would not shift the demand curve for a good or service?
    a. a change in the price of a related good
    b. a change in the price of the good or service
    c. a change in expectations about the price of the good or service
    d. a change in income

31. The term quantity supplied refers to
    a. the quantity of a good or service that a firm is willing and able to supply at a given price.
    b. a table that shows the relationship between the price of a product and the quantity of the product supplied.
    c. a curve that shows the relationship between the price of a product and the quantity of the product demanded.
    d. none of the above

32. Which of the following is the textbook's definition of a supply schedule?
    a. the quantity of a good or service that a firm is willing to supply at a given price
    b. a table that shows the relationship between the price of a product and the quantity of the product supplied
    c. a curve that shows the relationship between the price of a product and the quantity of the product demanded
    d. none of the above

33. Which of the following is the textbook's definition of a supply curve?
    a. the quantity of a good or service that a firm is willing to supply at a given price
    b. a table that shows the relationship between the price of a product and the quantity of the product supplied
    c. a curve that shows the relationship between the price of a product and the quantity of the product supplied
    d. none of the above

34. Which of the following is consistent with the law of supply?
    a. An increase in price causes an increase in the quantity supplied, and a decrease in price causes a decrease in the quantity supplied.
    b. A change in price causes a shift of the supply curve.
    c. Supply shifts are caused not by a single variable but most likely by a number of different variables.
    d. All of the above are consistent with the law of supply.

35. Refer to the graphs below. Each graph refers to the supply for digital music players. Which of the graphs illustrates the impact of an increase in the price of an input?

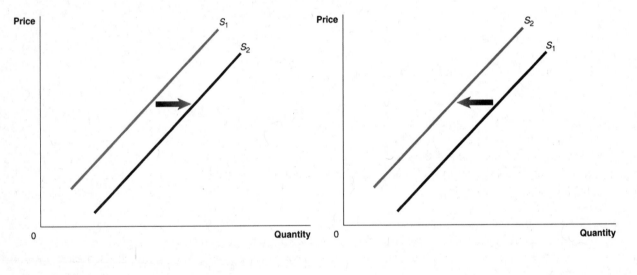

    a. the graph on the left
    b. the graph on the right
    c. both graphs
    d. neither graph

36. Refer to the graphs below. Each graph refers to the supply for digital music players. Which of the graphs illustrates the impact of an increase in productivity?

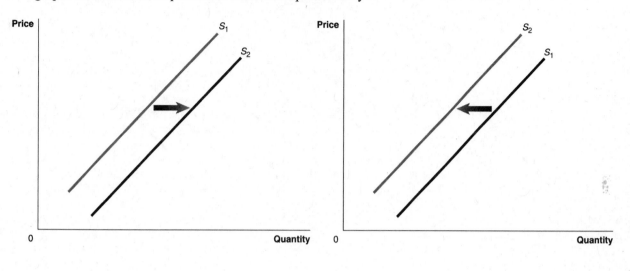

    a.   the graph on the left
    b.   the graph on the right
    c.   both graphs
    d.   neither graph

37. Refer to the graphs below. Each graph refers to the supply for digital music players. Which of the graphs illustrates the impact of an increase in the price of a substitute in production?

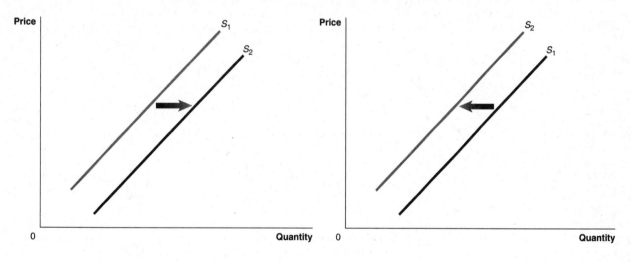

    a.   the graph on the left
    b.   the graph on the right
    c.   both graphs
    d.   neither graph

38. Refer to the graphs below. Each graph refers to the supply for digital music players. Which of the graphs illustrates the impact of an increase in the expected future price of the product?

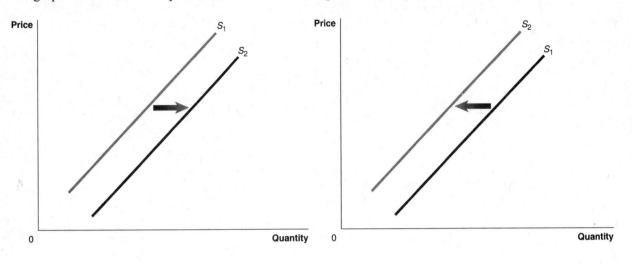

    a.   the graph on the left
    b.   the graph on the right
    c.   both graphs
    d.   neither graph

39. Refer to the graphs below. Each graph refers to the supply for digital music players. Which of the graphs illustrates the impact of an increase in the number of firms in the market?

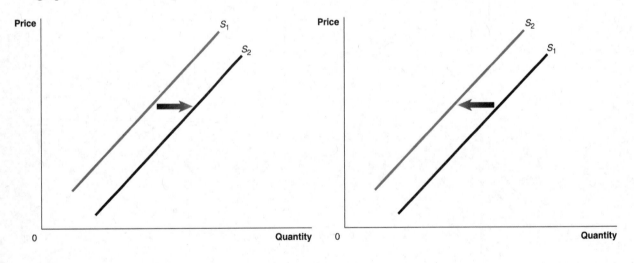

    a.   the graph on the left
    b.   the graph on the right
    c.   both graphs
    d.   neither graph

40. Refer to the graph below. Which of the following moves illustrates what happens when there is a change in a determinant of the supply for digital music players other than the price of players?

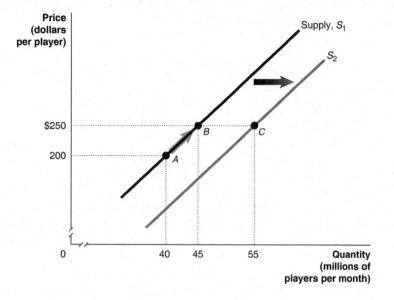

a. the move from *A* to *B*
b. the move from *B* to *C*
c. either the move from *A* to *B* or from *A* to *C*
d. none of the above

41. Refer to the graph below. Which of the following moves illustrates what happens when a change in the price of digital music players affects the market supply for players?

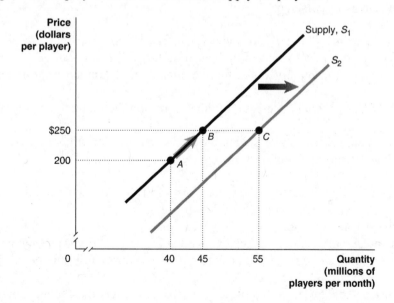

a. the move from *A* to *B*
b. the move from *A* to *C*
c. either the move from *A* to *B* or from *A* to *C*
d. none of the above

42. Which of the following would shift the supply of Red Bull to the left?
    a. an increase in the price of Red Bull
    b. an increase in the price of inputs used to produce Red Bull
    c. a decrease in the expected future price of Red Bull
    d. all of the above

43. A surplus exists in a market if the actual price is
    a. equal to the equilibrium price.
    b. below the equilibrium price.
    c. above the equilibrium price.
    d. either above or below the equilibrium price.

44. If a shortage exists in a market we know that the actual price is
    a. below equilibrium price and quantity demanded is greater than quantity supplied.
    b. above equilibrium price and quantity demanded is greater than quantity supplied.
    c. above equilibrium price and quantity supplied is greater than quantity demanded.
    d. below equilibrium price and quantity supplied is greater than quantity demanded.

45. An early frost in the apple orchards of Washington State would cause
    a. an increase in the demand for apple juice, increasing equilibrium price.
    b. an increase in the supply of apple juice, decreasing equilibrium price.
    c. a decrease in the demand for apple juice, decreasing equilibrium price.
    d. a decrease in the supply of apple juice, increasing equilibrium price.

46. Which of the following would definitely result in a higher price in the market for tennis shoes?
    a. demand increases and supply decreases
    b. demand and supply both decrease
    c. demand decreases and supply increases
    d. demand and supply both increase

47. Suppose that the income of buyers in a market increases and a technological advancement also occurs. What would we expect to happen in the market for a normal good?
    a. The equilibrium price would increase, but the impact on the amount sold in the market would be ambiguous.
    b. The equilibrium price would decrease, but the impact on the amount sold in the market would be ambiguous.
    c. Equilibrium quantity would increase, but the impact on equilibrium price would be ambiguous.
    d. Both equilibrium price and equilibrium quantity would increase.

48. If both demand and supply decrease in the market for Red Bull, how will equilibrium be affected?
    a. Equilibrium price and equilibrium quantity will rise.
    b. Equilibrium price and equilibrium quantity will fall.
    c. Equilibrium price will rise, but the impact on equilibrium quantity is ambiguous.
    d. The impact on equilibrium price will be ambiguous, but the equilibrium quantity will fall.

49. How will a decrease in the expected future price of Red Bull affect the demand and supply of Red Bull?
    a. Demand will rise and supply will fall.
    b. Demand will rise and supply will rise.
    c. Demand will fall and supply will rise.
    d. Demand will fall and supply will fall.

50. How will a decrease in the expected future price of Red Bull affect the equilibrium price and quantity?
    a. Equilibrium price and equilibrium quantity will rise.
    b. Equilibrium price will fall, and equilibrium quantity will rise.
    c. Equilibrium price will rise; the impact on equilibrium quantity is ambiguous.
    d. Equilibrium price will fall; the impact on equilibrium quantity is ambiguous.

Short Answer Questions

1. What evidence can be used to support the following statement? "Tickets to the World Series and the Super Bowl do not sell at their equilibrium prices."

    _____

    _____

    _____

    _____

    _____

2. In response to a surplus, a firm will lower a product's price until the quantity supplied equals quantity demanded. But prices of some goods will fall more quickly than others. What type of good would a firm lower the price of quickly in response to a surplus?

    _____

    _____

    _____

    _____

3. Explain the difference between a shortage and scarcity.

    _____

    _____

    _____

    _____

4. During 2009 there were over 100,000 people on waiting lists for kidney, lung, and other organ transplant operations. By law, organ donors and their families in the United States may not be paid for the donated organs. If payments for organ donations were made legal in the United States, would this affect the demand or the quantity demanded for organ transplants?

_____

_____

_____

_____

_____

5. The demand for health care in the United States is expected to rise throughout the first part of the twenty-first century. Which of the variables that influence market demand is most responsible for this expected increase?

_____

_____

_____

6. Briefly comment on the following statement: "An increase in demand always leads to an increase in supply."

_____

_____

_____

True/False Questions

T F 1. A market demand curve demonstrates the quantity that each consumer is willing to buy at each possible price.

T F 2. The law of demand states that, holding everything else constant, increases in price cause decreases in demand.

T F 3. The price of lobsters is higher in the spring than in the summer, even though demand is greater in the summer. The lower summer price results from increases in the supply of lobsters in the summer.

T F 4. As a result of a surplus, the price in a market will fall; quantity supplied falls and quantity demanded rises until equilibrium is reached.

T F 5. An increase in income causes demand for a normal good to increase.

T F 6. Big Macs are normal goods because the demand for Big Macs increased during the most recent recession in the United States.

T F 7.   Inferior goods are goods that are of lesser quality than other similar goods.

T F 8.   Substitution and income effects are used to explain the law of supply.

T F 9.   A negative technological change will shift the supply curve for a product to the left.

T F 10. Increases in the supply of flat-screen televisions led to lower prices and increased quantity demanded for these televisions.

T F 11. An increase in the price of a complement for good A will decrease the demand for good A.

T F 12. As "baby boomers" age, the demand for large houses is expected to increase.

T F 13. If both demand and supply increase over time, equilibrium price and equilibrium quantity will also rise.

T F 14. A change in price will not cause a change in demand or supply.

T F 15. Competitive markets have many buyers and many sellers.

Answers to the Self-Test

Multiple-Choice Questions

Question	Answer	Comment
1	b	In this example, the quantity of players demanded per month is 35 million when the price per player is $250.
2	c	Quantity demanded is the amount of a good or service that a consumer is willing and able to buy at a given price. See page 66 in the textbook.
3	b	The demand schedule is a table, not a curve or a single quantity demanded at a given price. See page 66 in the textbook.
4	c	This is the definition of demand curve. See page 66 in the textbook.
5	d	This is the definition of market demand. See page 66 in the textbook.
6	b	The demand curve is downward sloping. There is an inverse relationship between price and quantity demanded, meaning that price and quantity demanded move in opposite directions.
7	a	The demand curve is downward sloping, so as the price falls the quantity demanded rises.
8	c	The consumers' demand curve is downward sloping. There is an inverse relationship between price and quantity demanded. Price and quantity demanded move in opposite directions.
9	d	The law of demand states that there is an inverse relationship between the price of a product and the quantity of the product demanded, and the substitution and income effects explain the law of demand.
10	c	According to the law of demand, there is an inverse relationship between the price of a product and the quantity of the product demanded.
11	c	Along with the substitution effect, the income effect helps to explain why a demand curve is downward sloping. (Note that the income effect only works in this direction for normal goods.)
12	b	The substitution effect helps to explain why a demand curve is downward sloping. See page 67 in the textbook.
13	d	The term *ceteris paribus* is Latin for "all else equal."
14	a	This graph shows an increase in demand. When the price of a substitute good rises, the demand for the good in question also rises.
15	b	Demand decreases when the price of a complementary good increases.
16	a	This graph shows an increase in demand. When income increases, the demand for any normal good also increases.
17	a	This graph shows an increase in demand. When tastes for a product increase, the

demand for the good in question also increases.

18	a	This graph shows an increase in demand. When population increases, the demand for the good in question also increases.
19	a	This graph shows an increase in demand. When the expected future price of a product increases, the demand for the good in question today also increases.
20	b	When two goods are complements, the more consumers buy of one the more they will buy of the other.
21	a	Substitutes are goods and services that can be used for the same purpose.
22	b	An increase in the price of a good will lead to a decrease in the demand for a complement for the good.
23	d	An increase in the price of a complement will decrease demand for the good.
24	b	The term inferior good means consumers will buy less of a good as income rises.
25	a	The term normal good means consumers will buy more of a good as their income increases.
26	b	Anything that causes a demand curve to shift also causes a change in demand.
27	a	Anything that causes movement along a single demand curve also causes a change in quantity demanded. The only factor that can change quantity demanded is a change in the price of the product.
28	b	When any variable that affects demand changes, demand shifts. (The sole exception to this rule is changes in the price of the product.)
29	a	Anything that causes a movement along a single demand curve also causes a change in quantity demanded. The only factor that can change quantity demanded is a change in the price of the product.
30	b	A change in the price of a good or service does not cause a shift in the demand curve. It would cause a movement along the demand curve.
31	a	Quantity supplied is the quantity of a good or service that a firm is willing to supply at a given price. See page 74 in the textbook.
32	b	A table that shows the relationship between the price of a product and the quantity of the product supplied is called the supply schedule. See page 74 in the textbook.
33	c	A curve that shows the relationship between the price of a product and the quantity of the product supplied is called a supply curve. Quantity supplied is the quantity of a good or service that a firm is willing to supply at a given price. See page 74 in the textbook.
34	a	This is the law of supply. See page 75 in the textbook.
35	b	This graph shows a decrease in supply. When the price of an input increases, supply decreases.
36	a	This graph shows an increase in supply. When productivity increases, supply increases.
37	b	This graph shows a decrease in supply. When the price of a substitute in production increases, supply for the good in question decreases because more of the substitute is produced and less of the good in question is produced.
38	b	This graph shows a decrease in supply. When the expected future price of a product increases, supply for the good in question decreases today because less of the good will be produced today and more will be produced in the future to take advantage of the higher future price.
39	a	This graph shows an increase in supply. When the number of firms in the market increases, market supply increases.
40	b	A determinant of supply other than price will cause a shift in the supply curve. In this case, the supply increases or the supply curve shifts to the right.
41	a	If the price of a good changes that will cause a movement along the supply curve. This movement from *A* to *B* is an increase in the quantity supplied.
42	b	An increase in the price of inputs will decrease supply (shift supply to the left).

43	c	If the actual price is above the equilibrium price, the quantity supplied is greater than the quantity demanded, so there is a surplus.
44	a	If the actual price is below the equilibrium price, the quantity demanded is greater than the quantity supplied, so there is a shortage.
45	d	If there is a frost, it will destroy some of the apples, which will cause the price of apples to rise. Because apples are an input in the production of apple juice, the supply of apple juice will decrease, resulting in an increase in the equilibrium price of apple juice.
46	a	The price will rise when the demand increases and the supply decreases, though the effect on the equilibrium quantity will be ambiguous.
47	c	Both the demand and supply shift to the right, which will cause an increase in the equilibrium quantity and an ambiguous effect on the price.
48	d	The decrease in demand and decrease in supply both reduce the equilibrium quantity, but the decrease in demand reduces the equilibrium price while the decrease in supply increases the equilibrium price. As a result, the equilibrium price may rise or fall.
49	c	A decrease in the expected future price discourages consumers from making purchases in the current period but encourages sellers to increase sales in the current period.
50	d	The lower demand for Red Bull reduces price and quantity, while the increase in supply reduces price but increases quantity.

Short Answer Responses

1. Tickets for these events typically sell out soon after they are offered to the public. Many of these tickets are later resold at prices higher than the original prices buyers paid for them. This implies that the quantity demanded for the tickets is greater than the quantity supplied at the original prices. The prices the tickets are first sold at are below their equilibrium levels.

2. Prices of perishable goods such as fresh fish, baked goods, milk, and fruit are likely to be lowered quickly. A key factor is the product's durability. Services are the most perishable products, but a head of lettuce is not much more durable. However, cars and home appliances can be stored as inventories for quite some time without spoiling.

3. A shortage exists when the price for a product is less than the equilibrium price. If the price is allowed to rise to its equilibrium level, the shortage will be eliminated. But the product will be scarce whether the market price is above, below, or equal to its equilibrium value. Every economic product is scarce because unlimited human wants exceed society's limited productive resources.

4. Because the price of organs and transplant operations would rise, this would affect quantity demanded rather than demand. An increase in the price of organs and transplant operations would typically decrease the quantity demanded. But it is unlikely that the quantity demanded would change very much, if at all, because there are no good substitutes for the operations.

5. Demographics are most responsible for this change. As more members of the so-called baby boom generation reach retirement age, their demand for health care will increase. (Most health care spending is for care of those over age 60.)

6.   An increase in demand results in an increase in the equilibrium price and equilibrium quantity. As the equilibrium price rises, the quantity supplied also increases. However, supply itself does not shift, so there is no increase in supply. An increase in supply will be caused only by one of the determinants of supply, not an increase in demand.

True/False Answers

1.   F   The demand curve shows the quantity that all consumers would collectively demand at each possible price.
2.   F   Increases in price cause decreases in quantity demanded, not demand.
3.   T   Even though demand increases in the summer, the supply increases even more.
4.   T   A surplus would cause firms to want to decrease their supply to reduce their inventories. As the price falls, the quantity demanded increases and the quantity supplied decreases.
5.   T   A normal good is one for which demand increases as income rises.
6.   F   Because the demand for Big Macs rose during the most recent U.S. recession, that indicates Big Macs are actually inferior goods.
7.   F   Inferior goods are ones that you buy less of as your income rises.
8.   F   Substitution and income effects explain the law of demand, not supply.
9.   T   If something causes technology to decrease, the supply will decrease.
10.   T   As the supply increased, the market price fell, which caused a downward movement along the demand curve for flat-screen televisions; that is, there was an increase in quantity demanded.
11.   T   Complements, such as coffee and creamer, are consumed together. If the price of one increases, consumers will buy less of the related good.
12.   F   Older people often downsize their homes, so the demand for large homes is expected to decrease as baby boomers age.
13.   F   An increase in both demand and supply will increase equilibrium quantity, but the equilibrium price will be ambiguous.
14.   T   A change in price causes a change in the quantity demanded or quantity supplied, not demand or supply.
15.   T   A competitive market must have many buyers and many sellers.

CHAPTER 4 | Economic Efficiency, Government Price Setting, and Taxes

Chapter Summary and Learning Objectives

4.1 Consumer Surplus and Producer Surplus (pages 98–102)

Distinguish between the concepts of consumer surplus and producer surplus. Although most prices are determined by demand and supply in markets, the government sometimes imposes *price ceilings* and *price floors*. A **price ceiling** is a legally determined maximum price that sellers may charge. A **price floor** is a legally determined minimum price that sellers may receive. Economists analyze the effects of price ceilings and price floors using *consumer surplus* and *producer surplus*. **Marginal benefit** is the additional benefit to a consumer from consuming one more unit of a good or service. The demand curve is also a marginal benefit curve. **Consumer surplus** is the difference between the highest price a consumer is willing to pay for a good or service and the price the consumer actually pays. The total amount of consumer surplus in a market is equal to the area below the demand curve and above the market price. **Marginal cost** is the additional cost to a firm of producing one more unit of a good or service. The supply curve is also a marginal cost curve. **Producer surplus** is the difference between the lowest price a firm is willing to accept for a good or service and the price it actually receives. The total amount of producer surplus in a market is equal to the area above the supply curve and below the market price.

4.2 The Efficiency of Competitive Markets (pages 102–105)

Understand the concept of economic efficiency. Equilibrium in a competitive market is **economically efficient**. **Economic surplus** is the sum of consumer surplus and producer surplus. Economic efficiency is a market outcome in which the marginal benefit to consumers from the last unit produced is equal to the marginal cost of production and where the sum of consumer surplus and producer surplus is at a maximum. When the market price is above or below the equilibrium price, there is a reduction in economic surplus. The reduction in economic surplus resulting from a market not being in competitive equilibrium is called the **deadweight loss**.

4.3 Government Intervention in the Market: Price Floors and Price Ceilings (pages 105–112)

Explain the economic effect of government-imposed price floors and price ceilings. Producers or consumers who are dissatisfied with the market outcome can attempt to convince the government to impose price floors or price ceilings. Price floors usually increase producer surplus, decrease consumer surplus, and cause a deadweight loss. Price ceilings usually increase consumer surplus, reduce producer surplus, and cause a deadweight loss. The results of the government imposing price ceilings and price floors are that some people win, some people lose, and a loss of economic efficiency occurs. Price ceilings and price floors can lead to a **black market**, where buying and selling take place at prices that violate government price regulations. Positive analysis is concerned with what is, and normative analysis is concerned with what should be. Positive analysis shows that price ceilings and price floors cause deadweight losses. Whether these policies are desirable or undesirable, though, is a normative question.

4.4   The Economic Impact of Taxes (pages 112–117)
Analyze the economic impact of taxes. Most taxes result in a loss of consumer surplus, a loss of producer surplus, and a deadweight loss. The true burden of a tax is not just the amount paid to government by consumers and producers but also includes the deadweight loss. The deadweight loss from a tax is the excess burden of the tax. **Tax incidence** is the actual division of the burden of a tax. In most cases, consumers and firms share the burden of a tax levied on a good or service.

Appendix: Quantitative Demand and Supply Analysis (pages 127–131)
Use quantitative demand and supply analysis.

Chapter Review

Chapter Opener: Should the Government Control Apartment Rents? (page 97)
Rent control is an example of a price ceiling. Rent controls exist in about 200 cities in the United States. Although the rules that govern rent control are complex and vary by city, rent control drives up the demand and price for apartments not subject to the controls. Like any price control, rent control also has many unintended consequences including lower quality of rent-controlled units, black markets, and unwanted, inefficient side conditions.

📖 **Study Hint**
Read *Solved Problem 4-3* and *An Inside Look* from this chapter to reinforce your understanding of the impact of rent control on the demand and supply of apartments.

 4.1   Consumer Surplus and Producer Surplus (pages 98–102)
Learning Objective: Distinguish between the concepts of consumer surplus and producer surplus.

Consumer surplus is the difference between the highest price a consumer is willing to pay and the price the consumer actually pays. **Producer surplus** is the difference between the lowest price a firm would be willing to accept and the price it actually receives.

Marginal benefit is the additional benefit to a consumer from consuming one more unit of a good or service. The height of a market demand curve at a given quantity measures the marginal benefit to someone from consuming that quantity. Consumer surplus refers to the difference between this marginal benefit and the market price the consumer pays. Total consumer surplus is the difference between marginal benefit and price for all quantities bought by consumers. Total consumer surplus is equal to the area below the demand curve and above the market price for the number of units consumed.

Marginal cost is the additional cost to a firm of producing one more unit of a good or service. The height of a market supply curve at a given quantity measures the marginal cost of this quantity. Producer surplus refers to the difference between this marginal cost and the market price the producer receives. Total producer surplus equals the area above the supply curve and below price for all quantities sold.

📖 **Study Hint**
You probably have bought something you thought was a bargain. If you did, the difference between what you would have been willing to pay and what you did pay was your consumer surplus. Consumers differ

in the value they place on the same item but typically pay the same price for the item. Those who value an item the most receive the most consumer surplus. For producers, the marginal cost of producing a good rises as more is produced, but the price producers receive remains constant. As a result, the difference between the price producers receive and their marginal cost of production—their producer surplus—falls as more is produced. Be sure you understand Figures 4-3 and 4-4 and the explanation of these figures in the textbook.

Extra Solved Problem 4-1
Consumer and Producer Surplus for the NFL Sunday Ticket
Supports Learning Objective 4.1: Distinguish between the concepts of consumer surplus and producer surplus.

DirecTV and the DISH Network are both providers of satellite television service. But only DirecTV offers its customers the option of subscribing to the NFL Sunday Ticket. In 2008, subscribers to this service paid $299 for the right to watch every regular season NFL Sunday game broadcast, except for those games played on Sunday evenings. This option is especially attractive to fans who have moved to cities that do not offer regular broadcasts of the games of their favorite teams. Television stations typically offer games played by teams with the most local interest. A long-time fan of the New York Giants or Denver Broncos who moved to Illinois would have to settle for watching the Chicago Bears most Sunday afternoons—unless the fan had signed up for the DirecTV NFL Sunday Ticket.

Team Marketing Report estimated that the 2008 average ticket price for NFL games for all teams was $72.20 and the per-game average Fan Cost was about $396.36 (this includes four average price tickets, four small soft drinks, two small beers, four hot dogs, two game programs, parking, and two adult size caps).

Use this information to estimate consumer and producer surplus for the NFL Sunday Ticket.

Source: www.teammarketing.com

SOLVING THE PROBLEM:
Step 1: **Review the chapter material.**
   This problem is about consumer and producer surplus, so you may want to review the section "Consumer Surplus and Producer Surplus," which begins on page 98 in the textbook.
Step 2: **Identify the maximum price a consumer would pay for the NFL Sunday Ticket.**
   The consumers who benefit most from the NFL Sunday Ticket are those who have the strongest demand to watch their favorite team play on Sundays. Assume that an average season ticket holder found out prior to fall 2008 that he was being transferred by his employer to a location that required him to forego season tickets for himself and three family members. Using the Team Marketing estimate, he would save $396.36 for each home game that he and his family would no longer attend. If there are 8 home games, then his total savings would be $396.36 × 8 = $3,170.80. This is an estimate of the maximum price he would pay for the NFL Sunday Ticket. (Note that he would also be able to watch his team's away games but would probably be able to view these games from his home at no additional cost if he had not moved.)

Step 3: **Estimate the value of consumer surplus.**
For the average season ticket holder and his family, an estimate of the consumer surplus is: $3,170.80 − $299 = $2,871.80. Each family member who no longer attended home games can watch these games at home.

Step 4: **Identify the minimum price DirecTV would accept for the NFL Sunday Ticket.**
The NFL Package is offered to existing DirecTV customers as an additional viewing option. Therefore, only trivial additional costs are incurred by DirecTV: the customer's billing must be adjusted to reflect this option and the service must be "switched on" for this customer. Assume that this cost is zero.

Step 5: **Estimate the value of producer surplus.**
Because DirecTV receives $299 for the NFL Sunday Ticket, its producer surplus for this customer is: $299 − $0 = $299.

4.2 The Efficiency of Competitive Markets (pages 102–105)
Learning Objective: Understand the concept of economic efficiency.

Economic surplus is the sum of consumer and producer surplus. **Economic efficiency** is a market outcome in which the marginal benefit to consumers of the last unit produced is equal to its marginal cost of production and where the sum of consumer and producer surplus is at a maximum. When equilibrium is reached in a competitive market, the marginal benefit equals the marginal cost of the last unit sold. This means that equilibrium is an economically efficient outcome.

If less than the equilibrium output were produced, the marginal benefit of the last unit bought would exceed its marginal cost. If more than the equilibrium quantity were produced, the marginal benefit of this last unit would be less than its marginal cost. We can also think of the concept of economic efficiency in terms of economic surplus. When in equilibrium, the willingness of the consumer to pay for the last unit is equal to the lowest price a firm will be willing to accept. If less than the equilibrium output were produced, the willingness to pay for the last unit bought would exceed the minimum price that firms would be willing to accept. If more than equilibrium quantity were produced, the willingness to pay for this last unit would be less than the minimum price that producers would accept. A **deadweight loss** is the reduction in economic surplus resulting from a market not being in competitive equilibrium.

 Study Hint
Figure 4-7 illustrates the deadweight loss from producing at a point away from the equilibrium point in a competitive market. Keep in mind the idea that when the quantity of chai tea cups sold is 14,000 instead of 15,000, there is a loss of both producer surplus and consumer surplus. Consumers are hurt because there are 1,000 cups of tea they can't purchase even though the marginal benefit of those cups exceeds the equilibrium price. And producers are worse off because there are 1,000 cups of tea they aren't producing even though the price producers would receive for those cups at equilibrium exceeds the marginal cost of production.

Extra Solved Problem 4-2
Supports Learning Objective 4.2: Understand the concept of economic efficiency.

Suppose that the tickets for a Kelly Clarkson concert just went on sale in your local area. The tickets are selling for $25 each, the equilibrium price. Suppose that the willingness to pay of the last consumer to buy a ticket was $50 and the minimum that the producer was willing to accept was $10.

a. Is this market outcome economically efficient?

b. If not, what would need to occur for this market to become economically efficient?

SOLVING THE PROBLEM
Step 1: **Review the chapter material.**
This problem is about economic efficiency, so you may want to review the section "The Efficiency of Competitive Markets," which begins on page 102 in the textbook.
Step 2: **Compare the minimum price that the concert producer is willing to accept to the price the consumer is willing to pay.**
Because the value to the consumer of the last ticket sold is higher than the minimum price that the producer is willing to accept, the market is not efficient. The willingness to pay by the consumer must be equal to the minimum price that the producer is willing to accept in order for efficiency to be achieved.
Step 3: **Determine what needs to occur in the market for the market to become efficient.**
Because the willingness to pay is greater than the minimum the firm is willing to accept, there is additional consumer and producer surplus that could be gained by increasing the number of tickets sold. The number of tickets sold should increase until the willingness to pay of the last consumer is equal to the minimum that the producer is willing to accept.

4.3 Government Intervention in the Market: Price Floors and Price Ceilings (pages 105–112)
Learning Objective: Explain the economic effect of government-imposed price floors and price ceilings.

Though the sum of consumer and producer surplus is maximized at a competitive market equilibrium, individual consumers would be better off if they could pay a lower than equilibrium price and individual producers would be better off if they could sell at a higher than equilibrium price. Consumers and producers sometimes lobby government to legally require a market price different from the equilibrium price. These lobbying efforts are sometimes successful. During the Great Depression of the 1930s, farm prices fell to very low levels. Farmers were able to convince the federal government to raise prices by setting price floors for many agricultural prices.

A **price floor** is a legally determined minimum price that sellers may receive. A price floor encourages producers to produce more output than consumers want to buy at the floor price. The government often buys the surplus, which is equal to the quantity supplied minus the quantity demanded, at the floor price. The government may also pay farmers to take some land out of cultivation, which would decrease supply. The marginal cost of production exceeds the marginal benefit, and there is a deadweight loss, which represents a decline in efficiency due to the price floor.

> 📖 **Study Hint**
> In this chapter's ***Making the Connection: Price Floors in Labor Markets: The Debate over Minimum Wage Policy***, the minimum wage is identified as an example of a price floor. While there is some debate about the extent of employment losses from the minimum wage, the minimum wage—like any price floor set above equilibrium—will result in inefficiency. This inefficiency comes from two sources. Some of the labor surplus (unemployment) resulting from higher minimum wages comes from reductions in firm willingness to hire workers at higher wages (a decrease in the quantity of labor the firm demands), but

some of the unemployment also comes from a higher number of workers entering the labor market (an increase in the quantity of labor supplied). Higher wages increase the incentive for people who may not have been looking for work before the wage increase to start searching for a job. The entire difference between the new quantity of labor supplied by households and the new quantity of labor demanded by firms is the measure of unemployment.

Also, keep in mind that the focus here is not on evaluating whether the minimum wage is "good" or "bad". Those are questions for normative analysis, as defined in Chapter 1. The focus here is on the positive analysis of the impact, if any, the minimum wage will have on employment and efficiency.

A **price ceiling** is a legally determined maximum price that sellers may charge. Price ceilings are meant to help consumers who lobby for lower prices. Consumers typically lobby for price ceilings after a sharp increase in the price of an item on which they spend a significant amount of their budgets (for example, rent or gasoline). At the ceiling price, the quantity demanded is greater than the quantity supplied so that the marginal benefit of the last item sold (the quantity supplied) exceeds the marginal cost of producing it. Price ceilings result in a deadweight loss and a reduction of economic efficiency. Price ceilings create incentives for **black markets**, in which buying and selling take place at prices that violate government price regulations.

With any price floor or price ceiling, there are winners and losers from the policy. The deadweight loss associated with a given policy tells us that the gains to the winners are outweighed by the losses to the losers.

📖 Study Hint

An interesting question to consider is why politicians maintain agricultural price supports despite the significant costs their constituents pay for these programs. Part of the explanation is that because each individual incurs a small fraction of the total cost, it is hardly worth the trouble to register a complaint to lawmakers. But the benefits of price floors are concentrated among a few producers who have a strong incentive to lobby for the continuation of the price supports. Politicians act quite rationally by ignoring the interests of those who pay for these programs.

However, you may be swayed by the argument that a price ceiling is justified because its intent is to help low-income consumers afford a specific product. Though some low-income consumers may be among those who buy the product, there is no guarantee of this. For example, as mentioned in the text, a black market may arise, resulting in consumers paying at least as much as they would in the absence of the price ceiling. Or, given a shortage of apartments, a landlord can choose tenants based on their physical characteristics or their lifestyles. Suppose you were a landlord who owned an apartment subject to rent control. As a result, there are 5 potential tenants for one apartment you have to rent. The potential tenants include a male college student, a single female school teacher with a pet dog, a low-income retail worker with a spouse and two children, a medical doctor, and a lawyer. Assume that you can select any one of these as your tenant. Would you select the retail worker? What about the college student?

4.4	**The Economic Impact of Taxes (pages 112–117)**
	Learning Objective: Analyze the economic impact of taxes.

Government taxes on goods and services reduce the quantity produced. A tax imposed on producers of a product will shift the supply curve up by the amount of the tax. Consumers pay a higher price for the product, and there will be a loss of consumer surplus. Because the price producers receive after paying the tax falls, there is also a loss of producer surplus. The imposition of a tax will also cause a deadweight loss. **Tax incidence** is the actual division of the burden of the tax between buyers and sellers. The incidence of a tax is not dependent on who is legally required to collect and pay the tax. Tax incidence is determined by the degree to which the market price rises as a result of a tax. This rise, in turn, is determined by the willingness of suppliers to change the quantity of the good or service they offer and the willingness of consumers to change their quantity demanded as a result of the tax. If more than half of the tax is paid for by consumers in the form of higher prices, then the burden of the tax falls on the consumers. If less than half of the tax is paid for by consumers in the form of higher prices, then the burden of the tax falls on suppliers.

Study Hint

Estimating the impact of cigarette taxes is more complicated than it appears from Figure 4-10. This is because state excise taxes on cigarettes vary widely. In 2009, the tax per pack ranged from 7 cents in South Carolina to $3.46 in Rhode Island. In addition, some counties and cities impose their own taxes. The variation in taxes creates a black market that reduces legal sales of cigarettes and tax revenue in states with the highest tax rates. Bootleggers can earn illegal profits by buying cigarettes in states with low tax rates and selling them to retail stores in states with the highest taxes.

Appendix
Quantitative Demand and Supply Analysis (pages 127–131)
Learning Objective: Use quantitative demand and supply analysis.

Quantitative analysis supplements the use of demand and supply curves with equations. An example of the demand and supply for apartments in New York City is:

$$Q^S = -450,000 + 1,300P$$

$$Q^D = 3,000,000 - 1,000P.$$

Q^D and Q^S are the quantity demanded and quantity supplied of apartments per month, respectively. The coefficient of P in the first equation equals the change in quantity supplied for a one dollar per month change in price.

$$\frac{\Delta Q^S}{\Delta P} = 1,300$$

The coefficient of the price term in the second equation equals the change in quantity demanded for a one dollar per month change in price.

$$\frac{\Delta Q^S}{\Delta P} = -1,000$$

At the competitive market equilibrium, quantity demanded equals quantity supplied.

$$Q^D = Q^S \text{ or}$$

$$3,000,000 - 1,000P = -450,000 + 1,300P$$

Rearranging terms and solving for *P* yields the price at which quantity demanded equals the quantity supplied. This is the equilibrium price.

$$3{,}000{,}000 + 450{,}000 = 1{,}300P + 1{,}000P$$

$$3{,}450{,}000 = 2{,}300P$$

$$P = \$1{,}500$$

Substituting the equilibrium price into the equation for either demand or supply yields the equilibrium quantity.

$$Q^D = 3{,}000{,}000 - 1{,}000(1{,}500)$$

$$Q^D = 3{,}000{,}000 - 1{,}500{,}000$$

$$Q^D = 1{,}500{,}000$$

$$Q^S = -450{,}000 + 1{,}300P$$

$$Q^S = -450{,}000 + 1{,}300\,(1{,}500)$$

$$Q^S = 1{,}500{,}000$$

The demand equation can be used to determine the price at which the quantity demanded is zero.

$$Q^D = 3{,}000{,}000 - 1{,}000P$$

$$0 = 3{,}000{,}000 - 1{,}000P$$

$$-3{,}000{,}000 = -1{,}000P$$

$$P = (-3{,}000{,}000)/(-1{,}000)$$

$$P = \$3{,}000$$

The supply equation can be used to determine the price at which the quantity supplied equals zero.

$$Q^S = -450{,}000 + 1{,}300P$$

$$0 = -450{,}000 + 1{,}300P$$

$$450{,}000 = 1{,}300P$$

$$P = \$346.15$$

📖 **Study Hint**

The equations highlight an oddity of demand and supply analysis. The dependent variable in most graphs is the Y variable—the variable measured along the vertical axis—while the independent, or X variable, is measured along the horizontal axis. Economists assume that price changes cause changes in quantity, so the price is the independent variable. However, for historical reasons, our demand and supply graphs have it backwards, with price on the vertical axis and quantity on the horizontal axis. Make sure you recognize that even though the equations for demand and supply may be written to solve for the dependent variable Q^D or Q^S, those values are actually graphed on the X axis, not the Y axis.

Calculating Consumer Surplus and Producer Surplus

Demand and supply equations can be used to measure consumer and producer surplus. Figure 4A-1 uses a graph to illustrate demand and supply. Because the demand curve is linear, consumer surplus is equal to the area of the blue triangle in Figure 4A-1. The area of a triangle is ½ multiplied by the base of the triangle multiplied by the height of the triangle, or:

$$\tfrac{1}{2} \times (1,500,000) \times (3000 - 1,500) = \$1,125,000,000.$$

Producer surplus is calculated in a similar way. Producer surplus is equal to the area above the supply curve and below the line representing market price. The supply curve is a straight line, so producer surplus equals the area of the right triangle:

$$\tfrac{1}{2} \times (1,500,000) \times (1,500 - 346) = \$865,500,000.$$

Producer surplus in the market for rental apartments in New York City is about $865 million.

Economic surplus is the sum of the consumer surplus and the producer surplus, so economic surplus is as follows:

$$\$1,125,000,000 + \$865,500,000 = \$1,990,500,000.$$

Key Terms

Black market A market in which buying and selling take place at prices that violate government price regulations.

Consumer surplus The difference between the highest price a consumer is willing to pay for a good or service and the price the consumer actually pays.

Deadweight loss The reduction in economic surplus resulting from a market not being in competitive equilibrium.

Economic efficiency A market outcome in which the marginal benefit to consumers of the last unit produced is equal to its marginal cost of production and in which the sum of consumer surplus and producer surplus is at a maximum.

Economic surplus The sum of consumer surplus and producer surplus.

Marginal benefit The additional benefit to a consumer from consuming one more unit of a good or service.

Marginal cost The additional cost to a firm of producing one more unit of a good or service.

Price ceiling A legally determined maximum price that sellers may charge.

Price floor A legally determined minimum price that sellers may receive.

Producer surplus The difference between the lowest price a firm would be willing to accept for a good or service and the price it actually receives.

Tax incidence The actual division of the burden of a tax between buyers and sellers in a market.

Self-Test

(Answers are provided at the end of the Self-Test.)

Multiple-Choice Questions

1. What is the name of a legally determined minimum price that sellers may receive?
   a. a price ceiling
   b. a price floor
   c. marginal benefit
   d. consumer surplus

2. What is the name of a legally determined maximum price that sellers may charge?
   a. a price ceiling
   b. a price floor
   c. marginal benefit
   d. consumer surplus

3. Some people believe there should be a legally determined maximum price in the gasoline market. Such a limit on the price of gasoline would be an example of
   a. a price floor.
   b. a price ceiling.
   c. an equilibrium price.
   d. rent control.

4. In response to information regarding the salaries of executives at firms receiving bailout funds in the United States, some people have called for a limit on the salaries paid to executives. Such a limit on the compensation executives can receive is an example of
   a. a price floor.
   b. a price ceiling.
   c. an equilibrium price.
   d. rent control.

5. Which of the following is the definition of consumer surplus?
   a. the additional benefit to a consumer from consuming one more unit of a good or service
   b. the additional cost to a firm of producing one more unit of a good or service
   c. the difference between the highest price a consumer is willing to pay and the price the consumer actually pays
   d. the difference between the lowest price a firm would have been willing to accept and the price it actually receives

6. Which of the following is the definition of producer surplus?
   a. the additional benefit to a consumer from consuming one more unit of a good or service
   b. the additional cost to a firm of producing one more unit of a good or service
   c. the difference between the highest price a consumer is willing to pay and the price the consumer actually pays
   d. the difference between the lowest price a firm would have been willing to accept and the price it actually receives

7. Which of the following is the definition of marginal benefit?
   a. the additional benefit to a consumer from consuming one more unit of a good or service
   b. the additional cost to a firm of producing one more unit of a good or service
   c. the difference between the highest price a consumer is willing to pay and the price the consumer actually pays
   d. the difference between the lowest price a firm would have been willing to accept and the price it actually receives

8. Which of the following is the definition of marginal cost?
   a. the additional benefit to a consumer from consuming one more unit of a good or service
   b. the difference between the highest price a consumer is willing to pay and the price the consumer actually pays
   c. the additional cost to a firm of producing one more unit of a good or service
   d. the difference between the lowest price a firm would have been willing to accept and the price it actually receives

9. Refer to the graph below. What name other than demand curve can you give this curve?

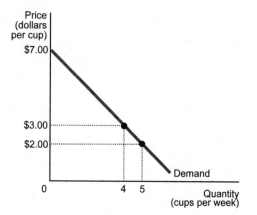

   a. the marginal cost curve
   b. the marginal benefit curve
   c. consumer surplus
   d. the price-equilibrium curve

10. Refer to the graph below. The graph shows an individual's demand curve for tea. At a price of $2.00, the consumer is willing to buy five cups of tea per week. More precisely, what does this mean?

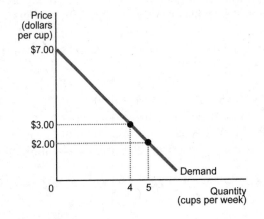

a. Marginal benefit equals marginal cost when five cups are consumed.
b. The total cost of consuming five cups is $2.00.
c. The marginal cost of producing five cups is $2.00.
d. The marginal benefit of consuming the fifth cup is $2.00.

11. Refer to the graph below. The graph shows an individual's demand curve for tea. If the price is $2.00, what is consumer surplus for the fourth cup of tea?

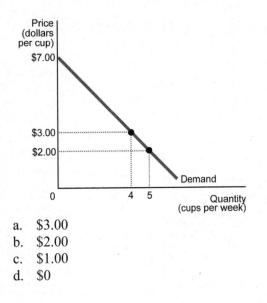

a. $3.00
b. $2.00
c. $1.00
d. $0

12. Refer to the graph below. The graph shows an individual's demand curve for tea. If the price is $3.00, what is consumer surplus for the fourth cup of tea?

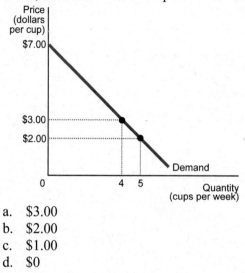

   a. $3.00
   b. $2.00
   c. $1.00
   d. $0

13. If the average price that cable subscribers are willing to pay for cable television is $208, but the actual price they pay is $81, how much is consumer surplus per subscriber?
   a. $208 + $81 = $289
   b. $208 − $81 = $127
   c. $81 + $127 = $208
   d. $81

14. Refer to the graph below. The graph shows the market demand for satellite TV service. If the market price is $81, which consumers receive consumer surplus in this market?

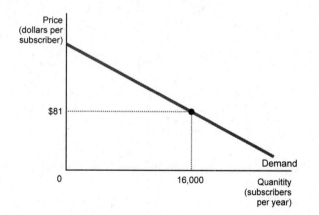

   a. those willing to pay something less than $81
   b. those willing to pay exactly $81
   c. those willing to pay more than $81
   d. all of the above

15. Refer to the graph below. When market price is $2.00, what is *producer surplus* from selling the 40th cup?

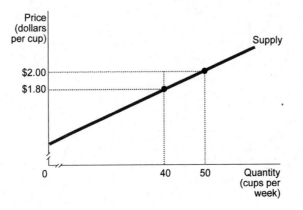

a. $72.00
b. $1.80
c. $0.20
d. $36.00

16. Refer to the graph below. How much is the marginal cost of producing the 50th cup?

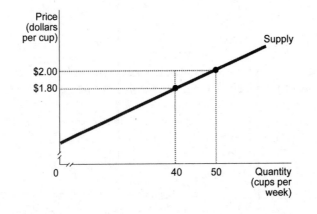

a. $100.00
b. $0.20
c. $2.00
d. None of the above; there is insufficient information to answer the question.

17. Refer to the graph below. To achieve economic efficiency, which output level should be produced?

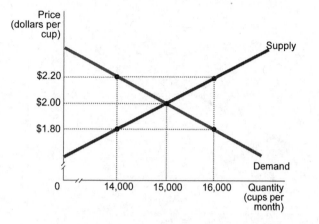

a. 14,000 cups per month, because at this level of output, marginal benefit is greater than marginal cost.
b. 15,000 cups per month, because at this level of output, marginal benefit is equal to marginal cost.
c. 16,000 cups per month, because at this level of output, marginal benefit is less than marginal cost.
d. All of the output levels above are efficient.

18. Refer to the graph below. To achieve economic efficiency, the level of output should be reduced when the quantity of cups produced equals

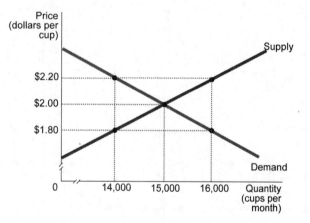

a. 14,000.
b. 15,000.
c. 16,000.
d. the quantity of cups demanded.

19. Refer to the graph below. When 14,000 cups of tea are produced per month, the marginal benefit of the 14,000ᵗʰ cup of tea is _____, the marginal cost of the 14,000ᵗʰ cup of tea is _____, and output is _____.

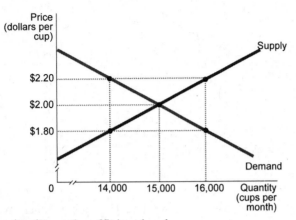

a. $2; $2; at the efficient level
b. $2.20; $1.80; above the efficient level
c. $2.20; $1.80; below the efficient level
d. $1.80; $2.20; below the efficient level

20. Refer to the graph below. When 15,000 cups of tea are produced and consumed per month, which of the following is true?

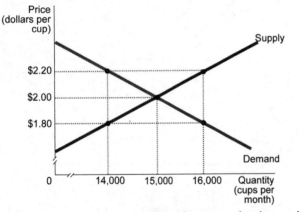

a. The sum of consumer and producer surplus is maximized.
b. The level of output is economically efficient.
c. The marginal benefit to buyers of the last cup of tea is equal to the marginal cost of producing the last cup of tea.
d. All of the above are true.

21. When is output inefficiently low?
a. when marginal benefit is greater than marginal cost
b. when marginal cost is greater than marginal benefit
c. when marginal cost is equal to marginal benefit
d. All of the above; any output level can be inefficiently low.

22. When a competitive market is in equilibrium, what is the economically efficient level of output?
    a. any output level where marginal benefit is greater than marginal cost
    b. any output level where marginal cost is greater than marginal benefit
    c. the output level where marginal cost is equal to marginal benefit
    d. all of the above

23. What does the sum of consumer surplus and producer surplus equal?
    a. economic efficiency
    b. economic surplus
    c. deadweight loss
    d. competitive equilibrium

24. Refer to the graph below. Assume this is a competitive market. Which of the following *does not* exist when the price is $2.00?

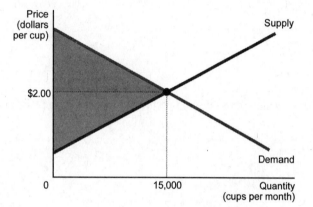

    a. economic efficiency
    b. economic surplus
    c. deadweight loss
    d. competitive equilibrium

25. Refer to the graph below. Compared to the competitive equilibrium, how much producer surplus is lost when the price is $2.20?

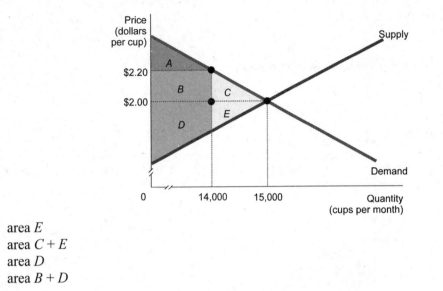

a. area E
b. area $C + E$
c. area D
d. area $B + D$

26. Refer to the graph below. Which area equals producer surplus when price is $2.20?

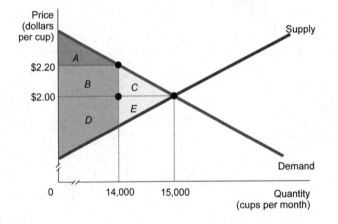

a. area E
b. area $C + E$
c. area $D + E$
d. area $B + D$

27. Refer to the graph below. Which area equals consumer surplus when price is $2.00?

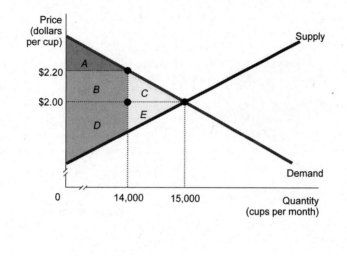

a.   area A
b.   area $B + C$
c.   area $A + B + C$
d.   area $B + C + D$

28. Refer to the graph below. Which area equals consumer surplus when price is $2.20?

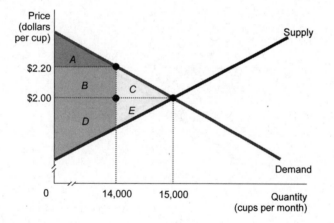

a.   area A
b.   area B
c.   area C
d.   area D

29. Refer to the graph below. If 14,000 cups of tea are produced, what area corresponds to deadweight loss?

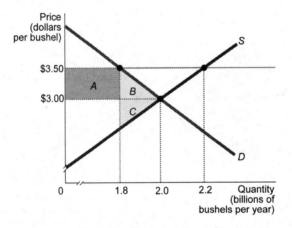

a. $A + B + C$
b. $B + C$
c. C
d. $C + E$

30. Refer to the graph below. After a price of $3.50 is imposed by the government in this market, what meaning do we give to area A?

a. Area A is consumer surplus transferred to producers.
b. Area A is additional consumer surplus that goes to existing consumers in the market.
c. Area A is a deadweight loss.
d. Area A is a surplus of wheat.

31. Refer to the graph below. After a price of $3.50 is imposed by the government in this market, what meaning do we give to area *B* + *C*?

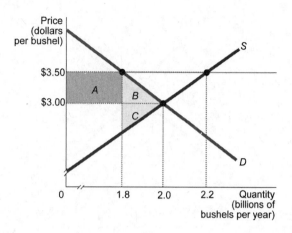

  a. producer surplus transferred to consumers
  b. additional consumer surplus to existing consumers in the market
  c. deadweight loss
  d. a surplus of wheat

32. Refer to the graph below. According to this graph, the existence of a minimum wage in the market for low-skilled workers results in:

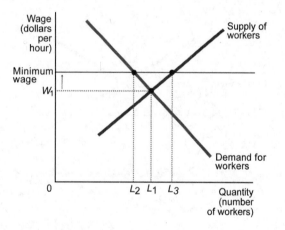

  a. an increase in wages and employment.
  b. an increase in wages but lower employment.
  c. a decrease in wages but higher employment.
  d. a decrease in wages and employment.

33. Refer to the graph below. According to this graph, the existence of a minimum wage in the market for low-skilled workers results in:

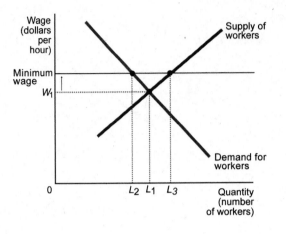

a. a shortage of workers.
b. a surplus of workers.
c. neither a shortage nor a surplus of workers.
d. a scarcity of workers.

34. Refer to the graph below. After rent control is imposed, area *A* represents:

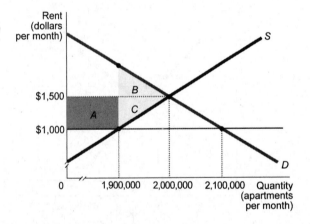

a. consumer surplus transferred from renters to landlords.
b. producer surplus transferred from landlords to renters.
c. a deadweight loss.
d. a shortage of apartments.

35. Refer to the graph below. After rent control is imposed, which area represents a deadweight loss?

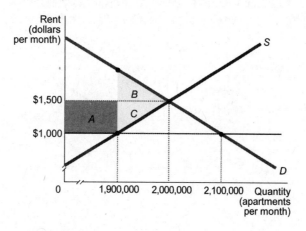

a. *A*
b. *A + B + C*
c. *B + C*
d. an area other than *A*, *B*, or *C*

36. Which of the following statements is correct?
    a. There is a shortage of every good that is scarce.
    b. There is no shortage of most scarce goods.
    c. Scarcity and shortage mean the same thing to economists.
    d. None of the above statements is correct.

37. Which of the following terms corresponds to a market in which buying and selling take place at prices that violate government price regulations?
    a. price conspiracy
    b. equilibrium
    c. competitive market
    d. black market

38. Refer to the graph below. Suppose that this market is operating under the established rent control of $1,000 per month. Then, a black market for rent-controlled apartments develops, and the apartments rent for $2,000 per month. What meaning does the sum of areas $A + E$ have in this situation?

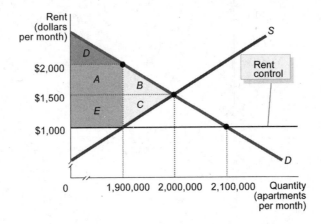

    a. consumer surplus transferred from renters to landlords
    b. producer surplus transferred from renters to landlords
    c. deadweight loss
    d. a surplus of apartments

39. Refer to the graph below. When a black market for rent-controlled apartments develops, what is the area of deadweight loss?

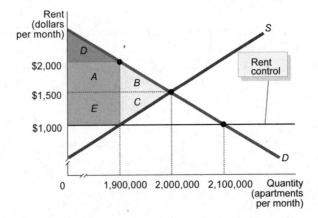

    a. none; the deadweight loss disappears.
    b. $B + C$
    c. $A + E$
    d. D

40. When the government imposes price floors or price ceilings, which of the following occurs?
    a. Some people win.
    b. Some people lose.
    c. There is a loss of economic efficiency.
    d. All of the above occur.

41. The term tax incidence refers to
    a. the type of product the tax is levied on.
    b. the amount of revenue collected by the government from a tax.
    c. the actual division of the burden of a tax.
    d. the actual versus the desired impact of a tax burden.

42. Refer to the graph below. A tax is imposed in this market that shifts the supply curve from S_1 to S_2. What price do producers receive after this tax is imposed?

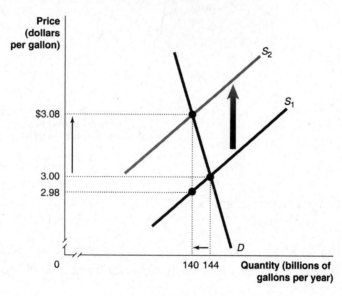

    a. $1.98
    b. $2.98
    c. $3.08
    d. None of the above

43. Refer to the graph below. A tax is imposed in this market that shifts the supply curve from S_1 to S_2. What area corresponds to the *excess burden* from the tax?

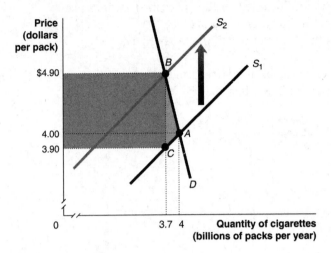

   a.   the dark gray area
   b.   the light gray area
   c.   the sum of the dark gray and light gray areas
   d.   an area not shown on this graph

44. Refer to the graph below. A tax is imposed in this market that shifts the supply curve from S_1 to S_2. What area corresponds to the revenue collected by the government from the tax?

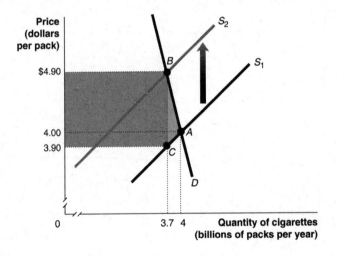

   a.   the dark gray area
   b.   the light gray area
   c.   the sum of the dark gray and light gray areas
   d.   an area not shown on this graph

45. Refer to the graph below. A tax is imposed in this market that shifts the supply curve from S_1 to S_2. In this graph, how much of the gas tax do consumers pay?

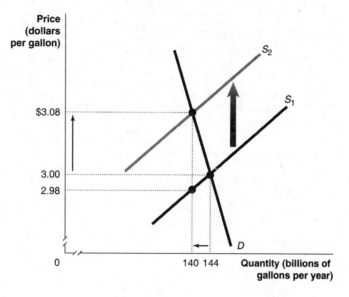

a. 2 cents per gallon
b. 8 cents per gallon
c. 10 cents per gallon
d. $1.50 per gallon

46. Refer to the graphs below. In each of the graphs, a curve has shifted as a result of a new social security tax. In which graph does the employer pay the entire social security tax?

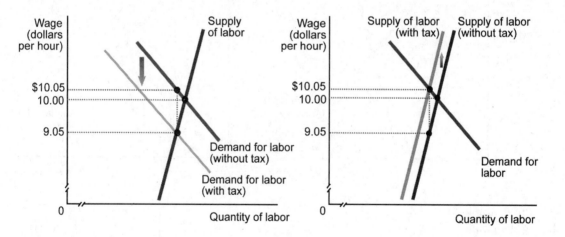

a. in the graph on the left
b. in the graph on the right
c. in both cases
d. in neither case

47. Refer to the graphs below. In each of the graphs, a curve has shifted as a result of a new social security tax. In which graph do the workers pay the entire social security tax?

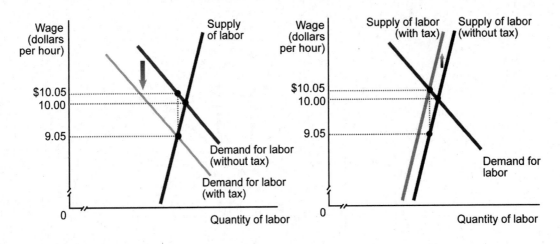

a. in the graph on the left
b. in the graph on the right
c. in both cases
d. in neither case

48. Refer to the graphs below. In each of the graphs, a curve has shifted as a result of a new social security tax. In which graph is the tax incidence larger on workers?

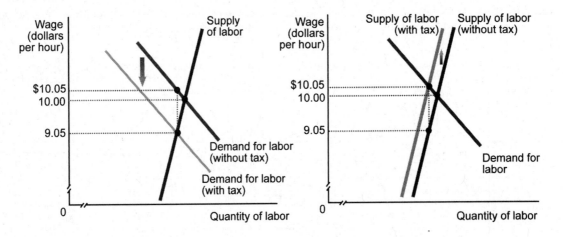

a. in the graph on the left
b. in the graph on the right
c. in neither case because the workers are not affected by the tax
d. in both cases the tax incidence is the same

49. Refer to the graph below. What is the deadweight loss (or excess burden) associated with the 10-cent tax on gasoline?

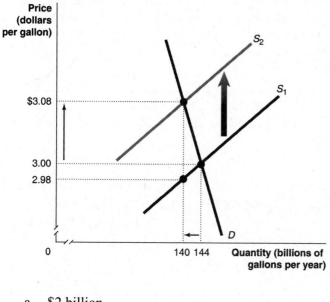

a. $2 billion
b. $1 billion
c. $3.2 billion
d. $800 million

50. Refer to the graph below. A tax imposed in the market for cigarettes shifts supply from S_1 to S_2. What is the excess burden of the cigarette tax?

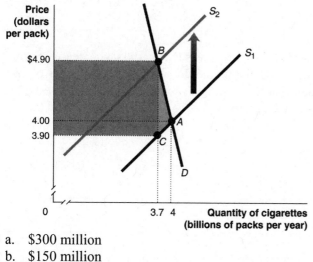

a. $300 million
b. $150 million
c. $270 million
d. $30 million

Short Answer Questions

1. Some economists oppose raising the minimum wage because they believe this would lead to a significant increase in unemployment among low-skilled workers. Is there an alternative to a higher minimum wage to raise the incomes of the working poor? Why do some economists favor raising the minimum wage?

   _____

   _____

   _____

2. Federal and state governments periodically raise excise taxes on cigarettes. Politicians often argue that these tax increases discourage smoking. What other motive is there for raising taxes on cigarettes?

   _____

   _____

   _____

3. One effect of rent control in New York City is a reduction in the number of apartment buildings. If rent control were eliminated, would this result in an increase in the number of apartment buildings and, therefore, lower rents for apartment dwellers?

   _____

   _____

   _____

4. Price floors have been imposed in markets for dairy products such as milk and cheese. Surplus dairy products are bought by the government to maintain the floor price. These surplus products must be stored in some location. As an alternative to storage, suppose a program was established to distribute surplus dairy products freely to the elderly and poor. Would this eliminate the government's storage problem?

   _____

   _____

   _____

5. The federal government has made several attempts to reduce agricultural surpluses that result from price floors. One such attempt was a program that paid farmers to reduce the amount of land they devoted to planting crops subject to price floors. What was the reason for the failure of this program? (Hint: Use one of the "three important ideas" from Chapter 1 to answer this question.)

   _____

   _____

   _____

True False Questions

T F 1. The total amount of consumer surplus in a market is equal to the area under the demand curve.

T F 2. Government intervention in agriculture in the United States increased significantly as a result of the Great Depression.

T F 3. A study of fast food restaurants in New Jersey and Pennsylvania found that increases in the minimum wage caused large increases in unemployment.

T F 4. Those people who lose because of rent control include landlords who abide by the law.

T F 5. It was Oliver Wendell Holmes who once said "Taxes are what we pay for a civilized society."

T F 6. The deadweight loss from a tax is equal to the revenue collected by government from the tax.

T F 7. Consumers will pay all of an increase in a sales tax only if the demand curve is a horizontal line at the market price.

T F 8. Economists who have studied the incidence of the social security tax have found that the tax burden is shared equally by employers and their employees.

T F 9. A tax is efficient if it imposes a small excess burden relative to the tax revenue it raises.

T F 10. One effect of rent control in New York City and London has been a large reduction in the number of apartment buildings.

T F 11. The Freedom to Farm Act was passed in Congress in 1996 to phase out price floors and government purchases of agricultural surpluses.

T F 12. Producer surplus refers to the surplus goods that result from price floors.

T F 13. Positive economic analysis is used to determine the economic results of price ceilings and price floors. Whether these price controls are desirable is a normative question.

T F 14. The earned income tax credit reduces the amount of tax lower income wage earners pay to the federal government.

T F 15. Economic efficiency results when the total benefit to consumers is equal to the total cost of production.

Answers to the Self-Test

Multiple-Choice Questions

Question	Answer	Comment
1	b	This is the definition of a price floor. See page 98 in the textbook.
2	a	This is the definition of a price ceiling. See page 98 in the textbook.
3	b	See page 98 in the textbook.
4	b	See page 98 in the textbook.
5	c	See page 98 in the textbook.
6	d	See page 102 in the textbook.
7	a	See the definition of marginal benefit on page 98 of the textbook.
8	c	See the definition of marginal cost on page 101 of the textbook.
9	b	Marginal benefit is the additional benefit to a consumer from consuming one more unit of a good or service, and price is a measure of that additional benefit, so the demand curve is also the marginal benefit curve.
10	d	The willingness of a consumer to pay $2 for five cups of tea per week means that the fifth cup consumed is worth exactly $2.00 to the consumer.
11	c	The fourth cup of tea has a marginal benefit of $3, and the consumer pays $2 for

		that cup, so consumer surplus is the difference of $1.
12	d	The fourth cup of tea has a marginal benefit of $3, and the consumer pays $3 for that cup, so consumer surplus is the difference of $0.
13	b	Consumer surplus is the difference between the price a consumer is willing to pay and the price actually paid.
14	c	These consumers participate in the market and receive consumer surplus equal to the difference between the highest price the consumers are willing to pay and the price they actually paid.
15	c	Producer surplus is the difference between the lowest price a firm would have been willing to accept ($1.80) and the price it actually receives ($2.00).
16	c	Price equals marginal cost, or the additional cost to a firm of producing one more unit of a good or service.
17	b	To achieve efficiency, output should be produced up until the marginal benefit to consumers is equal to the marginal cost to producers.
18	c	In this case, decreasing the level of output would increase efficiency. As output decreases, the gap between marginal cost and marginal benefit decreases, until the two are equal at 15,000 units of output.
19	c	Marginal benefit comes from the demand curve, marginal cost comes from the supply curve. When marginal benefit is greater than marginal cost, output is inefficiently low.
20	d	At equilibrium, marginal benefit equals marginal cost, and efficiency is achieved, which also implies that the sum of consumer and producer surplus is maximized.
21	a	Marginal benefit is less than marginal cost when the quantity of output produced is less than the equilibrium level of output.
22	c	When competitive markets are in equilibrium, marginal benefit equals marginal cost, and the quantity of output produced and sold is economically efficient.
23	b	Economic surplus equals the sum of consumer surplus and producer surplus. See page 103 in the textbook.
24	c	The equilibrium output level yields maximum economic efficiency; the market is in equilibrium, and the sum of consumer surplus and producer surplus yields the largest possible value. There is no deadweight loss.
25	a	Area E is the producer portion of the deadweight loss.
26	d	At a price of $2.20, only 14,000 cups will be produced per month. Producer surplus is the area below the $2.20 price and above the supply curve up to the 14,000 cups. This area is the trapezoid that includes areas B and D.
27	c	Consumer surplus is the area below the demand curve and above the price out to the number of units sold.
28	a	Consumer surplus is the area below the demand curve and above the market price.
29	d	Deadweight loss is the combination of lost consumer surplus (area C) and lost producer surplus (area E).
30	a	Producers capture some of the consumer surplus after market price increases to $3.50.
31	c	After the price of $3.50 is imposed by government, some producers and consumers no longer participate in the market, so a deadweight loss is created.
32	b	The minimum wage causes an excess of quantity supplied over quantity demanded, which corresponds to additional unemployment.
33	b	The minimum wage causes an excess of quantity supplied over quantity demanded, or a surplus of workers.
34	b	The lower price at which the first 1,900,000 apartments are rented benefits consumers who would have paid more in the absence of the rent control. So producer surplus is transferred from landlords to renters.

35	c	In the absence of the rent control, more landlords and renters would have participated in the market. This area shows that loss.
36	b	Scarcity and shortage are not the same thing. A shortage is the difference between quantity demanded and quantity supplied of a good when the market price is below the equilibrium price. Scarcity exists as long as the resources used to produce one thing could be used to produce another. There is no shortage of most scarce goods.
37	d	A market where buying and selling take place at prices that violate government price regulations is a black market. See page 109 in the textbook.
38	a	Renters would have paid $1,000 but now pay more. When price rises, consumer surplus decreases and producer surplus increases.
39	b	The black market does not change the deadweight loss.
40	d	Price controls have the consequences mentioned in all of these answers.
41	c	Tax incidence is the actual division of the burden of a tax between buyers and sellers in a market. See page 113 in the textbook.
42	b	Producers charge a price of $3.08 and give the government $0.10, leaving them effectively with $2.98 per gallon sold.
43	b	The excess burden from the tax is equivalent to the deadweight loss created by the tax.
44	a	That amount of revenue equals ($4.90 – $3.90) × 3.7 = $3.7 billion.
45	b	Consumers pay a price of $3.08, which is an 8-cent increase in price from the $3.00 equilibrium price. Producers receive $3.08 from consumers, pay 10 cents to the government, and keep $2.98 per pack.
46	d	Although the graph on the left shows that the firms are legally required to pay the tax, the legal requirement to pay a tax does not determine tax incidence. In both cases, workers see a 95-cent decrease in their wage after the tax, and employers see a 5 cent increase in the wage they pay their workers after the tax.
47	d	Although the graph on the right shows that the workers are legally required to pay the tax, the legal requirement to pay a tax does not determine tax incidence. In both cases, workers see a 95-cent decrease in their wage after the tax, and employers see a 5-cent increase in the wage they pay their workers after the tax.
48	d	It does not matter who pays the tax to the government, the tax incidence will remain the same. In both cases, workers see a 95-cent decrease in their wage after the tax, and employers see a 5-cent increase in the wage they pay their workers after the tax.
49	a	Deadweight loss is the area of the triangle with a height from $2.98 to $3.08 (height = $1) and a base from 140 billion to 144 billion (base = 4 billion). Using the formula for the area of a triangle: ½ base × height = ½ × $1 × 4 billion = $2 billion.
50	b	The area of the triangle that equals the deadweight loss (excess burden) of the tax is equal to ½ × 0.3 billion × $1 = $150 million

Short Answer Responses

1. Opponents of the minimum wage argue that raising the minimum wage will reduce employment, especially among workers with the least skills. An alternative policy is the earned income tax credit. Workers who do not owe any federal taxes receive payments from the federal government. This program increases the incomes of low-skilled workers without the risk of increasing unemployment. Despite these arguments against the minimum wage and the evidence from positive economic analysis that a higher minimum wage reduces employment, some economists still favor raising the minimum wage. They base their argument on normative economics. First, they believe the benefits of

higher wages to those still employed outweigh the costs to those thrown into unemployment. This is a value judgment; you are free to agree or disagree. Second, they argue that many low-income workers miss the earned income tax credit because they don't file tax returns.

2. Because cigarettes are addictive many smokers will pay higher prices for cigarettes rather than reduce the quantity they purchase. This results in greater government revenue from the cigarette taxes. Taxes on cigarettes and alcohol (often called "sin taxes") do not affect as many people as a sales tax or income tax. Therefore, politicians do not face as much public opposition to tax increases on these products.

3. Although this result is likely to occur eventually, it will take time for the elimination of rent controls to affect the quantity of apartments in New York City. The immediate effect would likely be an increase in rents on existing apartments. This is one reason why many New Yorkers oppose the elimination of rent control.

4. In fact, such a program was initiated in the 1980s. Although the storage problem was partially alleviated, some of the dairy products that are given away freely replace purchases made by the elderly and poor. The government still had to buy surplus dairy products.

5. The "important idea" that can be used to answer this question is: people respond to economic incentives. Given the opportunity to reduce the amount of land they used to grow crops, many farmers removed their least productive land from production and planted more on the land they did use. This program resulted in greater money payments to farmers—for the land they did not cultivate—and a smaller than expected reduction in crops harvested and sold.

True/False Answers

1. F The total amount of consumer surplus in a market is equal to the area under the demand curve above the market price.
2. T The government supported prices for the farmers because of the extremely low prices on agricultural goods.
3. F This study found only small increases in unemployment as a result of minimum wage increases.
4. T Producer surplus is typically reduced by rent control.
5. T See page 112 in the textbook.
6. F Government revenue is not a deadweight loss. This revenue will be used to provide goods and services to the economy.
7. F Consumers will pay all of an increase in a sales tax if the demand curve is a vertical line.
8. F Economists have found that the burden falls almost entirely on workers.
9. T See page 113 in the textbook.
10. T Landlords often sell or convert their buildings to other uses to avoid rent control regulations.
11. T See page 106 in the textbook.
12. F Producer surplus is the net benefit producers receive from participating in the market.
13. T Positive analysis tells us the cost and benefits associated with particular policy measures.
14. T The earned income credit is seen by some as a good alternative to the minimum wage.
15. F Economic efficiency results when the marginal benefit to consumers of the last unit produced equals the marginal cost of production.

CHAPTER 5

Externalities, Environmental Policy, and Public Goods

Chapter Summary and Learning Objectives

5.1   Externalities and Economic Efficiency (pages 134–137)
Identify examples of positive and negative externalities and use graphs to show how externalities affect economic efficiency. An **externality** is a benefit or cost to parties who are not involved in a transaction. Pollution and other externalities in production cause a difference between the **private cost** borne by the producer of a good or services and the **social cost**, which includes any external cost, such as the cost of pollution. An externality in consumption causes a difference between the **private benefit** received by the consumer and the **social benefit**, which includes any external benefit. If externalities exist in production or consumption, the market will not produce the optimal level of a good or service. This outcome is referred to as **market failure**. Externalities arise when property rights do not exist or cannot be legally enforced. **Property rights** are the rights individuals or businesses have to the exclusive use of their property, including the right to buy or sell it.

5.2   Private Solutions to Externalities: The Coase Theorem (pages 137–143)
Discuss the Coase theorem and explain how private bargaining can lead to economic efficiency in a market with an externality. Externalities and market failures result from incomplete property rights or from the difficulty of enforcing property rights in certain situations. When an externality exists, and the efficient quantity of a good is not being produced, the total cost of reducing the externality is usually less than the total benefit. According to the **Coase theorem**, if **transactions costs** are low, private bargaining will result in an efficient solution to the problem of externalities.

5.3   Government Policies to Deal with Externalities (pages 143–147)
Analyze government policies to achieve economic efficiency in a market with an externality. When private solutions to externalities are unworkable, the government sometimes intervenes. One way to deal with a negative externality in production is to impose a tax equal to the cost of the externality. The tax causes the producer of the good to internalize the externality. The government can deal with a positive externality in consumption by giving consumers a subsidy, or payment, equal to the value of the externality. Government taxes and subsidies intended to bring about an efficient level of output in the presence of externalities are called **Pigovian taxes and subsidies**. Although the federal government has sometimes used subsidies and taxes to deal with externalities, in dealing with pollution, it has more often used a command-and-control approach. A **command-and-control approach** involves the government imposing quantitative limits on the amount of pollution allowed or requiring firms to install specific pollution control devices. Direct pollution controls of this type are not economically efficient, however. As a result, Congress decided to use a system of tradable emissions allowances to reduce sulfur dioxide emissions.

5.4   Four Categories of Goods (pages 148–157)
Explain how goods can be categorized on the basis of whether they are rival or excludable, and use graphs to illustrate the efficient quantities of public goods and common resources. There are four categories of goods: private goods, public goods, quasi-public goods, and common resources. **Private goods** are both rival and excludable. **Rivalry** means that when one person consumes a unit of a good, no one else can consume that unit. **Excludability** means that anyone who does not pay for a good cannot consume it. **Public goods** are both nonrivalrous and nonexcludable. Private firms are usually not willing

to supply public goods because of free riding. **Free riding** involves benefiting from a good without paying for it. **Quasi-public goods** are excludable but not rival. **Common resources** are rival but not excludable. The **tragedy of the commons** refers to the tendency for a common resource to be overused. The tragedy of the commons results from a lack of clearly defined and enforced property rights. We find the market demand curve for a private good by adding the quantity of the good demanded by each consumer at each price. We find the demand curve for a public good by adding vertically the price each consumer would be willing to pay for each quantity of the good. The optimal quantity of a public good occurs where the demand curve intersects the curve representing the marginal cost of supplying the good.

Chapter Review

Chapter Opener: Economic Policy and the Environment (page 133)

Economic analysis is a useful tool in formulating efficient pollution policies. The Duke Energy Corporation is a participant in the federal government's program to reduce acid rain emissions through a market-based approach. Duke Energy and other utility companies are allowed to trade emissions allowances. Each allowance permits the holder to emit one ton of sulfur dioxide. Utilities are free to buy and sell allowances so long as they end up with one allowance for every ton of sulfur dioxide they emit.

5.1 | Externalities and Economic Efficiency (pages 134–137)

Learning Objective: Identify examples of positive and negative externalities and use graphs to show how externalities affect economic efficiency.

An **externality** is a benefit or cost that affects someone who is not directly involved in the production or consumption of a good or service. Positive externalities refer to benefits received from a good or service by consumers who do not pay for them. Negative externalities refer to costs incurred by individuals not involved in the production or consumption of a good or service. Externalities interfere with the economic efficiency of market equilibrium by causing a difference between the private cost of production and the social cost, or between the private benefit from consumption and the social benefit.

A **private cost** is a cost borne by the producer of a good or service. A **social cost** is the total cost of production, including both the private cost and any external cost. A **private benefit** is the benefit received by the consumer of a good or service. A **social benefit** is the total benefit from consuming a good, including both the private benefit and any external benefit.

A negative externality causes the social cost of production for a good to be greater than the private cost. As a result, more than the economically efficient level of output is produced. A positive externality causes the social benefit from the production of a good to be greater than the private benefit. As a result, less than the economically efficient level of output is produced. Externalities result from the absence of property rights for resources (for example, air) or inadequate legal enforcement of property rights. **Property rights** are the rights individuals or businesses have to the exclusive use of their property, including the right to buy or sell it.

Market failure refers to situations where the market fails to produce the efficient level of output. Figure 5-1 illustrates the effect of acid rain on the market for electricity and the deadweight loss that occurs due to a negative externality. Figure 5-2 illustrates the impact of a positive externality in the market for a college education and the deadweight loss caused by this externality.

📖 **Study Hint**

In chapter 4, you learned that the equilibrium price in a competitive market results in the economically efficient level of output, where marginal benefit equals marginal cost. That is still true, but only if the demand curve reflects all of the relevant marginal benefits in the market and the supply curve reflects all of the relevant marginal costs. If there are external benefits and costs that make the social and private costs unequal, then the market equilibrium will not be efficient.

Extra Solved Problem 5-1
The Influenza Pandemic of 1918
Supports Learning Objective 5.1: Identify examples of positive and negative externalities and use graphs to show how externalities affect economic efficiency.

From 1914 to 1918, World War I caused over 8 million military deaths, a total that dwarfed the number of deaths suffered in any previous war in history. But this total is much lower than the number of people who died during the influenza pandemic of 1918–19. There were at least 20 million, perhaps as many as 40 million, victims of the so-called "Spanish Flu" or "La Grippe." Ironically, many American soldiers who survived the war would carry the influenza virus home with them from Europe. An estimated 675,000 Americans died during the pandemic, ten times the number who died in the war. With no known cure for the deadly disease, public health officials distributed gauze masks for people to wear in public. Stores were forbidden to hold sales and railroads refused to carry passengers who did not have signed certificates stating that they were free of the virus. There were serious shortages of health care workers, morticians, and gravediggers, conditions not unlike those experienced during the Black Death of the Middle Ages.

a. Draw a graph illustrating the demand and supply for research directed at finding a cure for a highly contagious disease such as the 1918 flu. Assume that all research efforts are funded through private markets.

b. Describe how an externality causes an equilibrium level of output that is not economically efficient.

Source: "The Influenza Pandemic of 1918." http://www.stanford.edu/group/virus/uda/

SOLVING THE PROBLEM
Step 1:   Review the chapter material.
This problem is about externalities and efficiency, so you may want to review the section "Externalities and Economic Efficiency," which begins on page 134 in the textbook.

Step 2: **Draw a graph to illustrate the externality associated with privately funded research to cure influenza.**

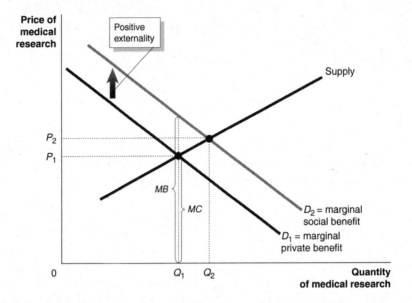

Step 3: **Describe how the externality causes a deviation from economic efficiency.**

There is a positive externality associated with medical research because of the external benefits the research generates. Assume that researchers had found a cure for the so-called "Spanish Flu" in 1918 at the beginning of the pandemic. The benefits to those people who would be protected from contracting the deadly disease would be substantial. If we estimate the benefit at $100 for each person, the external benefits range in the billions of dollars. Of course, medical research is by nature uncertain, and scientists and doctors can work many years without finding a cure for any disease. Private hospitals and research laboratories are likely to receive a relatively small amount of the social benefit from their efforts. As the graph in Step 2 shows, the demand curve for medical research that includes only private benefits will be below the demand curve that includes all social benefits. The private market equilibrium price and quantity would be P_1 and Q_1. At this point the marginal (social) benefit (MB) would exceed the marginal cost (MC). The economically efficient price and quantity would be P_2 and Q_2 where marginal (social) benefit is equal to marginal cost.

5.2 | Private Solutions to Externalities: The Coase Theorem (pages 137–143)

Learning Objective: Discuss the Coase theorem and explain how private bargaining can lead to economic efficiency in a market with an externality.

Ronald Coase argued that private bargaining may improve inefficient market results caused by externalities. The **Coase theorem** states that if transactions costs are low, private bargaining will result in an efficient solution to the problem of externalities. **Transactions costs** are the costs in time and other resources that parties incur in the process of agreeing to and carrying out an exchange of goods and services. Successful application of the Coase theorem requires that the bargaining parties have full information regarding the costs and benefits associated with the externalities and are willing to accept a reasonable agreement. In practice, private solutions are often not feasible because transactions costs are too high.

> 📖 **Study Hint**
> Because pollution generates a negative externality, many people believe the optimal or "efficient" level of pollution is zero pollution. However, there are not only benefits to cleaning up pollution—there are also costs to cleaning up pollution. As Figure 5-4 shows, declining marginal benefits and increasing marginal costs result in a level of pollution that is still positive. Only if the marginal benefit is equal to the marginal cost at 100% reduction of pollutants would zero pollution be efficient.

Extra Solved Problem 5-2

The Dog Next Door

Supports Learning Objective 5.2: Discuss the Coase theorem and explain how private bargaining can lead to economic efficiency in a market with an externality.

Assume that your next-door neighbor owns a large dog named Rufus that spends a significant amount of the night in the backyard. While in the yard, Rufus barks continuously and prevents you from getting a good night's sleep. Consider an attempt by you and your neighbor to come to an agreement that would deal with this negative externality.

a. What would you be willing to pay the neighbor to have him get rid of Rufus? What would the neighbor require in payment to get rid of Rufus?

b. Who will pay? Will you pay the neighbor to get rid of his dog, or will he pay you to listen to the dog bark?

SOLVING THE PROBLEM

Step 1: Review the chapter material.

This problem is about private solutions to externalities, so you may want to review the section "Private Solutions to Externalities: The Coase theorem," which begins on page 137 in the textbook.

Step 2: Consider the value to you of being able to sleep, and consider the value of Rufus to the neighbor.

You would be willing to pay the neighbor a dollar amount up to the value of the bark-free nights. Your neighbor would only agree to get rid of Rufus if you paid him an amount greater than the value he places on owning Rufus.

Step 3: Compare the value you place on quiet nights to the value the neighbor places on the ownership of the dog.

If the neighbor values the ownership of his dog more than you value a good night's rest, then the neighbor will pay you to listen to Rufus' barking. If you value a good night's rest more than the neighbor values owning Rufus, then you will pay the neighbor to get rid of his dog. But who pays also depends on the local government's regulations on barking dogs. If your town has a strict rule against dogs being allowed to bark at night, then your neighbor may need to pay you to allow him to keep his barking dog. In this case you would accept the payment only if it is greater than the value you place on a good night's sleep.

5.3 Government Policies to Deal with Externalities (pages 143–147)

Learning Objective: Analyze government policies to achieve economic efficiency in a market with an externality.

In the absence of private solutions to externalities, government intervention may be warranted. To achieve economic efficiency, governments may intervene in different ways. The government may impose a **Pigovian tax** or provide a **subsidy** to cause consumers and firms to internalize the externalities associated with production and consumption. The tax or subsidy would be equal to the dollar amount of the externality. To reduce pollution, governments have often used a command-and-control approach. A **command-and-control approach** refers to government-imposed quantitative limits on the amount of pollution firms are allowed to generate. Under this approach, the government may require installation of specific pollution control devices. Since 1990, a market-based approach of tradable permits has reduced emissions of sulfur dioxide from electric utilities at lower than expected cost. The success of this approach has led economists to advocate more extensive use of market-based approaches, and less use of command-and-control policies.

📖 Study Hint

At the end of chapter 4, you learned that taxes reduce efficiency and create deadweight loss. This is not necessarily the case when externalities are present. When externalities exist, taxes and subsidies can actually promote efficiency by encouraging demand and supply to better reflect the true marginal costs and marginal benefits to society.

5.4 Four Categories of Goods (pages 148–157)

Learning Objective: Explain how goods can be categorized on the basis of whether they are rival or excludable, and use graphs to illustrate the efficient quantities of public goods and common resources.

Goods may be classified into four categories based on whether their consumption is rival and/or excludable. If I consume one more unit of a product and that means you cannot consume the same unit, then the product is called **rival**. If anyone who wants to consume one unit of a product must pay for that unit, then the product is **excludable**. Products can be either rival or nonrivalrous and excludable or nonexcludable. This gives us four possible combinations of characteristics.

A **private good** is a good that is both rival and excludable. The economically efficient quantity of a private good can be supplied in a market without government intervention. Quasi-public goods are goods that are excludable but not rival. A **common resource** is a good that is rival but not excludable. There are typically externalities associated with common resources. The **tragedy of the commons** refers to the tendency for a common resource to be overused. The tragedy of the commons results from a lack of clearly defined and enforced property rights. A **public good** is a good that is both nonrivalrous and nonexcludable. **Free riding** refers to benefiting from a good without paying for it. Because of free riders, public goods are usually supplied by government rather than private firms.

In contrast with private goods, each consumer will consume the same quantity of a public good as every other consumer. The demand for a public good is determined by adding the price each consumer is willing to pay for each quantity of the good. Because no consumer can be excluded from receiving the good, it is difficult to determine consumers' true preferences and willingness to pay because of the free rider problem. Governments typically provide public goods, such as national defense, and determine the quantity supplied through cost-benefit analysis or a political process.

📖 Study Hint

Solved Problem 5-4, "Determining the Optimal Level of Public Goods," shows how we aggregate individual demand curves to determine the optimal level of public goods. For private goods, market demand is determined by summing the quantities individual consumers are willing and able to purchase at various prices. Because quantity is measured on the horizontal axis, adding the individual quantities together to determine the market quantity is called "horizontal summation."

For a public good, because the good is nonrivalrous, the units consumed by one individual are the same units consumed by other individuals in the market. The demand for a public good then comes from summing the individual marginal benefits associated with a given quantity of output. Because marginal benefit is measured on the vertical axis of a demand curve, we call this a "vertical summation" of the demand curves.

Key Terms

Coase theorem The argument of economist Ronald Coase that if transactions costs are low, private bargaining will result in an efficient solution to the problem of externalities.

Command-and-control approach An approach that involves the government imposing quantitative limits on the amount of pollution firms are allowed to emit or requiring firms to install specific pollution control devices.

Common resource A good that is rival but not excludable.

Excludability The situation in which anyone who does not pay for a good cannot consume it.

Externality A benefit or cost that affects someone who is not directly involved in the production or consumption of a good or service.

Free riding Benefiting from a good without paying for it.

Market failure A situation in which the market fails to produce the efficient level of output.

Pigovian taxes and subsidies Government taxes and subsidies intended to bring about an efficient level of output in the presence of externalities.

Private benefit The benefit received by the consumer of a good or service.

Private cost The cost borne by the producer of a good or service.

Private good A good that is both rival and excludable.

Property rights The rights individuals or businesses have to the exclusive use of their property, including the right to buy or sell it.

Public good A good that is both nonrivalrous and nonexcludable.

Rivalry The situation that occurs when one person's consuming a unit of a good means no one else can consume it.

Social benefit The total benefit from consuming a good or service, including both the private benefit and any external benefit.

Social cost The total cost of producing a good or service, including both the private cost and any external cost.

Tragedy of the commons The tendency for a common resource to be overused.

Transactions costs The costs in time and other resources that parties incur in the process of agreeing to and carrying out an exchange of goods or services.

Self-Test

(Answers are provided at the end of the Self-Test.)

Multiple-Choice Questions

1. What is the cost that affects someone who is not directly involved in the production or consumption of a good called?
   a. private cost
   b. indirect cost
   c. an externality
   d. all of the above

2. What is the term used to describe the total cost of producing a good which includes both private and external costs?
   a. private cost
   b. social cost
   c. externality
   d. all of the above

3. What is the difference between private benefit and social benefit?
   a. an external benefit
   b. private cost
   c. social cost
   d. a negative externality

4. What is the benefit received by the consumer of a good or service called?
   a. private benefit
   b. social benefit
   c. private cost
   d. a positive externality

5. Refer to the graphs below. In which of these markets is an externality present?

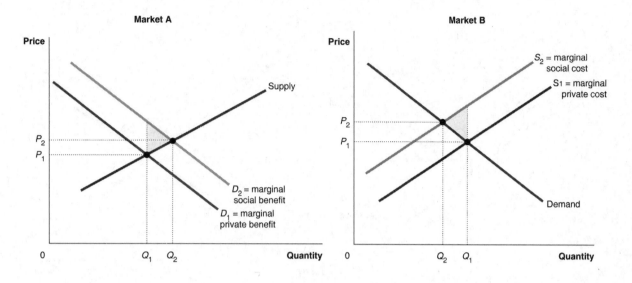

a. in Market A
b. in Market B
c. in both Market A and Market B
d. Neither market exhibits an externality.

6. Refer to the graphs below. Which of the following statements is correct?

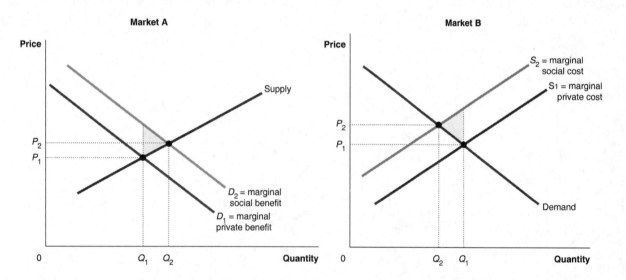

a. Market A exhibits a negative externality because the marginal private benefit exceeds the marginal social benefit.
b. Market B exhibits a negative externality because the marginal social cost exceeds the marginal private cost.
c. Market A exhibits a negative externality because the marginal social benefit exceeds the marginal private benefit.
d. Market B exhibits a positive externality because the marginal private cost exceeds the marginal social cost.

7. Refer to the graphs below. In which of the markets is the quantity Q_1 less than the economically efficient quantity?

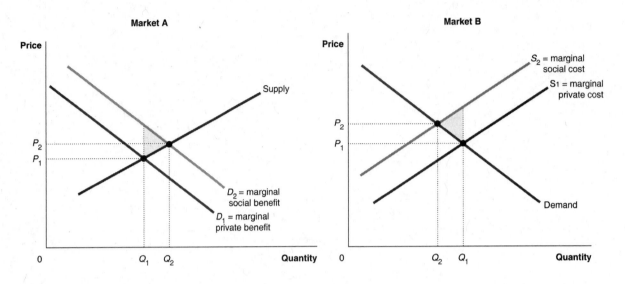

a.   in Market A
b.   in Market B
c.   in both markets
d.   in neither of the two markets

8. Refer to the graph below. The arrow in the graph refers to the difference between D_1 and D_2. What does this difference represent?

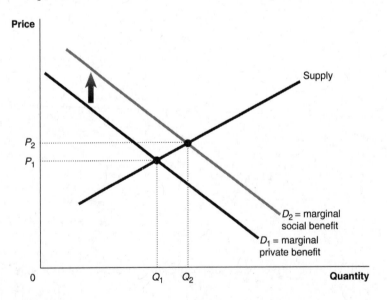

a.   an external benefit
b.   an external cost
c.   private cost
d.   social cost

9. Refer to the graph below. When an externality is present, which combination of price and quantity does the market yield without government intervention?

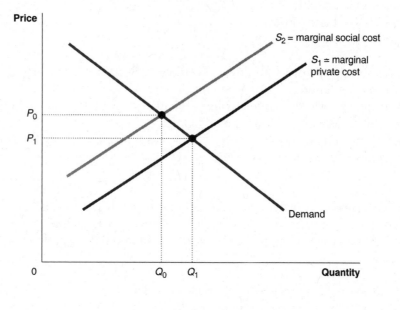

a. P_0, Q_0
b. P_1, Q_1
c. P_0, Q_1
d. P_1, Q_0

10. Fill in the blank. When a negative externality is present in producing a good or service, _____ of the good or service will be produced at market equilibrium.
a. too much
b. too little
c. the optimal quantity
d. none

11. What is the situation called in which the market fails to produce the efficient level of output?
a. an externality
b. market failure
c. external disequilibrium
d. the Coase theorem

12. When we talk about property rights in the discussion of externalities, which rights do we refer to?
a. the rights of individuals to pollute
b. the rights of individuals to have exclusive use of their property
c. the rights of individuals to buy but not sell their property
d. all of the above

13. What are the sources of externalities and market failure?
a. incomplete property rights
b. the difficulty of enforcing property rights in certain situations
c. both a. and b.
d. lack of understanding of the market system

14. What type of solution to externalities is the Coase theorem?
    a. a private solution to externalities
    b. a public solution to externalities
    c. the only solution to externalities
    d. the least preferred solution

15. Which of the following statements is correct according to Ronald Coase's argument for dealing with externalities and market failure?
    a. In some situations, a private solution to the problem of externalities can be found.
    b. Only public solutions exist for solving externalities.
    c. Completely eliminating an externality is almost always the most efficient solution.
    d. The only cure to externalities is taxation.

16. Which of the following is correct?
    a. Completely eliminating an externality is usually not economically efficient.
    b. As reductions in pollution increase, the additional benefits will decline.
    c. When levels of pollution are high, the marginal benefit of reducing pollution is also high.
    d. all of the above

17. The net benefit to society from reducing pollution is equal to
    a. the sum of the benefits of reducing pollution and the costs.
    b. the difference between the benefits of reducing pollution and the costs.
    c. the additional benefit plus the additional costs.
    d. the quantity of pollution, such as the tons of reduction in sulfur dioxide.

18. If we are considering further reductions in pollution, what rule should we follow to maximize the net benefit to society?
    a. The marginal benefit from another ton of reduction should be greater than the marginal cost.
    b. The marginal benefit from another ton of reduction should be less than the marginal cost.
    c. The marginal benefit from another ton of reduction should be equal to the marginal cost.
    d. The marginal benefit from another ton of reduction should equal zero.

19. Refer to the graph below. Which of the following is true when the reduction in sulfur dioxide equals seven tons?

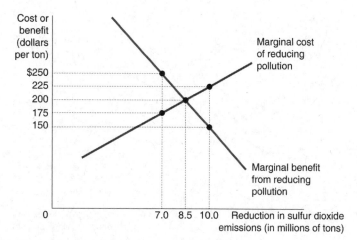

a. The marginal benefit of reducing sulfur dioxide emissions is greater than the marginal cost.
b. Further reductions will make society worse off.
c. The optimal amount of pollution reduction has been found.
d. all of the above

20. Refer to the graph below. Which of the following is true when the reduction in sulfur dioxide equals ten tons?

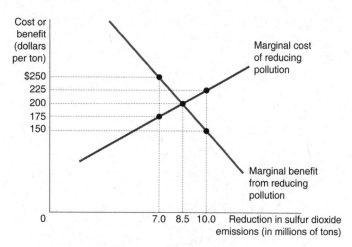

a. The marginal benefit of reducing sulfur dioxide emissions is greater than the marginal cost.
b. Further reductions will make society worse off.
c. The optimal amount of pollution reduction has been found.
d. all of the above

21. Refer to the graph below. How much reduction in sulfur dioxide can be considered economically efficient?

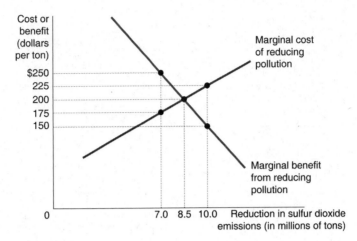

a. 7.0 million tons
b. 8.5 million tons
c. 10.0 million tons
d. all of the above

22. Refer to the graph below. What area represents the total benefit of increasing the reduction of sulfur dioxide from 7.0 million to 8.5 million tons?

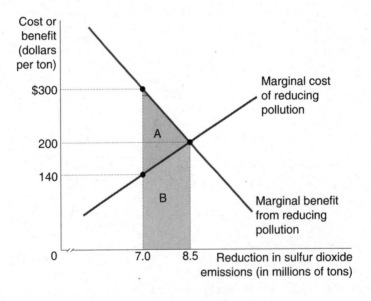

a. Area A
b. Area B
c. Area A + B
d. None of the above; the graph shows only marginal benefit.

23. Refer to the graph below. What area represents the total cost of increasing the reduction of sulfur dioxide from 7.0 million to 8.5 million tons?

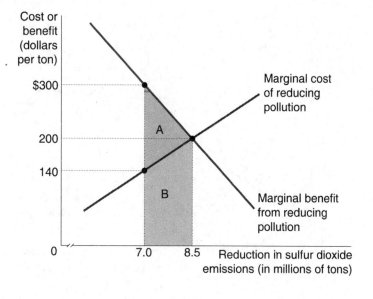

a. Area A
b. Area B
c. Area A + B
d. None of the above; the graph shows only marginal benefit.

24. Refer to the graph below. What is the net benefit of increasing the reduction of sulfur dioxide from 7.0 million to 8.5 million tons?

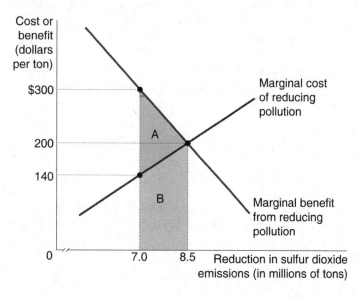

a. Area A
b. Area B
c. Area A + B
d. None of the above; the graph shows only marginal benefit.

25. Refer to the graph below. How much is the net benefit (in millions) of increasing the reduction of sulfur dioxide from 7.0 million tons to 8.5 million tons?

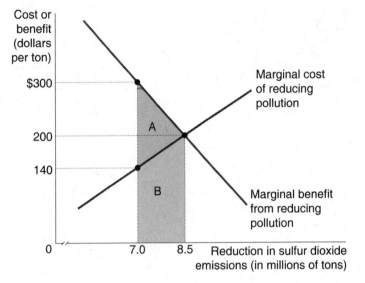

a. $255 million
b. $120 million
c. $200 million
d. none of the above

26. Which of the following assertions is made by Ronald Coase in finding an efficient solution to the problem of negative externalities?
    a. The solution usually depends on which party has a legal property right in the dispute.
    b. The solution does not depend on who has the property rights in the dispute.
    c. If we are to find a solution, property rights could not be enforced because they distort efficiency.
    d. In finding a solution, property rights are usually ignored.

27. Fill in the blanks. When there are many people involved, the transactions costs are often _____ than the net benefits from reducing an externality. In such cases, a private solution to an externality problem _____ feasible.
    a. higher; is
    b. higher; is not
    c. lower; is
    d. lower; is not

28. Fill in the blanks. According to the Coase theorem, if transactions costs are _____, private bargaining will result in an _____ solution to the problem of externalities.
    a. low; efficient
    b. low; inefficient
    c. high; efficient
    d. high; optimal

29. Refer to the graph below. Which of the following best represents a tax equal to the value of the negative externality?

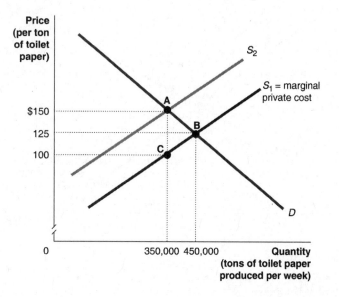

a. S_1
b. S_2
c. the vertical distance between S_1 and S_2
d. $P_2 - P_1$

30. Refer to the graph below. After the negative externality has been internalized, which point would best represent market equilibrium?

a. Point A
b. Point B
c. Point C
d. none of the above

31. Refer to the graph below. What Pigovian tax would push the market to efficiency?

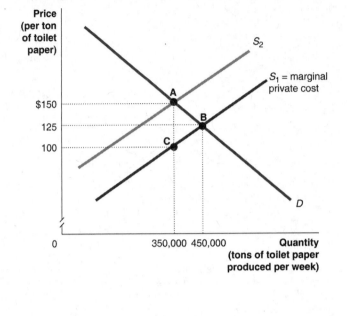

    a. $25
    b. $50
    c. $100
    d. $125

32. Refer to the graph below. To achieve economic efficiency, what should the magnitude of the arrow in the graph be equal to?

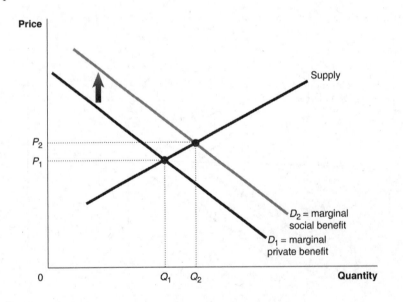

    a.   the amount of a subsidy
    b.   the amount of a tax
    c.   the amount of a price increase
    d.   the social benefit of education

33. What is the focus of a command-and-control approach to reducing pollution?
    a. imposing taxes intended to bring about an efficient level of output in the presence of externalities
    b. offering subsidies intended to bring about an efficient level of output in the presence of externalities
    c. imposing quantitative limits on the amount of pollution firms are allowed to generate
    d. trading emissions allowances to pollute for cash payments

34. What does the term excludability refer to?
    a. a situation in which one person's consumption of a good means that no one else can consume it
    b. the fact that anyone who does not pay for a good cannot consume it
    c. the idea that someone can benefit from a good without paying for it
    d. the possibility that public goods may become private goods

35. What does the term rivalry refer to?
    a. a situation in which one person's consumption of a good means that no one else can consume it
    b. the fact that anyone who does not pay for a good cannot consume it
    c. the idea that someone can benefit from a good without paying for it
    d. the possibility that public goods may become private goods

36. What does the term free riding refer to?
    a. a situation in which one person's consumption of a good means that no one else can consume it
    b. the fact that anyone who does not pay for a good cannot consume it
    c. the idea that someone can benefit from a good without paying for it
    d. the possibility that public goods may become private goods

37. Refer to the table below. From the examples given, which box applies to the concept of common resources?

A: Examples: Big Macs Levi's Jeans	B: Examples: Tuna in the ocean Public pasture land
C: Examples: Cable TV Toll road	D: Examples: National defense Court system

    a. A
    b. B
    c. C
    d. D

38. Refer to the table below. Which of the boxes applies to goods that are excludable and nonrivalrous?

A:	B:
Examples: *Big Macs* *Levi's Jeans*	*Examples:* *Tuna in the ocean* *Public pasture land*
C:	D:
Examples: *Cable TV* *Toll road*	*Examples:* *National defense* *Court system*

   a. A
   b. B
   c. C
   d. D

39. Refer to the graphs below. What procedure does this series of graphs show?

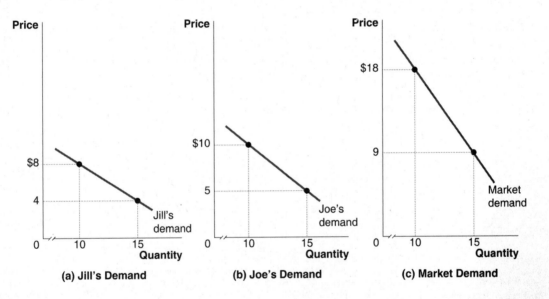

(a) Jill's Demand   (b) Joe's Demand   (c) Market Demand

   a. the construction of market demand for a private good
   b. the construction of market demand for a public good
   c. the construction of market demand for a rival good
   d. the construction of market demand for an excludable good

40. Refer to the graph below. What is the optimal quantity of this public good?

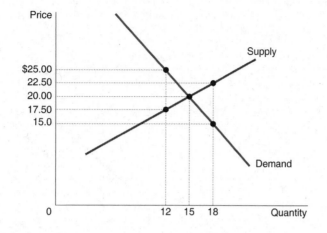

a. 12 units
b. 15 units
c. 18 units
d. none of the above

41. Refer to the table below. The table refers to the Solved Problem that begins on page 153 in the textbook. How many hours of protection maximize economic surplus?

DEMAND FOR PROTECTION			SUPPLY OF PROTECTION	
	Joe	Jill	Quantity (hours of protection)	Price (dollars per hour)
Price (dollars per hour)	Quantity (hours of protection)	Quantity (hours of protection)		
$20	0	1	1	$8
$18	1	2	2	$10
$16	2	3	3	$12
$14	3	4	4	$14
$12	4	5	5	$16
$10	5	6	6	$18
$8	6	7	7	$20
$6	7	8	8	$22
$4	8	9	9	$24
$2	9	10		

a. 1 hour
b. 9 hours
c. 5 hours
d. 6 hours

42. What is the tragedy of the commons?
a. The tragedy of the commons refers to the fact that some people benefit from a good without paying for it.
b. The tragedy of the commons is the tendency for some goods to be excluded from public consumption.
c. The tragedy of the commons refers to the fact that a good can be rival and excludable.
d. The tragedy of the commons refers to the tendency for a common resource to be overused.

43. Refer to the graphs below. Which graph best describes the move from an inefficient use of a common resource to an efficient use of it?

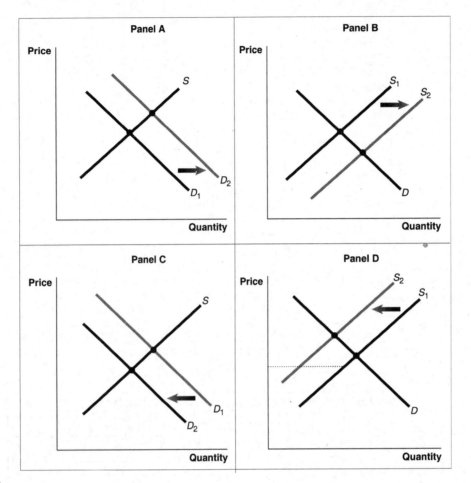

a. Panel A
b. Panel B
c. Panel C
d. Panel D

Short Answer Questions

1. Explain why the marginal benefit from reducing air pollution in the United States in 1970 was greater than the marginal benefit of reducing air pollution by an equivalent amount would be today.

_____

_____

_____

2. Steven Cheung of the University of Washington has written about the positive externalities associated with beekeeping and apple growing. Explain why the solution to this externalities problem is an application of the Coase theorem.

_____

_____

_____

3. Air and water pollution impose external costs on people without their consent. Why isn't it economically efficient to completely eliminate these external costs by reducing the amounts of air and water pollution to zero?

_____

_____

_____

_____

_____

4. Public radio and television stations periodically interrupt their regular broadcast schedules to solicit funds from their listeners and viewers. Why?

_____

_____

_____

_____

5. Ronald Coase argued that private solutions can solve externality problems without government intervention. Why is government intervention used more often than private bargaining to solve externality problems?

_____

_____

_____

_____

True/False Questions

T F 1. The benefits of reducing air pollution are much higher today than in 1970 because the level of air pollution has increased since 1970.

T F 2. The Coase theorem proves that government intervention is necessary to solve externalities problems.

T F 3. A common resource is a good that is excludable but not rival.

T F 4. A quasi-public good describes a good that it is excludable but not rival.

T F 5. The federal government rather than private firms provides national defense because consumers of national defense have an incentive to be free riders.

T F 6. Congress authorized a command-and-control approach to reducing sulfur dioxide emissions by electric utilities in 1990.

T F 7. A social benefit is the private benefit plus any external benefit from consuming a good or service.

T F 8. In the two years following the passage of the Clean Air Act of 1970 there was a decline in infant mortality in the United States.

T F 9. If the marginal cost of reducing emissions of some pollutant is greater than the marginal benefit, society will be better off if these emissions are increased.

T F 10. A.C. Pigou received the 1991 Nobel Prize in Economics for his work on finding private solutions to problems arising from externalities.

T F 11. Government payments to students to attend college are one way to internalize a positive externality.

T F 12. The 1983 requirement by the federal government to install catalytic converters on all new automobiles is an example of a command-and-control approach to reducing pollution.

T F 13. The actual cost to electric utilities of complying with Congress' program to reduce sulfur dioxide emissions in 2010 is greater than was originally estimated by the General Accounting Office in 1994.

T F 14. Most European governments favor a system of tradable emissions permits to reduce carbon dioxide emissions. The U.S. government favors a program that would require individual countries to reduce emissions by a specified amount.

T F 15. The demand for a public good is determined by adding the price each consumer is willing to pay for each quantity of the public good.

Answers to the Self-Test

Multiple Choice Questions

Question	Answer	Comment
1	c	An externality is a benefit or cost that affects someone who is not directly involved in the production or consumption of a good or service.
2	b	The social cost is the private cost plus any external cost resulting from production, such as the cost of pollution.
3	a	A positive externality causes there to be a difference between the *private benefit* from consumption and the social benefit.
4	a	The private benefit is the benefit received by the consumer of a good or service.
5	c	There is a difference between private and social benefits and/or costs in both markets.
6	b	When the social cost is greater than the private cost of production, the market suffers from a negative externality.

7	a	The economically efficient quantity of output in Market A is Q_2, where the marginal private cost equals the marginal social benefit.
8	a	An external benefit exists when the marginal social benefit is greater than marginal private benefit. The private market produces less than the efficient quantity.
9	b	The free market fails to account for external costs. The market produces too much output and charges too low a price when external costs are present.
10	a	When there is a negative externality in producing a good or service, too much of the good or service will be produced at market equilibrium. See page 135 in the textbook.
11	b	Market failure refers to situations where the market fails to produce the efficient level of output. (Option a, externality, is incorrect because an externality is only one type of market failure.)
12	b	Property rights refer to the rights individuals or businesses have to the exclusive use of their property, including the right to buy or sell it.
13	c	A main conclusion in the textbook is that externalities and market failures result from incomplete property rights or the difficulty of enforcing property rights in certain situations.
14	a	According to Coase, under some circumstances private solutions to the problem of externalities will occur.
15	a	According to Coase, under some circumstances private solutions to the problem of externalities will occur.
16	d	It is important to recognize that completely eliminating an externality is usually not economically efficient. For example, if emissions of sulfur dioxide fall to low levels, even people with asthma will no longer be affected. Further reductions in sulfur dioxide will have little additional benefit and a high marginal cost.
17	b	The net benefit to society from reducing pollution is equal to the difference between the benefit of reducing pollution and the costs.
18	c	It is optimal to reduce pollution up to the point where the marginal benefit of the last unit of pollution eliminated is equal to the marginal cost of eliminating that unit.
19	a	If the marginal benefit of reducing sulfur dioxide emissions is greater than the marginal cost, further reductions will make society better off.
20	b	Further reductions have an additional cost which is greater than the additional benefit. If the marginal benefit of reducing sulfur dioxide emissions is less than the marginal cost, further reductions will make society worse off. Refer to Figure 5-3 on page 139 in the textbook.
21	b	The economically efficient quantity is found where marginal benefit is equal to marginal cost.
22	c	The total benefit equals the area under the marginal benefit curve.
23	b	The total cost equals the area under the marginal cost curve.
24	a	The net benefit equals the total benefit minus the total cost.
25	b	The value of the benefits is $375 million or (1.5 million tons × $200 per ton) + (½ × 1.5 million tons × $100 per ton). The value of the costs is $255 million or (1.5 million tons × $140 per ton) + (½ × 1.5 million tons × $60 per ton). If the people who would benefit from a reduction in pollution could get together, they could offer to pay the electric utilities $255 million to reduce the pollution to the optimal level. After making the payment, they would still be left with a net benefit of $120 million. Because the net benefit (see previous question) equals area A, the value of net benefits is equal to ($300 − $140) × 0.5 × 1.5 million = $120 million.
26	a	See page 142 in the textbook.
27	b	When there are many people involved, the transactions costs are often higher than the net benefits from reducing the externality, so the cost of the transaction ends up

exceeding the gain from the transaction. In such cases, a private solution to an externality problem is not feasible.

28	a	The Coase theorem states that if transactions costs are low, private bargaining will result in an efficient solution to the problem of externalities.
29	c	The tax is equal to the difference between private cost and social cost.
30	a	At point A marginal social cost equals marginal benefit.
31	b	A $50 Pigovian tax is equal to the value of the negative externality of $50 (the distance between points A and C).
32	a	When there is a positive externality, a subsidy can bring about the efficient level of output.
33	c	In a command-and-control approach to reducing pollution, quantitative limits are set on the amount of pollution that firms are allowed to generate.
34	b	For example, private goods are excludable.
35	a	See page 148 in the textbook.
36	c	See page 148 in the textbook.
37	b	Common resources are rival and nonexcludable.
38	c	These goods are quasi-public goods.
39	b	To arrive at a demand curve for a public good we don't add quantities at each price, as with a private good. Instead, we add the price each consumer is willing to pay for each quantity of the public good. This gives us a value for the total dollar amount consumers as a group would be willing to pay for that quantity of the public good.
40	b	The optimal quantity of a public good will occur where the demand curve intersects the supply curve. When this quantity is produced, the sum of consumer surplus plus producer surplus is maximized.
41	d	For example, for every hour beyond 6, the supply curve is above the demand curve. Therefore, the additional benefits received will be less than the additional cost of supplying these hours. This results in a deadweight loss and a reduction in economic surplus. Joe is willing to pay $8, and Jill is willing to pay $10, for 6 hours of protection. Their total willingness to pay is equal to the price needed ($18) to provide six hours of protection. Joe and Jill are willing to pay more than the price needed to provide fewer than 6 hours of protection, but they are not willing to pay more than the price needed to provide more than 6 hours of protection.
42	d	The tragedy of the commons is the tendency for a common resource to be overused. A modern example is the forests in many poor countries.
43	d	See Figure 5-11 on page 156 in the textbook.

Short Answer Responses

1. Since the passage of the Clean Air Act in 1970, emissions of the six main forms of air pollution have fallen by almost half. With the lower level of air pollution, the marginal benefit (due to the reduction in illness, etc.) of reducing air pollution by an equivalent amount today would be much less.

2. Cheung noted that intervention by government was not necessary to address the problem because beekeepers and apple growers came to their own solution. Contracts are written between these two groups that specify payments between the parties.

3. The marginal cost of reducing the last amounts of air and water pollution—the amounts that would remain when nearly all forms of pollution were eliminated—would be very high. It might be necessary, for example, to ban all automobiles. The marginal benefit from reducing the last amounts of pollution would be low.

4. Public radio and television do not rely heavily on funding from commercial sponsors to cover their costs of production. Fund-raising programs are designed to solicit membership contributions to cover programming costs, but such contributions are voluntary. Free riding is common because people can enjoy programming without making contributions.

5. For most externalities problems, the number of individuals affected would require complex and costly private solutions. Often these parties do not have complete information regarding the costs and benefits associated with the externalities. Under these circumstances private solutions are not feasible.

True/False Answers

1. F   The level of air pollution is lower today than in 1970.
2. F   The Coase theorem states that private individuals may arrive at their own solutions to externalities.
3. F   A common resource is rival but not excludable.
4. T   This is the definition of a quasi-public good.
5. T   National defense is a public good.
6. F   In 1990, Congress enacted the tradable emissions allowances program.
7. T   This is the definition of social benefit.
8. T   See Making the Connection, "The Clean Air Act: How a Government Policy Reduced Infant Mortality," on page 138 in the textbook.
9. T   Emissions should be reduced up to the point where the marginal benefit is equal to the marginal cost of pollution reduction.
10. F   Ronald Coase received the Nobel Prize in Economics in 1991.
11. T   These government payments are Pigovian subsidies to help students internalize the positive externality associated with consuming education.
12. T   See page 145 in the textbook.
13. F   The actual cost of the program is much lower than original estimates.
14. F   The United States refused to sign the Kyoto Treaty, which required countries to reduce emissions by some fixed percentage. This would indicate that the U.S. government is not in favor of these blanket reductions.
15. T   See page 151 in the textbook.

The Responsiveness of Demand and Supply

Chapter Summary and Learning Objectives

6.1   The Price Elasticity of Demand and its Measurement (pages 168–174)
Define price elasticity of demand and understand how to measure it. **Elasticity** measures how much one economic variable responds to changes in another economic variable. The **price elasticity of demand** measures how responsive quantity demanded is to changes in price. The price elasticity of demand is equal to the percentage change in quantity demanded divided by the percentage change in price. If the quantity demanded changes more than proportionally when price changes, then the price elasticity of demand is greater than 1 in absolute value, and demand is **elastic**. If the quantity demanded changes less than proportionally when price changes, then the price elasticity of demand is less than 1 in absolute value, and demand is **inelastic**. If the quantity demanded changes proportionally when price changes, then the price elasticity of demand is equal to 1 in absolute value, and demand is **unit elastic**. **Perfectly inelastic demand** curves are vertical lines, and **perfectly elastic demand** curves are horizontal lines. Relatively few products have perfectly elastic or perfectly inelastic demand curves.

6.2   The Determinants of the Price Elasticity of Demand (pages 174–177)
Understand the determinants of the price elasticity of demand. The main determinants of the price elasticity of demand for a product are the availability of close substitutes, the passage of time, whether the good is a necessity or a luxury, how narrowly the market for the good is defined, and the share of the good in the consumer's budget.

6.3   The Relationship between Price Elasticity of Demand and Total Revenue (pages 177–181)
Understand the relationship between the price elasticity of demand and total revenue. **Total revenue** is the total amount of funds received by a seller of a good or service. When demand is inelastic, a decrease in price reduces total revenue, and an increase in price increases total revenue. When demand is elastic, a decrease in price increases total revenue, and an increase in price decreases total revenue. When demand is unit elastic, an increase or a decrease in price leaves total revenue unchanged.

6.4   Other Demand Elasticities (pages 181–183)
Define cross-price elasticity of demand and income elasticity of demand and understand their determinants and how they are measured. In addition to the elasticities already discussed, other important demand elasticities are the **cross-price elasticity of demand**, which is equal to the percentage change in quantity demanded of one good divided by the percentage change in the price of another good, and the **income elasticity of demand**, which is equal to the percentage change in the quantity demanded divided by the percentage change in income.

6.5   Using Elasticity to Analyze the Disappearing Family Farm (pages 183–185)
Use price elasticity and income elasticity to analyze economic issues. Price elasticity and income elasticity can be used to analyze many economic issues. One example is the disappearance of the family farm in the United States. Because the income elasticity of demand for food is low, the demand for food has not increased proportionally as incomes in the United States have grown. As farmers have become

more productive, they have increased the supply of most foods. Because the price elasticity of demand for food is low, increasing supply has resulted in continually falling food prices.

6.6   The Price Elasticity of Supply and its Measurement (pages 185–190)
Define price elasticity of supply and understand its main determinants and how it is measured. The **price elasticity of supply** is equal to the percentage change in quantity supplied divided by the percentage change in price. The supply curves for most goods are inelastic over a short period of time, but they become increasingly elastic over longer periods of time. Perfectly inelastic supply curves are vertical lines, and perfectly elastic supply curves are horizontal lines. Relatively few products have perfectly elastic or perfectly inelastic supply curves.

Chapter Review

Chapter Opener: Do People Respond to Changes in the Price of Gasoline? (page 167)

Higher prices reduce the quantity demanded in almost any market, including the market for gasoline. Even though many think of gasoline as a necessity, changes in the price definitely have an impact on the quantity of gasoline consumers purchase. The high gas prices of summer 2008 provide a recent example.

6.1 The Price Elasticity of Demand and its Measurement (pages 168–174)
Learning Objective: Define the price elasticity of demand and understand how to measure it.

Elasticity is a measure of how much one economic variable responds to changes in another economic variable. The **price elasticity of demand** is the responsiveness of the quantity demanded to a change in price, measured by dividing the percentage change in the quantity demanded of a product by the percentage change in the product's price. All elasticity formulas are stated as ratios of two percentage change values. Because of the law of demand, the sign of the price elasticity of demand is always negative. When economists refer to one elasticity being "larger" than another, they mean larger in absolute value (with the negative value turned into a positive value). So, for example, an elasticity of −3 is larger than an elasticity of −2.

Elastic demand means the percentage change in quantity demanded is greater than the percentage change in price, so price elasticity is greater than 1 in absolute value. **Inelastic demand** means the percentage change in quantity demanded is less than the percentage change in price, so price elasticity is less than 1 in absolute value. **Unit-elastic demand** means the percentage change in quantity demanded is equal to the percentage change in price, so price elasticity is equal to 1 in absolute value.

Because the value of the price elasticity of demand is different for each price and quantity combination, the *midpoint formula* is used to calculate elasticity values. In this formula, the change in quantity that results from a price change, $(Q_2 - Q_1)$ or ΔQ, is divided by the average of the quantities $(Q_2 + Q_1)/2$ to calculate the percentage change in quantity demanded. The percentage change in price is calculated by dividing the change in price, $(P_2 - P_1)$ or ΔP, by the average of these prices $(P_2 + P_1)/2$. The elasticity values obtained with the midpoint formula are the same for either a price increase or price decrease between P_2 and P_1.

There are two extreme cases of elasticity. A **perfectly inelastic demand curve** is vertical. If price elasticity of demand is zero, a change in price will not cause quantity demanded to change. A **perfectly elastic demand curve** is horizontal. If price elasticity of demand is very large (approaching infinity), even the smallest change in price will cause a very large change in quantity demanded (also approaching infinity).

📖 Study Hint

Your understanding of elasticity may be increased by rewriting the formula given in the textbook as:

$$E(lasticity) = \frac{\frac{\Delta Q}{Q_1 + Q_2}}{\frac{\Delta P}{P_1 + P_2}} = \frac{\Delta Q}{\Delta P} \times \frac{P_1 + P_2}{Q_1 + Q_2}$$

Because the slope of a linear, or straight-line, demand curve is constant and can be written $\Delta P / \Delta Q$, the elasticity formula can be rewritten as:

$$E = (1/slope) \times \frac{P_1 + P_2}{Q_1 + Q_2}$$

This formula illustrates several important points: (1) Elasticity is not equal to the slope of a linear demand curve. (2) Although a linear demand curve has a constant slope, the elasticity will be different for every segment of the demand curve. (3) Because relatively high values for price are associated with relatively low values for quantity demanded (and vice versa), the absolute values for elasticity will be high at high prices (demand is elastic) and relatively low at low prices (demand is inelastic). This can be shown by substituting price and quantity values for a given demand curve into the rewritten formula and observing the change in the ratio of $(P_2 + P_1)$ to $(Q_2 + Q_1)$.

Solved Problem 6-1 in the textbook gives you an opportunity to practice calculating the price elasticity of demand using an example of a Harry Potter book. If the price elasticity of demand is greater than 1 in absolute value, then demand is price elastic. If the price elasticity of demand is less than 1 in absolute value, then demand is price inelastic. Related end-of-chapter problem 1.6 in the textbook also offers more practice with demand elasticity calculations.

6.2 The Determinants of the Price Elasticity of Demand (pages 174–177)

Learning Objective: Understand the determinants of the price elasticity of demand.

There are five key determinants of the price elasticity of demand: (1) The availability of close substitutes, (2) the passage of time, (3) whether the product is a necessity or luxury, (4) the definition of the market, and (5) the share of the good in the consumer's budget.

The availability of close substitutes is the most important determinant of price elasticity of demand. In general, the price elasticity of demand for a product will be more elastic the more substitutes there are for the product or the closer the substitutes are to the product. Time is an important factor because consumers do not adjust their buying habits immediately following a price change. The more time that passes, the more elastic the demand for a product becomes. The demand for a luxury is more elastic than the demand for a necessity. The more narrowly the market for a product is defined, the more elastic the demand will be. The larger the portion of a consumer's budget that a good accounts for, the more elastic the demand for a good is.

> ### 📖 Study Hint
>
> Two important points to keep in mind: First, you should consider each of the five determinants separately from the others. A product that consumes a small part of a consumer's budget (this suggests demand would be relatively inelastic) may have several good substitutes (this suggests demand would be relatively elastic). Second, changes in the market price of any product will result in different values for price elasticity because each point on a demand curve will have a different price elasticity. Estimates of the price elasticity of demand, such as those cited in the text for breakfast cereals, use market prices for products at a particular time. Different market prices will usually result in different elasticity estimates.
>
> Look at *Making the Connection* "The Price Elasticity of Demand for Breakfast Cereal." You can see how the definition of the market affects the price elasticity of demand for the good. Post Raisin Bran is a very narrowly defined good and has an estimated price elasticity of demand of –2.5, which means it is very elastic. All family breakfast cereals are part of a more broadly defined market and have a less elastic demand. The market for all breakfast cereals is price inelastic and is the broadest of the markets for breakfast cereals discussed in the article.

Extra Solved Problem 6-2

Hailing a Cab in the Big Apple
Supports Learning Objective 6.2: Understand the determinants of the price elasticity of demand.

In New York City, the government sets the fares that taxi drivers can charge. In early 2002, Mayor Michael Bloomberg proposed a fare increase. As a result, some taxi drivers were upset. One driver was quoted as saying, "I get scared that we will start to lose passengers if rates go up and not gain a cent."

a. What was the driver assuming about the price elasticity of demand for taxi rides?

b. Which of the five determinants of elasticity would be the most important determinant of the price elasticity of demand for taxi rides in New York City?

SOLVING THE PROBLEM

Step 1: **Review the chapter material.**
This problem is about the price elasticity of demand, so you may want to review the section "The Determinants of the Price Elasticity of Demand," which begins on page 174 in the textbook.

Step 2: **Interpret the taxi-cab driver's assumption regarding the price elasticity of demand for taxi rides.**
The driver asserted that if the price of a cab ride rose, then the quantity demanded of rides would fall ("…we will start to lose passengers…"), but that the revenue he would receive from fares would be constant ("…we will…not gain a cent"). Therefore, the driver is assuming demand for cab rides is unit elastic. Or, if by "not gain a cent" the driver was actually predicting his revenues would fall, then he is assuming the demand for cab rides is elastic.

Step 3: **Determine which of the determinants of the elasticity of taxi-cab rides in New York City is the most important.**
The most important determinant of the price elasticity of demand is typically the availability of substitutes. On most occasions consumers can choose to travel by subway, bus, or taxi. Some consumers may drive their own automobiles. For many residents and tourists, driving

their own cars is impractical or more expensive than the others because of the difficulty and expense associated with finding parking spaces.

Source: Jayson Blair, "Some Taxi Drivers Say a Fare Increase Would Be Bad for Business," *New York Times*, February 24, 2002.

6.3 The Relationship between Price Elasticity of Demand and Total Revenue (pages 177–181)

Learning Objective: Understand the relationship between the price elasticity of demand and total revenue.

Changes in price and quantity demanded cause changes in the total revenue received by firms. **Total revenue** is the total amount of funds received by the seller of a good or service, calculated by multiplying price per unit by the number of units sold. This is also total spending on the product by consumers. Changes in total revenue are related to the price elasticity of demand. If demand is elastic, a change in price (increase or decrease) will result in a change in total revenue in the opposite direction. If demand is inelastic, a change in price will result in a change in total revenue in the same direction as the change in price. When demand is unit elastic, a change in price (increase or decrease) results in no change in total revenue.

📖 Study Hint

The relationship between elasticity and changes in revenue is very important. Setting and changing the price of a product are among the most important decisions firms make. But firms may not know the elasticity of demand for a product before a pricing decision is made. One way to estimate the elasticity is through a market experiment. *Making the Connection* "Determining the Price Elasticity of Demand through Market Experiments" describes how variations in the prices of DVDs can be used to help determine the price elasticity. This experimentation is especially important for new products where a firm cannot rely on the past relationship between price and quantity demanded.

Solved Problem 6-3 explains how price and total revenue do not always move in the same direction. If demand is price inelastic, then price and total revenue do move together. However, if the demand is price elastic, then price and total revenue will move in the opposite direction from one another, with revenue falling when price increases and rising when price decreases.

6.4 Other Demand Elasticities (pages 181–183)

Learning Objective: Define the cross-price elasticity of demand and the income elasticity of demand and understand their determinants and how they are measured.

The **cross-price elasticity of demand** is the percentage change in quantity demanded of one good divided by the percentage change in price of the other good. Because substitutes are products that can be used for the same purpose, an increase in the price of one of the products will lead to an increase in the quantity demanded of the substitute product. Therefore, the cross-price elasticity of demand will be positive when two goods are substitutes. Complements are products that are used together. An increase in the price of a product will lead to a decrease in the quantity demanded of its complement. Therefore, the cross-price elasticity of demand for these goods will be negative.

📖 **Study Hint**
Students often have trouble remembering that the cross-price elasticity of demand for goods that are substitutes is positive and negative for goods that are complements. "But two goods that are complements go together, so shouldn't they be positively related and have a positive cross-price elasticity?" is an example of the kind of confusion that sometimes results. The intuition that complementary goods go together in some way is correct. That implies that the quantities of the two goods will be positively related. However, the cross-price elasticity doesn't measure how the quantities of the two goods are related. Rather, the cross-price elasticity measures how the quantity of one good responds to a change in price of the other good. Keep that in mind when thinking about the rationale for the cross-price elasticity of demand for substitute and complementary goods.

The **income elasticity of demand** is a measure of the responsiveness of quantity demanded to changes in income, measured by the percentage change in quantity demanded divided by the percentage change in income. An increase in income leads to an increase in the quantity demanded of a normal good. Therefore, the income elasticity of demand for a normal good is positive. A good is a luxury if the income elasticity is greater than 1. A good is a necessity if the income elasticity is positive but less than 1. A good is inferior if the quantity demanded falls when income increases. Therefore, the income elasticity of demand for an inferior good is negative.

📖 **Study Hint**
Remember that, unlike the price elasticity of demand, whether cross-price or income elasticity is greater or less than 1 isn't as important as whether it is greater or less than zero. While we focus only on the number for price elasticity of demand (and less on the negative sign in front of the number), whether cross-price and income elasticities are positive or negative numbers is crucially important.

   Also, be careful not to confuse the price elasticity of demand with other elasticities like the cross-price and income elasticities. For example, if you find that the price elasticity of demand for iPods is −2.5, that finding provides no information about whether iPods are normal or inferior goods. Similarly, the finding that demand has an elasticity of −2.5 does not allow you to predict whether iPods are substitutes or complements for other goods. A price elasticity of demand equal to −2.5 tells you only that demand for iPods is elastic in response to a change in the price of iPods. How the demand for iPods changes when income or the prices of related goods change cannot be determined simply from the price elasticity of demand.

Extra Solved Problem 6-4
The Demand for Margarine
Supports Learning Objective 6.4: Define the cross-price elasticity of demand and the income elasticity of demand and understand their determinants and how they are measured.

Suppose that the table that follows gives the demand this month for margarine in the city of Breadville. Each of the quantity columns, (b) and (c), is a different demand schedule. Column (a) shows the price of margarine. Column (b) shows the quantity demanded of margarine for a fixed price of butter and a fixed income. Comparing columns (b) and (c), we can see that the price of butter rises.

(a) price of margarine (dollars per pound)	(b) Quantity demanded of margarine (price of butter is $1.00 per pound and family income is $30,000) [hundreds of pounds]	(c) Quantity demanded of margarine (price of butter is $1.60 per pound and family income is $30,000) [hundreds of pounds]
$1.60	24.02	32.91
1.40	25.00	34.25
1.20	26.18	35.87
1.00	27.65	37.89
0.80	29.57	40.51

a. Calculate the cross-price elasticity of demand for margarine using the midpoint formula given a change in the price of butter from $1.00 per pound to $1.60 per pound. (Hint: use columns (b) and (c).)

b. What can you say about the relationship between margarine and butter?

SOLVING THE PROBLEM
Step 1:   Review the chapter material.
This problem is about the other elasticities of demand, so you may want to review the section "Other Demand Elasticities," which begins on page 181 in the textbook.

Step 2:   Calculate the cross-price elasticity of demand using the midpoint method.
You can choose to analyze any row in the table, and you will get the following results. The price of butter rises from $1.00 to $1.60 per pound, while the quantity demanded of margarine rises from 24.02 hundred pounds to 32.91 hundred pounds. The cross-price elasticity of demand is 0.68.

Step 3:   Interpret the cross-price elasticity of demand.
Because the cross-price elasticity of demand is positive, we know that margarine and butter are substitutes. We can also see that the response of the quantity demanded of margarine to the price change in butter is relatively small, which means that an increase in the price of butter did not cause consumers to strongly switch from buying butter to buying margarine.

 6.5 Using Elasticity to Analyze the Disappearing Family Farm (pages 183–185)

Learning Objective: Use price elasticity and income elasticity to analyze economic issues.

The demand for many agricultural commodities (for example, wheat) is price inelastic, while the income elasticity for these commodities is low (positive but less than one). Technological change has caused large increases in the supply of agricultural commodities over time. Because of the low income elasticity of demand for these commodities, demand has increased much less than supply. This has resulted in decreases in the relative prices of many agricultural commodities and falling revenues for farmers. At the same time, the technological improvements have meant fewer farmers are needed to produce agricultural commodities.

📖 **Study Hint**

The decline in the relative price of agricultural products is an example of how knowledge of elasticity explains an important economic and social issue. *Solved Problem 6-5,* "Using Price Elasticity to Analyze Policy toward Illegal Drugs," is another excellent application of elasticity to an economic issue. How much consumption of cocaine will be affected by a change in price depends on the price elasticity of demand for cocaine. If the price elasticity is high in absolute value, then the decrease in price that would result from legalization could nearly triple consumption. If the price elasticity is low, then there will be only a slight increase in cocaine consumption. You can test your understanding further by completing related problems 5.2 and 5.3 on page 200 in the textbook.

6.6 **The Price Elasticity of Supply and its Measurement (pages 185–190)**
Learning Objective: Define the price elasticity of supply and understand its main determinants and how it is measured.

The **price elasticity of supply** is the responsiveness of the quantity supplied to a price change, measured by dividing the percentage change in the quantity supplied of a product by the percentage change in the product's price. Because of the law of supply, this elasticity will have a positive numerical value. The longer the time period firms have to respond to a price change, the greater the elasticity of supply. Like demand, supply can be "perfectly" elastic or "perfectly" inelastic if it is horizontal (perfectly elastic) or vertical (perfectly inelastic).

📖 **Study Hint**

Making the Connection "Why Are Oil Prices So Unstable?" explains how the elasticity of demand and supply affects the price of oil. In the short run, demand and supply are both relatively inelastic, so a reduction in the supply of oil will cause a large increase in the price of oil, but only a small change in the equilibrium quantity of oil produced and consumed. In the long run, consumers and firms have time to adjust their consumption preferences and productive capacity, so the demand and supply curves are relatively elastic. A change in the supply of oil has a smaller effect on the equilibrium price of oil in the long run. Use that analysis to help you solve part c of Extra Solved Problem 6-6 below.

Extra Solved Problem 6-6

Ethanol and Biodiesel
Supports Learning Objective 6.6: Define the price elasticity of supply and understand its main determinants and how it is measured.

Suppose that this summer your state government passes an immediate tax rebate to all citizens who use ethanol and biodiesel fuels in their automobiles. This causes the demand for ethanol and biodiesel to increase significantly. The main inputs for these alternative fuels are soy and corn. Because the supply of soy and corn are fixed for a given summer, the supply of these alternative fuels is fixed.

a. What is the price elasticity of supply when the supply of a good is fixed?

b. Using a graph of demand and supply in the market for alternative fuels, explain what happens to the equilibrium price and quantity of alternative fuels in the summer that this rebate is introduced.

c. How would you expect the price elasticity of supply for alternative fuels to change over time, if at all?

SOLVING THE PROBLEM

Step 1: **Review the chapter material.**

This problem is about the price elasticity of supply, so you may want to review the section "The Price Elasticity of Supply and its Measurement," which begins on page 185 in the textbook.

Step 2: **Interpret the fixed supply of alternative fuels and what that means in terms of the price elasticity of supply.**

If the supply is fixed, the quantity supplied is constant regardless of the market price, that is, supply is perfectly inelastic and is a vertical line. A vertical line has a price elasticity of supply of zero.

Step 3: **Apply the increase in demand and the vertical supply curve to the market for alternative fuels, and consider what determinants of the price elasticity might affect elasticity of supply over time.**

The equilibrium quantity will be unaffected, and the increase in demand will cause only an increase in the market price. Over time the elasticity of supply will increase, and the supply curve will become flatter, causing the quantity to increase in the long run with a smaller increase in price.

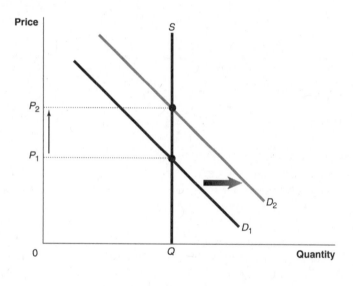

Key Terms

Cross-price elasticity of demand The percentage change in quantity demanded of one good divided by the percentage change in the price of another good.

Elastic demand Demand is elastic when the percentage change in quantity demanded is *greater* than the percentage change in price, so the price elasticity is *greater* than 1 in absolute value.

Elasticity A measure of how much one economic variable responds to changes in another economic variable.

Income elasticity of demand A measure of the responsiveness of quantity demanded to changes in income, measured by the percentage change in quantity demanded divided by the percentage change in income.

Inelastic demand Demand is inelastic when the percentage change in quantity demanded is *less* than the percentage change in price, so the price elasticity is *less* than 1 in absolute value.

Perfectly elastic demand The case where the quantity demanded is infinitely responsive to price, and the price elasticity of demand equals infinity.

Perfectly inelastic demand The case where the quantity demanded is completely unresponsive to price, and the price elasticity of demand equals zero.

Price elasticity of demand The responsiveness of the quantity demanded to a change in price, measured by dividing the percentage change in the quantity demanded of a product by the percentage change in the product's price.

Price elasticity of supply The responsiveness of the quantity supplied to a change in price, measured by dividing the percentage change in the quantity supplied of a product by the percentage change in the product's price.

Total revenue The total amount of funds received by a seller of a good or service, calculated by multiplying price per unit by the number of units sold.

Unit-elastic demand Demand is unit elastic when the percentage change in quantity demanded is *equal to* the percentage change in price, so the price elasticity is equal to 1 in absolute value.

Self-Test

(Answers are provided at the end of the Self-Test.)

Multiple-Choice Questions

1. What do economists use the concept of elasticity for?
   a. to explain how producers respond to consumers' needs
   b. to measure how one economic variable responds to changes in another economic variable
   c. to define the slope of supply and demand curves
   d. all of the above

2. If you know the value for price elasticity of demand, then which of the following can you compute?
   a. the effect of a price change on the quantity demanded
   b. the responsiveness of the quantity supplied of a good to changes in its price
   c. the price elasticity of supply
   d. all of the above

3. What is the name given to the responsiveness of the quantity supplied of a good to a change in its price?
   a. price elasticity of supply
   b. price elasticity of demand
   c. income elasticity
   d. cross-price elasticity

4. Who benefits from the concept of elasticity?
   a. business managers
   b. policymakers
   c. both business managers and policymakers
   d. neither business managers nor policymakers; only economists benefit from it

5. How is the responsiveness of the quantity demanded to a change in price measured?
   a. by dividing the percentage change in the product's price by the percentage change in the quantity demanded of a product
   b. by multiplying the percentage change in the product's price by the percentage change in the quantity demanded of a product
   c. by dividing the percentage change in the quantity demanded of a product by the percentage change in the product's price
   d. by multiplying the percentage change in the quantity demanded of a product by the percentage change in the product's price

6. Which of the following measures is more sensitive to the units chosen for quantity and price?
   a. price elasticity of demand
   b. price elasticity of supply
   c. the slope of a demand or supply curve
   d. cross-price elasticity

7. How do economists avoid confusion over units in the computation of elasticity?
   a. by using index numbers rather than whole numbers
   b. by using percentage changes rather than simple differences
   c. by using aggregate values rather than single values
   d. by using the same number as the value of the slope of the curve

8. Which of the following statements about the slope and the price elasticity of demand is correct?
   a. The slope is calculated using percentage changes in quantity and price, whereas elasticity is calculated using simple numerical changes.
   b. The slope is calculated using changes in quantity and price, whereas elasticity is calculated using percentage changes.
   c. Both the slope and elasticity must be calculated using percentage changes.
   d. Neither the slope nor the value of elasticity can be calculated using simple numerical changes.

9. Which of the following is true about the value of the price elasticity of demand?
   a. The value is always negative.
   b. The value is always positive.
   c. The value may be positive or negative depending on the value of the slope of the demand curve.
   d. The value is positive when the slope is negative and negative when the slope is positive.

10. If we find that the price elasticity of demand for hamburgers is −1.3 while the price elasticity of demand for textbooks is −0.6, which of the following can we say is true?
    a. The law of demand is violated in both the market for hamburgers and the market for textbooks.
    b. The demand for hamburgers is more elastic than the demand for textbooks.
    c. A 10% increase in the price of hamburgers will result in a 13% increase in the quantity of hamburgers demanded.
    d. Consumers like hamburgers more than they like textbooks.

11. What happens when the quantity demanded is very responsive to changes in price?
    a. The percentage change in quantity demanded will be greater than the percentage change in price.
    b. The percentage change in quantity demanded will be less than the percentage change in price.
    c. The percentage change in quantity demanded will be equal to the percentage change in price.
    d. The percentage change in quantity demanded will be unrelated to the percentage change in price.

12. When the percentage change in quantity demanded is greater than the percentage change in price, which of the following is true?
    a. The price elasticity of demand will be greater than 1 in absolute value.
    b. Demand is inelastic.
    c. There are few substitutes for the good in question.
    d. All of the above are true.

13. Which of the following is true if quantity demanded is not very responsive to price?
    a. The percentage change in quantity demanded will be less than the percentage change in price.
    b. The price elasticity of demand will be less than 1 in absolute value.
    c. Demand is inelastic.
    d. All of the above are true.

14. If a 20% increase in the price of Red Bull energy drinks results in a decrease in the quantity demanded of 25%, the price elasticity of demand is
    a. −25.
    b. −0.8.
    c. −1.25.
    d. −20.

15. If a 20% increase in the price of Red Bull energy drinks results in a decrease in the quantity demanded of 25%, we say demand for Red Bull is _____ in this range.
    a. inelastic
    b. elastic
    c. unit elastic
    d. vertical

16. Refer to the graph below which shows two potential demand curves in the market for photocopies at a printing company. If you start at point A on D_1, what is the percentage change in price when price falls from $30 to $20? Use the midpoint formula to calculate this percentage change.

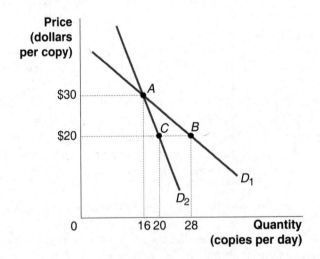

    a. price falls by 10%
    b. price falls by 25%
    c. price falls by 40%
    d. price falls by 45%

17. Refer to the graph below which shows two potential demand curves in the market for photocopies at a printing company. If you start at point A on D_1, what is the percentage change in quantity demanded when price falls from $30 to $20? Use the midpoint formula to calculate this percentage change.

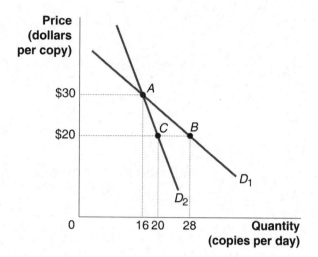

a. quantity demanded rises by 22%
b. quantity demanded rises by 4%
c. quantity demanded rises by 55%
d. quantity demanded falls by 40%

18. Refer to the graph below which shows two potential demand curves in the market for photocopies at a printing company. When price falls from $30 to $20, demand is _____ between points A and C on D_2 and demand is _____ between points A and B on D_1.

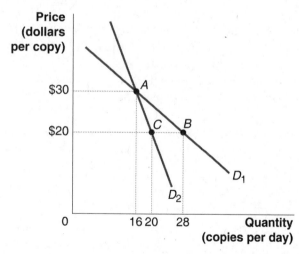

a. inelastic; elastic
b. elastic; elastic
c. inelastic; inelastic
d. elastic; inelastic

19. Refer to the graph below which shows two potential demand curves in the market for photocopies at a printing company. Between points A and B on D_1, what is the price elasticity of demand?

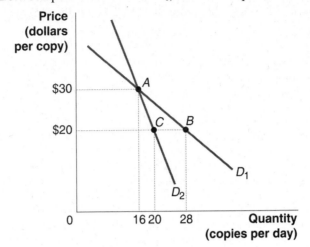

    a.   −1.2
    b.   −1.4
    c.   −0.83
    d.   −12

20. Which of the following would occur when calculating price elasticity between two points on a demand curve if we are not using the midpoint formula?
    a.   The value of elasticity we would get would be the same whether we apply it to price increases or to price decreases.
    b.   We would get a different value for price increases than for price decreases.
    c.   The values we would get would be the same if the demand curve is downward sloping.
    d.   The values would always coincide with the value of the slope of the demand curve, especially if the demand curve is linear.

21. Which of the following does the midpoint formula use to compute elasticity?
    a.   the averages of the initial and final quantity and the initial and final price
    b.   the differences between initial and final prices and quantities
    c.   the sums of the initial and final prices and quantities
    d.   the product of the initial and final prices and quantities

22. When quantity demanded is completely unresponsive to price, what is the value of price elasticity of demand?
    a.   zero
    b.   1
    c.   a number between zero and 1
    d.   a negative number

23. If demand is perfectly elastic, then what is the impact of an increase in price?
    a.   a decrease in quantity demanded to zero
    b.   no change in quantity demanded
    c.   a change in quantity demanded exactly equal to the change in price
    d.   a very small change in quantity demanded

24. Which of the following is the most important determinant of price elasticity of demand?
    a. the availability of substitutes
    b. the passage of time
    c. the difference between necessities and luxuries
    d. the definition of the market

25. Which of the following is a true statement?
    a. The more substitutes available for a product, the greater the price elasticity of demand.
    b. The more time that passes, the more elastic the demand for a product becomes.
    c. The demand curve for a luxury is more elastic than the demand curve for a necessity.
    d. All of the above are true.

26. Which of the following is a true statement?
    a. The fewer substitutes available for a product, the greater the price elasticity of demand.
    b. The more time that passes, the more inelastic the demand for a product becomes.
    c. The demand curve for a luxury is less elastic than the demand curve for a necessity.
    d. The more narrowly defined a product is, the larger the price elasticity of demand.

27. The price elasticity of demand for a particular brand of raisin bran is, in absolute value,
    a. larger than the price elasticity of demand for all breakfast cereals.
    b. the same as the price elasticity of demand for all breakfast cereals.
    c. smaller than the price elasticity of demand for all types of breakfast cereals.
    d. neither larger nor smaller than the price elasticity of demand for any other type of cereal.

28. Fill in the blanks. In general, the price elasticity of demand for a good will be _____ elastic the _____ the share of the good in the average consumer's budget.
    a. less; smaller
    b. more; smaller
    c. less; larger
    d. unit; larger

29. Sarah spends 2% of her weekly budget on chewing gum, and she spends 50% of her weekly budget on books. All else equal, we would expect her demand for chewing gum to be
    a. more elastic than her demand for books.
    b. less elastic than her demand for books.
    c. elastic.
    d. unit elastic.

30. What is total revenue?
    a. the total amount of funds a firm receives from selling a good or service
    b. an amount calculated by multiplying price per unit by the number of units sold
    c. an amount that increases when price increases if demand is inelastic
    d. all of the above

31. When demand is inelastic, what is the relationship between price and total revenue?
    a. They move in the same direction.
    b. They move in opposite directions.
    c. They always remain unchanged.
    d. They are entirely unrelated.

32. When demand is elastic, how will an increase in price affect total revenue?
    a.   Total revenue will rise.
    b.   Total revenue will fall.
    c.   Total revenue will be unaffected by the change in price.
    d.   Total revenue may rise or fall, but the effect will depend on the size of the price change.

33. Refer to the graphs below which show two potential demand curves in the market for photocopies at a printing company. In which of the two graphs does a price decrease lead to an increase in total revenue?

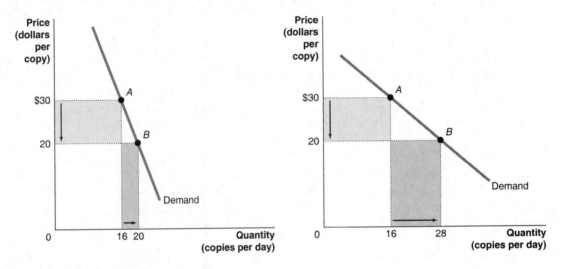

    a.   in the graph on the left
    b.   in the graph on the right
    c.   in both graphs
    d.   in neither graph

34. When an increase in the quantity demanded is not large enough to make up for a decrease in price, total revenue falls. Which graph is more applicable to this statement?

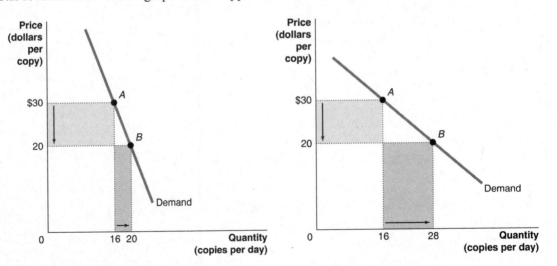

a. the graph on the left
b. the graph on the right
c. both graphs
d. neither graph

35. What is the effect of a cut in price when demand is inelastic?
a. an increase in total revenue
b. a decrease in total revenue
c. no effect on total revenue
d. a change in total revenue by an amount equal to the cut in price

36. When is a change in price exactly offset by a proportional change in quantity demanded, leaving revenue unaffected?
a. never
b. when demand is elastic
c. when demand is inelastic
d. when demand is unit elastic

37. Refer to the graph below which shows the demand for DVDs. What happens to price elasticity as we move down the demand curve?

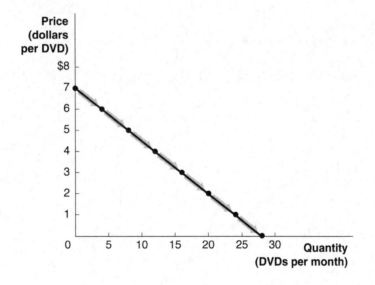

a. It rises.
b. It falls.
c. It remains the same.
d. It rises up to the midpoint, and then it falls.

38. Refer to the graph below which shows the demand for DVDs. What happens to total revenue as we move down the demand curve?

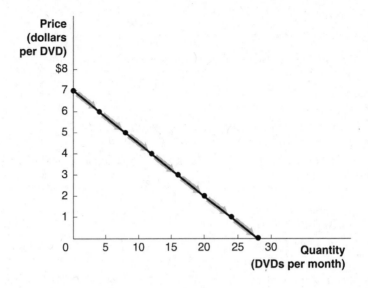

   a. It rises.
   b. It falls.
   c. It remains the same.
   d. It rises up to the midpoint, and then it falls.

39. In the graph of demand in the market for DVDs below, when the price is $6, demand

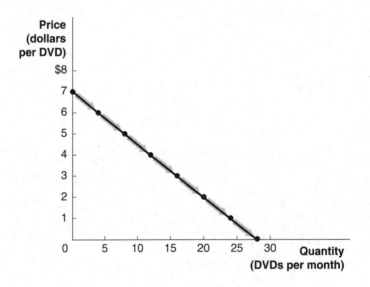

   a. is elastic.
   b. is inelastic.
   c. is unit elastic.
   d. cannot be determined from the graph.

40. Fill in the blanks: An increase in the price of a substitute for iPods will lead to _____ in quantity demanded of iPods, so the cross-price elasticity of demand will be _____.
    a. an increase; positive
    b. an increase; negative
    c. a decrease; positive
    d. a decrease; negative

41. Fill in the blanks: An increase in the price of a complement for DVDs will lead to _____ in the quantity demanded of DVDs, so the cross-price elasticity of demand will be _____.
    a. an increase; positive
    b. an increase; negative
    c. a decrease; positive
    d. a decrease; negative

42. What is the cross-price elasticity of demand for two products that are unrelated?
    a. zero
    b. 1
    c. infinite
    d. negative

43. If Amazon.com raises its prices by 10 percent and, as a result, the quantity of books demanded on Barnesandnoble.com increases by 35 percent, what do consumers consider the two Web sites to be?
    a. close substitutes
    b. close complements
    c. unrelated
    d. identical

44. If the quantity demanded of a good increases as income increases, then that good must be which of the following?
    a. a necessity
    b. a luxury
    c. a normal good
    d. an inferior good

45. If the income elasticity of SUVs is greater than 1, what is the good considered?
    a. a necessity
    b. a luxury
    c. a substitute good
    d. an inferior good

46. The income elasticity for peanut butter is −3. This defines peanut butter as what type of good?
    a. a good with elastic demand
    b. an inferior good
    c. a good that is a complement for jelly
    d. a necessity

47. What is true about quantity demanded if a good is considered a necessity?
    a. It is very responsive to changes in income.
    b. It is not very responsive to changes in income.
    c. It is unrelated to changes in income.
    d. It is always the same regardless of price changes.

48. Which of the following is true about what happens to the quantity demanded of an inferior good?
    a. It rises when income rises.
    b. It falls when income increases.
    c. It does not change with changes in price.
    d. It does not change with changes in income.

49. Suppose that an innovation in harvesting technology increases the supply of corn. Corn farmers will experience an increase in total revenue when
    a. the supply of corn is inelastic.
    b. the supply of corn is elastic.
    c. the demand for corn is inelastic.
    d. the demand for corn is elastic.

50. When demand increases, equilibrium price will rise _____ when supply is _____ elastic.
    a. more; more
    b. less; less
    c. more; less
    d. None of the above. Supply elasticity does not affect the impact of a shift in demand on the equilibrium price.

Short Answer Questions

1. Some people believe that changes in the price of gasoline have no effect on purchases of gasoline. They see gasoline as a necessity that will be purchased in the same amounts regardless of the price. If this were truly the case, what does that imply about the shape of the demand curve for gasoline? Do you think the demand curve for gasoline really does have that shape?

    _____

    _____

    _____

2. Phil Sanders, an economics major who recently graduated from a local college, was hired as a consultant by the Middletown City Council. A member of the Council proposed lowering fares for public transportation (buses and trolleys). He reasoned that the lower price would increase both the number of people using public transportation and revenue from fares. The increased revenue would be used to buy new buses. When he estimated price elasticities of demand, Sanders found that the price elasticity of demand for both bus and trolley service was −0.6. What advice should Sanders give the City Council?

    _____

    _____

    _____

3. Assume that economic growth causes incomes to rise in the United States by 5 percent. Use the income elasticities of demand from Making the Connection "Price Elasticity, Cross-Price Elasticity, and Income Elasticity in the Market for Alcoholic Beverages" on page 183 in the textbook to estimate the change in the quantities demanded for beer, wine, and spirits.

_____

_____

_____

4. The Los Angeles Lakers basketball team and the Los Angeles Kings hockey team play their home games in the Staples Center. The seating capacity of the Staples Center is just under 19,000. Although Lakers games are often sold out, the number of tickets sold to Kings games, some concerts, and other non-sports events is often less than 14,000. What is the price elasticity of supply for the Staples Center?

_____

_____

5. A low income elasticity of demand for wheat is one of the reasons given in the textbook for the reduction in the number of family farms in the United States. Why is the income elasticity for wheat low? Is wheat an inferior good?

_____

_____

_____

True/False Questions

T F 1.   The price elasticity of demand measures the responsiveness of demand for a product to a change in the product's price.

T F 2.   The demand for all breakfast cereals is more elastic than the demand for a specific brand of cereal.

T F 3.   If the demand for a product is elastic, a decrease in price results in an increase in revenue.

T F 4.   The cross-price elasticity of demand for two complements is positive.

T F 5.   The midpoint formula is used to ensure that there is only one value of the price elasticity of demand between two points on the same demand curve.

T F 6.   One reason for the decline in wheat prices from 1950 to 2009 (measured in terms of prices in 2009) is a price elasticity of demand that is less than 1 in absolute value.

T F 7.   During recessions, the demand for inferior goods will rise.

T F 8.   If the supply for a product is inelastic, an increase in price will increase total revenue.

T F 9.   A supply curve that is a horizontal line is perfectly elastic.

T F 10. If a product has a unit-elastic demand, an increase in income does not affect revenue.

T F 11. The larger the share of a good in the average consumer's budget, the more elastic demand for that good is.

T F 12. A perfectly elastic demand curve will be a horizontal line.
T F 13. A perfectly inelastic demand curve will have a price elasticity equal to 1 in absolute value.
T F 14. A good with an income elasticity of demand equal to 1.2 is a normal good.
T F 15. A good with an income elasticity of demand equal to 1.2 is a luxury good.

Answers to the Self-Test

Multiple-Choice Questions

Question	Answer	Comment
1	b	Economists use the concept of elasticity to measure how one economic variable responds to changes in another economic variable.
2	a	Price elasticity of demand measures the effect of a change in price on the quantity demanded.
3	a	The responsiveness of the quantity supplied of a good to changes in its price is called price elasticity of supply.
4	c	Elasticity is an important concept not just for business managers but for policymakers as well.
5	c	The responsiveness of the quantity demanded to a change in price is measured by dividing the percentage change in the quantity demanded of a product by the percentage change in the product's price.
6	c	The measurement of slope is sensitive to the units chosen for quantity and price. For this reason, we use percentage changes to compute responsiveness.
7	b	Percentage changes are not dependent on units of measurement.
8	b	The value we compute for the slope can change dramatically depending on the units we use for quantity and price. To avoid this confusion over units, economists use percentage changes when measuring the price elasticity of demand.
9	a	If we calculate the price elasticity of demand for a price cut, the percentage change in price will be negative, and the percentage change in quantity demanded will be positive. Similarly, if we calculate the price elasticity of demand for a price increase, the percentage change in price will be positive and the percentage change in quantity will be negative. Therefore, the price elasticity of demand is always negative.
10	b	In comparing elasticities, we are usually interested in their relative size. So, we often drop the minus sign and compare their absolute values. Because 1.3 is greater than 0.6, the price elasticity of demand in the market for hamburgers is greater.
11	a	In other words, the absolute value of elasticity will be greater than one, so the absolute value of the numerator will be greater than the absolute value of the denominator in the elasticity formula.
12	a	If the quantity demanded is responsive to changes in price, the percentage change in quantity demanded will be greater than the percentage change in price, and the price elasticity of demand will be greater than 1 in absolute value. In this case, demand is elastic.
13	d	When the quantity demanded is not very responsive to price, the percentage change in quantity demanded will be less than the percentage change in price, and the price elasticity of demand will be less than 1 in absolute value. In this case, demand is inelastic.
14	c	Price elasticity of demand is calculated as the percentage change in the quantity demanded divided by the percentage change in price.

15	b	The percentage change in quantity demanded is greater than the percentage change in price, resulting in a price elasticity of demand that is greater than 1 in absolute value. This is elastic demand.
16	c	The percentage change in price is the change in the price divided by the average price, which is (30−20)/25 = 40%.
17	c	The decrease in price increases quantity demanded from 16 to 28. Using the midpoint formula, that is a percentage change of (28−16)/22 = 55%.
18	a	Between points *A* and *C*, the percentage change in quantity demanded is smaller than the percentage change in price. Between points *A* and *B*, the percentage change in quantity demanded is greater than the price.
19	b	The percentage change in quantity demanded is 55%, and the percentage change in price is −40%. The price elasticity of demand is (55%/−40%) = −1.4.
20	b	We could run into a problem because we get a different value for the price elasticity of demand for price increases than for price decreases. To avoid this problem, we use the midpoint formula to compute elasticity.
21	a	The midpoint formula uses the average of the initial and final quantity and the initial and final price to compute elasticity.
22	a	If a demand curve is perfectly inelastic, an increase in price causes the quantity demanded to remain the same, so there is no (or zero) response in quantity demanded.
23	a	Refer to Table 6-1 on page 173 in the textbook.
24	a	The textbook asserts that the availability of substitutes is the most important determinant of the price elasticity of demand.
25	d	All of these statements are correct. Read pages 174–177 in the textbook.
26	d	The price elasticity of demand for a narrowly defined market (for example, *Tide* has many substitutes) will be greater than the price elasticity of demand for a broadly defined market (laundry detergent).
27	a	The more substitutes available for a product, the greater the price elasticity of demand. Also, the more narrowly defined a product is, the larger the price elasticity of demand.
28	a	Goods that take only a small fraction of a consumer's budget tend to have inelastic demand. For example, the share of the average consumer's budget that is spent on salt is very low. As a result, even a doubling of the price of salt is likely to result in only a small decline in the quantity of salt demanded.
29	b	Because Sarah spends less of her weekly budget on chewing gum, her demand for chewing gum should be less elastic than her demand for goods that take up a larger portion of her weekly budget.
30	d	Total revenue is the total amount of funds a firm receives from selling a good or service. Total revenue is calculated by multiplying price per unit by the number of units sold.
31	a	An increase in price raises total revenue, and a decrease in price reduces total revenue when demand is inelastic.
32	b	An increase in price reduces total revenue, and a decrease in price raises total revenue when demand is elastic.
33	b	In the graph on the right the price decrease raises revenue from ($30 × 16) = $480 to ($20 × 28) = $560. You can also see that the increase in revenue from decreasing price equals 12 copies (28 − 16) multiplied by $20, or $240. This is greater than the decrease in revenue from decreasing price (($30 − $20) × 16 = $160).
34	a	Demand is inelastic when price falls from $30 to $20, so the decrease in price results in a decrease in revenue.

35	b	When demand is inelastic, a cut in price will decrease total revenue.
36	d	When demand is unit elastic, a change in price is exactly offset by a proportional change in quantity demanded, leaving revenue unaffected. Therefore, when demand is unit elastic, neither a decrease in price nor an increase in price affects revenue.
37	b	At higher prices, demand is more elastic, and at lower prices, demand is less elastic and eventually becomes inelastic.
38	d	Total revenue is highest at the midpoint of the demand curve and decreases as the price moves away from the midpoint price.
39	a	Above the midpoint of a linear demand curve, demand is elastic.
40	a	An increase in the price of a substitute will lead to an increase in demand for the substitute product, so the cross-price elasticity of demand will be positive.
41	d	An increase in the price of a complement will lead to a decrease in quantity demanded for the complementary product, so the cross-price elasticity of demand will be negative.
42	a	If the two products are unrelated, the cross-price elasticity of demand will be zero.
43	a	If consumers buy more from Barnesandnoble.com when Amazon.com raises prices, then the two Web sites are considered by consumers to be close substitutes.
44	c	If the quantity demanded of a good increases as income increases, then the good is a normal good. Normal goods are often further subdivided into luxury goods and necessity goods.
45	b	A good is a luxury if demand is very responsive to changes in income, so that a 10 percent increase in income results in more than a 10 percent increase in quantity demanded. Expensive jewelry or vacation homes are examples of luxuries.
46	b	Any good with a negative income elasticity is an inferior good. Note that whether the income elasticity is greater or less than 1 does not predict whether the price elasticity of demand for that good is greater or less than 1 in absolute value.
47	b	A good is a necessity if demand is not very responsive to changes in income, so that a 10 percent increase in income results in less than a 10 percent increase in quantity demanded. Food and clothing are examples of necessities.
48	b	A good is inferior if quantity demanded falls when income increases. Ground beef with a high fat content is an example of an inferior good.
49	d	An increase in supply will cause a decrease in the equilibrium price and an increase in the equilibrium quantity. For total revenue to increase as the price falls, demand must be elastic.
50	c	When supply is less elastic (steeper), any change in demand will have a stronger effect on equilibrium price.

Short Answer Responses

1. If the price of gasoline really had no effect on the purchases of gasoline, then the demand for gasoline would be vertical. However, as the chapter opener points out, higher gasoline prices do affect the quantity of gasoline consumers purchase. When gas prices rose to around $4 per gallon in the summer of 2008, gas purchases were nearly 6% lower than in the previous year.

2. Sanders should advise the City Council members to not lower price, as this would result in lower revenue from fares. In fact, if the Council wishes to increase revenue, then the proper course would be to raise fares because demand is inelastic.

3. To determine the changes in quantity demanded it is necessary to multiply the income elasticity for these three goods by the percentage change in income. The income elasticities are: beer (−0.09), wine (5.03), and spirits (1.21). Multiplying these values by 5% (0.05) yields the following changes in quantity demanded: beer (−0.5%), wine (+25.2%), and spirits (+6.1%).

4. Assuming that temporary seating is not added to or removed from the Staples Center for different events, the price elasticity of supply is zero. This means that the supply curve is a vertical line at the quantity supplied of 19,000. The number of tickets sold for different events reflects quantity demanded, not quantity supplied.

5. Wheat has a low income elasticity because there is a small increase in the demand for goods made from wheat as incomes rise. Wheat would be an inferior good only if demand decreased as incomes rose. This was not the case from 1950 through 2009. The income elasticity of demand for wheat was positive but less than 1.

True/False Answers

1. F The price elasticity of demand measures the responsiveness of quantity demanded, rather than demand, for a product to a change in the product's price.
2. F The more narrowly the market is defined, the more elastic the demand for the product is.
3. T With an elastic demand, the price and total revenue move in the opposite direction of one another.
4. F Cross-price elasticity of demand is negative for complements.
5. T See page 170.
6. T See Figure 6-4 on page 184.
7. T As income falls, the demand for inferior goods increases.
8. F If demand, not supply, is inelastic, then an increase in price will increase total revenue.
9. T See Table 6-6 on page 188.
10. F A product has a unit-elastic demand if changes in price, not income, do not affect revenue.
11. T If the good is a large share of the budget, and the price increases, then we are more likely to significantly reduce our consumption of the good.
12. T See Table 6-1 on page 173.
13. F A perfectly inelastic demand curve will have a price elasticity equal to zero.
14. T If income elasticity is positive, then the good is a normal good.
15. T A luxury good has an income elasticity of more than 1.

CHAPTER 7 | Firms, the Stock Market, and Corporate Governance

Chapter Summary and Learning Objectives

7.1 Types of Firms (pages 204–206)

Categorize the major types of firms in the United States. There are three types of firms: A **sole proprietorship** is a firm owned by a single individual and not organized as a corporation. A **partnership** is a firm owned jointly by two or more persons and not organized as a corporation. A **corporation** is a legal form of business that provides the owners with limited liability. An **asset** is anything of value owned by a person or a firm. The owners of sole proprietorships and partnerships have unlimited liability, which means there is no legal distinction between the personal assets of the owners of the business and the assets of the business. The owners of corporations have **limited liability**, which means they can never lose more than their investment in the firm. Although only 20 percent of firms are corporations, they account for the majority of revenue and profit earned by all firms.

7.2 The Structure of Corporations and the Principal–Agent Problem (pages 206–208)

Describe the typical management structure of corporations and understand the concepts of separation of ownership from control and the principal–agent problem. **Corporate governance** refers to the way in which a corporation is structured and the impact a corporation's structure has on the firm's behavior. Most corporations have a similar management structure: The shareholders elect a board of directors that appoints the corporation's top managers, such as the chief executive officer (CEO). Because the top management often does not own a large fraction of the stock in the corporation, large corporations have a **separation of ownership from control**. Because top managers have less incentive to increase the corporation's profits than to increase their own salaries and their own enjoyment, corporations can suffer from the **principal–agent problem**. The principal–agent problem exists when the principals—in this case, the shareholders of the corporation—have difficulty getting the agent—the corporation's top management—to carry out their wishes.

7.3 How Firms Raise Funds (pages 208–213)

Explain how firms raise the funds they need to operate and expand. Firms rely on retained earnings—which are profits retained by the firm and not paid out to the firm's owners—or on using the savings of households for the funds they need to operate and expand. With **direct finance**, the savings of households flow directly to businesses when investors buy **stocks** and **bonds** in financial markets. With **indirect finance**, savings flow indirectly to businesses when households deposit money in saving and checking accounts in banks and the banks lend these funds to businesses. Federal, state, and local governments also sell bonds in financial markets, and households also borrow funds from banks. When a firm sells a bond, it is borrowing money from the buyer of the bond. The firm makes a **coupon payment** to the buyer of the bond. The **interest rate** is the cost of borrowing funds, usually expressed as a percentage of the amount borrowed. When a firm sells stock, it is selling part ownership of the firm to the buyer of the stock. **Dividends** are payments by a corporation to its shareholders. The original purchasers of stocks and bonds may resell them in stock and bond markets, such as the New York Stock Exchange. The performance of the U.S. stock market is often measured using stock market indexes. The three most widely followed stock indexes are the Dow Jones Industrial Average, the S&P 500, and the NASDAQ composite index.

7.4   Using Financial Statements to Evaluate a Corporation (pages 213–215)
Understand the information provided in corporations' financial statements. A firm's **income statement** sums up its revenues, costs, and profit over a period of time. A firm's **balance sheet** sums up its financial position on a particular day, usually the end of a quarter or year. A balance sheet records a firm's assets and liabilities. A **liability** is anything owed by a person or a firm. Firms report their **accounting profit** on their income statements. Accounting profit does not always include all of a firm's **opportunity cost**. **Explicit cost** is a cost that involves spending money. **Implicit cost** is a nonmonetary opportunity cost. Because accounting profit excludes some implicit costs, it is larger than **economic profit**.

7.5   Corporate Governance Policy (pages 215–219)
Understand the role of government in corporate governance. Because their compensation often rises with the profitability of the corporation, top managers have an incentive to overstate the profits reported on their firm's income statements. During the early 2000s, it became clear that the top managers of several large corporations had done this, even though intentionally falsifying financial statements is illegal. The *Sarbanes-Oxley Act* of 2002 took several steps intended to increase the accuracy of financial statements and increase the penalties for falsifying them. During the late 2000s, the financial crisis revealed that many financial firms held assets that were far riskier than investors had realized.

Appendix: Tools to Analyze Firms' Financial Information (pages 227–235)
Understand the concept of present value and the information contained on a firm's income statement and balance sheet.

Chapter Review

Chapter Opener: Facebook: From Dorm Room to Wall Street (page 203)
In 2004, Mark Zuckerberg, a college sophomore at the time, started Facebook. As Facebook's popularity expanded, the costs of running the business grew as well, and the company looked for sources of funding to continue operating the business. While, as of 2009, Facebook was still a private company controlled by its founder, public companies face similar hurdles in managing and securing funding for their businesses.

Types of Firms (pages 204–206)
Learning Objective: Categorize the major types of firms in the United States.

In the United States, there are three basic legal structures a firm can assume. A **sole proprietorship** is a firm owned by a single individual and not organized as a corporation. A **partnership** is a firm owned by two or more persons and not organized as a corporation. Owners of sole proprietorships and partnerships have control of their day-to-day operations, but they are subject to unlimited liability. There is no legal distinction between the owners' personal assets and those of the firms they own. As a result, employees or suppliers have a legal right to sue if they are owed money by these firms, even if this requires the owners to sell their personal assets.

A **corporation** is a legal form of business that provides owners with limited liability. **Limited liability** is the legal provision that shields owners of a corporation from losing more than they have invested in the firm. The profits of corporations are taxed twice in the United States, and corporations are more difficult to organize and run than sole proprietorships and partnerships. Despite these disadvantages, limited liability and the possibility of raising funds by issuing stock make corporations an attractive form of business.

Extra Solved Problem 7-1

The Risks of Private Enterprise: The "Names" of Lloyd's of London
Supports Learning Objective 7.1: Categorize the major types of firms in the United States.

The world famous insurance company Lloyd's of London got its start in London in the 1600s. Ship owners would come to Edward Lloyd's coffeehouse to find someone to insure (or "underwrite") their ships and cargo for a fee. Coffeehouse customers—merchants and ship owners themselves—who agreed to insure ships would make payment from their personal funds if a ship was lost at sea. By the late 1700s, each underwriter would recruit investors known as "Names" and use the funds raised to back insurance policies sold to a wide variety of clients.

By the 1980s, 34,000 people around the world had invested in Lloyd's as Names. A series of disasters in the 1980s and 1990s—earthquakes, oil spills, etc.—resulted in huge payments made on Lloyd's insurance policies. It had become clear that Lloyd's was not a corporation and the Names did not have the limited liability that a corporation's stockholders have. Many Names lost far more than they had invested. Some of those who invested in Lloyd's had the financial resources to absorb their losses, but others did not. Tragically, as many as 30 Names may have committed suicide as a result of their losses. By 2008, only 1,100 Names remained invested in Lloyd's. New rules allow insurance companies to underwrite Lloyd's policies for the first time, and Names now provide only about 20 percent of Lloyd's funds.

a. What characteristic of Lloyd's of London's business organization was responsible for the financial losses suffered by the Names who had invested in Lloyd's?

b. In the early 2000s, firms such as Enron and WorldCom suffered severe losses after it was discovered that executives of the firms had falsified financial statements to deceive investors. How were the losses suffered by Enron and WorldCom stockholders different from the losses suffered by Lloyd's of London's Names?

SOLVING THE PROBLEM:

Step 1:   Review the chapter material.
This problem is about firms and corporate governance, so you may want to review the section "Types of Firms," which begins on page 204 in the textbook.

Step 2:   What characteristic of Lloyd's of London's business organization was responsible for the financial losses suffered by the Names who had invested in Lloyd's?
Lloyd's of London was a partnership. A disadvantage of partnerships, as well as sole proprietorships, is the unlimited personal liability of the owners of the firm. The liability Lloyd's partners, or Names, incurred went beyond the amount of funds they invested in the company. Therefore, when the insurance company was hit with a series of financial losses, some of the Names suffered severe financial losses.

Step 3:   How were the losses suffered by Enron and WorldCom stockholders different from the losses suffered by Lloyd's of London's Names?
Enron and WorldCom were corporations, so their stockholders had limited liability. Their losses were limited to the amount they had invested in these firms.

7.2 The Structure of Corporations and the Principal–Agent Problem (pages 206–208)

Learning Objective: Describe the typical management structure of corporations and understand the concepts of separation of ownership from control and the principal–agent problem.

Corporate governance is the way corporations are structured and the effect that structure has on the firm's behavior. Shareholders in a corporation elect a board of directors to represent their interests. The board of directors appoints a chief executive officer (CEO) to run day-to-day operations and may appoint other top managers. Managers may serve on the board of directors (they are referred to as inside directors). Outside directors are directors who do not have a management role in the firm. In corporations, there is a **separation of ownership from control.** In most large corporations the top management, rather than the shareholders, control day-to-day operations. The separation of ownership from control is an example of a **principal–agent problem**—a problem caused by an agent pursuing his own interests rather than the interests of the principal who hired him.

📖 Study Hint

Read **Solved Problem 7-2** in the textbook to strengthen your understanding of the principal–agent problem. This Solved Problem explains how the principal–agent problem is easily extended to the relationship between management and workers. Managers would like workers to work as hard as possible, while workers would sometimes prefer to shirk. It may be difficult for management to determine whether a worker is working sufficiently hard or not.

7.3 How Firms Raise Funds (pages 208–213)

Learning Objective: Explain how firms raise the funds they need to operate and expand.

To finance expansion, firms can use some of their profits, called retained earnings, rather than pay the profits to owners as dividends. Firms may obtain external funds in two ways. **Indirect finance** is the flow of funds from savers to borrowers through financial intermediaries such as banks. Intermediaries raise funds from savers to lend to firms and other borrowers. **Direct finance** is the flow of funds from savers to firms through financial markets. Direct finance usually takes the form of the borrower selling a financial security to a lender.

A financial security is a document that states the terms under which the funds have passed from the buyer of the security to the borrower. There are two main types of financial securities. A **bond** is a financial security that represents a promise to repay a fixed amount of funds. When a firm sells a bond to raise funds, it promises to pay the purchaser of the bond an interest payment each year for the term of the loan as well as the final payment (or principal) of the loan. The interest payments on a bond are referred to as **coupon payments**. The **interest rate** is the cost of borrowing funds, usually expressed as a percentage of the amount borrowed. If the coupon is expressed as a percentage of the face value of the bond, then we have the coupon rate of the bond.

If the face value of a bond is $1,000 and the annual interest payment on the bond is $60, then the coupon rate is

$$\frac{\$60}{\$1,000} = 0.06 \text{ or } 10 \text{ percent}$$

A **stock** is a financial security that represents partial ownership of a firm. As an owner of the firm, a shareholder is entitled to a share of the corporation's profits. Management decides how much profit to reinvest in the firm (retained earnings). The remaining profits are paid to stockholders as **dividends**.

There is a broad market for previously owned stocks and bonds. Changes in the prices of these financial instruments represent future expectations of the profits likely to be earned by the firms that issued them. Changes in the prices of bonds issued by a corporation reflect investors' perceptions of the firm's ability to make interest payments as well as the prices of newly issued bonds. A previously issued bond with a coupon payment of $80 and a principal of $1,000 is less attractive than a newly issued bond with a coupon payment of $100 and a principal of $1,000. The price of the previously issued bond must fall, and its interest rate must rise, to induce investors to buy it.

> 📖 **Study Hint**
>
> The double taxation of corporate profits—once via the corporate profits tax and again via the income tax on shareholders' dividends—gives corporations an incentive to raise funds more through debt (bonds) than equity (stocks). Some economists have criticized the corporate profits tax because it gives corporations an incentive to incur debt solely to reduce taxes.
>
> **_Making the Connection_** "Following Abercrombie & Fitch's Stock Price in the Financial Pages" provides a thorough explanation of how to read the stock pages in the newspaper using Abercrombie & Fitch as an example.

Extra Solved Problem 7-3

Google's Stocks

Supports Learning Objective 7.3: Explain how firms raise the funds they need to operate and expand.

On September 1, 2009, Google's stock closed at a price of $472.14 per share and the trading volume for the day was 1,902,811. The trading volume is the number of shares that traded on the secondary market for that day.

a. How much financial capital did the trading of these stocks raise for Google to use for expansion?

b. How could Google raise additional funds for growth?

SOLVING THE PROBLEM

Step 1:   Review the chapter material.

This problem is about how firms raise funds, so you may want to review the section "How Firms Raise Funds," which begins on page 208 in the textbook.

Step 2:   Discuss the secondary market for stocks and the impact on funds available for Google to expand.

In the feature **_Don't Let This Happen to YOU!_** "When Google Shares Change Hands, Google Doesn't Get the Money," you will find a description of secondary markets. The majority of stocks that are bought and sold on a daily basis are being traded in the secondary market. Trading in the secondary market does not raise additional funds for Google.

Step 3:   Consider the options that Google has to raise funds for growth.

There are three main options for a firm to obtain funds for growth. A firm can save some of its profits, called retained earnings. It can borrow money from a bank. Or it can issue more stocks or bonds and sell them directly to the public. All of these options are available to Google.

Source: http://finance.yahoo.com/q?s=goog

 Using Financial Statements to Evaluate a Corporation (pages 213–215)
Learning Objective: Understand the information provided in corporations' financial statements.

A firm must accurately disclose its financial condition to enable potential investors to make informed decisions about the firm's stock and bond offerings. The Securities and Exchange Commission (SEC) requires publicly owned firms to report their performance according to generally accepted accounting principles.

There are two main types of financial statements. An **income statement** is a financial statement that sums up a firm's revenues, costs, and profit over a period of time. The income statement is used to compute the firm's **accounting profit**, which is the firm's net income measured by revenue minus operating expenses and taxes paid. Economic profit—measured by a firm's revenue minus all of its implicit and explicit costs—provides a better indication than accounting profit of how successful a firm is. **Opportunity cost** is the highest-valued alternative that must be given up to engage in an activity. Opportunity costs can include both **explicit costs** that involve spending money and **implicit costs** that are nonmonetary costs. One significant implicit cost is the cost of investor's funds, measured as the value of those funds in their highest-alternative use. If a firm fails to provide investors with at least a normal rate of return, it will not be able to retain investors and will not be able to remain in business over the long run.

A **balance sheet** is a financial statement that sums up a firm's financial position on a particular day, usually the end of a quarter or year. The balance sheet summarizes a firm's assets and liabilities. An **asset** is anything of value owned by a person or a firm. A **liability** is anything owed by a person or a firm. The difference between the value of assets and liabilities is the firm's net worth.

📖 **Study Hint**

Keep in mind that, while accounting profit is useful in measuring whether a company is earning enough revenue to pay its bills, economic profit is a more accurate measure of how successful a firm is. Firms that are earning accounting profits may not be earning economic profits. Even though such a firm may look healthy financially, if the opportunity costs of producing are greater than revenues, then there are alternative uses of the company's resources that would be more profitable. Firms that do not earn economic profits will not remain in business over the long run.

Extra Solved Problem 7-4

Accounting Profit versus Economic Profit
Supports Learning Objective 7.4: Understand the information provided in corporations' financial statements.

Suppose that Sally decides to open a business. Opening Sally's Sassy Salon will cost $200,000 for the necessary capital equipment. Sally is considering two options for financing her new beauty salon. The first option she is considering is to borrow $100,000 and take $100,000 from her savings. The second option is to take $200,000 from her savings to start the business. Suppose that her savings account is earning 5 percent interest and the loan that her bank offered her also has a 5 percent interest rate.

a. What is the explicit cost of opening Sally's Sassy Salon if she chooses the first option? If she chooses the second option? What is the implicit cost of opening Sally's Sassy Salon using the first option? The second option?

b. Which option will give Sally the higher economic profit? The higher accounting profit?

SOLVING THE PROBLEM

Step 1:   **Review the chapter material.**

This problem is about financial statements, so you may want to review the section "Using Financial Statements to Evaluate a Corporation," which begins on page 213 in the textbook.

Step 2:   **Determine the implicit and explicit costs of each option.**

The explicit costs would be costs that require an outlay of money, for example, the interest on the loan, and the implicit costs would be the foregone interest on her savings. The first option has an explicit cost of $0.05 \times \$100,000 = \$5,000$ and an implicit cost of $0.05 \times \$100,000 = \$5,000$. The second option has no explicit cost and has $0.05 \times \$200,000 = \$10,000$ in implicit costs.

Step 3:   **Evaluate the economic and accounting profit for Sally's Sassy Salon.**

Assuming that her revenue will be unaffected by her choice of how she finances her new firm, we can see that the explicit cost of the second option is lower than the first option. This means that the second option would have a higher accounting profit. If we consider all of the costs, both explicit and implicit, then we are calculating the economic profit. In this case, the explicit cost plus implicit cost is the same for both options, so the economic profit would be the same for either option.

7.5	**Corporate Governance Policy (pages 215–219)**

Learning Objective: Understand the role of government in corporate governance.

During 2001 and 2002, the importance of providing accurate financial information through financial statements was illustrated by several major financial scandals. The *Sarbanes-Oxley Act of 2002* was passed in response to these scandals. The act requires corporate directors and chief executive officers to have greater accountability for the accuracy of their firms' financial statements. Beginning in 2007, the U.S. economy suffered its worst financial crisis since the Great Depression, stemming from problems in the subprime mortgage industry. Borrowers who were unable to afford their mortgages began to default, and, as housing prices fell, banks and other private financial firms who had securitized these mortgages began to fail. New regulations were considered to increase oversight over banks and other financial firms that securitize mortgages.

📖 Study Hint

One result, likely an unintended one, of the Sarbanes-Oxley Act was to increase the demand for newly hired accountants. For example, the accounting firm Ernst and Young hired 4,500 undergraduate accounting students in 2005, an increase of 30 percent from the previous year.

Source: "Jobs: Accountants are kings among grads," *CNNMoney*, June 5, 2005.
http://money.cnn.com/2005/06/pf/accountant.jobs.reut/index.htm?ccc=yes

Appendix

Tools to Analyze Firms' Financial Information (pages 227–235)

Learning Objective: Understand the concept of present value and the information contained on a firm's income statement and balance sheet.

Using Present Value to Make Investment Decisions

Most people value funds they have today more highly than funds they will receive in the future. **Present value** is the value in today's dollars of funds to be paid or received in the future. Someone who lends money expects to be paid back the amount of the loan and some additional interest. If someone lends $1,000 for one year at 10 percent interest, the value of money received in the future is:

$$\$1,000 \times (1 + 0.10) = \$1,100.$$

Dividing this expression by $(1 + 0.10)$ and adjusting terms:

$$\$1,000 = \frac{\$1,000}{(1.10)}$$

Writing this more generally:

$$\text{Present Value} = \frac{\text{Future Value}}{(1+i)}$$

The present value formula for funds received any number of years in the future (n represents the number of years) is:

$$\text{Present Value} = \frac{\text{Future Value}_n}{(1+i)^n}$$

The present value formula can be used to calculate the price of a financial asset. The price of a financial asset should be equal to the present value of the payments to be received from owning that asset. The general formula for the price of a bond is:

$$\text{Bond Price} = \frac{\text{Coupon}_1}{(1+i)} + \frac{\text{Coupon}_2}{(1+i)^2} + \dots + \frac{\text{Coupon}_n}{(1+i)^n} + \frac{\text{Face Value}}{(1+i)^n}$$

In this formula,

Coupon$_1$ is the coupon payment, or interest payment, to be received after one year.
Coupon$_2$ is the coupon payment after two years.
Coupon$_n$ is the coupon payment in the year the bond matures.
Face Value is the face value of the bond to be received when the bond matures.
The interest rate on comparable newly issued bonds is i.

The price of a share of stock should be equal to the present value of the dividends, or the profits paid to shareholders, that investors expect to receive as a result of owning the stock. The general formula for the price of a stock is:

$$\text{Stock Price} = \frac{\text{Dividend}_1}{(1+i)} + \frac{\text{Dividend}_2}{(1+i)^2} + \ldots$$

Unlike a bond, a stock has no maturity date, so the stock price is the present value of an infinite number of dividend payments. Unlike coupon payments, which are written on the bond and can't be changed, dividend payments are uncertain. If dividends grow at a constant rate, the formula for determining the price of a stock is:

$$\text{Stock Price} = \frac{\text{Dividend}}{(i - \text{Growth Rate})}$$

Dividend refers to the dividend currently received, and Growth Rate is the rate at which dividends are expected to grow.

Going Deeper into Financial Statements

Corporations disclose substantial information about their business operations and financial position to investors. This information is provided for two reasons. First, participants in financial markets demand the information. Second, some of this information meets the requirements of the U.S. Securities and Exchange Commission. The key sources of information about a corporation's profitability and financial position are its income statement and balance sheet. Income statements summarize a firm's revenues, costs, and profit over a time period (for example, one year). These statements list the firm's revenues and its cost of revenue (also called its costs of sales or cost of goods sold). The difference between a firm's revenues and costs is its profit. Operating income is the difference between revenue and operating expenses. Investment income is income earned on holdings of investments such as government and corporate bonds. The net income that firms report on income statements is referred to as their after-tax accounting profit.

A balance sheet summarizes a firm's financial position on a particular day. An asset is anything of value owned by the firm. A liability is a debt or obligation owed by the firm. **Stockholders' equity** is the difference between the value of a corporation's assets and the value of its liabilities, also known as net worth. Balance sheets list assets on the left side and liabilities and net worth or stockholders' equity on the right side. The value on the left side of the balance sheet must equal the value on the right side. Current assets are assets the firm could convert into cash quickly. Goodwill represents the difference between the purchase price of a company and the market value of its assets. Current liabilities are short-term debts. Long-term liabilities include long-term bank loans and outstanding corporate bonds.

Key Terms

Accounting profit A firm's net income, measured by revenue minus operating expenses and taxes paid.

Asset Anything of value owned by a person or a firm.

Balance sheet A financial statement that sums up a firm's financial position on a particular day, usually the end of a quarter or year.

Bond A financial security that represents a promise to repay a fixed amount of funds.

Corporate governance The way in which a corporation is structured and the effect a corporation's structure has on the firm's behavior.

Corporation A legal form of business that provides owners with protection from losing more than their investment should the business fail.

Coupon payment An interest payment on a bond.

Direct finance A flow of funds from savers to firms through financial markets, such as the New York Stock Exchange.

Dividends Payments by a corporation to its shareholders.

Economic profit A firm's revenues minus all of its implicit and explicit costs.

Explicit cost A cost that involves spending money.

Implicit cost A nonmonetary opportunity cost.

Income statement A financial statement that sums up a firm's revenues, costs, and profit over a period of time.

Indirect finance A flow of funds from savers to borrowers through financial intermediaries such as banks. Intermediaries raise funds from savers to lend to firms (and other borrowers).

Interest rate The cost of borrowing funds, usually expressed as a percentage of the amount borrowed.

Liability Anything owed by a person or a firm.

Limited liability The legal provision that shields owners of a corporation from losing more than they have invested in the firm.

Opportunity cost The highest-valued alternative that must be given up to engage in an activity.

Partnership A firm owned jointly by two or more persons and not organized as a corporation.

Principal–agent problem A problem caused by an agent pursuing his own interests rather than the interests of the principal who hired him.

Separation of ownership from control A situation in a corporation in which the top management, rather than the shareholders, control day-to-day operations.

Sole proprietorship A firm owned by a single individual and not organized as a corporation.

Stock A financial security that represents partial ownership of a firm.

Key Terms—Appendix

Present value The value in today's dollars of funds to be paid or received in the future.

Stockholders' equity The difference between the value of a corporation's assets and the value of its liabilities; also known as net worth.

Self-Test

(Answers are provided at the end of the Self-Test.)

Multiple-Choice Questions

1. Which of the following statements is true?
    a. In the United States, most firms are organized as corporations.
    b. In the United States, there are more partnerships than sole proprietorships.
    c. In the United States, corporations account for the majority of total revenue and profits earned by all firms.
    d. all of the above

2. Which of the following types of firms have limited liability?
    a. a corporation
    b. a sole proprietorship
    c. a partnership
    d. all of the above

3. Your friend asks you to join him in the new Internet business he is setting up as a partnership. If you invest $10,000 in the business, what is the limit to your liability?
    a. $10,000
    b. $100,000
    c. $1,000
    d. There is no limit to your liability.

4. Which of the following is true about liability for a corporation?
    a. The owners of a corporation have limited liability.
    b. The owners of a corporation have unlimited liability.
    c. The owners of a corporation may or may not be subject to unlimited liability.
    d. The owners of a corporation do not face any constraints with regard to liability issues.

5. In which of the following cases is there a legal distinction between the personal assets of the owners of the firm and the assets of the firm?
    a. sole proprietorships
    b. partnerships
    c. corporations
    d. in both the case of sole proprietorships and the case of partnerships

6. When a corporation fails, which of the following is true?
    a. The owners can always lose more than the amount they have invested in the firm.
    b. The owners can never lose more than the amount they have invested in the firm.
    c. The owners will always lose less than the amount they have invested in the firm.
    d. What the owners lose is unrelated to liability laws.

7. Your friend asks you to join him in the new Internet business he is setting up as a corporation. If you invest $10,000 in the business, what is the limit to your liability?
   a. $10,000
   b. $100,000
   c. $1,000
   d. There is no limit to your liability.

8. In the United States, how many times are corporate profits taxed?
   a. once
   b. twice
   c. three times
   d. often more than three times

9. Refer to Figure 7-1 in the textbook. Which type of firms account for the majority of revenue earned in the United States in 2009?
   a. sole proprietorships
   b. corporations
   c. partnerships
   d. none of the above

10. Refer to Figure 7-1 in the textbook. Which type of firm accounts for the majority of the profits earned by different business organizations in the United States in 2009?
    a. sole proprietorships
    b. partnerships
    c. corporations
    d. none of the above

11. Fill in the blanks. According to the textbook, there are more than _____ corporations in the United States, but only _____ have annual revenues of more than $50 million.
    a. 20 million; 1.2 million
    b. 18 million; 2 million
    c. 8 million; 5,000
    d. 5 million; 32,000

12. How much of the total corporate profits in the United States is earned by large firms?
    a. about 10 percent of all U.S. corporate profits
    b. one-half of all U.S. corporate profits
    c. more than 85 percent of all U.S. corporate profits
    d. 99 percent of all U.S. corporate profits

13. What is corporate governance?
    a. Corporate governance is a structure imposed on all corporations by the Securities and Exchange Commission.
    b. Corporate governance is the way in which corporations are structured and the impact a corporation's structure has on the firm's behavior.
    c. Corporate governance is the division of business firms among proprietorships, partnerships, and corporations.
    d. Corporate governance is the relationship between corporations and the government officials in the states in which firms operate.

14. What term do economists use to refer to the conflict between the interests of shareholders and the interests of top management?
    a. corporate governance
    b. a principal–agent problem
    c. gold plating
    d. capture theory

15. How can a firm obtain funds for an expansion of its operation?
    a. by reinvesting profits
    b. by recruiting additional owners to invest in the firm
    c. by borrowing funds from relatives, friends, or a bank
    d. all of the above

16. Which of the following refers to a flow of funds from savers to firms through financial markets?
    a. indirect finance
    b. direct finance
    c. business finance
    d. financial borrowing

17. What is the name given to the interest payments on a bond?
    a. coupon payments
    b. the cost of borrowing funds
    c. the face value of the bond
    d. capital gains

18. What are the payments by a corporation to its shareholders?
    a. stocks
    b. dividends
    c. retained earnings
    d. interest

19. If Proctor and Gamble (manufacturer of Tide, Crest, and Pampers) sells a bond with a face value of $10,000 and agrees to pay $800 of interest per year to bond purchasers, what is the interest rate paid on the bond?
    a. 2%
    b. 4%
    c. 8%
    d. 10%

20. If Kimberly-Clark (manufacturer of Kleenex, Huggies, and Cottonelle) sells a bond with a face value of $5,000 and an interest rate of 5%, what is the coupon payment on the bond?
    a. $250
    b. $500
    c. $1,000
    d. $1,500

21. An increase in a firm's stock price most likely reflects which of the following?
    a. concern that the firm will soon go out of business
    b. optimism about the firm's profit prospects
    c. a higher cost of new external funds
    d. All of the above would increase the price of a firm's stock.

22. What are markets in which newly issued claims are sold to initial buyers by the issuer called?
    a. primary markets
    b. secondary markets
    c. tertiary markets
    d. initial public offerings

23. Investors resell existing stocks to each other in what type of market?
    a. a primary market
    b. a secondary market
    c. a bond market
    d. a dividend market

24. If Mark Zuckerberg, the owner and founder of Facebook, decides to open up ownership of his company to the public, the initial public offering of stock in Facebook will take place in what type of market?
    a. a primary market
    b. a secondary market
    c. a bond market
    d. a coupon market

25. Which of the following is the most important of the over-the-counter markets?
    a. the New York Stock Exchange
    b. the American Stock Exchange
    c. the NASDAQ
    d. the S&P 500

26. In the United States, the Securities and Exchange Commission requires publicly owned firms to report their performance in financial statements using standard methods. What are these methods called?
    a. Standard and Poor's Accounting Standards
    b. generally accepted accounting principles
    c. Moody's Investors Service Standards
    d. U.S. Standard Financial Practices

27. If investors become more optimistic about a firm's profit prospects, and the firm's managers want to expand the firm's operations as a result, what will happen to the price of the company's stock?
    a. It will rise.
    b. It will fall.
    c. It will remain constant.
    d. It may rise for a while, but then fall.

28. To answer the three basic questions: what to produce, how to produce it, and what price to charge, what does a firm's management need to know?
    a. the firm's revenues and costs
    b. the value of the property and other assets the firm owns
    c. the firm's debts, or other liabilities, that it owes to another person or business
    d. all of the above

29. Which of the following sums up a firm's revenues, costs, and profit over a period of time?
    a. the balance sheet
    b. the income statement
    c. the firm's accounting profit
    d. the firm's economic profit

30. An income statement starts with the firm's revenue and subtracts its operating expenses and taxes paid. What is the remainder called?
    a. net income
    b. gross income
    c. economic profit
    d. explicit cost

31. Which of the following is considered an explicit cost?
    a. the cost of labor
    b. the cost of materials
    c. the cost of electricity
    d. All of the above are explicit costs.

32. What term do economists use to refer to the minimum amount that investors must earn on the funds they invest in a firm, expressed as a percentage of the amount invested?
    a. opportunity cost
    b. the normal rate of return
    c. explicit cost
    d. economic profit

33. Accounting profit is equal to which of the following?
    (i) Total revenue – explicit costs
    (ii) Total revenue – opportunity costs
    (iii) Economic profit + implicit costs
    a. (i) only
    b. (ii) only
    c. (iii) only
    d. (i) and (iii) only

34. In which of the following industries do investors require a higher rate of return?
    a. in more risky industries
    b. in less risky industries
    c. in more established industries, such as electric utilities
    d. in any industry (Investors always need to receive high rates of return regardless of the type of investment or the risk involved.)

35. Which of the following statements is correct?
    a. Economic profit equals the firm's revenues minus its explicit costs.
    b. Accounting profit equals the firm's revenues minus all of its costs, implicit and explicit.
    c. Accounting profit is larger than economic profit.
    d. all of the above

36. What is a balance sheet?
    a. a summary of a firm's financial position on a particular day
    b. a summary of revenues, costs, and profit over a particular period of time
    c. a firm's net income measured by revenue less operating expenses and taxes paid
    d. a list of anything owed by a person or business

37. What do you obtain by subtracting the value of a firm's liabilities from the value of its assets?
    a. income
    b. net worth
    c. economic profit
    d. accounting profit

38. Which set of incentives does the top management of a corporation have?
    a. an incentive to attract investors and to keep the firm's stock price high
    b. an incentive to attract investors and to keep the firm's stock price low
    c. an incentive to discourage investors and to keep the firm's stock price high
    d. an incentive to discourage investors and to keep the firm's stock price low

39. Which of the following is true? Top managers who are determined to cheat and hide the true financial condition of their firms can
    a. deceive investors but never outside auditors.
    b. deceive outside auditors but never investors.
    c. deceive investors and sometimes also deceive outside auditors.
    d. deceive other managers but never the company's investors or its outside auditors.

40. The landmark *Sarbanes-Oxley Act of 2002* mandated that
    a. chief executive officers personally certify the accuracy of financial statements.
    b. financial analysts and auditors shall disclose whether any conflicts of interest might exist that could limit their independence in evaluating a firm's financial condition.
    c. managers shall be held accountable and face stiff penalties (including long jail sentences) for not meeting their responsibilities.
    d. all of the above be satisfied.

41. What does the term "insiders" refer to in the realm of corporate management?
    a. Insiders are auditors who have access to the corporation's financial statements.
    b. Insiders are members of top management who also serve on a firm's board of directors.
    c. Insiders are managers who have connections with people on independent auditing boards.
    d. An insider is anyone who is not part of a public corporation but who knows something that the public at large does not know.

42. What are the names of the two organizations established by Congress to help increase the volume of lending in the home mortgage market?
    a. Bank of America and Lehman Brothers
    b. Fannie Mae and Freddie Mac
    c. Mick and Mack
    d. Sarbanes and Oxley

43. One of the causes of the financial crisis that began in 2007 was a dramatic decrease in the value of mortgage-backed securities when housing prices began to fall. What does it mean to securitize a mortgage?
    a. To securitize a mortgage is to bundle mortgages together and sell them to investors.
    b. To securitize a mortgage is to buy insurance that guarantees your mortgage will be paid even if you lose your job.
    c. To securitize a mortgage is to offer a mortgage to a borrower whose credit is below average.
    d. To securitize a mortgage is to purchase a mortgage from Fannie Mae or Freddie Mac.

Short Answer Questions

1. Owners of successful sole proprietorships may choose to change their firms to corporations to raise money to finance expansion and limit the owner's liability. But this will also subject the firm to the principal–agent problem. Why don't sole proprietorships face the principal–agent problem?

   _____

   _____

   _____

2. Why did the passage of the Sarbanes-Oxley Act lead to an increase in the demand for accountants?

   _____

   _____

   _____

   _____

3. In addition to salary and benefits, the compensation of the top managers of many corporations includes shares of company stock or options to buy the stock at a favorable price. Why?

   _____

   _____

   _____

   _____

4. Explain why a firm that reports a profit on its income statement may actually suffer an economic loss.

_____

_____

_____

_____

5. Publicly owned firms in the United States are required to report their performance in financial statements using generally accepted accounting principles. These statements are examined closely by private firms and investors. Why did the public disclosure of the statements of Enron and WorldCom fail to provide investors with advance warning of serious financial problems that resulted in billions of dollars of shareholders' losses?

_____

_____

_____

_____

True/False Questions

T F 1. In the United States, Standard and Poor's requires publicly owned firms to report their performance in financial statements.

T F 2. If investors expect a firm to earn economic profits, the firm's share price will rise, providing a dividend for shareholders.

T F 3. Indirect finance refers to raising funds through financial intermediaries such as banks.

T F 4. A disadvantage of organizing a firm as a sole proprietorship or a partnership is that owners have limited liability.

T F 5. A disadvantage of organizing a firm as a corporation is that the firm is subject to the principal–agent problem.

T F 6. Profits that are reinvested in a firm rather than paid to the firm's owners are called retained earnings.

T F 7. The most important of the so-called "over-the-counter" stock markets is the New York Stock Exchange.

T F 8. The larger a firm's profits are, the higher its stock price.

T F 9. The price of a bond is equal to the present value of dividends, or the profits paid out by the firm that issues the bond.

T F 10. The unexpected rise in the price of Google stock in 2004 led to the passage of the Sarbanes-Oxley Act.

T F 11. Over 70 percent of firms in the United States are sole proprietorships.

T F 12. The day-to-day operations of a corporation are run by the firm's board of directors.

T F 13. An advantage of organizing a firm as a partnership is that the partners share the risks of owning the firm.

T F 14. The legal and financial problems incurred by Enron, WorldCom, and other well-known firms were due to the unlimited liability of the firms' owners.

T F 15. Economic profit is equal to a firm's revenue minus its operating expenses and taxes paid for a given time period.

Answers to the Self-Test

Multiple-Choice Questions

Question	Answer	Comment
1	c	Based on data for 2009, corporations accounted for 83 percent of revenue and 70 percent of the profits earned by all firms in the United States. See Figure 7-1 on page 205 in the textbook.
2	a	The owners of corporations have limited liability, while sole proprietorships and partnerships have unlimited liability.
3	d	Partnerships are firms owned jointly by two or more people, and there is no limit to liability.
4	a	Most large firms are organized as corporations. A corporation is a legal form of business that provides the owners with limited liability.
5	c	Unlimited liability means there is no legal distinction between the personal assets of the owners of the firm and the assets of the firm. In sole proprietorships and partnerships, the owners are not legally distinct from the firms they own.
6	b	Limited liability is the legal provision that shields owners of a corporation from losing more than they have invested in the firm.
7	a	Liability for owners of a corporation is limited to the amount invested in the firm.
8	b	Corporate profits are taxed twice—once at the corporate level and again when investors receive a share of corporate profits (revenues less expenses).
9	b	Although only 20 percent of all firms are corporations, corporations account for the majority of revenue and profits earned by all firms.
10	c	Corporations account for a majority of the total revenue and profits earned by businesses.
11	d	There are more than 5 million corporations in the United States, but only 32,000 have annual revenues of more than $50 million. We can think of these 32,000 firms—including Microsoft, General Electric, and Google—as representing "big business."
12	c	There are more than 5 million corporations in the United States, but only 32,000 have annual revenues of more than $50 million. We can think of these 32,000 firms—including Microsoft, General Electric, and Exxon-Mobil—as representing "big business." These large firms account for more than 85 percent of all U.S. corporate profits.
13	b	The way in which corporations are structured and the impact a corporation's structure has on the firm's behavior is referred to as corporate governance.
14	b	The fact that top managers do not own the entire firm means they may have an incentive to decrease the firm's profits by spending money to purchase private jets or schedule management meetings at luxurious resorts. This problem

occurs when agents—in this case, a firm's top management—pursue their own interests rather than the interests of the principal who hired them—in this case, the shareholders of the corporation.

15 d All of these are ways in which firms raise the funds they need to expand their operations.

16 b A flow of funds from savers to firms through financial markets is known as direct finance. Direct finance usually takes the form of firms selling savers financial securities.

17 a A coupon payment is the interest payment on a bond, usually expressed as a percentage of the amount borrowed.

18 b Dividends are payments by a corporation to its shareholders.

19 c The interest rate on a bond is calculated as the ratio of the coupon payment to the face value of the bond.

20 a The annual coupon payment will be the face value of the bond multiplied by the interest rate.

21 b Higher stock prices mean that investors are more optimistic about the firm's profit prospects.

22 a Primary markets are those in which newly issued claims are sold to initial buyers by the issuer.

23 b When stocks and bonds are resold, they are traded in secondary markets.

24 a New issues of stocks and bonds are sold in primary markets.

25 c The stocks of many computer and other high-technology firms—including Microsoft and Apple—are traded on the NASDAQ.

26 b In most high-income countries, government agencies establish standard requirements for information that is disclosed in order for publicly owned firms to sell stocks and bonds. In the United States, this government agency is the Securities and Exchange Commission. To maintain consistency, all firms are required to use generally accepted accounting principles.

27 a Changes in the value of a firm's stocks and bonds offer important information for a firm's managers, as well as for investors. An increase in the stock price means that investors are more optimistic about the firm's profit prospects, and the firm's managers may wish to expand the firm's operations as a result.

28 d To answer these questions, a firm's management needs the following information: The firm's revenues and costs, the value of the property and other assets the firm owns, and the firm's liabilities.

29 b A firm's income statement sums up the firm's revenues, costs, and profits over a period of time.

30 a A firm's net income is revenue less expenses and taxes paid in a given time period.

31 d Firms pay explicit labor costs to employees. They have many other explicit costs as well, such as the cost of the electricity used to light their office buildings.

32 b Economists refer to the minimum amount that investors must earn on the funds they invest in a firm, expressed as a percentage of the amount invested, as a normal rate of return.

33 d Accounting profit equals a firm's revenue minus its explicit costs. This is equivalent to adding a firm's economic profit and implicit costs.

34 a The necessary rate of return that investors must receive to continue investing in a firm varies from firm to firm. If the investment is risky, then investors will require a high rate of return to compensate them for the risk.

35	c	Because accounting profit excludes some implicit costs, it will be larger than economic profit.
36	a	A firm's balance sheet sums up its financial position on a particular day, usually the end of a quarter or a year.
37	b	We can think of the net worth as what the firm's owners would be left with if the firm closed, its assets sold, and its liabilities paid off. Investors can determine a firm's net worth by inspecting its balance sheet.
38	a	The top management of a firm has at least two reasons to attract investors and keep the firm's stock price high. First, a higher stock price increases the funds the firm can raise when it sells a given amount of stock. Second, to reduce the principal–agent problem, boards of directors will often tie the salaries of top managers to the firm's stock price or to the profitability of the firm.
39	c	This is what the textbook argues in "Corporate Governance Policy," beginning on page 215 in the textbook.
40	d	Each of the responses is a provision of the Sarbanes-Oxley Act.
41	b	"Insiders" are members of top management of a firm who also serve on the firm's board of directors.
42	b	Fannie Mae (the Federal National Mortgage Association) and Freddie Mac (the Federal Home Loan Mortgage Association) were established to increase the volume of lending in the home mortgage market.
43	a	When groups of mortgages are bundled together and sold to investors, they are securitized.

Short Answer Responses

1. The principal–agent problem is used to describe the consequence of separating ownership and management. There is no such division with a sole proprietorship and no principal–agent problem because the principal is also the agent.

2. The Act requires senior executives of publicly owned firms to have greater accountability for the accuracy of their firms' reporting and created a board to oversee the auditing of companies' financial reports. Because of the financial scandals of 2001 and 2002, there is a demand on the part of government officials and analysts for transparent and accurate financial information, and a demand for accountants who can provide and verify this information.

3. Tying the compensation of managers to the stock price of the firms they manage provides a greater incentive to pursue strategies that enhance profitability. Members of corporate boards of directors choose this form of compensation, in part, in response to the principal–agent problem.

4. An income statement reports a firm's accounting profit, which is net income measured by revenue minus explicit costs—operating expenses and taxes paid—over a period of time. Because the income statement does not account for the implicit costs incurred by the firm, accounting profit will be greater than economic profit. Economic profit is computed by subtracting both explicit and implicit costs from total revenue.

5. Ultimately the accuracy of a firm's statements depends on the integrity of corporate officials and the accountants who audit these statements. If some corporate officials deliberately choose to provide incomplete and misleading information in their financial statements, then analysts may be persuaded that their firms are more profitable than they actually are.

True/False Answers

1. F This is the responsibility of the Securities and Exchange Commission.
2. F An increase in the share price results in a capital gain.
3. T This is the definition of indirect finance.
4. F These firms have unlimited liability.
5. T The managers of a corporation are typically not the owners, so the principal–agent problem may arise.
6. T This is the definition of retained earnings.
7. F The most important "over-the-counter" market is the National Association of Securities Dealers' Automated Quotation System (NASDAQ).
8. T See page 211 in the textbook.
9. F This statement confuses stocks with bonds. The price of stock is equal to the present value of dividends.
10. F The Sarbanes-Oxley Act came about to prevent future accounting scandals like those of Enron and WorldCom in 2001.
11. T See Figure 7-1 on page 205 in the textbook.
12. F The chief executive officer of a corporation is appointed by the board of directors to conduct the firm's day-to-day operations.
13. T A partnership allows owners to share risk.
14. F The legal problems resulted from the stock incentive system associated with top management's pay. The capital gains and dividends that these managers received from their own shares of stock were higher due to their manipulation of the financial statements.
15. F This is the definition of accounting profit.

CHAPTER 8 | Comparative Advantage and the Gains from International Trade

Chapter Summary and Learning Objectives

8.1 The United States in the International Economy (pages 238–241)

Discuss the role of international trade in the U.S. economy. International trade has been increasing in recent decades, in part because of reductions in *tariffs* and other barriers to trade. A **tariff** is a tax imposed by a government on imports. The quantity of goods and services the United States imports and exports has been continually increasing. **Imports** are goods and services bought domestically but produced in other countries. **Exports** are goods and services produced domestically but sold to other countries. Today, the United States is the leading exporting country in the world, and about 20 percent of U.S. manufacturing jobs depend on exports.

8.2 Comparative Advantage in International Trade (pages 241–243)

Understand the difference between comparative advantage and absolute advantage in international trade. **Comparative advantage** is the ability of an individual, a business, or a country to produce a good or service at the lowest **opportunity cost**. **Absolute advantage** is the ability to produce more of a good or service than competitors when using the same amount of resources. Countries trade on the basis of comparative advantage, not on the basis of absolute advantage.

8.3 How Countries Gain from International Trade (pages 243–249)

Explain how countries gain from international trade. **Autarky** is a situation in which a country does not trade with other countries. The **terms of trade** is the ratio at which a country can trade its exports for imports from other countries. When a country specializes in producing goods where it has a comparative advantage and trades for the other goods it needs, the country will have a higher level of income and consumption. We do not see complete specialization in production for three reasons: Not all goods and services are traded internationally, production of most goods involves increasing opportunity costs, and tastes for products differ across countries. Although the population of a country as a whole benefits from trade, companies—and their workers—that are unable to compete with lower-cost foreign producers lose. Among the main sources of comparative advantage are climate and natural resources, relative abundance of labor and capital, technology, and *external economies*. **External economies** are reductions in a firm's cost that result from an increase in the size of an industry. A country may develop a comparative advantage in the production of a good, and then as time passes and circumstances change, the country may lose its comparative advantage in producing that good and develop a comparative advantage in producing other goods.

8.4 Government Policies That Restrict International Trade (pages 249–255)

Analyze the economic effects of government policies that restrict international trade. **Free trade** is trade between countries without government restrictions. Government policies that interfere with trade usually take the form of *tariffs*, *quotas*, or *voluntary export restraints* (VERs). A **tariff** is a tax imposed by a government on imports. A **quota** is a numerical limit imposed by a government on the quantity of a good that can be imported into the country. A **voluntary export restraint (VER)** is an agreement negotiated between two countries that places a numerical limit on the quantity of a good that can be imported by one country from the other country. The federal government's sugar quota costs U.S.

consumers $3.44 billion per year, or about $1,150,000 per year for each job saved in the sugar industry. Saving jobs by using tariffs and quotas is often very expensive.

8.5 The Arguments Over Trade Policies and Globalization (pages 255–260)
Evaluate the arguments over trade policies and globalization. The **World Trade Organization (WTO)** is an international organization that enforces international trade agreements. The WTO has promoted **globalization**, the process of countries becoming more open to foreign trade and investment. Some critics of the WTO argue that globalization has damaged local cultures around the world. Other critics oppose the WTO because they believe in **protectionism**, which is the use of trade barriers to shield domestic firms from foreign competition. The WTO allows countries to use tariffs in cases of **dumping**, when an imported product is sold for a price below its cost of production. Economists can point out the burden imposed on the economy by tariffs, quotas, and other government interferences with free trade. But whether these policies should be used is a normative decision.

Appendix: Multinational Firms (pages 272–277)
Understand why firms operate in more than one country.

Chapter Review

Chapter Opener: Is a Government "Buy American" Policy a Good Idea for U.S. Firms like Caterpillar? (page 237)
The stimulus package passed by Congress in 2009 initially included provisions that would require all manufactured goods bought with stimulus money to be made in the United States. This "Buy American" provision was intended to increase the number of jobs created by the stimulus bill overall. However, some U.S. firms protested the bill, arguing that the restrictions on foreign imports were likely to result in retaliation from foreign countries that might limit U.S. exports into their countries. For firms like Caterpillar that sell construction equipment to those foreign countries, these restrictions would have hurt business rather than helped it.

8.1 The United States in the International Economy (pages 238–241)
Learning Objective: Discuss the role of international trade in the U.S. economy.

Imports are goods and services bought domestically but produced in other countries. A **tariff** is a tax imposed by a government on imports. **Exports** are goods and services produced domestically but sold to other countries. Tariff rates in the United States have fallen, and international trade has increased significantly since 1930. The United States is the world's largest exporter, although exports and imports are a smaller fraction of GDP in the United States than in most other countries.

📖 Study Hint
International trade is a controversial topic among politicians and the general public. You may have formed opinions about trade based on comments made through newspaper and magazine articles and conversations with family and friends. In every country there are winners and losers from international trade. Remember that the analysis presented here is positive analysis, not normative.

Extra Solved Problem 8-1
Chinese Tire Tariff
Supports Learning Objective 8.1: Discuss the role of international trade in the U.S. economy.

In September of 2009, President Barack Obama announced that he would impose a three-year tariff on some tires imported from China. A statement from the White House explained that the President's intention was to "remedy the clear disruption to the U.S. tire industry." In the first year of the plan, a 35 percent tax on imports of passenger car and light truck tires from China will be imposed. In year two, the tariff will fall to 30 percent, and in year three the tariff will fall to 25 percent.

Source: http://edition.cnn.com/2009/WORLD/asiapcf/09/12/us.china.tires/

Explain the impact of the tariff on exports and imports in the United States.

SOLVING THE PROBLEM:

Step 1:   **Review the chapter material.**
This problem asks you to interpret the effect of trade on the United States, so you may want to review section "The United States in the International Economy," which begins on page 238 in the textbook.

Step 2:   **Explain the impact on imports and exports if the tariff were to remain in place.**
A tariff will cause Chinese tires to become more expensive in the United States. This makes it more difficult for Chinese firms to compete with U.S. firms. The tariff would cause imports to fall and U.S. firms would be able to sell more tires at a higher price. However, U.S. firms that have used Chinese tires in producing vehicles will find their costs rising, which might lead them to raise prices and reduce production and employment.

8.2	**Comparative Advantage in International Trade (pages 241–243)**

Learning Objective: Understand the difference between comparative advantage and absolute advantage in international trade.

Comparative advantage is the ability of an individual, a firm or a country to produce a good or service at a lower opportunity cost than another individual, firm, or country. Mutually beneficial trade between two parties is possible when they specialize in the production of the goods and services for which they have a comparative advantage and trade for the goods and services for which they have comparative disadvantage in production. Comparative advantage is the basic argument in favor of free domestic trade as well as free international trade.

📖 **Study Hint**
Absolute advantage and comparative advantage were explained in Chapter 2 on pages 44–47. Review **Solved Problem 2-2** on page 48 from that chapter to ensure you understand these two concepts.

Extra Solved Problem 8-2

Supports Learning Objective 8.2: Understand the difference between comparative advantage and absolute advantage in international trade.

Suppose that the United States and China each produce only two goods, wheat and shirts. Further assume that these two countries use only labor to produce the two goods. Use the productivity information in this table to answer the questions below.

	Output per hour of work	
	Wheat	**Shirts**
United States	2 bushels	10 shirts
China	1 bushel	8 shirts

a. Who has the absolute advantage in the production of wheat? Who has absolute advantage in the production of shirts?

b. Who has the comparative advantage in the production of wheat? Who has comparative advantage in the production of shirts? What good should the United States specialize in? What good should China specialize in?

SOLVING THE PROBLEM:

Step 1: **Review the chapter material.**

This problem is about comparative advantage, so you may want to review the section "Comparative Advantage in International Trade," which begins on page 241 in the textbook.

Step 2: **Determine who has the absolute advantage in the production of each good.**

To determine absolute advantage, you should begin by looking at each good individually and ask yourself the question "Who can produce more of the good?" The United States can produce more wheat than China, so the United States has the absolute advantage in the production of wheat. The United States can also produce more shirts, so the United States also has the absolute advantage in the production of shirts.

Step 3: **Determine who has the comparative advantage in the production of each good by calculating opportunity costs.**

For the United States to produce 1 bushel of wheat, it must give up 5 shirts, while China must give up 8 shirts for the same bushel of wheat. The United States gives up less to produce wheat, so it has the comparative advantage in the production of wheat. To produce 1 shirt, the United States must give up 1/5 of a bushel of wheat, while China gives up only 1/8 bushel of wheat. Therefore, China has the comparative advantage in the production of shirts.

Step 4: **Determine specialization by looking at the comparative advantage.**

To receive gains from trade, countries should specialize in the good in which they have a comparative advantage and then trade that good for goods from other countries. In this case, the United States should specialize in the production of wheat and China should specialize in the production of shirts.

8.3 How Countries Gain from International Trade (pages 243–249)
Learning Objective: Explain how countries gain from international trade.

The gains from trade can be illustrated with an example of two countries that produce the same two goods under conditions of autarky. **Autarky** is a situation in which a country does not trade with other countries. When each country specializes in the production of the good for which it has a comparative advantage and trades some of this good for some of the good produced by the other country, (a) total production of both goods can be greater than it would be under conditions of autarky and (b) total consumption of both goods in both countries can be greater with trade than under conditions of autarky.

The **terms of trade** is the ratio at which a country can trade its exports for imports from other countries. Although countries as a whole are made better off from trade, trade can harm firms and workers in industries that produce goods at a higher cost than foreign competitors.

📖 Study Hint
Read **Solved Problem 8-3** "The Gains from Trade," which describes the gains from trade in David Ricardo's famous cloth and wine example. In this example, Portugal and England each gain from trade. Portugal can specialize in wine, while England specializes in the production of cloth. The two countries can make themselves better off through trade Be sure you understand the example in the textbook where Japan and the United States are both able to consume more cell phones and digital music players after trade than under autarky.

In reality, countries do not specialize completely in the goods in which they have the comparative advantage. This lack of complete specialization is because some goods are not traded internationally, opportunity costs increase as production increases, and consumers in different countries have different preferences for products. There are several reasons why a country may have a comparative advantage in producing a particular good. A firm in one country may have a relatively low opportunity cost in the production of a good because of favorable climate, abundant supplies of certain natural resources, or relatively abundant supplies of labor or capital. Another source of comparative advantage is superior technology in one country. Comparative advantage may also result from external economies. **External economies** are reductions in a firm's costs that result from an expansion in the size of an industry.

📖 Study Hint
Raymond Vernon provided the following classic example of the importance of external economies. Anyone who lives in or has visited New York City, Manhattan in particular, knows that prices for most goods and services are higher there than in most other cities. Real estate and transportation are expensive, streets are crowded, and firms must pay employees a premium to compensate for the high cost of living. Yet, the garment and financial industries located in Manhattan continue to thrive despite these disadvantages. For both of these industries, ready access to suppliers, customers, and competitors are important assets. Personal contacts and face-to-face meetings are critical to the success of doing business. The large market size and concentration of related businesses offered by New York City are more important assets than the lower cost of real estate and transportation offered by locations outside of Manhattan.

8.4 Government Policies That Restrict International Trade (pages 249–255)
Learning Objective: Analyze the economic effects of government policies that restrict international trade.

Free trade refers to trade between countries that is without government restrictions. Free-trade policies offer benefits to consumers of imported goods and allow for a more efficient allocation of resources than is possible when international trade is restricted by tariffs or other trade barriers. But free trade also harms domestic firms that are less efficient than their foreign competitors.

While a tariff is a tax on imports imposed by the government, a **quota** is a numerical limit imposed by the government on the quantity of a good that can be imported into the country. A **voluntary export restraint (VER)** is an agreement negotiated between two countries that places a numerical limit on the quantity of a good that can be imported by one country from the other country. The imposition of these barriers to free trade creates a deadweight loss for the domestic economy.

📖 **Study Hint**
Figures 8-6 and 8-7 illustrate the deadweight losses that result from the imposition of a tariff or quota. Tables 8-5 and 8-6 describe the costs of trade restrictions in a different but compelling manner. The tables list estimates of the per-job cost to consumers of saving jobs in industries protected by trade restrictions. Those who favor restrictions on international trade must be willing to argue that these high costs of preserving jobs in domestic industries are justified. See *Solved Problem 8-4*, "Measuring the Economic Effect of a Quota," for additional practice with analyzing the deadweight losses associated with a quota. If the United States imposes a quota on the number of apples that can be imported into the country, then the price of apples will increase and the quantity of apples that can be purchased will decrease. This causes a decrease in consumer surplus and a deadweight loss to the economy.

8.5 The Arguments Over Trade Policies and Globalization (pages 255–260)
Learning Objective: Evaluate the arguments over trade policies and globalization.

Debates over the merits of free trade and policies to restrict trade date back to the beginning of the United States. After World War II, government officials from the United States and Europe negotiated an international agreement to reduce trade barriers and promote free trade. Some interest groups began to oppose free trade policies in the 1990s. You have probably heard the term globalization. **Globalization** refers to the process of countries becoming more open to foreign trade and investment. Opposition to globalization is based on the fear that low-income countries are at risk of losing their cultural identity as multinational countries sell Western goods in their markets and relocate factories in their countries to take advantage of low-cost labor.

Protectionism is the use of trade barriers to shield domestic firms from foreign competition and is demanded by those who wish to preserve domestic jobs in certain industries or who believe that certain domestic industries should be protected from foreign competition for reasons of national security. **Dumping** refers to selling a product for a price below the cost of production. If a country is able to establish that foreign firms have dumped products on the domestic market, then they are allowed under international agreements to impose tariffs on these products. The **World Trade Organization (WTO)** is an international organization that oversees international trade agreements.

📖 **Study Hint**

Arguments for and against free trade and globalization offer you an opportunity to analyze important policy issues in an objective manner using positive analysis. You may have formed opinions about these issues after reading or seeing reports of low wages and poor working conditions offered by multinational corporations in developing countries. *Making the Connection* "The Unintended Consequences of Banning Goods Made with Child Labor" explains how in some developing countries the alternative to working in a multinational firm is begging or illegal activity. Positive analysis predicts that, as incomes rise in countries, families rely less on child labor. Whether this result is enough to justify child labor involves normative analysis.

Extra Solved Problem 8-5
Sunlight—Bah, Humbug!
Supports Learning Objective 8.5: Evaluate the arguments over trade policies and globalization.

Arguments over international trade are nothing new. Alexander Hamilton called for the protection of so-called "infant industries" in the United States, and farming interests have long espoused trade restrictions to prevent consumers from buying cheaper food products from abroad. Although the countries and industries have changed over time, the arguments over trade restrictions have not. The 19th century French economist, Frédèric Bastiat, satirized French opponents of free trade in writing a petition to the French government supposedly from the manufacturers of "candles, waxlights, lamps, candlesticks, street lamps…generally of everything connected with lighting." Bastiat's "petition" has been reprinted many times and often appears in textbooks because of its clever theme as well as its applicability to the arguments of 21st century "petitioners." Here is a brief excerpt from the "petition:"

> We are suffering from the intolerable competition of a foreign rival, placed, it would seem, in a condition so superior to ours for the production of light that he absolutely inundates our national market with it at a price fabulously reduced. The moment he shows himself, our trade leaves us—all consumers apply to him; and a branch of native industry, having countless ramifications, is all at once rendered completely stagnant. This rival…is no other than the sun…

> What we pray for is, that it may please you to pass a law ordering the shutting up of all windows, skylights, dormer-windows, outside and inside shutters, curtains, blinds…all openings, holes, chinks, clefts, and fissures by or through which the light of the sun has been in use to enter houses, to the prejudice of the meritorious manufacturers with which we flatter ourselves we have accommodated our country—a country which, in gratitude, ought not to abandon us now to strife so unequal.

Source: Frédèric Bastiat, *Social Fallacies*, translated by Patrick James Stirling, Santa Anna, CA: Register Publishing, 1944, pp. 60–61.

Cite arguments from chapter 8 that are similar to those raised in Bastiat's petition.

SOLVING THE PROBLEM:
Step 1:   Review the chapter material.

This problem is about arguments over trade policies, so you may want to review the section "The Arguments Over Trade Policies and Globalization," which begins on page 255 in the textbook.

Step 2: **Cite arguments from chapter 8 that are similar to those raised in Bastiat's petition.**
In describing protectionism, Hubbard and O'Brien write:

> For as long as international trade has existed, governments have attempted to restrict it to protect domestic firms...protectionism causes losses to consumers and eliminates jobs in domestic industries that use the protected product...Supporters of protectionism argue that free trade reduces employment by driving domestic firms out of business...jobs are lost, but jobs are also lost when more-efficient domestic firms drive less-efficient domestic firms out of business...No economic study has ever found a long-term connection between the total number of jobs available and the level of tariff protection for domestic industries.

Source: Hubbard/O'Brien *Microeconomics,* (3rd ed.), Prentice Hall, 2010, pages 257-258.

As Bastiat might have said: "plus ça change, plus c'est la même chose." ("The more things change, the more they stay the same.")

Appendix
Multinational Firms (pages 272–277)
Learning Objective: Understand why firms operate in more than one country.

Multinational enterprises are firms that conduct operations in more than one country.

A Brief History of Multinational Enterprises

Two innovations made it possible for firms to coordinate operations on several continents. The first was the completion of the transatlantic cable in 1866, which made possible instant communication by telegraph between the United States and Europe. The second was the development of more efficient steam engines, which reduced the cost and increased the speed of long ocean voyages.

Foreign direct investment is the purchase or building by a domestic firm of a facility in a foreign country. **Foreign portfolio investment** is the purchase by an individual or firm of stocks or bonds issued in another country. In the early 20th century, most U.S. firms expanded abroad through foreign direct investment because the stock and bond markets in other countries were often too poorly developed to make foreign portfolio investment practical.

Strategic Factors in Moving from Domestic to Foreign Markets

Today, most large U.S. corporations have established facilities overseas because they expect to increase their profitability by doing so. Firms might expect to increase their profits through overseas operations for five reasons:

1. To avoid tariffs or the threat of tariffs.
2. To gain access to raw materials.
3. To gain access to low-cost labor.
4. To minimize exchange-rate risk.
5. To respond to industry competition.

Most newly established U.S. firms begin by selling only in the United States. If successful, they will begin to export, using foreign firms to market and distribute their products. If firms' exporting efforts are successful, they may establish their own overseas marketing and distribution networks. Finally, the firms will establish their own production facilities in foreign countries.

Challenges to U.S. Firms in Foreign Markets

Firms face costs from expanding into foreign markets that differ from the costs of operating in domestic markets. One problem is that tastes differ between consumers in foreign and domestic markets. Products that are popular in one country may not be as popular in another country because of cultural differences or foreign government restrictions.

Competitive Advantages of U.S. Firms

U.S. firms possess certain competitive advantages when operating in foreign countries. Some firms, such as Coca-Cola and McDonald's, have strong name recognition. Some firms possess a significant technological edge over foreign rivals, and other firms have developed efficient, low-cost production methods. Some firms have proven to be better at designing and rapidly bringing to market new products than their foreign competitors.

> 📖 Study Hint
>
> Many people believe that when U.S. firms locate production facilities in other countries the level of employment and wages in the U.S. decline. *Making the Connection* "Have Multinational Corporations Reduced Employment and Lowered Wages in the United States?" explains that wages of U.S. workers are determined by their productivity. Competition from low-wage workers in other countries has little impact on the wages of U.S. workers.

Key Terms

Absolute advantage The ability to produce more of a good or service than competitors when using the same amount of resources.

Autarky A situation in which a country does not trade with other countries.

Comparative advantage The ability of an individual, a firm, or a country to produce a good or service at a lower opportunity cost than competitors.

Dumping Selling a product for a price below its cost of production.

Exports Goods and services produced domestically but sold in other countries.

External economies Reductions in a firm's costs that result from an increase in the size of an industry.

Free trade Trade between countries that is without government restrictions.

Globalization The process of countries becoming more open to foreign trade and investment.

Imports Goods and services bought domestically but produced in other countries.

Opportunity cost The highest-valued alternative that must be given up to engage in an activity.

Protectionism The use of trade barriers to shield domestic firms from foreign competition.

Quota A numerical limit imposed by a government on the quantity of a good that can be imported into the country.

Tariff A tax imposed by a government on imports.

Terms of trade The ratio at which a country can trade its exports for imports from other countries.

Voluntary export restraint (VER) An agreement negotiated between two countries that places a numerical limit on the quantity of a good that can be imported by one country from the other country.

World Trade Organization (WTO) An international organization that oversees international trade agreements.

Key Terms—Appendix

Foreign direct investment The purchase or building by a domestic firm of a facility in a foreign country.

Foreign portfolio investment The purchase by an individual or a firm of stocks or bonds issued in another country.

Multinational enterprise A firm that conducts operations in more than one country.

Self-Test

(Answers are provided at the end of the Self-Test.)

Multiple-Choice Questions

1. The sugar quota in the United States creates winners and losers. Which of these groups ends up being a winner?
   a. U.S. producers of sugar
   b. U.S. companies that use sugar
   c. U.S. consumers
   d. all of the above groups

2. Since 1930, what has generally happened to tariff rates?
   a. Tariff rates have risen.
   b. Tariff rates have fallen.
   c. Tariff rates have remained the same.
   d. Tariffs rates have fluctuated up and down.

3. Goods and services produced domestically but sold to other countries are called
   a. imports.
   b. exports.
   c. tariffs.
   d. net exports.

4. Which of the following is true about the importance of trade in the U.S. economy?
   a. Exports and imports have steadily declined as a fraction of U.S. GDP.
   b. While exports and imports have been steadily rising as a fraction of GDP, not all sectors of the U.S. economy have been affected equally by international trade.
   c. Only a few U.S. manufacturing industries depend on trade.
   d. all of the above

5. Refer to the graph below. The figure is a representation of the pattern of U.S. international trade. Which trend line shows exports?

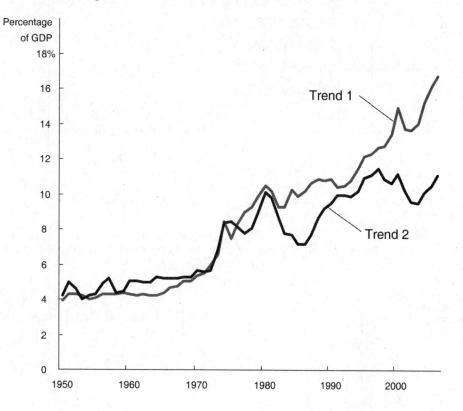

   a. Trend 1
   b. Trend 2
   c. Both lines show exports.
   d. Both lines show imports.

6. Refer to the bar graph below. The graph shows the eight leading exporting countries. The values are the shares of total world exports of merchandise and commercial services. In which of the first four positions does the United States come in?

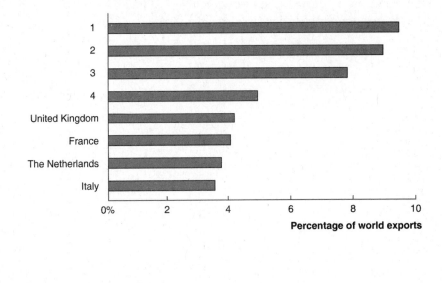

a. 1
b. 2
c. 3
d. 4

7. Refer to the bar graph below. The graph shows the importance of international trade to several countries. In which position does the United States come in?

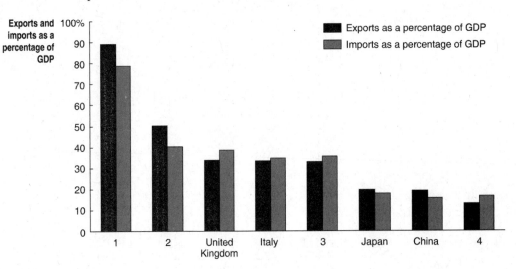

a. 1
b. 2
c. 3
d. 4

8. If a country has a comparative advantage in the production of a good, then that country
    a. also has an absolute advantage in producing that good.
    b. should allow another country to specialize in the production of that good.
    c. has a lower opportunity cost in the production of that good.
    d. all of the above

9. You and your neighbor pick apples and cherries. If you can pick apples at a lower opportunity cost than your neighbor can, which of the following is true?
    a. You have a comparative advantage in picking apples.
    b. Your neighbor is better off specializing in picking cherries.
    c. You can trade some of your apples for some of your neighbor's cherries and both of you will end up with more of both fruit.
    d. All of the above are true.

10. What is absolute advantage?
    a. The ability of an individual, firm, or country to produce more of a good or service than competitors using the same amount of resources.
    b. The ability of an individual, firm, or country to produce a good or service at a lower opportunity cost than other producers.
    c. The ability of an individual, firm, or country to consume more goods or services than others at lower costs.
    d. The ability of an individual, firm, or country to reach a higher production possibilities frontier by lowering opportunity costs.

11. Fill in the blanks. Countries gain from specializing in producing goods in which they have a(n) _____ advantage and trading for goods in which other countries have a(n) _____ advantage.
    a. absolute; absolute
    b. absolute; comparative
    c. comparative; absolute
    d. comparative; comparative

12. Consider the table below. The table shows the quantity of two goods that a worker can produce per day in a given country. Which of the following statements is true?

Output per day of work		
	Food	Clothing
Country A	6	3
Country B	1	2

    a. Country A has an absolute advantage in the production of both goods.
    b. Country B has an absolute advantage in the production of both goods.
    c. Both countries have an absolute advantage in the production of both goods.
    d. Neither country has an absolute advantage in the production of either good.

13. Consider the table below. The table shows the quantity of two goods that a worker can produce per day in a given country. Which of the following statements is true?

Output per day of work		
	Food	Clothing
Country A	6	3
Country B	1	2

    a.   Country A has a comparative advantage in the production of both goods.
    b.   Country B has a comparative advantage in the production of both goods.
    c.   Country A has a comparative advantage in the production of food.
    d.   Country B has a comparative advantage in the production of food.

14. In the real world, specialization is not complete. Why do countries not completely specialize?
    a.   because not all goods are traded internationally
    b.   because production of most goods involves increasing opportunity costs
    c.   because tastes for products differ
    d.   all of the above

15. Which of the following is a source of comparative advantage?
    a.   autarky
    b.   absolute advantage
    c.   the relative abundance of capital and labor
    d.   all of the above

16. The term external economies refers to
    a.   the process of turning inputs into goods and services.
    b.   the reduction of production costs due to increased capacity utilization.
    c.   the reduction of costs resulting from increases in the size of an industry in a given area.
    d.   the benefits an industry derives from other industries located nearby.

17. Refer to the graph below of the market for lumber in the United States. Assuming autarky, what is the equilibrium price of lumber?

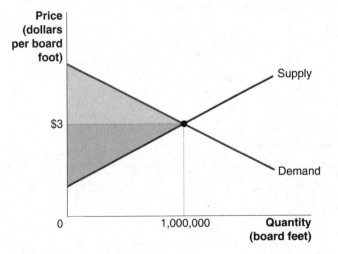

   a. $3 per board foot
   b. less than $3 per board foot
   c. $333,333 per board foot
   d. $1,000,000 per board foot

18. Refer to the graph below of the market for lumber in the United States. Under autarky, which area represents consumer surplus?

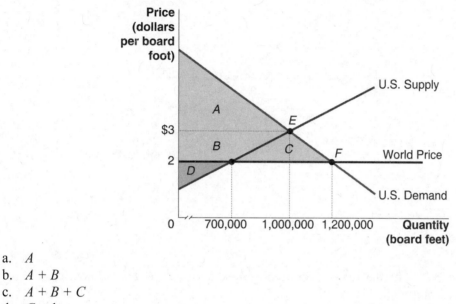

   a. *A*
   b. *A* + *B*
   c. *A* + *B* + *C*
   d. *C* only

19. Refer to the graph below of the market for lumber in the United States. Under autarky, which area represents the total economic surplus?

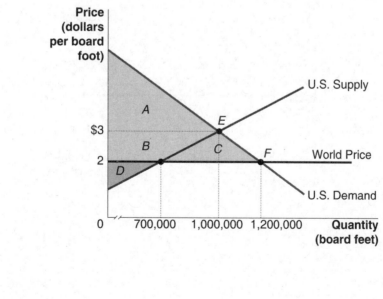

   a. *A*
   b. *A* + *B*
   c. *A* + *B* + *C*
   d. *A* + *B* + *D*

20. Refer to the graph below of the market for lumber in the United States. How many board feet of lumber are imported when imports are allowed into the United States?

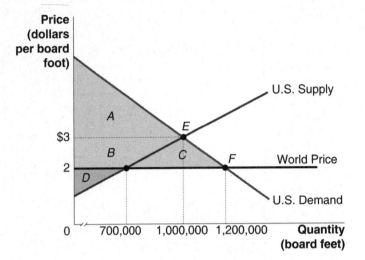

a. 1,000,000
b. 500,000
c. 700,000
d. 1,200,000

21. Refer to the graph below of the market for lumber in the United States. Which area represents domestic producer surplus with free trade?

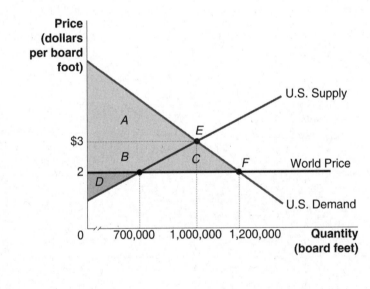

a. A
b. $A + B$
c. $A + B + D$
d. D

22. Refer to the graph below of the market for lumber in the United States. If the world price is $2 and the United States. imports lumber with no trade restrictions, what area represents consumer surplus?

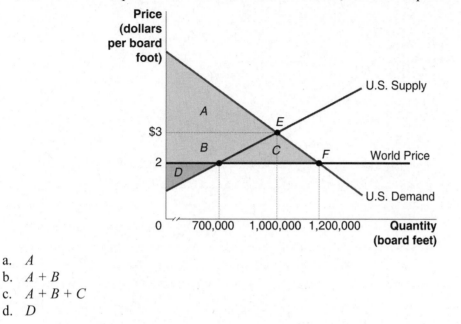

a. *A*
b. *A + B*
c. *A + B + C*
d. *D*

23. Refer to the graph below of the market for lumber in the United States. Which area represents the increase in economic surplus from opening the economy to imports?

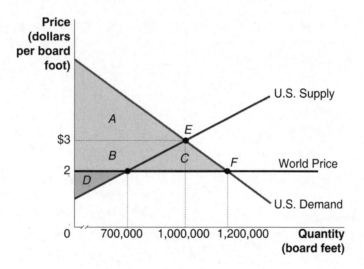

a. Area *A*
b. Area *B + C*
c. Area *C*
d. Area *D*

24. Refer to the graph below of the market for lumber in the United States. The figure shows the effect of a $0.50 per board foot tariff on lumber. Which area represents the deadweight loss from this tariff?

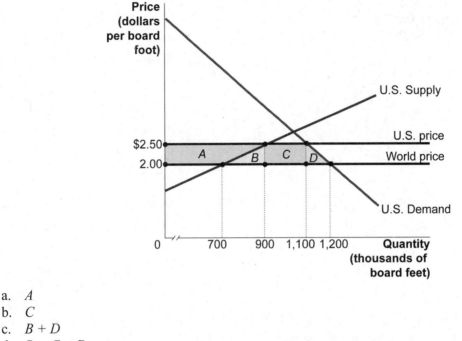

   a. *A*
   b. *C*
   c. *B* + *D*
   d. *B* + *C* + *D*

25. Refer to the graph below of the market for lumber in the United States. The graph shows the effect of a $0.50 per board foot tariff on lumber. What is the quantity of lumber supplied (in thousands of board feet) by domestic producers after the tariff?

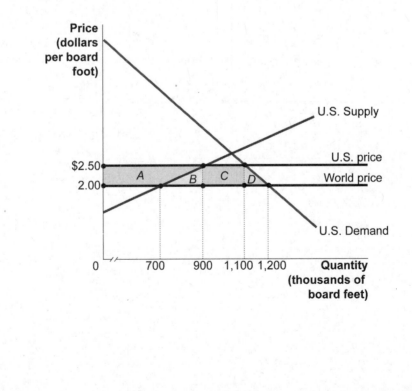

   a. 700
   b. 900
   c. 1,100
   d. 1,200

26. Refer to the graph below of the market for lumber in the United States. The graph shows the effect of a $0.50 per board foot tariff on lumber. What is the reduction in U.S. lumber consumption (in thousands of board feet) as a result of the tariff?

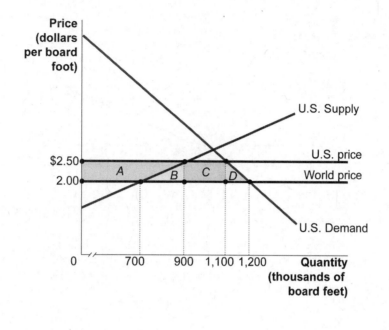

a. 100
b. 200
c. 300
d. 500

27. Refer to the graph below of the market for lumber in the United States. The graph shows the effect of a $0.50 per board foot tariff on lumber. Which area represents the revenue collected by government from the tariff?

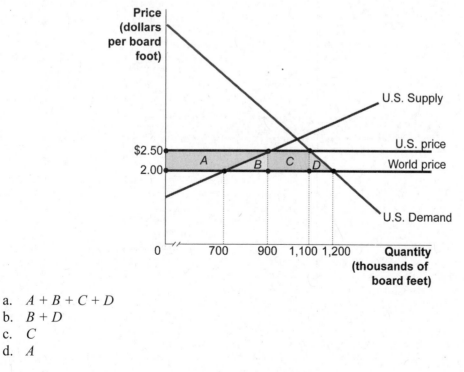

a. $A + B + C + D$
b. $B + D$
c. C
d. A

28. Refer to the graph below of the market for lumber in the United States. The graph shows the effect of a $0.50 per board foot tariff on lumber. How much revenue is collected by the government from the tariff?

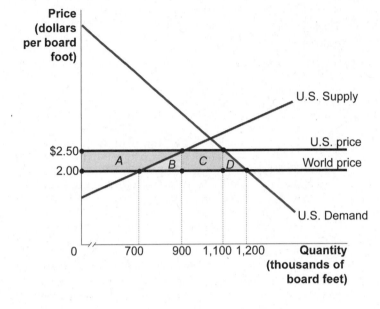

a. $100,000
b. $300,000
c. $400,000
d. $500,000

29. Refer to the graph below of the market for lumber in the United States. The graph shows the effect of a $0.50 per board foot tariff on lumber. What is the deadweight loss associated with the tariff?

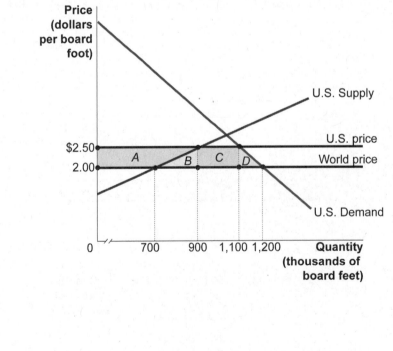

a. $100,000
b. $75,000
c. $50,000
d. $25,000

30. What is a quota?
    a. A quota is a numerical limit on the quantity of a good that can be imported.
    b. A quota is an agreement negotiated between two countries that places a numerical limit on the quantity of a good that can be imported by one country from the other country.
    c. A quota is the same thing as a voluntary export restraint.
    d. All of the above

31. What is a voluntary export restraint?
    a. a numerical limit on the quantity of a good that can be imported
    b. an agreement negotiated between two countries that places a numerical limit on the quantity of a good that can be imported by one country from the other country
    c. a quota imposed by the WTO
    d. the same as a tariff

32. In the United States and Japan, the cost of saving jobs through trade barriers such as tariffs and quotas is
    a. relatively low in both countries.
    b. relatively high in both countries.
    c. relatively high in the United States but relatively low in Japan.
    d. relatively low in the United States but relatively high in Japan.

33. Which of the following groups of people are significant sources of opposition to the World Trade Organization (WTO)?
    a. people who want to protect domestic firms
    b. people who believe that low-income countries gain at the expense of high-income countries
    c. people who favor globalization
    d. all of the above oppose the WTO

34. The opponents of globalization contend that
    a. globalization destroys cultures.
    b. globalization causes factories to relocate from low-income to high-income countries.
    c. globalization means that workers in poor countries lose jobs.
    d. all of the above occur as a result of globalization.

35. The use of trade barriers to shield domestic companies from foreign competition is called
    a. protectionism.
    b. dumping.
    c. globalization.
    d. patriotism.

36. Which of the following arguments is used to justify protectionism?
    a. Tariffs and quotas save jobs.
    b. Tariffs and quotas protect national security.
    c. Tariffs and quotas protect infant industries.
    d. All of the above are used to justify protectionism.

37. Which of the following statements about NAFTA is correct?
    a. NAFTA resulted in reduced consumption for the countries involved.
    b. NAFTA led to an overall loss of jobs.
    c. NAFTA reduced wages for both U.S. and Mexican workers.
    d. None of the above is correct.

38. What is the name given to the sale of a product for a price below its cost of production?
    a. bargain pricing
    b. cut-throat pricing
    c. grim-trigger pricing
    d. dumping

39. How does the World Trade Organization allow countries to determine whether dumping has occurred?
    a. The WTO determines that dumping has occurred if a product is imported for a lower price than it sells for on the home market.
    b. The WTO determines that dumping has occurred if a product is exported for a lower price than it sells for on the home market.
    c. The WTO determines that dumping has occurred if firms are selling products for a price that exceeds the cost of production.
    d. The WTO determines that dumping has occurred if some brands in the country sell for lower prices than other brands in the same country.

40. Which of the following is an example of positive economic analysis?
    a. measuring the impact of the sugar quota on the U.S. economy
    b. asserting that the sugar quota is bad public policy and should be eliminated
    c. justifying the profits of U.S. sugar companies based on the number of workers they employ
    d. All of the above are examples of positive economic analysis.

Short Answer Questions

1. The textbook notes that: "The effect of a quota is very similar to the effect of a tariff." If the effects are similar, why would a nation impose a quota rather than a tariff on an imported good?

   _____

   _____

   _____

2. Tables 8-5 and 8-6 list the high cost of trade restrictions to consumers in the United States and Japan for each job saved in several product markets. Because the number of jobs saved is much smaller than the number of consumers who must pay high prices to save these jobs, why do the governments of the United States and Japan maintain these trade restrictions?

   _____

   _____

   _____

3. Comparative advantage is used to explain why nations export products that they can produce at a lower opportunity cost than other nations. How, then, can one explain why the United States both exports and imports automobiles?

_____

_____

_____

_____

_____

4. David Ricardo's explanation of comparative advantage is considered to be one of the most important contributions to the history of economic thought. Why is comparative advantage so important?

_____

_____

_____

_____

_____

5. The World Trade Organization (WTO) allows member nations to impose tariffs on imported products if dumping can be demonstrated. Why is it difficult to prove accusations of dumping?

_____

_____

_____

True/False Questions

T F 1. As a percentage of GDP, U.S. imports and exports have both decreased during the past 20 years.
T F 2. In The Netherlands, imports and exports represent a larger fraction of GDP than in any other country.
T F 3. The United States is the leading exporting country in the world.
T F 4. One reason why countries do not specialize completely in production is that not all goods and services are traded internationally.

T F 5.   Caterpillar supported the "Buy American" provision in the 2009 stimulus package because it guaranteed that more dollars would be spent on goods produced by Caterpillar.

T F 6.   Firms in Dalton, Georgia developed a comparative advantage in carpet-making because of external economies.

T F 7.   Between 1994, when the North American Free Trade Agreement (NAFTA) went into effect, and 2008, the number of jobs in the U.S. declined by 23 million. Some of this decrease was due to NAFTA.

T F 8.   Barriers to international trade include health and safety requirements that are more strictly imposed on imported goods than goods produced by domestic firms.

T F 9.   The Smoot-Hawley Tariff of 1930 lowered average tariff rates in the United States by about 50 percent.

T F 10. One reason why countries do not specialize completely in production is that complete specialization requires countries to have an absolute advantage in the products they produce.

T F 11. Although countries gain overall from international trade, some individuals are harmed, including some workers who lose their jobs.

T F 12. The terms of trade refers to the length of trade agreements (for example, NAFTA) signed by officials from countries that are parties to these agreements.

T F 13. Each year the United States exports about 50 percent of its wheat crop.

T F 14. Economic surplus in a country that does not engage in international trade is always greater than economic surplus in a country that does engage in international trade.

T F 15. A tariff imposed on imports of textiles will raise the price of textiles in the importing country and create a deadweight loss in the domestic textile market.

Answers to the Self-Test

Multiple-Choice Questions

Question	Answer	Comment
1	a	The sugar quota creates winners—U.S. sugar companies and their employees—and losers—U.S. companies that use sugar, their employees, and U.S. consumers who must pay higher prices for goods that contain sugar.
2	b	Tariff rates have fallen. In the 1930s, the United States charged an average tariff rate above 50 percent. Today, the average rate is less than 2 percent.
3	b	Imports are goods and services bought domestically but produced in other countries. Exports are goods and services produced domestically but sold to other countries.
4	b	Not all sectors of the U.S. economy have been affected equally by international trade.
5	b	Exports have been less than imports since 1982.
6	a	The United States is the leading exporting country, accounting for about 10 percent of total world exports.
7	c	International trade is less important to the United States than to most other countries, with the exception of Japan.
8	c	The country with a lower opportunity cost of production has a comparative advantage in the production of that good.
9	d	If you can pick apples at a lower opportunity cost than your neighbor can, you have a comparative advantage in picking apples. Your neighbor is better off specializing in picking cherries, and you are better off specializing in picking apples. You can then trade some of your apples for some of your neighbor's cherries and both of you will end up with more of both fruit.
10	a	Absolute advantage is the ability of an individual, firm, or country to produce more of a good or service than competitors using the same amount of resources.

11	d	Countries gain from specializing in producing goods in which they have a comparative advantage and trading for goods in which other countries have a comparative advantage.
12	a	Country A can produce more food and more clothing in one day than Country B.
13	c	A worker in Country A can produce 6 times as many units of food as a worker in Country B but only 1.5 times as many units of clothing. Country A is more efficient in producing food than clothing relative to Country B.
14	d	These are the three reasons given in the textbook. See page 246.
15	c	The main sources are: climate and natural resources, the relative abundance of labor and capital, technology, and external economies.
16	c	The advantages include the availability of skilled workers, the opportunity to interact with other companies in the same industry, and being close to suppliers. These advantages result in lower costs to firms located in the area. Because these lower costs result from increases in the size of the industry in an area, economists refer to them as external economies.
17	a	When the U.S. does not trade with other nations, the domestic price is also the equilibrium price.
18	a	Autarky refers to equilibrium without international trade. Area A is consumer surplus when price equals the domestic price, or $3 per board foot.
19	d	The total economic surplus is the area between the demand and supply curves out to the domestic equilibrium.
20	b	Imports will equal 500,000 board feet, which is the difference between U.S. consumption and U.S. production at the world price.
21	d	With free trade and a price of $2, only 700,000 board feet of lumber will be produced domestically, so producer surplus is area D.
22	c	With free trade, consumer surplus is the area below demand but above the price of $2.
23	c	Area C is additional consumer surplus that did not exist under autarky.
24	c	The areas B and D represent deadweight loss.
25	b	After the tariff is imposed, the quantity supplied domestically is 900 board feet, at a price of $2.50.
26	a	At a price (before the tariff) of $2.00, U.S. consumption is 1,200 thousand. After the tariff is imposed, U.S. consumption falls to 1,100 thousand, so the decrease is 100 thousand.
27	c	Government revenue equals the tariff multiplied by the number of board feet imported, or area A.
28	a	Government revenue equals the tariff multiplied by the number of board feet imported, or $.50 \times (1,100,000 - 900,000) = \$0.50 \times 200,000 = \$100,000$.
29	b	The deadweight loss is equal to area B plus area D. Both are triangles. The value of area B is $\frac{1}{2} \times 200,000 \times \$0.50 = \$50,000$ and the value of area D is $\frac{1}{2} \times 100,000 \times \$0.50 = \$25,000$, so the sum of the two areas is $75,000.
30	a	A quota is a numerical limit on the quantity of a good that can be imported, and it has an effect similar to a tariff.
31	b	This is the definition of a voluntary export restraint.
32	b	Tables 8-5 and 8-6 show how expensive it is to save jobs in each country.
33	a	The WTO favors the opening of trade and opposes most trade restrictions.
34	a	Some believe that free trade and foreign investment destroy the distinctive cultures of many countries.
35	a	Protectionism is the use of trade barriers to shield domestic companies from foreign competition.

36	d	According to the textbook, all of these reasons, in addition to protecting high wages, are used to justify protectionism.
37	d	The results of NAFTA were the opposite of those listed.
38	d	Dumping is selling a product for a price below its cost of production.
39	b	Although there are problems with this method for determining whether dumping has occurred, the WTO determines that dumping has occurred if a country exports a product at a lower price than it sells the product for domestically.
40	a	Positive analysis concerns "what is." Measuring the impact of the sugar quota on the U.S. economy is an example of positive analysis.

Short Answer Responses

1. Quotas may be used to restrict trade when there are legal and political obstacles to raising tariffs. Quotas may also be used when there is a desire to limit imports by a specified amount. It is difficult to know the impact of a tariff rate on the amount of imports before the tariff is imposed.

2. Because the benefits are concentrated among relatively few workers and producers, these workers and their employers have strong incentives to lobby for trade restrictions. Although many consumers are negatively affected, the impact is widely spread so that no individual has a strong incentive to lobby for the removal of the trade restrictions.

3. Real markets are more complex than the simple models used to explain comparative advantage. Automobiles are not standardized products that all look and perform in exactly the same way. One reason why the United States imports automobiles from some nations (for example, Japan) is that these nations specialize in producing the types of automobiles that appeal to certain consumers (consumers who desired relatively small fuel-efficient cars). The United States exports different types of automobiles that appeal to consumers with different tastes in automobiles (for example, SUVs).

4. Comparative advantage explains why domestic and international trade is mutually beneficial under very general conditions, even when one of the parties to a trade has an absolute advantage in both traded goods. Specialization can improve the opportunities for consumption for all countries involved in trade, not just the countries that can produce the largest quantities of goods.

5. Dumping (selling a good below its cost of production) is difficult to prove for two main reasons. First, it can be difficult to measure the true cost of production for firms from countries different from the country where the dumping allegedly occurred. Second, what is dumping to a firm harmed by the practice may be normal business practice to the firm that does the selling.

True/False Answers

1. F   U.S. imports and exports have both increased as a fraction of GDP.
2. T   See Figure 8-3 on page 240 in the textbook.
3. T   Exports from the United States account for approximately 9.5 percent of total world exports, the largest of any country in the world. See page 239 in the textbook.
4. T   Because not all goods are traded internationally, countries will have to produce some goods domestically to satisfy the demands of domestic consumers.
5. F   Caterpillar opposed the "Buy American" provision, fearing that countries would retaliate by imposing trade barriers that would increase the cost of U.S. goods in foreign countries.
6. T   See Making the Connection "Why is Dalton, Georgia, the Carpet-Making Capital of the

World?" on page 248 in the textbook.

7.   F   The number of jobs *increased* by about 23 million during this time period.

8.   T   These are examples of non-tariff barriers to trade.

9.   F   The Smoot-Hawley Tariff raised average tariffs rates to more than 50 percent.

10.   F   A country need not have an absolute advantage in producing any good in order to specialize and gain from trade.

11.   T   There are winners and losers in international trade, and the workers in the industry that competes with the imported goods may lose their jobs.

12.   F   The terms of trade refers to the ratio at which goods trade between two countries.

13.   T   See page 239 in the textbook.

14.   F   Free trade increases economic surplus.

15.   T   Tariffs are similar to taxes and result in an increase in the price of the good. The resulting decrease in consumption and production creates a deadweight loss.

CHAPTER 9 | Consumer Choice and Behavioral Economics

Chapter Summary and Learning Objectives

9.1 Utility and Consumer Decision Making (pages 280–288)

Define utility and explain how consumers choose goods and services to maximize their utility. **Utility** is the enjoyment or satisfaction that people receive from consuming goods and services. The goal of a consumer is to spend available income so as to maximize utility. **Marginal utility** is the change in total utility a person receives from consuming one additional unit of a good or service. The **law of diminishing marginal utility** states that consumers receive diminishing additional satisfaction as they consume more of a good or service during a given period of time. The **budget constraint** is the amount of income consumers have available to spend on goods and services. To maximize utility, consumers should make sure they spend their income so that the last dollar spent on each product gives them the same marginal utility. The **income effect** is the change in the quantity demanded of a good that results from the effect of a change in the price on consumer purchasing power. The **substitution effect** is the change in the quantity demanded of a good that results from a change in price making the good more or less expensive relative to other goods, holding constant the effect of the price change on consumer purchasing power.

9.2 Where Demand Curves Come From (pages 288–291)

Use the concept of utility to explain the law of demand. When the price of a good declines, the ratio of the marginal utility to price rises. This leads consumers to buy more of that good. As a result, whenever the price of a product falls, the quantity demanded increases. We saw in Chapter 1 that this is known as the *law of demand*. The market demand curve can be constructed from the individual demand curves for all the consumers in the market.

9.3 Social Influences on Decision Making (pages 291–296)

Explain how social influences can affect consumption choices. Social factors can have an effect on consumption. For example, the amount of utility people receive from consuming a good often depends on how many other people they know who also consume the good. There is a **network externality** in the consumption of a product if the usefulness of the product increases with the number of consumers who use it. There is also evidence that people like to be treated fairly and that they usually attempt to treat others fairly, even if doing so makes them worse off financially. This result has been demonstrated in laboratory experiments, such as the ultimatum game. When firms set prices, they take into account consumers' preference for fairness. For example, hardware stores often do not increase the price of snow shovels to take advantage of a temporary increase in demand following a snowstorm.

9.4 Behavioral Economics: Do People Make Their Choices Rationally? (pages 296–300)

Describe the behavioral economics approach to understanding decision making. **Behavioral economics** is the study of situations in which people act in ways that are not economically rational. **Opportunity cost** is the highest-valued alternative that must be given up to engage in an activity. People would improve their decision making if they took into account nonmonetary opportunity costs. People sometimes ignore nonmonetary opportunity costs because of the **endowment effect**—the tendency of people to be unwilling to sell something they already own even if they are offered a price that is greater than the price they would be willing to pay to buy the good if they didn't already own it. People would also improve their decision making if they ignored *sunk costs*. A **sunk cost** is a cost that has already been paid and cannot be recovered. Finally, people would improve their decision making if they were more realistic about their future behavior.

Appendix: Using Indifference Curves and Budget Lines to Understand Consumer Behavior (pages 309–323)
Use indifference curves and budget lines to understand consumer behavior.

Chapter Review

Chapter Opener: Can Oprah Get You to Buy a Kindle? (page 279)

In October 2008, Oprah Winfrey announced on her show that her new "favorite thing" was Amazon's e-reader, the Kindle. Immediately, sales of the Kindle rose dramatically. What is it about Oprah's endorsement that led to such growth in sales of the Kindle? Firms often hire celebrities to endorse their products with the expectation that the endorsements will increase their sales. In this chapter, we will examine how consumers make choices about their purchases.

9.1 Utility and Consumer Decision Making (pages 280–288)

Learning Objective: Define utility and explain how consumers choose goods and services to maximize their utility.

Utility is the enjoyment or satisfaction people receive from consuming goods and services. Economists assume consumers spend their limited budgets on the bundle of goods and services that provides them with the most utility, although utility cannot be measured exactly. If we assume that utility can be measured, then a certain number of *utils* (units of utility or satisfaction) are associated with each unit of a product.

Marginal utility (*MU*) is the change in total utility a person receives from consuming one additional unit of a good or service. The **law of diminishing marginal utility** states that consumers experience less additional satisfaction as they consume more of a good or service during a given period of time.

📖 Study Hint
Remember that diminishing marginal utility does not imply that increasing consumption reduces utility. Utility still rises even if marginal utility is falling.

Because consumers have limited income, they try to receive the most utility they can as they spend their income. A **budget constraint** refers to the limited amount of income available to consumers to spend on goods and services. The model of consumer behavior can be used to determine the optimal amounts of goods a consumer will purchase given (a) knowledge of the marginal utilities (*MU*) of the goods, (b) the prices of the goods, and (c) the consumer's budget constraint. This model applies a key economic principle you learned about in Chapter 1: optimal decisions are made at the margin.

The following information is taken from Table 9-2 on page 283 in the textbook. It is assumed that the price of pizza is $2 per slice, the price of a cup of Coke is $1, and the consumer has $10 to spend on pizza and Coke.

Slices of pizza	*MU* per dollar (pizza)	Cups of Coke	*MU* per dollar (Coke)
1	10	1	20
2	8	2	15
3	5	3	10
4	3	4	5
5	1	5	3

The consumer maximizes utility by first buying the good for which the *MU* per dollar is higher. Because the first cup of Coke has a higher *MU* per dollar (20) than the *MU* per dollar from the first slice of pizza (10), the consumer will first spend $1 on a cup of Coke. Because of the law of diminishing marginal utility, the *MU* of Coke and pizza declines as more of each is consumed. The consumer will compare the *MU* per dollar of the next unit of each good in deciding how to spend his income. The consumer will maximize his utility when:

1. Marginal utility per dollar is equal for each good consumed, and
2. Total spending on all goods equals the income available.

The consumer's optimal consumption is 3 slices of pizza (at $2 each, spending $6 on pizza) and 4 Cokes (at $1 each, spending $4 on Coke). Total spending is equal to the consumer's budget, $10. Marginal utility per dollar is 5 for both pizza and Coke at this equilibrium.

The rule of equal marginal utility per dollar can be used to analyze a consumer's response to a price change. Using the previous example, if the price of pizza were to fall to $1.50, then there would be a substitution and income effect on the quantity of pizza demanded.

Slices of pizza	*MU* per dollar (pizza)	Cups of Coke	*MU* per dollar (Coke)
1	13.3	1	20
2	10.7	2	15
3	6.7	3	10
4	4	4	5
5	1.3	5	3

The decrease in the price of pizza has raised the *MU* per dollar of pizza. Previously, the consumer's $10 budget was used to buy 3 slices of pizza and 4 cups of Coke. At the lower price of pizza, the same combination of goods costs only $8.50. This increase in purchasing power is the income effect of the price change. And the consumer will now purchase 4 slices of pizza but will still buy 4 Cokes as this is the consumption bundle where the entire budget is spent and the marginal utility per dollar of the last unit consumed is the same for both goods.

The **income effect** is the change in the quantity demanded of a good that results from a change in price caused by the altered consumer purchasing power, holding all other factors constant. If pizza is a normal good, then the income effect of a decrease in price will lead to an increase in the quantity demanded of pizza. If pizza is an inferior good, then the income effect of a decrease in price will lead to a decrease in the quantity demanded. The **substitution effect** is the change in quantity demanded of a good that results from a change in price that makes the good more or less expensive relative to other goods, holding constant the effect of the price change on consumer purchasing power.

Study Hint

The assumption that we can measure utility exactly is unrealistic. We can't strap a consumer into a chair and measure how many *utils* she receives from eating a slice of pizza. But it is realistic to assume a consumer can determine whether he or she prefers a certain amount of one product to an amount of another, or that he or she is indifferent between consuming two different products. Economists do not believe in "cardinal utility"—utility measured in utils. However, economists do believe in "ordinal utility"—that consumers can rank products, or combinations of products, based on their preferences.

Study Hint

You can memorize the rule that utility is maximized when marginal utility per dollar is equal across all goods, but it should make sense intuitively as well. Think about this simple example: You like both candy bars and ice cream cones. Ice cream cones cost three times as much as candy bars, and you would like an ice cream cone twice as much as you would like a candy bar. On one hand, you might be tempted to say that, because the candy bar is cheaper, that you should buy a candy bar. On the other hand, you might be tempted to say that, because you would like an ice cream cone more, that you should buy an ice cream cone. The reality is that you need to balance your relative desire for ice cream cones and candy bars with their relative prices. If an ice cream cone costs three times as much but you only like it twice as much as a candy bar, then the relative cost of that ice cream cone isn't worth the benefit you would receive. Rather, you should buy the candy bar. Mathematically, the $MU_{\text{ice cream}} = 2 \times MU_{\text{candy bar}}$ and $P_{\text{ice cream}} = 3 \times P_{\text{candy bar}}$ so that the marginal utility per dollar spent on ice cream is only two-thirds of the marginal utility per dollar spent on a candy bar. Spending the money on the candy bar will increase utility more than spending the money on the ice cream cone.

9.2 | Where Demand Curves Come From (pages 288–291)
Learning Objective: Use the concept of utility to explain the law of demand.

The substitution and income effects of price changes explain why demand curves for normal goods are downward sloping. As price decreases, the good becomes attractive relative to available substitutes, so the quantity demanded of the good will rise. This same price decrease causes an increase in the consumer's purchasing power, which causes an increase in the quantity demanded of normal goods. Although the substitution and income effects of price changes for inferior goods have opposite effects on quantity demanded, the income effect is typically quite small. So, as the price decreases, the quantity demanded will increase for nearly all goods. Economists have statistically estimated millions of demand curves using real-world data. In nearly every case, the demand curve slopes downward. The law of demand is based on real-world evidence, not economic theory alone.

Extra Solved Problem 9-2
Deriving Lee's Demand Curve for Ice Cream
Supports Learning Objective 9.2: Use the concept of utility to explain the law of demand.

The following table represents Lee's marginal utility per dollar for ice cream cones and cans of Lime Fizz as derived in Step 4 of Solved Problem 9-1 in the textbook. The optimal level of consumption, given Lee's $7 budget constraint and the price of $2 per cone and $1 per can of Lime Fizz, is 1 ice cream cone and 5 cans of Lime Fizz.

	Ice Cream Cones $2 each		Cans of Lime Fizz $1 each	
Quantity	*MU*	*MU/P*	*MU*	*MU/P*
1	30	15	40	40
2	25	12.5	35	35
3	20	10	26	26
4	15	7.5	18	18
5	10	5	15	15
6	5	2.5	7	7

a. Assume that the price per can of Lime Fizz remains $1.00. What is the optimal level of consumption if the price of an ice cream cone falls to $1.50? What is the optimal level of consumption if the price per cone falls to $1.00? (Hint: Continue to purchase units with the highest marginal utilities per dollar.)

b. Use the optimal consumption bundles for each of the three prices of ice cream cone to derive Lee's demand curve for ice cream cones.

SOLVING THE PROBLEM

Step 1:   Review the chapter material.

This problem is about optimal consumption bundles and how to derive a demand curve, so you may want to review the section "Where Demand Curves Come From," which begins on page 288 in the textbook.

Step 2:   Calculate the marginal utility per dollar of spending for each of the two prices proposed in part (a).

Because only the price of ice cream cones is changing we can focus on the marginal utility of ice cream cones. See the table below for the results of the calculations:

	Ice Cream Cones $1.50 each		Ice Cream Cones $1.00 each	
Quantity	*MU*	*MU/P*	*MU*	*MU/P*
1	30	20	30	30
2	25	17	25	25
3	20	13	20	20
4	15	10	15	15
5	10	7	10	10
6	5	3	5	5

Step 3:   Determine the optimal consumption bundle for Lee given his $7 budget for each of the new possible prices of ice cream cones.

At a price of $1.50 per ice cream cone, Lee will consume 2 ice cream cones and 4 cans of Lime Fizz as this is the point where the marginal utilities per dollar are closest and still within the $7.00 budget. Similarly, when the price is $1.00 per cone, Lee will consume 3 ice cream cones and 4 cans of Lime Fizz.

Step 4: **Use the optimal bundles to generate Lee's demand curve for ice cream cones.**
At a price of $2.00, Lee will consume 1 ice cream cone. At $1.50 per cone, Lee will consume 2 cones and at $1 per cone, he will consume 3 cones.

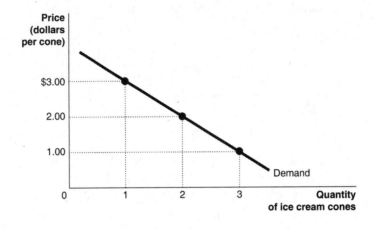

9.3 Social Influences on Decision Making (pages 291–296)
Learning Objective: Explain how social influences can affect consumption choices.

Consumer decisions appear to be influenced by the actions and perceptions of other consumers. Some people obtain utility from consuming goods that others consume. Firms use celebrity endorsements to sell products because consumers often wish to be identified with products used by celebrities. Celebrity endorsements can be particularly effective when consumers believe celebrities are knowledgeable about the products they endorse. For example, consumers know that Tiger Woods is knowledgeable about golf clubs and therefore trust his endorsement.

Consumer decisions can be affected by **network externalities**, a situation in which the usefulness of a product increases with the number of consumers who use it. For example, you will not find a fax machine useful if no one else owns one. Consumers' willingness to buy new technologies, such as Blu-ray DVD players, is enhanced when they know many others have bought them, because this will ensure these technologies will be available in the future and that complementary products—such as DVDs in the Blu-ray format—will be widely available.

Recent studies of consumer behavior indicate consumers think about fairness when they make decisions, which means that consumers may decrease their well-being financially for the sake of fairness. For example, some restaurant diners may leave a good tip even though they do not expect to visit that restaurant again. Even economic experiments, like the Ultimatum Game, show that fairness often plays a role in making decisions.

Firm realize that consumers value fairness. Tickets for Broadway plays, concerts, and sporting contests are often priced below their equilibrium levels. These decisions appear to be a response to consumers' concerns that the equilibrium prices would be unfairly high.

📖 **Study Hint**

Prior to the 1970s, owners of foreign-made automobiles often had difficulty locating parts for their cars and mechanics who could repair them. One would usually need hard-to-find metric wrenches to do even simple repair work. The rapid increase in oil and gasoline prices beginning in 1973 caused a surge in demand for the smaller, more fuel-efficient automobiles offered by Japanese and German automakers. By the late twentieth century, foreign manufacturers had gained significant market share in the United States. The availability of parts, mechanics, and tools was no longer an issue for buyers of domestic or foreign automobiles. This is an example of the importance of network externalities.

Extra Solved Problem 9-3

Supports Learning Objective 9.3: Explain how social influences can affect consumption choices.

In 2009, Olympic hero Michael Phelps and singer Chris Brown gave advertisers another lesson in the risks of paying big money to celebrities to endorse their products. Soon after a photograph of Phelps smoking marijuana was printed in a British tabloid, Kellogg cancelled its contract with the swimmer. Brown shocked music fans after he allegedly battered singing star and girlfriend Rihanna. Brown had earlier appeared in ads for Doublemint gum. The best celebrity endorsement deals for firms, of course, feature those who are well-known both for their achievements in the world of sports (Peyton Manning, Michael Jordan) and entertainment (Jerry Seinfeld, Beyoncé) as well as for their ability to avoid scandal. But another important factor is the public's belief in the credibility of the celebrity endorser. One of the best examples of this is star pitchman and former heavyweight boxing champion George Foreman. Foreman has appeared in ads for Meineke Mufflers and has endorsed his own line of clothing, but his greatest success has been from sales of The George Foreman "Lean Mean Grilling Machine." Salton Inc., the manufacturer of the Grilling Machine, paid Foreman over $130 million to endorse its product over a ten-year period. An important part of Foreman's success is his amiable persona, in contrast with the sullen image he had in his early boxing years. The public also trusts Foreman, especially when it comes to food. "He has a well-chronicled history of enjoying food—lots of it," says Rich Kenah, director of marketing for Global Athletics and Marketing firm in Boston. "So he is credible on the subject…"

Foreman tries all products—gathering approvals from his wife and children—before agreeing to endorse them. John Bellamy, CEO of Knockout Group Inc., says Foreman went so far as to put an ethics clause in Knockout's contract prohibiting it from selling the company to anyone involved in alcohol, tobacco, pornography, or gambling. "The most important thing to him is image," Bellamy says.

Sources: A.K. Cabell, "Celebrity Endorsements Reach for the Stars," brandchannel.com, June 2, 2003. "George Foreman: Marketing Champ of the World," *BusinessWeek Online*. December 20, 2004. Charisse Jones, "Ad Track: Scandals tarnish celebrity endorsement," USA Today, February 22, 2009.

a. Why do consumers buy products endorsed by George Foreman?

b. Contrast Foreman's success with the endorsement failures of celebrities such as Michael Phelps and Chris Brown.

SOLVING THE PROBLEM:

Step 1:   Review the chapter material.

This problem is about celebrity endorsements that influence the choices consumers make, so you may want to review the section "Social Influences on Decision Making," which begins on page 291 in the textbook.

Step 2: **Why do consumers buy products endorsed by George Foreman?**

Part of Foreman's appeal stems from his personality. Many consumers know and like Foreman and want to own products he endorses because they know other people who own these products. Consumers may also believe Foreman is knowledgeable about the products he endorses, such as the "Lean Mean Grilling Machine" and his line of men's clothing.

Step 3: **Contrast Foreman's success with the endorsement failures of celebrities such as Michael Phelps and Chris Brown.**

Phelps and Brown received adverse publicity for behavior that made companies unwilling to continue using them in their advertising campaigns. In contrast, Foreman carefully selects the products he endorses and does not have a history of controversial behavior.

9.4 Behavioral Economics: Do People Make Their Choices Rationally? (pages 296–300)

Learning Objective: Describe the behavioral economics approach to understanding decision making.

Some economists have questioned whether consumers make decisions rationally. Consumers sometimes make poor choices. **Behavioral economics** studies situations in which people make choices that do not appear to be economically rational. Among the most important reasons for poor choices are: failure to account for nonmonetary opportunity costs, failure to ignore sunk costs, and being unrealistic about future behavior.

📖 Study Hint

Sunk costs should be ignored not only by consumers but by government officials and even baseball executives. Before the 2002 baseball season, Allard Baird, the general manager of the Kansas City Royals, decided to release pitcher José Rosado. Writing about this decision, Rany Jazayerdi wrote: "[I]t's the first piece of evidence…that Baird understands…sunk costs. Rosado was paid $3.5 million to make five starts in 2000…$3.25 million again in 2001 to do absolutely nothing. He's already guaranteed $533,000 this year…it must be awfully tempting to keep him on the roster…in hope that, after so much time and so much money, their investment might finally pay some dividends…Baird cut Rosado because he compared Rosado to the other [pitching] options…and came to the…conclusion that the only thing Rosado had on [other pitchers] is service time and income."

Source: Rany Jazayerdi, "Rany on the Royals: Cutting Bait," posted on the Web site www.baseballprospectus.com, March 12, 2002.

Appendix
Using Indifference Curves and Budget Lines to Understand Consumer Behavior (pages 309–323)

Learning Objective: Use indifferent curves and budget lines to understand consumer behavior.

Consumer Preferences

Rather than assume utility is measured in utils, it is more realistic to assume that consumers rank different combinations of goods and services by how much utility they provide. If a consumer is presented with two alternative consumption bundles (A and B), one can assume she will be able to decide on one of the following:

1. the consumer prefers A to B, or
2. the consumer prefers B to A, or
3. the consumer is indifferent between A and B because she receives equal utility from A and B.

Economists assume that the consumer's preferences are transitive. This means that if a consumer prefers A to B and B to C, then she must prefer A to C. Given the assumptions made, we can draw a map of a consumer's preferences using indifference curves. An **indifference curve** is a curve that shows the combinations of consumption bundles that give the consumer the same utility. Indifference curves assume that consumption bundles consist of various amounts of only two goods. Each possible combination of two goods—for example, cans of Coca-Cola and slices of pizza—has an indifference curve passing through it. A consumer is indifferent among all the consumption bundles that are on the same indifference curve.

In a graph of indifference curves, the further to the right a curve is the greater the utility it represents. Along an indifference curve, the slope indicates the rate at which a consumer is willing to trade off one good for another, keeping total utility constant. This rate is called the **marginal rate of substitution (MRS)**. The MRS decreases as we move down the indifference curve. This decrease in the MRS means the indifference curves are bowed in or convex.

Indifference curves do not cross. If two indifference curves (I_1 and I_2) crossed, they would share a common point (point X). (See Figure 9A-2 on page 311). Assume that Y is a point on I_2 so that the consumer would be indifferent between points X and Y. Assume that point Y lies on the portion of I_2 that is above I_1. Z is another point on I_1 so that the consumer is indifferent between X and Z. Because of the transitivity assumption, the consumer should be indifferent between points Z and Y, but Y represents more of both Coke and pizza. The violation of the transitivity assumption proves that indifference curves cannot cross.

📖 Study Hint

Be sure you understand Figure 9A-1 on page 310 and Figure 9A-2 on page 311 and the description of these graphs in the textbook. Notice that the indifference curves do not bend backward, or become positively sloped. This means that receiving more Coke and pizza always increases utility. If indifference curves were positively sloped, this would mean that receiving more of one good (for example, pizza) would lower consumer utility and require more of the other good to maintain utility at the same level. (Positively sloped indifference curves are sometimes used to model economic "bads" such as pollution and risk.)

The Budget Constraint

A consumer's budget constraint is the amount of income the consumer has to spend on goods and services. Knowing a consumer's income and the prices of two goods he or she can buy allows us to draw a budget line in a graph with the amount of either good measured on the vertical and horizontal axes of the graph. The vertical intercept of the budget line is the maximum amount of a good (for example, cans of Coke) that can be bought with the consumer's income (for example, $10) and the price of the good (for example, $1). The horizontal intercept of the budget line is the maximum of the other good (for example, slices of pizza) that can be bought with the consumer's income.

The slope of the budget constraint is constant and is equal to the ratio of the price of pizza (the good measured on the horizontal axis) to the price of Coke (the good measured along the vertical axis) multiplied by –1.

📖 **Study Hint**

Budget lines are similar to the production possibilities frontiers introduced in chapter 2, but they identify possible consumption choices rather than production options. Figure 9A-3 on page 312 illustrates a budget line for Dave, a representative consumer. Points on the budget line represent combinations of two goods that are affordable and use up all available income. Points inside the budget line represent affordable combinations of the two goods that leave some income unspent, and points above the budget line represent unaffordable consumption bundles.

Choosing the Optimal Consumption of Pizza and Coke

To maximize utility, a consumer needs to be on the highest indifference curve, given the consumer's budget constraint. The combination of goods that will maximize utility subject to a consumer's budget constraint is at the tangency of the budget line with an indifference curve. If the price of one of the goods changes, then the budget line will change. For example, when the price of pizza decreases to $1, more consumption bundles can be purchased than were previously possible. The change in the budget line from a price decrease results in a new combination of goods that will maximize utility.

By changing the price of one of the goods and determining the amount of the good that will be purchased after the price change, one can derive the demand curve for the good. Indifference curves and budget constraints can be used to analyze the income and substitution effects from a price change. Assume that a consumer is maximizing utility at the tangency of a budget line and indifference curve I_1. Assume a change in the price of pizza from $2 to $1. The budget line changes to reflect the price change and the lines' new slope. The consumer maximizes utility at the tangency of the new budget line and indifference curve I_2 as in Figure 9A-6.

When the price of a good changes, the slope of the budget line also changes, and there will be a new tangency between the new budget line and an indifference curve. For example, when the price of a good measured on the x axis falls, the budget line rotates outward. The consumer will maximize utility where the new flatter budget line will be tangent to a new indifference curve. The law of demand predicts that a decrease in the price of a good will result in an increase in the quantity demanded.

📖 **Study Hint**

It is much easier to understand how the optimal combination of goods is determined and how price changes change the optimal combination with graphs rather than with words alone. Be sure you understand the graphs in Figures 9A-4 through 9A-6.

Drawing a line parallel to the new budget line (that is, with the new line's slope) tangent to the I_1 illustrates the substitution effect of the price change. The change in consumption from the tangency of a line parallel to the new budget line and I_1 to the tangency of the new budget line and I_2 illustrates the income effect of the change in price. Increases in income shift the budget line outward and enable consumers to reach higher indifference curves.

The Slope of the Indifference Curve, the Slope of the Budget Line, and the Rule of Equal Marginal Utility Per Dollar Spent

At the point of optimal consumption, the *MRS* is equal to the ratio of the price of the product on the horizontal axis to the price of the product on the vertical axis. The slope of the indifference curve is the rate at which a consumer is *willing* to trade off one good for the other. The slope of the budget line is the rate at which a consumer is *able* to trade off one good for the other. Only at the point of optimal consumption is the rate at which a consumer is willing to trade off one good for the other equal to the rate which she can trade off one good for the other.

Indifference curves and budget lines can be used to explain the rule of equal marginal utility per dollar. When a consumer moves downward along an indifference curve, more of one good (for example, pizza) and less of another good (for example, Coke) is consumed but utility is constant. Moving along an indifference curve results in a loss in utility equal to the change in the quantity of Coke multiplied by the marginal utility of Coke:

$$-\text{Change in the quantity of Coke} \times MU_{Coke}$$

and a gain in utility equal to the change in the quantity of pizza multiplied by the marginal utility of pizza:

$$\text{Change in the quantity of pizza} \times MU_{Pizza.}$$

The loss in utility from consuming less Coke equals the gain in utility from consuming more pizza because the consumer remains on the same indifference curve. The change in utility can be written:

$$-(\text{Change in the quantity of Coke} \times MU_{Coke}) = (\text{Change in the quantity of pizza} \times MU_{Pizza}).$$

This can be rewritten:

$$(-\text{Change in the quantity of Coke})/(\text{Change in the quantity of pizza}) = (MU_{Pizza}/MU_{Coke}) = MRS.$$

Because the slope of the indifference curve (*MRS*) equals the slope of the budget line at the point of optimal consumption then:

$$MU_{Pizza}/P_{Pizza} = MU_{Coke}/P_{Coke}$$

Rewriting this equation yields marginal utility per dollar:

$$\frac{MU_{pizza}}{P_{pizza}} = \frac{MU_{Coke}}{P_{Coke}}$$

Key Terms

Behavioral economics The study of situations in which people make choices that do not appear to be economically rational.

Budget constraint The limited amount of income available to consumers to spend on goods and services.

Endowment effect The tendency of people to be unwilling to sell a good they already own even if they are offered a price that is greater than the price they would be willing to pay to buy the good if they didn't already own it.

Income effect The change in the quantity demanded of a good that results from the effect of a change in price on consumer purchasing power, holding all other factors constant.

Law of diminishing marginal utility The principle that consumers experience diminishing additional satisfaction as they consume more of a good or service during a given period of time.

Marginal utility (*MU*) The change in total utility a person receives from consuming one additional unit of a good or service.

Network externality A situation in which the usefulness of a product increases with the number of consumers who use it.

Opportunity cost The highest-valued alternative that must be given up to engage in an activity.

Substitution effect The change in the quantity demanded of a good that results from a change in price making the good more or less expensive relative to other goods, holding constant the effect of the price change on consumer purchasing power.

Sunk cost A cost that has already been paid and cannot be recovered.

Utility The enjoyment or satisfaction people receive from consuming goods and services.

Key Terms—Appendix

Indifference curve A curve that shows the combinations of consumption bundles that give the consumer the same utility.

Marginal rate of substitution (*MRS*) The rate at which a consumer would be willing to trade off one good for another.

Self-Test

(Answers are provided at the end of the Self-Test.)

Multiple-Choice Questions

1. If increasing your consumption of pizza from 3 to 4 slices increases your utility, which of the following must be true?
   a. The marginal utility of the 4th slice of pizza is equal to the total utility of 4 slices of pizza.
   b. The marginal utility of the 4th slice of pizza is greater than the marginal utility of the 3rd slice of pizza.
   c. The marginal utility of the 4th slice of pizza is positive.
   d. The marginal utility of the 3rd slice of pizza is negative.

2. If marginal utility is negative, what must be true about total utility?
   a. Total utility increases with additional consumption.
   b. Total utility decreases with additional consumption.
   c. Total utility remains constant regardless of the number of units consumed.
   d. Total utility equals zero.

3. Which of the following statements concerning total utility and marginal utility is correct?
   a. Marginal utility is usually larger than total utility.
   b. Total utility is the sum of marginal utilities.
   c. Marginal utility is the sum of total utility.
   d. Marginal utility is maximized when total utility is zero.

4. According to the law of diminishing marginal utility, as the consumption of a particular good increases,
   a. total utility increases by more and more.
   b. marginal utility increases.
   c. total utility decreases.
   d. marginal utility decreases.

5. Refer to the table below. Total utility derived from consuming three ice cream cones equals

Ice Cream Cones	Total Utility	Marginal Utility
1	10	?
2	18	?
3	?	6
4	28	?
5	?	2

   a. 34.
   b. 6.
   c. 22.
   d. 24.

6. Refer to the table below. The marginal utility from consuming the second ice cream cone equals

Ice Cream Cones	Total Utility	Marginal Utility
1	10	?
2	18	?
3	?	6
4	28	?
5	?	2

   a. 10.
   b. 9.
   c. 8.
   d. 18.

7. Refer to the table below. The total utility from consuming 5 ice cream cones is equal to

Ice Cream Cones	Total Utility	Marginal Utility
1	10	?
2	18	?
3	?	6
4	28	?
5	?	2

a. 28.
b. 29.
c. 30.
d. 2.

8. Refer to the graph below. Marginal utility is

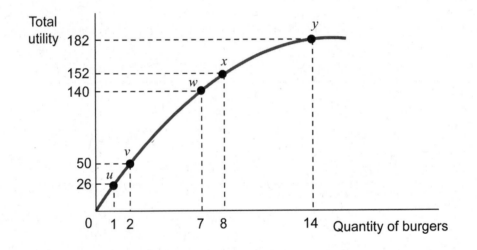

a. greater at points *u* and *v* than at points *w* and *x*.
b. greater at points *w* and *x* than at points *u* and *v*.
c. the same at points *u* and *v* as at points *w* and *x*.
d. greatest at point *y*.

9. Refer to the graph below. From the information in the graph, we can deduce that the marginal utility curve would be

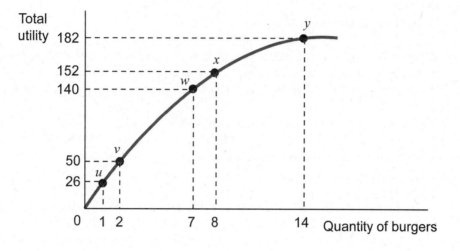

a. downward sloping.
b. upward sloping.
c. horizontal.
d. vertical.

10. What is a budget constraint?
a. The limited amount of income available to consumers to spend on goods and services.
b. The amount of income that yields equal marginal utility per dollar spent.
c. The amount of utility that a consumer receives from spending a limited amount of income on goods and services.
d. The amount of money necessary to purchase a given combination of goods.

11. According to economists, decisions to increase an activity, such as consumption, are based on
a. an evaluation of the incremental implications of that decision, that is, an evaluation of what happens at the margin.
b. an evaluation of the totality of the consequences of our actions, both past and present.
c. the maximization of opportunity cost.
d. the maximization of social welfare.

12. Refer to the inequality below. The marginal utility per dollar spent on good X is less than the marginal utility per dollar spent on good Y. According to the rule of equal marginal utility per dollar spent, what can a consumer do to increase total utility from consumption of goods X and Y?

$$\frac{\text{Marginal utility of good X}}{\text{Price of good X}} < \frac{\text{Marginal utility of good Y}}{\text{Price of good Y}}$$

a. increase the consumption of good X
b. increase the consumption of good Y
c. increase the consumption of both goods
d. decrease the consumption of both goods

13. A consumer maximizes total utility from a limited amount of income when
    a. choosing more of one good and less of another increases utility.
    b. choosing more of one good and less of another no longer increases utility.
    c. marginal utility is maximized.
    d. marginal utility per dollar spent on each good is highest.

14. Suppose you have a fixed amount of income to spend on two goods, X and Y. The price of good X is $P_x = \$10$ and the price of good Y is $P_y = \$5$. The marginal utility of X is $MU_x = 60$ utils and the marginal utility of Y is $MU_y = 15$ utils. How should consumption of X and Y change, if at all, to increase utility?
    a. Consumption of good X should increase, and consumption of good Y should decrease.
    b. Consumption of good X should decrease, and consumption of good Y should increase.
    c. The current combination of goods maximizes total utility; consumption should remain the same.
    d. The consumption of goods X and Y should both increase.

15. Refer to the table below. As stated in the first row, the income of the consumer (I) equals $20. The price of good X (P_x) equals $4.00 and the price of good Y (P_y) equals $2.00. Total utility derived from consuming X and Y is listed. What is the marginal utility per dollar spent on the 5th unit of good X?

I = $20.00				P_x = $4.00	P_y = $2.00		
X	Total Utility	MU_x	MU_x / P_x	Y	Total Utility	MU_y	MU_y / P_y
0	0	-		0	0	-	
1	40			1	35		
2	65			2	55		
3	85			3	70		
4	100			4	80		
5	108			5	84		
6	114			6	85		

    a. 8
    b. 4
    c. 2
    d. 1.5

16. Refer to the table below. As stated in the first row, the income of the consumer (I) equals $20. The price of good X (P_x) equals $4.00 and the price of good Y (P_y) equals $2.00. Total utility derived from consuming X and Y is listed. What combination of goods X and Y will maximize utility subject to the consumer's budget constraint?

I = $20.00		P_x = $4.00		P_y = $2.00			
X	Total Utility	MU_x	MU_x / P_x	Y	Total Utility	MU_y	MU_y / P_y
0	0	-		0	0	-	
1	40			1	35		
2	65			2	55		
3	85			3	70		
4	100			4	80		
5	108			5	84		
6	114			6	85		

a. 6 units of X and 6 units of Y
b. 5 units of X and 0 units of Y
c. 3 units of X and 4 units of Y
d. 4 units of X and 3 units of Y

17. Refer to the table below. As stated in the first row, the income of the consumer (I) equals $20. The price of good X (P_x) equals $3.00 and the price of good Y (P_y) equals $2.00. Total utility derived from consuming X and Y is listed. What combination of goods X and Y will maximize utility subject to the consumer's budget constraint?

I = $20.00		P_x = $3.00		P_y = $2.00			
X	Total Utility	MU_x	MU_x / P_x	Y	Total Utility	MU_y	MU_y / P_y
0	0	-		0	0	-	
1	40			1	35		
2	65			2	55		
3	85			3	70		
4	100			4	80		
5	108			5	84		
6	114			6	85		

a. 6 units of X and 6 units of Y
b. 6 units of X and 1 unit of Y
c. 4 units of X and 3 units of Y
d. 4 units of X and 4 units of Y

18. Fill in the blank. The substitution effect is the change in the quantity demanded of a good that results from _____, holding constant the effect of the price change on consumer purchasing power.
a. a change in the price of a substitute for the good
b. a change in price making the good more or less expensive relative to other goods
c. an increase in the usefulness of a product as the number of consumers who use it increases
d. the tendency of people to be unwilling to sell something they own

19. Fill in the blank. The income effect is the change in the quantity demanded of a good that results from _____, holding all other factors constant.
    a. the effect of a change in price on consumer purchasing power
    b. a change in price, making the good more or less expensive relative to other goods
    c. an increase in the usefulness of a product as the number of consumers who use it increases
    d. the tendency of people to be unwilling to sell something they own

20. How do the income and substitution effects work when the price of a normal good decreases?
    a. Both the income effect and the substitution effect cause an increase in the quantity demanded of the good.
    b. Both the income effect and the substitution effect cause a decrease in the quantity demanded of the good.
    c. The income effect causes an increase in the quantity demanded of the good, and the substitution effect causes a decrease in the quantity demanded of the good.
    d. The income effect causes a decrease in the quantity demanded of the good, and the substitution effect causes an increase in the quantity demanded of the good.

21. How do the income and substitution effects work when the price of an inferior good decreases?
    a. Both the income effect and the substitution effect cause an increase in the quantity demanded of the good.
    b. Both the income effect and the substitution effect cause a decrease in the quantity demanded of the good.
    c. The income effect causes an increase in the quantity demanded and the substitution effect causes a decrease in the quantity demanded.
    d. The income effect causes a decrease in the quantity demanded and the substitution effect causes an increase in the quantity demanded.

22. If the income effect of a price change for an inferior good is larger than the substitution effect, the demand curve will be
    a. downward sloping.
    b. upward sloping.
    c. horizontal.
    d. vertical.

23. Refer to the graph below. The graph shows your weekly demand for pizza. How was this demand curve constructed?

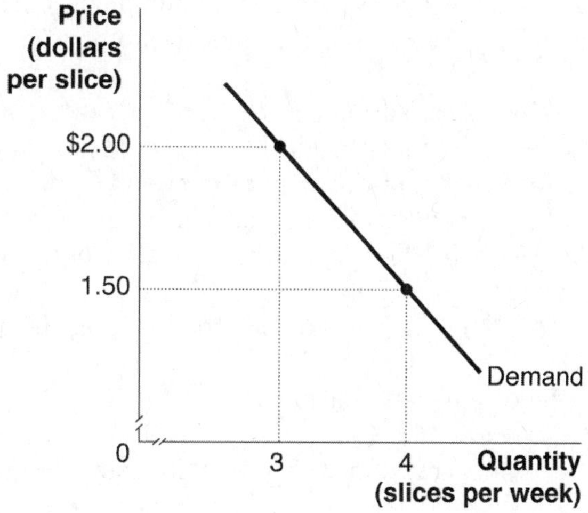

a. by computing your optimal consumption of pizza at the various prices shown, all else the same
b. by computing your consumption of pizza when the price of pizza remains constant
c. by computing your consumption of pizza when both the price of pizza and the number of slices you consume per week remain constant
d. by computing your consumption of pizza at various prices, regardless of utility gained

24. What are the characteristics of Giffen goods?
a. Giffen goods have downward-sloping demand curves.
b. Giffen goods are normal, not inferior goods.
c. Giffen goods are inferior goods for which the income effect is greater than the substitution effect when price changes.
d. All of the above are characteristics of Giffen goods.

25. Which of the following factors best explains why consumers might prefer to go to a restaurant that was similar to another restaurant in terms of décor and food choices but had fewer customers?
a. the presence of network externalities
b. the idea that some people receive utility from goods they believe are popular
c. income and substitution effects
d. switching costs

26. Whenever consumption takes place publicly, what does your decision to buy a product depend on?
a. The decision depends only on the characteristics of the product.
b. The decision depends only on how many other people are buying the product.
c. The decision depends both on the characteristics of the product and on how many other people are buying the product.
d. The decision depends on factors other than the characteristics of the product and on how many people are buying it.

27. What happens when network externalities are present?
    a. The usefulness of telecommunications equipment rises.
    b. The usefulness of networks diminishes with the number of consumers who enter them.
    c. The usefulness of a product increases with the number of consumers who use it.
    d. The usefulness of a product decreases as the number of products rises.

28. What happens when a product is path dependent?
    a. The technology used to produce the product has a specific growth path.
    b. The product can sell for a higher price when it is new and there are no similar products consumers can buy than when it is older and consumers can choose to buy substitutes for the product.
    c. The cost of switching to a product with a better technology gives the product with the initial technology an advantage.
    d. The path that a product follows depends on the firm that uses the best technology to produce it.

29. What are the potential effects of path dependence?
    a. market failure
    b. a loss of efficiency if the government chooses to intervene in markets where there is path dependence
    c. a reduction in switching costs
    d. All of the above are potential results of path dependence.

30. In considering consumers' attitudes toward fairness, which of the following have economists found to be true?
    a. People are interested mainly in making themselves as well off as possible.
    b. People attempt to treat others fairly, even if doing so makes them worse off financially.
    c. People attempt to treat others fairly but only if doing so makes them better off financially.
    d. People usually ignore fairness when making spending decisions.

31. Many people donate to charity and leave tips to servers in restaurants even when they will never visit the restaurant again. Economists consider this type of behavior to be
    a. irrational, because these actions make people worse off financially.
    b. rational, because it shows that people value fairness even when this behavior makes people worse off financially.
    c. rational only if other people observe this behavior.
    d. All of the above are consistent with the general view of fairness.

32. In the ultimatum game, if neither the allocator nor the recipient cared about fairness, what would be the optimal distribution of $20.00?
    a. $19.99 for the allocator and $0.01 for the recipient
    b. $10.00 for the allocator and $10.00 for the recipient
    c. $19.99 for the recipient and $0.01 for the allocator
    d. $20.00 for the allocator and nothing for the recipient

33. In the ultimatum game, when the allocator and the recipient care about fairness, how is the distribution of $20.00 affected?
    a. Allocators receive everything and recipients receive nothing.
    b. Recipients usually reject offers of less than a 10 percent share.
    c. Allocators usually offer recipients a very small share.
    d. Allocators and recipients always end up sharing the $20.00 equally.

34. Refer to the graph below which shows the demand and supply of tickets for a Broadway play. At what price is there a shortage of tickets?

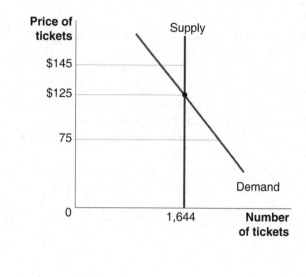

   a. at $75
   b. at $125
   c. at $145
   d. at all three prices

35. Refer to the graph below which shows the demand and supply of tickets for a Broadway play. When the play's producers take fairness into account, which of the following would most likely occur?

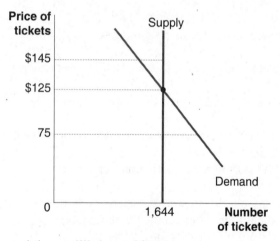

   a. The market price will equal the equilibrium of $125.
   b. Producers will charge $75 for a ticket even though the result would be a shortage.
   c. Producers will charge $145 for a ticket in anticipation of stronger demand.
   d. Producers will raise ticket prices gradually as demand strengthens over time.

36. Fill in the blanks. Which of the following has been found by researchers in surveys of consumers? Most people consider it _____ for firms to raise their prices following an increase in costs _____ to raise prices following an increase in demand.
   a. fair; and fair
   b. fair; but unfair
   c. unfair; but fair
   d. unfair; and unfair

37. Fill in the blanks. Researchers have found that sometimes firms will give up some profits in the _____ to keep their customers happy and increase their profits in the _____ .
    a. short run; long run
    b. long run; short run
    c. sale of some goods; sale of other goods
    d. early stages of product development; mature market

38. Based the textbook's description of Alan Krueger's study, which of the following statements best describes the policy the National Football League (NFL) uses to set the prices of Super Bowl tickets?
    a. The NFL attempts to set ticket prices at their equilibrium levels.
    b. The NFL sets prices at less than equilibrium levels to allow corporate sponsors and teams to resell tickets at higher prices.
    c. The NFL sets prices at greater than equilibrium levels to discourage ticket scalping.
    d. The NFL sets prices at less than equilibrium levels to avoid alienating football fans.

39. What do economists call the study of situations in which people act in ways that do not appear to be economically rational?
    a. normative economics
    b. rational economics
    c. behavioral economics
    d. the economics of fairness

40. Which of the following mistakes do consumers commonly commit when making decisions?
    a. They take into account monetary costs but ignore nonmonetary opportunity costs.
    b. They fail to ignore sunk costs.
    c. They are unrealistic about their future behavior.
    d. All of the above are mistakes consumers commonly commit when making decisions.

41. According to the endowment effect, people are unwilling to sell a good they already own in which of the following situations?
    a. if they are offered a price greater than the price they would pay if they did not already own the good
    b. if they are offered a price lower than the price they would have to pay to replace the good
    c. if they can't replace the good
    d. if the good was a gift that had great sentimental value

42. Which of the following reasons do economists use to explain why people are overweight?
    a. People undervalue the utility to be received in the future.
    b. People overvalue the utility from current choices.
    c. People's preferences are not consistent over time.
    d. All of the above explain why people are overweight.

Short Answer Questions

1. Is it possible for a normal good to have an upward-sloping demand curve? Explain briefly.

_____

_____

_____

_____

_____

_____

2. A Congressional representative explained his support for a spending project in his district by arguing "The bridge that is being built has cost the taxpayers of the United States $15 million. If we don't spend an additional $20 million to finish the bridge, the initial $15 million will be wasted. We owe it to the taxpayers to finish this project." Explain the decision-making mistake the representative made in this statement.

_____

_____

_____

_____

3. In Table 9-2 (page 283) in the textbook, you have a budget of $10 to spend on pizza and Coke, and the price of pizza is $2 per slice while the price of Coke is $1.00 per cup. You would maximize your utility by consuming 3 slices of pizza and 4 cups of Coke. What quantities of Coke and pizza would you consume if your budget increased to $13? What does your answer tell you about whether Coke and pizza are normal or inferior goods?

_____

_____

_____

_____

4. Some consumers argued that VHS video recorders used technology that was inferior to the technology used by Sony Betamax recorders. Nevertheless, VHS technology dominated the market for video recorders, and by the end of the twentieth century, Betamax recorders were so rare that their owners found it nearly impossible to purchase movies taped in Betamax format. Is this an example of market failure?

_____

_____

_____

_____

5. Approximately 20 percent of U.S. adults smoke cigarettes despite the documented health risks associated with smoking. Explain how the prevalence of smoking can be cited as an example of irrational decision making.

_____

_____

_____

_____

True/False Questions

T F 1. If total utility increases when you consume more of a good, then marginal utility must also be increasing as consumption rises.

T F 2. Marginal utility is the total utility a person receives from consuming one additional unit of a good or service.

T F 3. One of the conditions for maximizing utility is that total spending on goods must be equal to the amount available to be spent.

T F 4. For an inferior good, a price decrease increases a consumer's purchasing power and causes the quantity demanded to increase.

T F 5. Gary Becker and Kevin Murphy are among the economists who believe that social factors such as culture, customs, and religion do not explain the choices consumers make.

T F 6. Economists use the phrase "network externalities" to describe the role technology plays in explaining why consumers buy products that other consumers are already buying.

T F 7. Switching costs can explain why consumers buy products that have inferior technologies.

T F 8. A Giffen good has an upward-sloping demand curve.

T F 9. When the price of a normal good decreases, the substitution effect causes the quantity demanded to increase. When the price of an inferior good decreases, the substitution effect causes the quantity demanded to decrease.

T F 10. Economists believe that it is possible to measure utility in units called "utils."

T F 11. When economists state "optimal decisions are made at the margin" they mean that most decisions people make involve doing a little more of one thing or a little more of an alternative.

T F 12. Firms pay celebrities to endorse their products because they believe this will increase the demand for these products.

T F 13. Firms will sometimes not raise their prices, even when there is a large increase in demand for their products, because they fear consumers will consider the price increases unfair.

T F 14. Consumers often commit the mistake of ignoring sunk costs when they make decisions.

T F 15. The endowment effect is used to describe the mistake a consumer makes when he accounts for the monetary costs of his decisions but ignores the nonmonetary opportunity costs.

Answers to the Self-Test

Multiple-Choice Questions

Question	Answer	Comment
1	c	If utility increases from increased consumption, marginal utility is positive.
2	b	Figure 9-1 on page 282 in the textbook shows this clearly.
3	b	The table in Figure 9-1 on page 282 in the textbook confirms this fact.
4	d	According to the law of diminishing marginal utility, consumers experience diminishing additional satisfaction as they consume more of a good or service during a given period of time.
5	d	Total utility is the sum of marginal utilities. Therefore, total utility = 18 + 6 = 24.
6	c	Marginal utility is the additional utility caused by the consumption of one additional ice cream cone, so 18 − 10 = 8.
7	c	The marginal utility of the 5th ice cream cone is 2. Adding that to total utility from 4 ice cream cones yields 28 + 2 = 30.
8	a	As total utility increases, marginal utility decreases.
9	a	As total utility increases, marginal utility decreases, so the marginal utility curve would be downward sloping.
10	a	This is the definition of a budget constraint. See page 281 in the textbook.
11	a	Optimal decisions are made at the margin.
12	b	Increasing the consumption of good Y causes the marginal utility of good Y to decrease, thus lowering the numerator of that fraction and bringing both fractions into equality.
13	b	When a consumer maximizes utility subject to the budget constraint, the marginal utility of the last dollar spent on each good is the same.
14	a	Apply the utility maximizing rule. Because the marginal utility per dollar spent on X (60/10) is greater than the marginal utility per dollar spent on Y (15/5), the quantity of X consumed should increase. As the quantity consumed of good X increases, the MUx decreases, lowering the numerator and bringing both fractions closer to equality. At the same time, the quantity consumed of Y should decrease. This will increase the MU_Y, making both fractions equal.
15	c	The marginal utility of the 5th unit of good X is 8, and the price of X is $4, so the marginal utility per dollar spent on X is 2.
16	c	The marginal utility per dollar spent on the third unit of X (20/$4 = 5) equals the marginal utility per dollar spent on the fourth unit of Y (10/$2 = 5).
17	d	The marginal utility per dollar spent on the fourth unit of X (15/$3 = 5) equals the marginal utility per dollar spent on the fourth unit of Y (10/$2), and the consumer spends all of her income: $12 on X (4 units × $3 = $12) and $8 on Y (4 units × $2 = $8).

18	b	This is the definition of the substitution effect.
19	a	This is the definition of the income effect.
20	a	The lower price increases purchasing power and lowers the opportunity cost of consuming the good.
21	d	The income effect for an inferior good moves quantity demanded in the opposite direction from the substitution effect. A decrease in price increases purchasing power, which reduces the quantity demanded of the inferior good, while the lower price increases the quantity demanded of the inferior good.
22	b	When the price of an inferior good falls, the income and substitution effects work in opposite directions: The income effect causes consumers to decrease the quantity of the good they demand, whereas the substitution effect causes consumers to increase the quantity of the good they demand. It is possible, then, that consumers might actually buy less of a good when the price falls. If this happened, then the demand curve would be upward sloping.
23	a	A consumer responds optimally to the fall in the price of a product by consuming more of that product. When the price of pizza falls from $2 per slice to $1.50, the optimal quantity of slices consumed rises from 3 to 4. We assume that tastes and preferences, income, the price of related goods, and price expectations remain constant. When we graph this result, we have the consumer's demand curve.
24	c	For a demand curve to be upward sloping, the good would have to be an inferior good, and the income effect would have to be larger than the substitution effect. Goods that have both of these characteristics are called Giffen goods.
25	b	Although economists have traditionally believed social influences on consumer choice are unimportant, some consumers appear to receive utility from consuming goods that are popular with other consumers.
26	c	Whenever consumption takes place publicly, many consumers will base their purchasing decisions on what other consumers buy. Examples include eating in restaurants, attending sporting events, and wearing clothes or jewelry. In all these cases, the decision to buy a product will depend partly on the characteristics of the product and partly on how many other people are buying the product.
27	c	There are network externalities in the consumption of a product if the usefulness of the product increases with the number of consumers who use it. For example, if you owned the only telephone in the world, it would not be very useful.
28	c	Once a product becomes established, consumers may find it too costly to switch to a new product that contains a better technology. The selection of products may be *path dependent*. That means that because of switching costs, the technology that was first available may have advantages over better technologies that were developed later.
29	a	Some economists have argued that because of path dependence and switching costs, network externalities can result in market failures.
30	b	There is a great deal of evidence that people like to be treated fairly and that they usually attempt to treat others fairly, even if doing so makes them worse off financially. Tipping servers in restaurants is an example.
31	b	There are many other examples where people willingly part with money when they are not required to do so and when they receive nothing material in return. The most obvious example is making donations to charity.
32	a	If neither the allocator nor the recipient cared about fairness, optimal play in the ultimatum game is straightforward: The allocator should propose a division of the money in which the allocator receives $19.99 and the recipient receives $0.01. The allocator has maximized his or her gain. The recipient should accept the division, because the alternative is to reject the division and receive nothing at all.

33	b	When the ultimatum game experiment is carried out, both allocators and recipients act as if fairness is important. Allocators usually offer recipients at least a 40 percent share of the money, and recipients almost always reject offers of less than a 10 percent share.
34	a	At this price, the quantity demanded is greater than the quantity supplied.
35	b	The theater could raise the price, but a concern for fairness will lead them to keep the price of tickets at $75, even though the result is a shortage of tickets.
36	b	Most people consider it fair for firms to raise their prices following an increase in costs but unfair to raise prices following an increase in demand.
37	a	Kahneman, Knetsch, and Thaler have concluded that firms may sometimes not raise their prices when quantity demanded for their products is greater than the quantity supplied out of fear that in the long run they will end up losing customers who believe the price increases were unfair (see page 295).
38	d	When asked whether it would "be fair for the NFL to raise the [price of tickets] to $1,500 if that is still less than the amount most people are willing to pay for tickets," 92 percent of the fans surveyed answered "no." Even 83 percent of the fans who had paid more than $1,500 for their tickets answered "no." Krueger concluded that whatever the NFL might gain in the short run from raising ticket prices, it would more than lose in the long run from alienating football fans.
39	c	See page 296 in the textbook.
40	d	Consumers commonly commit the following three mistakes when making decisions: They take into account monetary costs but ignore nonmonetary opportunity costs. They fail to ignore sunk costs. They are overly optimistic about their future behavior. See page 296 in the textbook.
41	a	The endowment effect is the tendency of people to be unwilling to sell something they already own even if they are offered a price that is greater than the price they would be willing to pay to buy the good if they didn't already own it.
42	d	Because people are unrealistic about their future behavior, they underestimate the costs of choices—like overeating or smoking—that they make today. One way they could avoid this problem is to be realistic about their future behavior.

Short Answer Responses

1. No. Assume that the price of a normal good (apples) increased. The substitution effect from this price change would cause the quantity of apples demanded to decrease. Because apples are a normal good, the income effect would cause the quantity demanded to decrease also. If apples were an inferior good, then the income effect would cause quantity demanded to increase. Apples would have an upward-sloping demand curve only if (a) they were an inferior good and (b) the income effect of the price increase was greater than the substitution effect.

2. The representative fails to recognize that the $15 million spent on bridge construction is a sunk cost that should be ignored when deciding whether the project merits additional spending so that the bridge can be finished. The representative should ignore the money that has already been spent and explain why the additional expenditure of $20 million is justified.

3. You should consume the quantity of pizza and Coke that makes the marginal utility per dollar equal and spends your entire budget. If the budget increases to $13, you would want to consume 4 slices of pizza and 5 cups of Coke to maximize your utility. Because the increase in income resulted in an increase in the quantity demanded of both Coke and pizza, the goods must both be normal goods.

4. Some economists argue that because of switching costs and path dependence, network externalities can result in market failure. In their view, the triumph of VHS technology can be seen as market failure. But other economists, such as Stephen Margolis and Stan Leibowitz, argue that network externalities do not lock consumers into using inferior technology and that the evidence that Betamax technology was truly superior is unconvincing. This is an area where there is no consensus opinion among mainstream economists. (See page 293 in the textbook.)

5. This is an example of people being unrealistic about their future behavior. Those who are addicted to nicotine have difficulty quitting because of the withdrawal effects, including nervousness, irritability, and weight gain. As a result, the decision to quit smoking is put off into the future even though the withdrawal effects will not be avoided. Many adults who smoke might like to quit in the long run, but their short-run decisions are inconsistent with their long-run goals.

True/False Answers

1. F   Total utility increases, even if marginal utility (the change in total utility from consuming one more unit) decreases.
2. F   Marginal utility is the *increase* in total utility a person receives from consuming one additional unit of a good or service.
3. T   To maximize utility we must spend our total budget.
4. F   This describes the income effect for a normal good, not an inferior good.
5. F   These economists believe that the mentioned factors *do* influence decision making.
6. T   The product becomes more useful as more consumers purchase and use the product.
7. F   Switching costs can explain why consumers continue to use a previously purchased product that presently contains inferior technology.
8. T   For Giffen goods, as the price increases so does the quantity demanded. Giffen goods are inferior goods that have an income effect that is stronger than the substitution effect.
9. F   If the price of either a normal good or an inferior good decreases, the substitution effect will cause quantity demanded to increase. It is the direction of the income effect that is different across normal and inferior goods.
10. F   At one time, some economists believed that this might be possible.
11. T   Marginal decision making involves small, incremental changes.
12. T   Consumers may buy products endorsed by celebrities to be fashionable or to feel closer to the celebrities.
13. T   See the section entitled "Does Fairness Matter?" that begins on page 293.
14. F   In fact, consumers should ignore sunk costs when they make decisions, but they often don't.
15. F   The endowment effect is the tendency of people to be unwilling to sell a good they already own even if they are offered a price that is greater than the price they would be willing to pay to buy the good if they didn't already own it.

CHAPTER 10 | Technology, Production, and Costs

Chapter Summary and Learning Objectives

10.1 Technology: An Economic Definition (pages 326–327)
Define technology and give examples of technological change. The basic activity of a firm is to use inputs, such as workers, machines, and natural resources, to produce goods and services. The firm's **technology** is the processes it uses to turn inputs into goods and services. **Technological change** refers to a change in the ability of a firm to produce a given level of output with a given quantity of inputs.

10.2 The Short Run and the Long Run in Economics (pages 327–331)
Distinguish between the economic short run and the economic long run. In the **short run**, a firm's technology and the size of its factory, store, or office are fixed. In the **long run**, a firm is able to adopt new technology and to increase or decrease the size of its physical plant. **Total cost** is the cost of all the inputs a firm uses in production. **Variable costs** are costs that change as output changes. **Fixed costs** are costs that remain constant as output changes. **Opportunity cost** is the highest-valued alternative that must be given up to engage in an activity. An **explicit cost** is a cost that involves spending money. An **implicit cost** is a nonmonetary opportunity cost. The relationship between the inputs employed by a firm and the maximum output it can produce with those inputs is called the firm's **production function**.

10.3 The Marginal Product of Labor and the Average Product of Labor (pages 331–335)
Understand the relationship between the marginal product of labor and the average product of labor. The **marginal product of labor** is the additional output produced by a firm as a result of hiring one more worker. Specialization and division of labor cause the marginal product of labor to rise for the first few workers hired. Eventually, the **law of diminishing returns** causes the marginal product of labor to decline. The **average product of labor** is the total amount of output produced by a firm divided by the quantity of workers hired. When the marginal product of labor is greater than the average product of labor, the average product of labor increases. When the marginal product of labor is less than the average product of labor, the average product of labor decreases.

10.4 The Relationship between Short-Run Production and Short-Run Cost (pages 335–337)
Explain and illustrate the relationship between marginal cost and average total cost. The **marginal cost** of production is the increase in total cost resulting from producing another unit of output. The marginal cost curve has a U shape because when the marginal product of labor is rising, the marginal cost of output is falling. When the marginal product of labor is falling, the marginal cost of output is rising. When marginal cost is less than average total cost, average total cost falls. When marginal cost is greater than average total cost, average total cost rises.

10.5 Graphing Cost Curves (page 338)
Graph average total cost, average variable cost, average fixed cost, and marginal cost. **Average fixed cost** is equal to fixed cost divided by the level of output. **Average variable cost** is equal to variable cost divided by the level of output. Figure 10-5 on page 339 in the text book shows the relationship among marginal cost, average total cost, average variable cost, and average fixed cost. It is one of the most important graphs in microeconomics.

10.6   Costs in the Long Run (pages 338–343)
Understand how firms use the long-run average cost curve in their planning. The **long-run average cost curve** shows the lowest cost at which a firm is able to produce a given level of output in the long run. For many firms, the long-run average cost curve falls as output expands because of **economies of scale**. **Minimum efficient scale** is the level of output at which all economies of scale have been exhausted. After economies of scale have been exhausted, firms experience **constant returns to scale**, where their long-run average cost curve is flat. At high levels of output, the long-run average cost curve turns up as the firm experiences **diseconomies of scale**.

Appendix: Using Isoquants and Isocosts to Understand Production and Cost (pages 355–365)
Use isoquants and isocost lines to understand production and cost.

Chapter Review

Chapter Opener: Sony Uses a Cost Curve to Determine the Price of Radios (page 325)

The introduction to the chapter uses a story related by Sony Corporation chairman Akio Morita regarding the behavior of his firm's average costs of production. Sony's cost per unit, or average cost, changes as it increases its rate of output. At first, average cost falls as output increases, but eventually increases as output increases further. The U shape of Sony's average total cost curve is typical of most firms' average total cost curves.

10.1 Technology: An Economic Definition (pages 326–327)
Learning Objective: Define technology and give examples of technological change.

Technology is the processes a firm uses to turn inputs into outputs of goods and services. **Technological change** is a change in the ability of a firm to produce a given level of output with a given quantity of inputs. Positive technological change results from changes such as rearranging the layout of a store and purchasing faster or more reliable machinery. Positive technological change causes more output to be produced from the same inputs or the same output from fewer inputs. Negative technological change may result from changes such as hiring less-skilled workers or damage to buildings due to inclement weather. The result is a decline in the quantity of output that can be produced from a given quantity of inputs.

📖 Study Hint
Do not confuse technological change with invention. An invention is the development of a new product or process for making a product. An invention or discovery of new information, such as a chemical formula, is not technological change. Technological change results from the application of new or old knowledge to a production process. *Making the Connection* "Improving Inventory Control at Wal-Mart" provides an example of technological change in which Wal-Mart uses electronic point-of-sale information and just-in-time (JIT) delivery to manage its inventories and supply chain to fulfill the needs of the customer and grow the business. A number of other firms have followed in Wal-Mart's footsteps by incorporating JIT and electronic inventory controls into their production process to increase their efficiency.

Extra Solved Problem 10-1
Technological Change: Wright and Wrong
Supports Learning Objective 10.1: Define technology and give examples of technological change.

Decades can pass before a new idea is developed to the point where it can be widely used. For instance, the Wright brothers first achieved self-propelled flight at Kitty Hawk, North Carolina, in 1903. But their plane was very crude, and it wasn't until the introduction of the DC-3 by Douglas Aircraft in 1936 that regularly scheduled intercity flights became common in the United States. Similarly, the development of the first digital electronic computer—the ENIAC—occurred in 1945, but the first IBM personal computer was not introduced until 1981. It wasn't until the 1990s that widespread use of computers began to have a significant effect on the productivity of American business.

In 1999, Hershey Foods, manufacturer of Hershey's bars and Reese's Peanut Butter Cups, installed a new software program designed by the German company SAP to coordinate almost all of the company's operations. Unfortunately, it took Hershey many months to get the software to work properly. During the period when the software was not working well, Hershey failed to send out some shipments and other shipments contained less candy than they were supposed to have. Software problems made it difficult for Hershey to keep track of what had been shipped and to whom it had been shipped. The company lost $150 million worth of sales before the problem was corrected and the software began to work as intended.

Sources: For DC-3 and ENIAC, David Mowery and Nathan Rosenberg, "Twentieth Century Technological Change," in Stanley L. Engerman and Robert Gallman, eds., *The Cambridge Economic History of the United States, Vol. III: The Twentieth Century*, Cambridge: Cambridge University Press, 2000. For Hershey: Emily Nelson and Evan Ramstad, "Trick or Treat: Hershey's Biggest Dud Has Turned Out to Be Its New Technology," *Wall Street Journal*, October 29, 1999 and "Hershey Foods Warns 1999 Earnings Will Be Worse Than Initially Feared," *Dow Jones Business News*, December 28, 1999.

a. Define technology and technological change.

b. Was the Wright Brothers' 1903 flight at Kitty Hawk an example of technological change? Was the development of the ENIAC computer an example of technological change?

c. Explain why the widespread use of computers in the 1990s resulted in positive technological change.

d. Did Hershey's use of a new software program in 1999 result in positive or negative technological change?

SOLVING THE PROBLEM:
Step 1: **Review the chapter material.**
This problem is about technology and technological change, so you may want to review the section "Technology: An Economic Definition," which begins on page 326 in the textbook.
Step 2: **Define technology and technological change.**
A firm's technology is the process it uses to turn inputs into outputs of goods and services. Technological change is the change in the ability to produce a given level of output with a given quantity of inputs.
Step 3: **Was the Wright Brothers' 1903 flight at Kitty Hawk an example of technological change? Was the development of the ENIAC computer an example of technological change?**
Neither the Wright Brothers' 1903 flight at Kitty Hawk nor the development of ENIAC represents technological change because there was no impact on the ability of firms to produce output with a different quantity of inputs.

Step 4:   **Explain why the widespread use of computers in the 1990s resulted in positive technological change.**
The widespread use of computers led to an improvement in productivity. Many firms were able to produce the same output of goods and services with fewer inputs or more output with the same quantity of inputs.

Step 5:   **Did Hershey's use of a new software program in 1999 result in positive or negative technological change?**
The initial use of the software produced negative technological change because Hershey's output was less with the same quantity of inputs. After the "bugs" were eliminated, the use of this software produced positive technological change.

10.2   **The Short Run and the Long Run in Economics (pages 327–331)**
Learning Objective: Distinguish between the economic short run and the economic long run.

The **short run** is a period of time during which at least one of the firm's inputs is fixed. The **long run** is a period of time long enough to allow a firm to vary all of its inputs, to adopt new technology, and to increase or decrease the size of its physical plant. **Total cost** is the cost of all the inputs a firm uses in production. **Variable costs** are costs that change as output changes. **Fixed costs** are costs that remain constant as output changes.

$$\text{Total Cost } (TC) = \text{Fixed Cost } (FC) + \text{Variable Cost } (VC)$$

In the long run, all costs are variable because the quantities of all inputs are variable.

Total costs can also be divided into explicit and implicit costs. An **explicit cost** is a cost that involves spending money. An **implicit cost** is a nonmonetary opportunity cost. Recall from Chapters 1 and 2 that the **opportunity cost** of an activity is the highest-valued alternative that must be given up to engage in the activity. Opportunity costs can include both explicit and implicit costs.

The **production function** is the relationship between the inputs employed by the firm and the maximum output it can produce with those inputs. In the short run, at least one input is fixed, so the short-run production function shows the level of output the firm can produce with different levels of the variable inputs and a constant quantity of the fixed input. The long-run production function shows the maximum quantity of output the firm can produce using various levels of all inputs. Knowing how many inputs are required to produce a given level of output allows you to determine the total cost of production as well. The **average total cost** is total cost divided by the quantity of output produced. The average total cost curve often has a U shape.

Study Hint

An example may help you to understand the difference between a short-run and a long-run production function. Your hometown probably has a theater, stadium, or auditorium. Various events are held at these venues during the year, some of which may sell out while others do not. In the short run, the size of the facility is a fixed input and variations in crowd size can be accommodated by changes in the use of variable inputs (such as ticket takers, ushers, parking attendants, and food at refreshment stands). It is unlikely that the owners will decide to increase or decrease the capacity of the facility unless they expect a permanent change in average expected attendance. Such a permanent change could be the result of an increase or decrease in the population served by the facility or the acquisition or loss of a permanent tenant; for example, a professional sports franchise or a philharmonic orchestra. Expanding or contracting the size of the facility (usually by tearing down the existing structure and building a new one) is an example of a long-run production decision. See *Making the Connection* "Fixed Costs in the Publishing Industry" for a discussion of fixed costs in the editing and marketing of books. Because the number of editors, designers, and marketing people does not vary with the number of copies of books that are sold in a given year, publishers treat the salaries and benefits of people in these job categories as fixed costs.

Extra Solved Problem 10-2

Apple Picking

Supports Learning Objective 10.2: Distinguish between the economic short run and the economic long run.

Suppose that you own an apple orchard and the following chart represents the number of apples that can be picked from your orchard on a per-hour basis with a given quantity of capital equipment, such as baskets and ladders.

Quantity of Workers	Apples	Fixed Cost	Variable Cost	Total Cost	Cost per Apple (Average Total Cost)
0	0	$10	$0		
1	100	10	5		
2	210	10	10		
3	290	10	15		
4	340	10	20		
5	360	10	25		

a. Complete the table above by calculating the total cost and the average total cost.

b. Does the total cost in the table represent your short-run or long-run total cost?

SOLVING THE PROBLEM

Step 1:   Review the chapter material.

This problem is about distinguishing short-run and long-run costs, so you may want to review the section, "The Short Run and the Long Run in Economics," which begins on page 327 in the textbook.

Step 2: **Answer question (a) by computing the total cost and the average total cost.**

Total cost is calculated by adding the fixed costs to the variable costs. The average total cost is the total cost divided by the quantity. The table below provides the results of the calculations.

Quantity of Workers	Apples	Fixed Cost	Variable Cost	Total Cost	Cost per Apple (Average Total Cost)
0	0	$10	$0	$10	–
1	100	10	5	15	$ 0.15
2	210	10	10	20	0.10
3	290	10	15	25	0.09
4	340	10	20	30	0.09
5	360	10	25	35	0.10

Step 3: **Answer question (b) by determining whether the costs and production function shown in the table are representative of the short run or the long run.**

To determine whether this is the short run or the long run, we need to determine if all inputs are variable or if at least one input is fixed. In the description of the problem, we see that the number of ladders and baskets is fixed, so we are looking at the short-run condition. This is reinforced by the fact that your orchard is experiencing a positive and constant fixed cost.

10.3 The Marginal Product of Labor and the Average Product of Labor (pages 331–335)

Learning Objective: Understand the relationship between the marginal product of labor and the average product of labor.

The **marginal product of labor** is the additional output a firm produces as a result of hiring one more worker. The increases in marginal product of labor that occur at low rates of output result from specialization and the division of labor. Consider for instance, a firm that initially employs only one worker. Adding a second or third worker, for example, would typically reduce the time the workers spend moving from one activity to the next and allow them to become more specialized at their tasks. At some point, adding more of a variable input, such as labor, to the same amount of a fixed input, such as capital, will cause the marginal product of the variable input to decline. This principle is called the **law of diminishing returns**. When the marginal product of labor is decreasing, but still positive, total output increases, but at a decreasing rate.

The **average product of labor** is the total output produced by a firm divided by the quantity of workers. When the marginal product of labor is greater than the average product of labor, the average product of labor must be increasing. When the marginal product of labor is less than the average product of labor, the average product of labor must be decreasing. The marginal product of labor equals the average product of labor for the quantity of workers where the average product of labor is at a maximum.

📖 **Study Hint**
The relationship between the marginal product of labor and average product of labor is similar to many other marginal-average relationships. You will better understand the relationship between the two after reviewing the example of GPAs illustrated in Figure 10-3. Also read *Making the Connection* "Adam Smith's Famous Account of the Division of Labor in a Pin Factory" for a discussion of how the division of labor can increase the average output per worker. Smith describes how workers become very specialized in a particular part of the production process with the division of labor and, thus, become more productive.

Extra Solved Problem 10-3

Apple Picking—Continued
Supports Learning Objective 10.3: Understand the relationship between the marginal product of labor and the average product of labor.

Suppose that you own an apple orchard and the following chart represents the number of apples that can be picked from your orchard on a per-hour basis with the given capital equipment, including five baskets.

Quantity of Workers	Quantity of Baskets	Apples	Marginal Product of Labor	Average Product of Labor
0	5	0		
1	5	100		
2	5	210		
3	5	290		
4	5	340		
5	5	360		

a. Complete the table above by calculating the marginal product of labor and the average product of labor.

b. Describe the relationship between marginal product of labor and the orchard's total production. Does the law of diminishing returns apply to the orchard's production?

c. Describe the relationship between the marginal product of labor and the average product of labor.

SOLVING THE PROBLEM
Step 1:   Review the chapter material.
This problem is about marginal and average product of labor, so you may want to review the section "The Marginal Product of Labor and the Average Product of Labor," which begins on page 331 in the textbook.

Step 2: **Answer question (a) by computing the marginal product of labor and the average product of labor.**

The marginal product of labor is the additional output a firm produces as a result of hiring one more worker. This is calculated by dividing the change in the quantity of apples produced by the change in the quantity of labor used to produce the apples. The average product of labor is the total output produced by a firm divided by the quantity of workers used to produce that output. The results of these calculations are displayed in the table below.

Quantity of Workers	Quantity of Baskets	Apples	Marginal Product of Labor	Average Product of Labor
0	5	0		
1	5	100	100	100
2	5	210	110	105
3	5	290	80	97
4	5	340	50	85
5	5	360	20	72

Step 3: **Answer question (b) by explaining the relationship between the marginal product and the total output.**

When the marginal product is increasing rapidly, the firm's total output increases rapidly. As the gains from specialization and the division of labor are exhausted, an additional increase in labor causes the marginal product to fall. Total output continues to increase but at a decreasing rate as the marginal product falls. See Figure 10-2 on page 332 in the textbook to see an example of this.

Step 4: **Answer question (c) by describing the relationship between the marginal product of labor and the average product of labor.**

When the marginal product of labor is greater than the average product of labor, the average product of labor will increase. When the marginal product of labor is lower than the average product of labor, the average product of labor will decrease. The marginal product of the second worker is 110, which is higher than the average product of 100 apples per worker, causing the average product of two workers to rise from 100 to 105. When the third worker is hired, only 80 additional apples are picked, which is less than the average of 105. The addition of the third worker whose marginal product was less productive than average pulls down the average product from 105 to 97. (See the GPA example on page 334 in the textbook for an example of how the marginal value drives the average value.)

10.4 **The Relationship between Short-Run Production and Short-Run Cost (pages 335–337)**

Learning Objective: Explain and illustrate the relationship between marginal cost and average total cost.

In the short run, the behavior of the marginal product of the variable factor is represented in the behavior of marginal cost. **Marginal cost** is the change in a firm's total cost from producing one more unit of a good or service. The U shape of the average total cost curve is determined by the shape of the marginal cost curve. Marginal cost (*MC*) can be expressed mathematically as

$$MC = \frac{\Delta TC}{\Delta Q}$$

where Δ represents "change in," *TC* is total cost, and *Q* is output.

The law of diminishing returns explains the behavior of the marginal product of the variable factor in the short run. This is illustrated in the table that is part of Figure 10-4 on page 336 in the textbook. The table in this figure shows how the marginal product of labor rises for the first and second workers, and the marginal cost falls as these first two workers are hired. As diminishing returns set in, the marginal product of labor falls and the marginal cost rises as the last four workers are hired. The marginal cost of production falls and then rises—a U shape—because the marginal product of labor rises and then falls.

📖 **Study Hint**

Solved Problem 10-4 shows how, as diminishing returns set in, the average and marginal costs of production rise. Work related end-of-chapter problems 4.5 and 4.6 for further help in understanding the law of diminishing returns and its relationship to costs.

10.5 **Graphing Cost Curves (page 338)**
Learning Objective: Graph average total cost, average variable cost, average fixed cost, and marginal cost.

Several related average cost measures can be described mathematically.

Remember that average total cost (*ATC*) equals total cost (*TC*) divided by the quantity of output produced.

$$ATC = \frac{TC}{Q}$$

Average fixed cost (*AFC*) equals fixed cost divided by the quantity of output produced.

$$AFC = \frac{FC}{Q}$$

Average variable cost (*AVC*) equals variable cost divided by the quantity of output produced.

$$AVC = \frac{VC}{Q}$$

Average total cost (ATC) can then be calculated as the sum of average fixed cost and average variable cost.

$$ATC = AFC + AVC$$

The *MC*, *ATC*, and *AVC* curves are all U-shaped. Here are key points about these curves:

- The *MC* curve intersects the *AVC* and *ATC* curves at their minimum points.
- When *MC* is below *AVC* or *ATC*, it causes them to decrease, and when *MC* is above *AVC* or *ATC*, it causes them to increase.
- As output increases, the difference between *ATC* and *AVC* (this is equal to *AFC*) gets smaller because *AFC* gets smaller and smaller as output increases.

📖 Study Hint

To draw the curves accurately, it is best to draw the *MC* curve first. Then draw *ATC*, but start by putting your pencil or pen on the *MC* curve and drawing the left half of *ATC* so that it curves up and to the left. Go back to the *MC* curve and then draw the right half of *ATC* so that it curves up and to the right. This ensures that the minimum point of *ATC* is where *ATC* crosses *MC*. Follow the same procedure to draw *AVC* below *ATC*. When you draw the left half of *AVC*, make sure that the difference between *ATC* and *AVC* becomes greater as output decreases. When you draw the right half of *AVC*, make the difference between *ATC* and *AVC* smaller as output increases. Remember that the difference between *ATC* and *AVC* is *AFC* (average fixed cost), which gets smaller as output increases.

Extra Solved Problem 10-5

Apple Picking—Continued
Supports Learning Objective 10.5: Graph average total cost, average variable cost, average fixed cost, and marginal cost.

Suppose that you own an apple orchard and the following chart represents the quantity of apples that can be picked from your orchard per hour with a given quantity of capital equipment, such as baskets and ladders.

Quantity of Workers	Apples	Fixed Cost	Variable Cost	Total Cost	Cost per Apple (*ATC*)	*MC*	*AVC*	*AFC*
0	0	10	0	10				
1	100	10	5	15				
2	210	10	10	20				
3	290	10	15	25				
4	340	10	20	30				
5	360	10	25	35				

a. Complete the table above by calculating the average total cost, marginal cost, average variable cost, and the average fixed cost.

b. Graph the marginal cost, average total cost, average variable cost, and average fixed cost curves.

SOLVING THE PROBLEM

Step 1:   Review the chapter material.

To complete this problem you may want to review the section "Graphing Cost Curves" on page 338 in the textbook.

Step 2: **Answer question (a) by computing the marginal cost, the average variable cost, and the average fixed cost.**

The average total cost is the total cost divided by the quantity of output. The average fixed cost is the fixed cost divided by the quantity of output produced. Average variable cost is calculated by dividing variable cost by the quantity of units produced. The marginal cost is the change in a firm's total cost from producing one more unit of a good or service. The results of these calculations are presented below. (Hint: Don't make the mistake of using the quantity of workers in these calculations; use the quantity of apples produced.)

Quantity of Workers	Apples	Fixed Cost	Variable Cost	Total Cost	Cost per Apple (*ATC*)	*MC*	*AVC*	*AFC*
0	0	10	0	10				
1	100	10	5	15	$0.15	$.05	$.050	$.100
2	210	10	10	20	0.10	.05	.047	.048
3	290	10	15	25	0.09	.06	.052	.034
4	340	10	20	30	0.09	.10	.059	.029
5	360	10	25	35	0.10	.25	.069	.028

Step 3: **Answer question (b) by graphing the cost curves.**

To graph each of the average cost curves and the marginal cost curve, consider what the cost is for each given quantity. The graph of the curves is as follows:

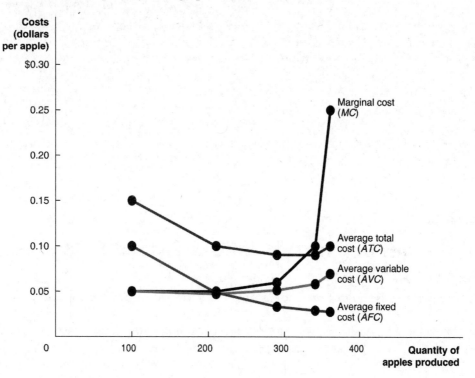

10.6 Costs in the Long Run (pages 338–343)

Learning Objective: Understand how firms use the long-run average cost curve in their planning.

There are no fixed costs in the long run, so total cost equals variable cost. In the short run, managers of firms decide how they will operate their current store, office, or factory. In the long run, managers decide whether the firm would be more profitable if the store, office, or factory were made larger or smaller.

A **long-run average cost curve** shows the lowest cost at which the firm is able to produce a given quantity of output in the long run, when no inputs are fixed. **Economies of scale** is the situation when a firm's long-run average total costs fall as it increases output. **Constant returns to scale** is the situation when a firm's long-run average costs remain unchanged as it increases output. **Minimum efficient scale** is the level of output at which all economies of scale have been exhausted. **Diseconomies of scale** is the situation when a firm's long-run average costs rise as it increases output.

Economies of scale may result from several factors. The firm's technology may make it possible to increase production with a smaller than proportional increase in at least one input. As output expands, both workers and managers may become more specialized, enabling them to be more productive. Large firms may be able to purchase inputs at lower costs than smaller competitors. Diseconomies of scale result when managers have difficulty coordinating a firm as it grows in scale.

📖 Study Hint

Long-run average cost curves, such as those shown in *Solved Problem 10-6*, are drawn as smooth U-shaped curves. Do not confuse these curves with short-run average total cost curves. Read *Don't Let This Happen to YOU!* "Don't Confuse Diminishing Returns with Diseconomies of Scale," which explains why there are different explanations for the U shape of the short-run and long-run curves. The smooth long-run average cost curve is similar to the optical illusion of a motion picture. A motion picture is essentially a series of still photographs that when projected sequentially (and rapidly) give the viewer the illusion of live, continuous motion. Similarly, the long-run average cost curve is made up of a series of short-run *ATC* curves, each of which contributes a small portion (one point) of the long-run average cost curve. As the plant size increases or decrease, the effect of the plant size on the production cost (that is, economies and diseconomies of scale) determines the shape of the long-run average cost curve. The shape of the short-run average cost curve, however, is determined by diminishing returns.

Appendix
Using Isoquants and Isocosts to Understand Production and Cost (pages 355–365)

Learning Objective: Use isoquants and isocost lines to understand production and cost.

The chapter covers the relationship between a firm's level of production and its costs. This appendix looks more closely at how firms choose the *combination of inputs* to produce a given level of output.

Isoquants

Firms search for the cost-minimizing combination of inputs that will allow them to produce a given level of output. The cost-minimizing combination of inputs depends on technology and input prices. An

isoquant is a curve showing all the combinations of two inputs, such as capital and labor, that will produce the same level of output. The farther an isoquant is from the origin—the farther to the right on the graph—the more output the firm is producing. There are many isoquants, one for every possible level of output.

The **marginal rate of technical substitution (*MRTS*)** is the rate at which a firm is able to substitute one input for another while keeping the level of output constant. The slope of an isoquant becomes less steep as one moves downward along the isoquant. This is a consequence of diminishing returns.

> 📖 **Study Hint**
> Figure 10A-1 illustrates three isoquants, each of which represents various combinations of capital (measured on the vertical axis) and labor (measured on the horizontal axis) that enable Jill to produce a given number of pizzas per week. Isoquants are similar to indifference curves in several respects. If you understand the analysis of indifference curves in the appendix to Chapter 9, then you should understand isoquants.

Isocost Lines

The relationship between the quantity of inputs used and the firm's total cost can be shown with an **isocost line**. An isocost line shows all the combinations of two inputs, such as capital and labor, that have the same total cost. An isocost line intersects the vertical axis at the maximum amount of an input (for example, capital) that can be purchased with a given budget, or total cost. The same isocost line intersects the horizontal axis at the maximum amount of another input (for example, labor) that can be purchased with the same budget. One input is substituted for another as one moves along an isocost line, but the total expenditure on inputs is the same. The slope of an isocost line is constant and equals the change in the quantity of one input (capital) divided by the change in the quantity of the other input (labor). The slope of an isocost line is equal to the ratio of the price of the input on the horizontal axis divided by the price of the input on the vertical axis, multiplied by negative 1. A change in the price of an input causes the slope to change, which is a rotation of the isocost line. Higher levels of total cost shift the isocost line outward, and lower levels of cost shift the isocost line inward.

> 📖 **Study Hint**
> Figure 10A-2 on page 357 in the textbook illustrates an example of an isocost line. The analysis of isocost lines is similar to the analysis of budget lines in the appendix to Chapter 9.

Choosing the Cost-Minimizing Combination of Capital and Labor

If diminishing returns exist, there will be only one combination of inputs that will produce a given amount of output at the lowest total cost. The lowest cost combination of inputs that will produce a given level of output is found at the tangency of an isocost line with the isoquant that represents the given output level. At the point of cost minimization, the *MRTS* is equal to the price of the input measured on the horizontal axis (for example, the wage rate or price of labor) divided by the price of the input measured on the vertical axis (for example, the rental price of capital).

The cost-minimizing choice of inputs is determined jointly by available production technology and input prices. A change in technology affects the position of isoquants and may affect the choice of inputs. If input prices change, then the position of isocost lines will change and the choice of inputs may also change.

Moving along an isoquant, the output is constant while the amounts of two inputs change. The marginal product of capital (MP_K) equals the change in output from using an additional unit of capital. The marginal product of labor (MP_L) equals the change in output from using an additional unit of labor. Because the loss in output from using lower capital equals the gain in output from using more workers along an isoquant,

–Change in the quantity of capital $\times$ MP_K = Change in the quantity of labor $\times$ MP_L.

Rewriting this equation:

$$-\frac{\text{Change in the quantity of capital}}{\text{Change in the quantity of labor}} = MRTS = \frac{MP_L}{MP_K}$$

The slope of the isocost line equals the wage rate (w) divided by the rental price of capital (r). At the point of cost minimization, the slope of the isoquant equals the slope of the isocost line. Therefore:

$$\frac{MP_L}{MP_K} = \frac{w}{r}$$

or, after rearranging, $\dfrac{MP_L}{w} = \dfrac{MP_K}{r}$

The last equation implies that to minimize cost, a firm should hire inputs up to the point where the last dollar spent on each input results in the same increase in output.

📖 Study Hint

Solved Problem 10A-1 explains how Jill can find the cost minimizing combination of inputs to produce pizza. A firm should purchase or hire inputs up to the point where the ratio of the marginal product to the price of the input is the same for every input used. If one input has a higher marginal product for the last dollar spent, then the firm should hire more of that input and less of the other input to minimize the costs of production.

The Expansion Path

An **expansion path** is a curve that shows a firm's cost-minimizing combination of inputs for every level of output. The expansion path represents the least-cost combination of inputs to produce a given level of output in the long run when the firm is able to vary the levels of all of its inputs. In the short run, at least one of the firm's inputs is fixed. The expansion of output is possible only by varying the firm's variable input(s), so the firm's minimum total costs of production are lower in the long run than in the short run.

Key Terms

Average fixed cost Fixed cost divided by the quantity of output produced.

Average product of labor The total output produced by a firm divided by the quantity of workers.

Average total cost Total cost divided by the quantity of output produced.

Average variable cost Variable cost divided by the quantity of output produced.

Constant returns to scale The situation when a firm's long-run average costs remain unchanged as it increases output.

Diseconomies of scale The situation when a firm's long-run average costs rise as the firm increases output.

Economies of scale The situation when a firm's long-run average costs fall as it increases output.

Explicit cost A cost that involves spending money.

Fixed costs Costs that remain constant as output changes.

Implicit cost A nonmonetary opportunity cost.

Law of diminishing returns The principle that, at some point, adding more of a variable input, such as labor, to the same amount of a fixed input, such as capital, will cause the marginal product of the variable input to decline.

Long run The period of time in which a firm can vary all its inputs, adopt new technology, and increase or decrease the size of its physical plant.

Long-run average cost curve A curve showing the lowest cost at which a firm is able to produce a given quantity of output in the long run, when no inputs are fixed.

Marginal cost The change in a firm's total cost from producing one more unit of a good or service.

Marginal product of labor The additional output a firm produces as a result of hiring one more worker.

Minimum efficient scale The level of output at which all economies of scale are exhausted.

Opportunity cost The highest-valued alternative that must be given up to engage in an activity.

Production function The relationship between the inputs employed by a firm and the maximum output it can produce with those inputs.

Short run The period of time during which at least one of a firm's inputs is fixed.

Technological change A change in the ability of a firm to produce a given level of output with a given quantity of inputs.

Technology The processes a firm uses to turn inputs into outputs of goods and services.

Total cost The cost of all the inputs a firm uses in production.

Variable costs Costs that change as output changes.

Key Terms—Appendix

Expansion path A curve that shows a firm's cost-minimizing combination of inputs for every level of output.

Isocost line All the combinations of two inputs, such as capital and labor, that have the same total cost.

Isoquant A curve that shows all the combinations of two inputs, such as capital and labor, that will produce the same level of output.

Marginal rate of technical substitution (*MRTS*) The rate at which a firm is able to substitute one input for another while keeping the level of output constant.

Self-Test

(Answers are provided at the end of the Self-Test.)

Multiple-Choice Questions

1. The processes a firm uses to turn inputs into outputs of goods and services is _____.
   a. technology
   b. technological change
   c. the short run
   d. the production function

2. The term used to describe a change in the ability of a firm to produce a given level of output with a given level of inputs is called _____.
   a. technology
   b. technological change
   c. the long run
   d. the production function

3. What is the short run?
   a. a period of time during which a firm can vary all of its inputs
   b. a period of time during which a firm can adopt a new technology
   c. a period of time during which a firm can increase or decrease the size of its physical plant
   d. a period of time during which at least one of the firm's inputs is fixed

4. Which costs are affected by the level of output produced?
   a. fixed costs
   b. variable costs
   c. all costs
   d. sunk costs

5. If the number of people in a publishing company does not go up or down with the quantity of books it publishes, then how should we categorize the salaries and benefits paid to these employees?
   a. They are part of fixed cost.
   b. They are part of variable cost.
   c. They are an implicit cost.
   d. They are not considered a part of the cost of production.

6. Which of the following is known as the highest-valued alternative that must be given up in order to engage in an activity?
   a. opportunity cost
   b. explicit cost
   c. total cost
   d. variable cost

7. Refer to the table below. Which of the following costs are implicit costs?

Paper	$20,000
Wages	$48,000
Lease payment for copy machines	$10,000
Electricity	$6,000
Lease payment for store	$24,000
Foregone salary	$30,000
Foregone interest	$3,000
Total	$141,000

    a. the foregone salary and interest
    b. the lease payments
    c. the payments for paper, wages, and electricity
    d. all of the above

8. Which of the following are sometimes called accounting costs?
    a. economic costs
    b. implicit costs
    c. explicit costs
    d. total variable costs

9. What is the production function?
    a. the representation of the firm's costs
    b. the relationship between the inputs employed by a firm and the maximum output it can produce with those inputs
    c. the total cost divided by the quantity of output produced
    d. all of the above

10. Fill in the blanks. When graphing a conventional short-run production function, we place _____ on the horizontal axis and _____ on the vertical axis.
    a. output; the variable input
    b. the variable input; the fixed input
    c. the fixed input; the variable input
    d. the variable input; output

11. Refer to the graphs below. Which graph is representative of a typical average total cost curve?

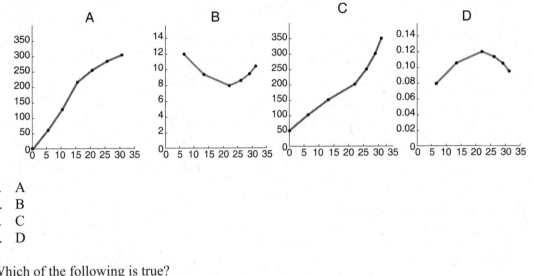

a. A
b. B
c. C
d. D

12. Which of the following is true?
    i.   Total cost = fixed cost + variable cost
    ii.   Total cost = explicit costs + implicit costs
    iii.   Economic cost = accounting cost + implicit costs
a. i only
b. ii only
c. i and ii only
d. i, ii, and iii

13. What is the additional output that a firm produces as a result of hiring one more worker called?
a. the production function
b. average total cost
c. marginal product of labor
d. average product of labor

14. Refer to the table below. When do diminishing returns in the production of pizzas start?

QUANTITY OF WORKERS	QUANTITY OF PIZZA OVENS	QUANTITY OF PIZZAS	MARGINAL PRODUCT OF LABOR
0	2	0	—
1	2	200	200
2	2	450	250
3	2	550	100
4	2	600	50
5	2	625	25
6	2	640	15

a. when the second worker is hired
b. when the third worker is hired
c. when the fourth worker is hired
d. when the fifth worker is hired

15. Refer to the graph below. In moving along the curve from point A to point B, which of the following is more likely to occur?

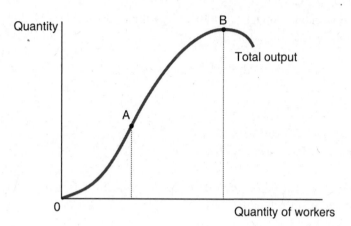

a. specialization
b. diminishing returns
c. division of labor
d. none of the above

16. Refer to the graph below. From the origin up until point A,

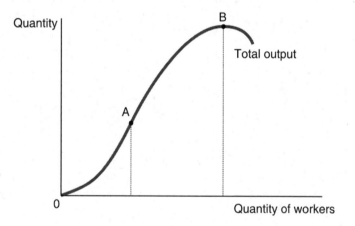

a. output increases at an increasing rate.
b. output increases at a decreasing rate.
c. output increases at a constant rate.
d. the effect of diminishing returns is greater than the effect of specialization.

17. Which of the following statements about the relationship between marginal product of labor and average product of labor is correct?
    a. Whenever the marginal product of labor is less than the average product of labor, the average product of labor must be increasing.
    b. Whenever the marginal product of labor is greater than the average product of labor, the average product of labor must be increasing.
    c. Whenever the marginal product of labor is greater than the average product of labor, the marginal product of labor must be decreasing.
    d. Whenever the marginal product of labor is less than the average product of labor, the marginal product of labor must be decreasing.

18. Which of the following refers to the total output produced by a firm divided by the quantity of workers?
    a. average total cost
    b. marginal cost
    c. average product of labor
    d. marginal product of labor

19. Refer to the graph below. Based on the relationship between marginal product and average product, which curve appears to be average product?

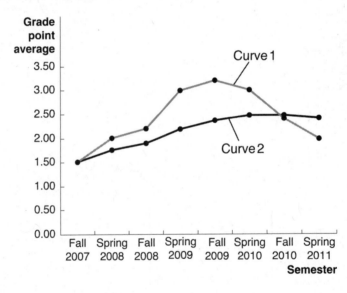

    a. Curve 1
    b. Curve 2
    c. Both curves appear to be average product curves.
    d. neither curve

20. Refer to the table below. What is the marginal cost of producing the 200th pizza?

Quantity of Workers	Quantity of Pizzas	Marginal Product of Labor	Total Cost of Pizzas
0	0	–	$800
1	200	200	1450
2	450	250	2100
3	550	100	2750
4	600	50	3400
5	625	25	4050
6	640	15	4700

a. $0.00
b. $2.60
c. $3.25
d. $650.00

21. Refer to the graph below. Based on the relationship between average total cost and marginal cost, which of the curves below appears to be average total cost?

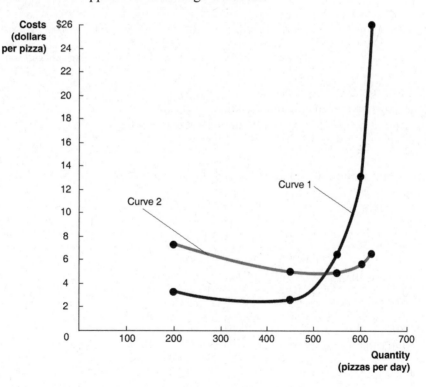

a. Curve 1
b. Curve 2
c. Both curves appear to be average cost curves.
d. neither curve

22. Refer to the graph below. For a certain output range (or quantity of pizzas produced per day), marginal cost is greater than average cost. What is this output range?

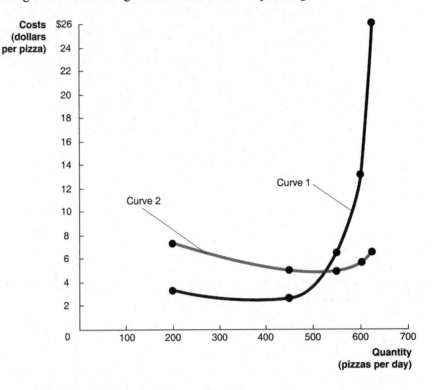

a. from zero to about 525 pizzas per day
b. the output range greater than about 525 pizzas per day
c. the entire output range, from zero to about 640 pizzas per day
d. exactly 640 pizzas per day

23. What do we obtain by dividing the fixed cost by the quantity of output produced?
    a. total variable cost
    b. average fixed cost
    c. total cost
    d. average variable cost

24. What cost measure is equal to *AFC* + *AVC*?
    a. total cost
    b. average total cost
    c. marginal cost
    d. total variable cost

25. Refer to the graph below. What does Curve 4 represent?

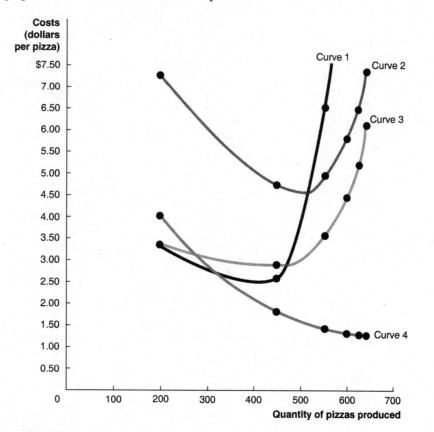

a. average variable cost
b. average total cost
c. average fixed cost
d. marginal cost

26. Refer to the graph below. At any level of output, what is the vertical distance between Curve 2 and Curve 3 equal to?

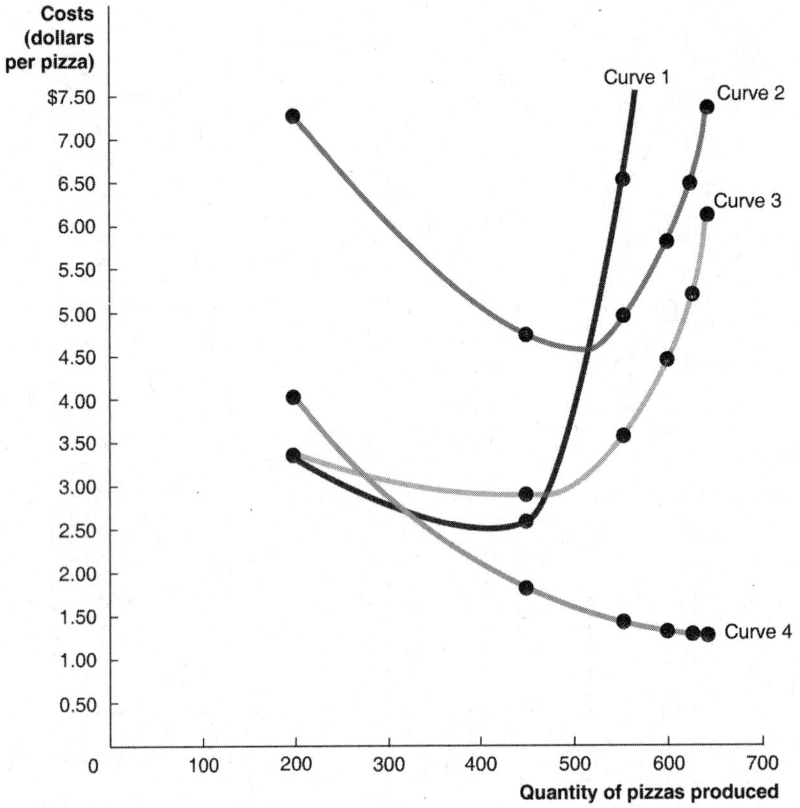

a. Curve 1
b. Curve 4
c. total cost
d. marginal cost

27. The following cost measures reach their minimum points when they are equal to the value of marginal cost, except one. Which cost measure is the exception?
   a. average variable cost
   b. average total cost
   c. average fixed cost
   d. There is no exception; all three measures above reach their minimum values when they are equal to the value of marginal cost.

28. What does the term "spreading the overhead" refer to?
   a. reducing average fixed cost by selling more output
   b. reducing average total cost by selling more output.
   c. reducing average variable cost by selling more output
   d. reducing total cost by selling more output

29. Refer to the graph below. How much is the value of total fixed cost?

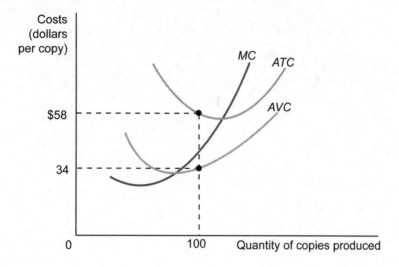

a. $2,400
b. $3,400
c. $5,800
d. None of the above; total fixed cost cannot be computed using this graph.

30. Refer to the table below. What is the marginal cost of producing the 640th pizza?

Quantity of Workers	Quantity of Ovens	Quantity of Pizzas	Cost of Ovens (Fixed cost)	Cost of Workers (Variable cost)	Total Cost of Pizzas
0	2	0	$800	$0	$800
1	2	200	800	650	1,450
2	2	450	800	1,300	2,100
3	2	550	800	1,950	2,750
4	2	600	800	2,600	3,400
5	2	625	800	3,250	4,050
6	2	640	800	3,900	4,700

a. $43.33
b. $650.00
c. $4050.00
d. $4700.00

31. Refer to the table below. What is the average total cost of producing 550 pizzas?

Quantity of Workers	Quantity of Ovens	Quantity of Pizzas	Cost of Ovens (Fixed cost)	Cost of Workers (Variable cost)	Total Cost of Pizzas
0	2	0	$800	$0	$800
1	2	200	800	650	1,450
2	2	450	800	1,300	2,100
3	2	550	800	1,950	2,750
4	2	600	800	2,600	3,400
5	2	625	800	3,250	4,050
6	2	640	800	3,900	4,700

    a. $5.00
    b. $6.48
    c. $13.00
    d. $26.00

32. What happens to the difference between average variable cost and average total cost as the level of output increases?
    a. the difference increases
    b. the difference decreases
    c. the difference remains the same
    d. the difference first increases then decreases

33. Which of the following statements is correct?
    a. In the long run, all costs are variable.
    b. In the long run, all costs are fixed.
    c. In the long run, there are no fixed or variable costs.
    d. In the long run, at least one input remains fixed.

34. Which of the following terms refers to the lowest cost at which a firm is able to produce a given level of output in the long run, when no inputs are fixed?
    a. the long-run marginal cost curve
    b. the long-run average cost curve
    c. the variable inputs curve
    d. economies of scale

35. What happens when firms experience economies of scale?
    a. Firms can produce more output in smaller plants.
    b. The firm's long-run average costs fall as output increases.
    c. The possibility of lowering long-run average costs is exhausted.
    d. Only a single plant size minimizes the long-run average cost of production.

36. Refer to the graph below. Which change in output represents economies of scale in bookselling?

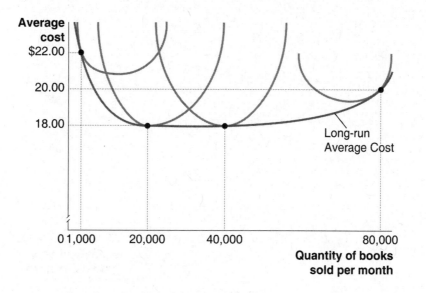

   a.   the move from 1,000 to 20,000 books sold per month
   b.   the move from 20,000 to 40,000 books sold per month
   c.   the move from 40,000 to 80,000 books sold per month
   d.   None of the above. Economies of scale cannot be achieved anywhere on the graph.

37. Refer to the graph below. Which level of output represents the minimum efficient scale?

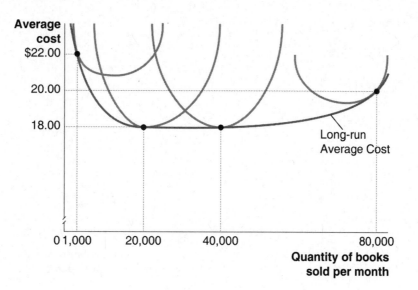

   a.   1,000 books
   b.   20,000 books
   c.   40,000 books
   d.   80,000 books

38. Refer to the graph below. In what output range do we find constant returns to scale?

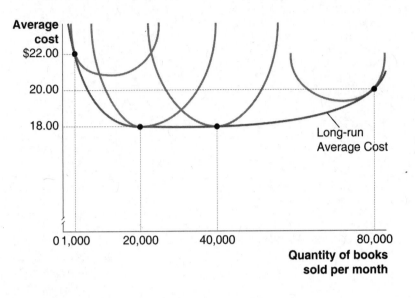

   a. between 0 and 1,000 books
   b. between 1,000 and 20,000 books
   c. between 20,000 and 40,000 books
   d. between 40,000 and 80,000 books

39. Refer to the graph below. Which bookstore is more likely to experience diseconomies of scale?

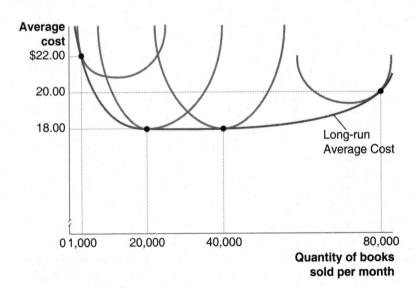

   a. a bookstore selling 1,000 books per month
   b. a bookstore selling 20,000 books per month
   c. a bookstore selling 40,000 books per month
   d. a bookstore selling 80,000 books per month

40. When does the law of diminishing returns apply?
    a. when there are diseconomies of scale
    b. in the short run only
    c. in the long run only
    d. in both the short run and the long run

Short Answer Questions

1. You are studying for your economics exam with a friend, and your friend tells you that he thinks that if a firm can spread overhead costs over larger levels of output as output expands, then marginal costs must decline. Explain the flaw in your friend's reasoning.

    _____

    _____

    _____

    _____

2. What is the difference between a sunk cost and an opportunity cost?

    _____

    _____

    _____

3. Figure 10-6 on page 340 in the textbook illustrates a bookstore's long-run average total cost curve. The average total cost of selling 60,000 books per month ($20) is greater than the average total cost of selling 40,000 books per month ($18). If the bookstore sells 60,000 books at a cost of $20 each, is it producing inefficiently?

    _____

    _____

4. The last column of Table 10-3 on page 331 in the textbook shows that the marginal product of labor at Jill Johnson's restaurant changes as additional workers are hired. The marginal product of labor of the second worker (250 pizzas) is greater than the marginal product of labor for any other worker. To make the most profit, should Jill hire two workers?

    _____

    _____

    _____

5. In his famous account of the division of labor in a pin factory, Adam Smith refers to "...the important business of making a pin..." Even in Smith's day, the total value of pin production in the United Kingdom was not a large fraction of total output. Why would Smith use the word "important" in referring to the production of a seemingly insignificant product?

_____

_____

_____

True/False Questions

T F 1.   In the short run, as the marginal product of labor (the variable factor) rises, marginal cost falls (assuming the wage rate remains constant as the quantity of labor hired changes).

T F 2.   The average product of labor equals the total output produced by a firm divided by the change in the quantity of workers.

T F 3.   Economies of scale result when the marginal product of labor rises as one more worker is hired in the short run.

T F 4.   Average fixed cost is constant in the short run.

T F 5.   Explicit costs are opportunity costs; implicit costs are not.

T F 6.   When the average product of labor increases, marginal cost decreases.

T F 7.   In the short run, the change in total cost is equal to the change in variable cost.

T F 8.   Isoquants are curves that represent all the combinations of two inputs that have the same total cost.

T F 9.   In the short run, if an increase in output causes average total cost to increase, then marginal cost must be greater than average total cost.

T F 10. The relationship between the inputs employed by a firm and the maximum output it can produce with those inputs is a production function.

T F 11. A technological change always results in the production of more output using the same inputs, or the same output using fewer inputs.

T F 12. In the long run, average fixed cost declines as output increases.

T F 13. According to the law of diminishing returns, as more workers are hired in the short run, the marginal product of labor always decreases.

T F 14. The average product of labor is the average of the marginal products of labor.

T F 15. In the long run, all costs are variable.

Answers to the Self-Test

Multiple-Choice Questions

Question	Answer	Comment
1	a	See the definition of technology on page 326 in the textbook.
2	b	See the definition of technological change on page 326 in the textbook.
3	d	See the definition of short run on page 327 in the textbook.
4	b	Variable costs are the costs that vary with the amount of output produced.
5	a	Read Making the Connection "Fixed Costs in the Publishing Industry" on page 328 in the textbook. The company's output is books published per year. The input in

question is the quantity of labor. Since the quantity of labor does not change when the number of books published changes, labor must be a fixed input in this production process.

6	a	See page 328 in the textbook.
7	a	Implicit costs are nonmonetary opportunity costs.
8	c	Explicit costs are sometimes called accounting costs.
9	b	The relationship between the inputs employed by a firm and the maximum output it can produce with those inputs is called the firm's production function.
10	d	The short-run production function shows the quantity of output that can be produced by a variable input (such as labor), while another input (such as capital) remains fixed.
11	b	Average total cost is typically U-shaped.
12	d	Each of the equations is true.
13	c	The additional output produced by a firm as a result of hiring one more worker is called the marginal product of labor.
14	b	The marginal product of labor starts to decrease when the third worker is hired.
15	b	Because of specialization and the division of labor, output will at first increase at an increasing rate, with each additional worker hired causing production to increase by a greater amount than did the hiring of the previous worker. After point A, hiring more workers while keeping the amount of machinery constant results in diminishing returns. Once point A, or the point of diminishing returns, has been reached, production increases at a decreasing rate.
16	a	Because of specialization and the division of labor, output will at first increase at an increasing rate, with each additional worker hired causing production to increase by a greater amount than did the hiring of the previous worker.
17	b	When marginal product is greater than average product, average product is rising. When marginal product is less than average product, average product is falling.
18	c	The average product of labor is the total output produced divided by the quantity of workers.
19	b	When marginal product is greater than average product, average product is rising.
20	c	Marginal cost is the change in total cost divided by a change in the level of output produced. The change in total cost from zero to 200 pizzas is $1450 – $800 = $650. The change in output is $200 – 0 = 200$. Therefore, marginal cost is $650/200 = $3.25.
21	b	When the marginal cost curve is above the average total cost curve, the average total cost curve rises, and when the marginal cost curve is below the average total cost curve, the average total cost curve falls.
22	b	Marginal cost is above average total cost when average total cost is rising.
23	b	Average fixed cost equals fixed cost divided by the quantity of output produced.
24	b	$ATC = AFC + AVC$.
25	c	Average fixed cost gets smaller and smaller as output increases.
26	b	$ATC – AVC = AFC$. Curve 4 represents AFC, average fixed cost.
27	c	When marginal cost equals average variable cost or average total cost, they must be at their minimums, but not average fixed cost, which decreases continuously as output increases.
28	a	Firms often refer to lowering average fixed cost by selling more output as "spreading the overhead." See page 338 in the textbook.
29	a	$ATC – AVC = AFC$, or $58 – $34 = $24. Then AFC × the quantity of copies produced = total fixed cost, or $24 × 100 = $2,400.
30	a	Marginal cost is the change in total cost divided by the change in output. As output increases from 625 to 640 pizzas, the total cost increases from $4,050 to

$4,700. Marginal cost is therefore $650/15 = $43.33.

31	a	Average total cost equals total cost divided by output produced. The total cost of producing 550 pizzas is $2,750, so average total cost is $2,750/550 = $5.00.
32	b	As output increases, the difference between average total cost and average variable cost decreases because average fixed cost gets smaller as output increases.
33	a	In the long run, all costs are variable. There are no fixed costs in the long run.
34	b	The long-run average cost curve shows the lowest cost at which the firm is able to produce a given level of output in the long run, when no inputs are fixed.
35	b	Economies of scale means that a firm's long-run average cost falls as it increases the quantity of output it produces.
36	a	For a small bookstore, the average total cost of selling 1,000 books per month would be $22 per book. By moving to a different short-run average total cost curve, the average total cost of selling 20,000 books would be only $18 per book. This decline in average cost represents the economies of scale that exist in bookselling.
37	b	The first quantity where economies of scale have been exhausted is 20,000.
38	c	A bookstore selling 20,000 books per month and a bookstore selling 40,000 books per month will experience constant returns to scale and have the same average cost.
39	d	Very large bookstores will experience diseconomies of scale, and their average costs will rise as sales increase beyond 40,000 books per month.
40	b	The law of diminishing returns applies in the short run, when at least one of the firm's inputs is fixed.

Short Answer Responses

1. Overhead costs are part of the fixed costs of production. Average fixed cost is calculated as fixed cost divided by total output. Marginal cost is calculated as the change in total cost divided by the change in output. Changes in cost reflect variable costs, not fixed costs. Your friend is correct that spreading out overhead costs results in a decrease in average fixed cost, but that is not related to marginal cost.

2. A sunk cost is not an opportunity cost because it has been paid in the past and cannot be avoided.

3. No. $20 is the lowest long-run average total cost of selling 60,000 books. The store can reduce its average total cost only by selling fewer books with a smaller scale (for example, with a smaller size store). As long as the firm is producing output on its long-run average cost curve, it is producing efficiently.

4. One cannot determine Jill's profit or the optimal number of workers to hire without knowing the selling price of her services and her firm's costs. In Table 10-3 the marginal product of labor of the sixth worker is only 15 pizzas, but if the revenue Jill earns from selling these pizzas is greater than the wage she pays to this worker, then her profits would increase (assuming that labor is the only variable factor of production in the short run).

5. Smith used the example of how a pin was produced to show how using specialization and a division of labor in production could cause an enormous increase in the productivity of a nation's scarce resources. The lessons learned from Smith's example can be applied to many more products with similar effects on productivity. It was the process, not the product, that was important to Smith.

True/False Answers

1. T See the section "Why Are the Marginal and Average Cost Curves U-Shaped?" beginning on page 335 in the textbook.
2. F The average product of labor is the total output produced by a firm divided by the total amount of workers, not the change in the quantity of workers.
3. F Economies of scale refers to changes in the average cost in the long run, not the short run.
4. F Fixed cost, not average fixed cost, is constant in the short run. Average fixed cost decreases as output expands in the short run.
5. F Implicit costs are the nonmonetary opportunity costs.
6. F When the marginal product of labor increases, marginal cost decreases.
7. T The change in total cost is equal to the change in marginal cost due to fixed costs being constant in the short run.
8. F Isocost lines represent all the combinations of two inputs that have the same total cost.
9. T If the quantity of output is such that marginal cost is greater than average total cost, then average total cost increases.
10. T See page 329 in the textbook.
11. F This describes only positive technological change. Technological change may also be negative.
12. F There are no fixed costs in the long run.
13. F In the short run, the marginal product of labor (the variable factor) increases initially but eventually decreases.
14. T See the section entitled "The Relationship between Marginal and Average Product" beginning on page 333 in the textbook.
15. T Because there are no fixed inputs in the long run, there are no fixed costs, and all costs are variable.

CHAPTER 11 | Firms in Perfectly Competitive Markets

Chapter Summary and Learning Objectives

11.1 Perfectly Competitive Markets (pages 369–371)

Explain what a perfectly competitive market is and why a perfect competitor faces a horizontal demand curve. A **perfectly competitive market** must have many buyers and sellers, firms must be producing identical products, and there must be no barriers to entry of new firms. The demand curve for a good or service produced in a perfectly competitive market is downward sloping, but the demand curve for the output of one firm in a perfectly competitive market is a horizontal line at the market price. Firms in perfectly competitive markets are **price takers** and see their sales drop to zero if they attempt to charge more than the market price.

11.2 How a Firm Maximizes Profit in a Perfectly Competitive Market (pages 371–374)

Explain how a firm maximizes profit in a perfectly competitive market. **Profit** is the difference between total revenue (*TR*) and total cost (*TC*). **Average revenue (*AR*)** is total revenue divided by the quantity of the product sold. A firm maximizes profit by producing the level of output where the difference between revenue and cost is the greatest. This is the same level of output where marginal revenue is equal to marginal cost. **Marginal revenue (*MR*)** is the change in total revenue from selling one more unit.

11.3 Illustrating Profit or Loss on the Cost Curve Graph (pages 374–379)

Use graphs to show a firm's profit or loss. From the definitions of profit and average total cost, we can develop the following expression for the relationship between total profit and average total cost: Profit = $(P - ATC) \times Q$. Using this expression, we can determine the area showing profit or loss on a cost-curve graph: The area of profit or loss is a box with a height equal to price minus average total cost (for profit) or average total cost minus price (for loss) and a base equal to the quantity of output.

11.4 Deciding Whether to Produce or to Shut Down in the Short Run (pages 379–382)

Explain why firms may shut down temporarily. In deciding whether to shut down or produce during a given period, a firm should ignore its *sunk costs*. A **sunk cost** is a cost that has already been paid and that cannot by recovered. In the short run, a firm continues to produce as long as its price is at least equal to its average variable cost. A perfectly competitive firm's **shutdown point** is the minimum point on the firm's average variable cost curve. If price falls below average variable cost, the firm shuts down in the short run. For prices above the shutdown point, a perfectly competitive firm's marginal cost curve is also its supply curve.

11.5 "If Everyone Can Do It, You Can't Make Money at It": The Entry and Exit of Firms in the Long Run (pages 382–388)

Explain how entry and exit ensure that perfectly competitive firms earn zero economic profit in the long run. **Economic profit** is a firm's revenues minus all its costs, implicit and explicit. **Economic loss** is the situation in which a firm's total revenue is less than its total cost, including all implicit costs. If firms make economic profits in the short run, new firms enter the industry until the market price has fallen enough to wipe out the profits. If firms make economic losses, firms exit the industry until the market price has risen enough to wipe out the losses. **Long-run competitive equilibrium** is the situation in which the entry and exit of firms has resulted in the typical firm breaking even. The **long-run supply curve** shows the relationship between market price and the quantity supplied.

11.6 Perfect Competition and Efficiency (pages 389–391)
Explain how perfect competition leads to economic efficiency. Perfect competition results in **productive efficiency**, which means that goods and services are produced at the lowest possible cost. Perfect competition also results in **allocative efficiency**, which means the goods and services are produced up to the point where the last unit provides a marginal benefit to consumers equal to the marginal cost of producing it.

Chapter Review

Chapter Opener: Perfect Competition in the Market for Organic Apples (page 367)
The market for organic apples has grown rapidly. In response to rising demand and high profits, many apple growers switched to organic methods. The entry of new firms rapidly increased supply, which decreased the price and profit associated with the production of organic apples. Today, the industry has the characteristics of a perfectly competitive market. Each apple producer has only a small share of the overall market; therefore each firm is a price taker.

11.1 Perfectly Competitive Markets (pages 369–371)
Learning Objective: Explain what a perfectly competitive market is and why a perfect competitor faces a horizontal demand curve.

A **perfectly competitive market** is a market that meets the conditions of (1) many buyers and sellers, (2) all firms selling identical products, and (3) no barriers to new firms entering the market. Prices in perfectly competitive markets are determined by the intersection of market demand and supply. Consumers and firms must accept the market price if they want to buy and sell in a competitive market.

A **price taker** is a buyer or seller that is unable to affect the market price. A firm in a perfectly competitive market is a price taker because it is very small relative to the market and sells exactly the same product as every other firm. Consumers are also price takers. Although the market demand curve has the normal downward shape, the demand curve for a perfectly competitive firm is horizontal at the market price because the firm is unable to affect the market price.

> 📖 **Study Hint**
> Spend some time reviewing Table 11-1 on page 368 because it provides an overview of the four market structures. This chapter focuses on perfect competition. You will see the other three market structures in the upcoming chapters. Differences across the three characteristics of the number of firms, the type of product, and the ease of entry are the key to defining which structure applies to a given market.

Extra Solved Problem 11-1
Supports Learning Objective 11.1: Explain what a perfectly competitive market is and why a perfect competitor faces a horizontal demand curve.

You and your sister have decided to start a petsitting business. You ask around your neighborhood and find that petsitting generally pays $20 per day. If the market for petsitting is perfectly competitive, what price will you charge for your petsitting services? What does this imply about the demand curve facing your new business?

SOLVING THE PROBLEM

Step 1: **Review the chapter material.**

This problem is about the definition of a perfectly competitive market and the effect of market structure on the firm's ability to control price, so you may want to review the section "Perfectly Competitive Markets," which begins on page 369 in the textbook.

Step 2: **Determine the price a perfectly competitive firm charges for its product or service.**

Firms in a perfectly competitive industry do not have the ability to affect the price. They are price takers who are unable to affect the market price no matter how much they produce. If you charge any more than the market equilibrium price $20 per day for petsitting, then customers will simply turn to alternative suppliers. Because an individual firm is such a small fraction of the market supply, no individual supplier can charge a price that is any different from the market price. Therefore, you will charge $20 per day for petsitting services. Because perfectly competitive firms are price takers, they face a demand curve that is horizontal at the market price. Therefore, you and your sister will face a demand curve that is horizontal at a market price of $20 per day in the petsitting market.

| 11.2 | **How a Firm Maximizes Profit in a Perfectly Competitive Market (pages 371–374)** |

Learning Objective: Explain how a firm maximizes profit in a perfectly competitive market.

Economists assume that the objective of a firm is to maximize profits. **Profit** is the difference between total revenue (*TR*) and total cost (*TC*):

$$\text{Profit} = TR - TC$$

Therefore, a firm will produce that quantity of output where the difference between *TR* and *TC* is as large as possible. A firm's **average revenue (*AR*)** equals total revenue divided by the number of units sold. Average revenue is the same as market price. For a firm in a perfectly competitive market, price is also equal to marginal revenue. **Marginal revenue (*MR*)** is the change in total revenue caused by producing and selling one more unit:

$$\text{Marginal Revenue} = MR = \frac{\Delta TR}{\Delta Q}$$

The marginal revenue curve for a perfectly competitive firm is the same as its demand curve.

The marginal cost (*MC*) of production for a perfectly competitive firm first falls, then rises. So long as *MR* exceeds *MC*, the firm's profits are increasing and production will increase. The firm's profits will decrease if production is increased beyond the output for which *MC* exceeds *MR*. The profit maximizing level of output is where *MR* = *MC*. Because *P* = *MR* for these firms, profit will be maximized when *P* = *MC*.

📖 **Study Hint**

You might be wondering, "Why would a seller produce a unit of output for which $MR = MC$, as it would not earn any profit from this last unit?" If $MR = MC$, then the firm is earning just enough revenue to cover the cost of producing the last unit of output. If the firm chose not to produce this unit of output, then it would stop producing at a point where $MR > MC$. The firm maximizes profit by continuing to expand production just to the point where $MR = MC$.

Extra Solved Problem 11-2

Cost and Revenue for Apples R' Us

Supports Learning Objective 11.2: Explain how a firm maximizes profit in a perfectly competitive market.

Sally Borts owns Apples R' Us, an orchard located in Washington State. Sally is one of about 7,500 apple producers in the United States who produced over 14 billion pounds of apples in 2008. That year, the average price of apples was 23 cents per pound (or $230 per 1,000 pounds). Sally's revenue and costs of production for various quantities of apples are shown in the table below.

Output (000 lbs.)	Total cost (000)	Marginal cost (000)	Total revenue (000)	Marginal revenue (price per 1,000 lbs)
0	$50	-----	$0	-----
1	150	$100	230	$230
2	235	85	460	230
3	330	95	690	230
4	430	100	920	230
5	550	120	1,150	230
6	720	170	1,380	230
7	950	230	1,610	230
8	1,270	320	1,840	230

Source: http://usapple.org/media/newsreleases/inr082109.pdf

a. Determine whether Apples R' Us is a perfectly competitive firm.

b. Explain how Sally will decide how much to produce.

SOLVING THE PROBLEM

Step 1: **Review the chapter material.**

This problem is about how a firm maximizes profit, so you may want to review the section "How a Firm Maximizes Profit in a Perfectly Competitive Market," which begins on page 371 in the textbook.

Step 2: **Determine if Apples R' Us is a perfectly competitive firm.**

Sally is one of thousands of apple producers, and her output is a small fraction of the total number of apples produced. Within each variety of apples (Red Delicious, McIntosh, Granny Smith, etc.) apple growers sell an identical product and new firms are free to enter the market. Therefore, Apples R' Us is a perfectly competitive firm. In addition, marginal revenue is constant, which means that price must also be constant, and the demand curve facing Apples R' Us must be horizontal. Price and marginal revenue are constant and the demand curve is horizontal only in a perfectly competitive market.

Step 3: **Explain how Sally will decide how much to produce.**
Sally should increase her production of apples so long as the marginal revenue exceeds her marginal cost of production. The profit-maximizing level of output is where marginal revenue equals marginal cost. Sally's marginal revenue equals the $230 price of a thousand pounds of apples. Therefore, Sally should produce up to 7 thousand pounds of apples. At 7 thousand pounds, her marginal cost is equal to the marginal revenue of $230, and she is maximizing her profit.

11.3 Illustrating Profit or Loss on the Cost Curve Graph (pages 374–379)
Learning Objective: Use graphs to show a firm's profit or loss.

Profit equals total revenue (*TR*) minus total cost (*TC*). Because *TR* equals price multiplied by quantity sold, this can be written as:

$$\text{Profit} = (P \times Q) - TC$$

Dividing both sides by Q:

$$\frac{\text{Profit}}{Q} = \frac{(P \times Q)}{Q} - \frac{TC}{Q}$$

Or:

$$\frac{\text{Profit}}{Q} = P - ATC$$

This equation means that profit per unit (or average profit) equals price minus average total cost. Multiplying both sides of the equation by Q yields an equation that tells us a firm's total profit is equal to the quantity produced multiplied by the difference between price and average total cost. ($P - ATC$ is called the profit margin per unit.)

$$\text{Profit} = (P - ATC) \times Q$$

Figure 11-4 on page 375 in the textbook illustrates the situation where the firm is making a profit. Figure 11-5 on page 378 illustrates the situations where the firm is either breaking even or suffering a loss. The firm will make a profit if $P > ATC$. The firm will break even if $P = ATC$. The firm will experience losses if $P < ATC$.

📖 **Study Hint**
Solved Problem 11-3 provides an example of an individual firm in a perfectly competitive market. Study this Solved Problem carefully and be sure you understand the graphs that show a firm's profit or loss. If properly drawn, graphs can help you to answer questions that would be more difficult to answer using only words or numbers. Here are tips to learning from these graphs:
(1) When a firm's demand curve intersects the *ATC* curve, price will exceed *ATC* for some level of output. That means the firm earns a profit.
(2) To show a firm suffering losses, the *ATC* curve is drawn everywhere above the demand curve, which would mean that the price is less than the average total cost.
(3) Always draw the demand curve and the *MC* curve first to determine the profit-maximizing output. This will make it easier to identify *ATC* and *AVC* at this same output.

<table>
<tr><td>**11.4**</td><td>**Deciding Whether to Produce or to Shut Down in the Short Run (pages 379–382)**
Learning Objective: Explain why firms may shut down temporarily.</td></tr>
</table>

In the short run, a firm suffering losses has two options: produce or shut down. The firm will produce the profit-maximizing output if its total revenue is greater than its total variable cost. In this situation, even though the firm is suffering a loss, it is earning enough revenue to cover all of its variable costs and at least some of its fixed costs. The firm's second option is to stop production by shutting down temporarily (producing zero output). During a temporary shutdown, a firm must still pay its fixed costs. If, by producing, the firm would lose an amount greater than its fixed costs (that is, the firm will not be able to cover all of its variable costs), then it will shut down.

A **sunk cost** is a cost that has already been paid and cannot be recovered. The firm should treat its sunk costs as irrelevant to its decision making.

The firm's marginal cost curve is its supply curve only for prices at or above average variable cost. The **shutdown point** is the minimum point on a firm's average variable cost curve. If the price falls below this point, the firm shuts down production in the short run. The market supply curve can be derived by adding up the quantity that each firm in the market is willing to supply at each price. For a given price, the quantity each firm in the market is willing to supply can be determined from the marginal cost curve, so a firm's supply curve is the portion of the marginal cost curve that lies above average variable cost.

📖 Study Hint

The decision to shut down is not the same as deciding to leave the market or go out of business. Many firms sell goods or services only in certain seasons. Examples include ski resorts, retail stores near summer resorts, and Christmas tree vendors. These firms shut down temporarily during the off season. Going out of business permanently, however, is a long-run decision. See *Making the Connection* "When to Close a Laundry" for an example of a firm that is not making a profit. The laundry had $3,300 per month in fixed costs and was losing $4,000 per month while operating. If the laundry closed down it would only lose $3,300 per month instead of $4,000, so the firm should shut down. The owner of the laundry brought in a new manager who reorganized the business so that it was now losing only $2,000 per month. Under this reorganization, the firm should stay in business because it is losing only $2,000 per month while operating compared to the $3,300 per month that would be lost if it shut down.

Extra Solved Problem 11-4

Apples R' Us—Continued
Supports Learning Objective 11.4: Explain why firms may shut down temporarily.

The table that follows represents costs for the perfectly competitive firm Apples R' Us. As in Extra Solved Problem 11-2, the market equilibrium price in this competitive market is $230 per thousand pounds of apples produced.

Output (000 lbs.)	Total cost (000)	Marginal cost (000)	Average variable cost (000)
0	$50	-----	
1	150	$100	
2	235	85	
3	330	95	
4	430	100	
5	550	120	
6	720	170	
7	950	230	
8	1,270	320	

a. Determine the rule that Apples R' Us will use to determine whether it will produce at various market prices.

b. Complete the "Average variable cost" column. Should the firm produce and sell apples if the price is $100 per 1,000 pounds of apples instead of $230 per 1,000 pounds, or should the firm shut down? What about a price of $85 per 1,000 pounds of apples?

SOLVING THE PROBLEM

Step 1: **Review the chapter material.**

This problem is about whether a firm should continue to produce or shut down at various possible market prices, so you may want to review the section "Deciding Whether to Produce or to Shut Down in the Short Run," which begins on page 379 in the textbook.

Step 2: **Determine the rule that Apples R' Us will use to determine whether they should produce at each price mentioned in the problem.**

Apples R' Us will compare the market price to the minimum value of average variable cost. If the price is greater than the minimum AVC, then the firm will produce where $MR = MC$. If the price is below the minimum AVC, then the firm will shut down in the short run. Apples R' Us should continue to produce in the short run as long as the price is greater than $93.33, which is the minimum value for AVC. If the price falls below $93.33, then the firm will shut down because its loss will be greater than its fixed cost.

Step 3: **Calculate AVC for the firm, and compare each price to the rule from Step 2 to determine whether the firm will produce or shut down at each given price.**

Output (000 lbs.)	Total cost (000)	Marginal cost (000)	Average variable cost (000)
0	$50	-----	----
1	150	$100	$100
2	235	85	92.50
3	330	95	93.33
4	430	100	95
5	550	120	100
6	720	170	111.67
7	950	230	128.57
8	1,270	320	152.50

The total cost of $50 that is paid even when output is zero represents the fixed costs of production. Because fixed costs do not change as output changes, this $50 fixed cost is part of cost for every level of output. Any costs greater than the $50 fixed cost must be variable costs then, and *AVC* is calculated as variable cost divided by output, as shown in the table above.

Apples R' Us will continue to produce in the short run when the price is $100 per thousand pounds of apples. The firm will choose to produce all levels of output where marginal revenue of $100 is at least as great as the marginal cost, and will maximize profit where marginal revenue equals marginal cost. Marginal revenue is equal to marginal cost at 4 thousand pounds of apples, so profit will be maximized when the firm produces 4 thousand pounds of apples. In this case, profit is *negative* $30, but the loss of $30 is a higher level of profit than the loss of $50 the firm would suffer if it shut down.

When the price falls to $85 per thousand pounds, the firm will shut down because the price has fallen below the minimum of *AVC*. In this case, the firm cannot collect enough revenue to cover its variable costs, so there is no money left over to pay down the fixed costs. Even though the $85 price is equal to the marginal cost of producing 2 thousand apples, producing 2 thousand apples would generate a *loss* for the firm of $65. If the firm chooses simply to shut down when the price is $85, then it will suffer a loss of only $50.

11.5 "If Everyone Can Do It, You Can't Make Money at It": The Entry and Exit of Firms in the Long Run (pages 382–388)

Learning Objective: Explain how entry and exit ensure that perfectly competitive firms earn zero economic profit in the long run.

In the long run, unless a firm can cover all of its costs it will shut down and exit the industry. **Economic profit** is a firm's revenues minus all its costs, implicit and explicit. An **economic loss** means a firm's total revenue is less than its total cost, including all implicit costs. If firms in a perfectly competitive market are earning economic profits in the short run, then new firms will have an incentive to enter the market so they, too, can earn an economic profit.

The entry of new firms shifts the industry supply curve to the right. As a result, the market price will fall. The entry of firms will continue until price is equal to average total cost. If firms in a perfectly competitive market are suffering losses in the short run, some of these firms will exit the industry because they will not be able to cover all of their costs. The exit of firms shifts the industry supply curve to the left. As a result, the market price will rise. The exit of firms will continue until price is equal to average total cost.

Long-run competitive equilibrium is the situation in which the entry and exit of firms have resulted in the typical firm breaking even. The **long-run supply curve** shows the relationship in the long run between market price and the quantity supplied. A constant cost industry is an industry in which the typical firm's long-run average costs do not change as the industry expands. This means that the firm will have a horizontal long-run supply curve. An increasing cost industry is an industry in which the typical firm's long-run average costs increase as the industry expands. This means the firm will have an upward-sloping long-run supply curve. A decreasing cost industry is an industry in which the typical firm's long-run average costs decrease as the industry expands. This means that the firm will have a downward sloping long-run supply curve.

Extra Solved Problem 11-5
Apples R' Us—Continued
Supports Learning Objective 11.5: Explain how entry and exit ensure that perfectly competitive firms earn zero economic profit in the long run.

Consider the perfectly competitive market in which Apples R' Us competes. Suppose that the price is $100 per thousand pounds of apples and that all firms face the same costs as those shown for Apples R' Us below.

Output (000 lbs.)	Total cost (000)	Marginal cost (000)	Average variable cost (000)
0	$50	-----	----
1	150	$100	$100
2	235	85	92.50
3	330	95	93.33
4	430	100	95
5	550	120	100
6	720	170	111.67
7	950	230	128.57
8	1,270	320	152.50

a. What will happen to the supply in this industry in the long run? What is the effect of this change in supply on price?

b. What will happen to the long-run profit of firms that remain in the market for apples?

SOLVING THE PROBLEM
Step 1: Review the chapter material.
This problem is about long-run losses, so you may want to review the section "'If Everyone Can Do It, You Can't Make Money at It': The Entry and Exit of Firms in the Long Run," which begins on page 382 in the textbook.

Step 2: Answer part (a) by determining what short-run profit looks like for a typical firm in the industry and discuss the incentive effect that this profit has on the firm.
If each firm has the same costs as Apples R' Us, each firm in the industry will be suffering a loss of $30 at the price of $100 per thousand pound of apples. These losses give firms an incentive to exit the industry in the long run because the owners of the firms could receive a greater return on their investment somewhere else.

Step 3: **Answer part (b) by determining how this incentive will alter the market supply curve and the profit of remaining firms.**

Because profits are negative, some firms will exit the apple market, which will cause the market supply curve to shift to the left. A decrease in supply will cause the market price for apples to rise. As firms exit the industry, the price will continue to rise up to the point where all remaining firms in the industry will be earning zero economic profit. The firms who remain are making the same return producing apples as could be achieved in their next best alternative, so there is no additional incentive for firms to exit the market.

Perfect Competition and Efficiency (pages 389–391)
Learning Objective: Explain how perfect competition leads to economic efficiency.

Productive efficiency is the situation in which a good or service is produced at the lowest possible cost. Perfect competition results in productive efficiency because the forces of competition drive the market price to the minimum average cost of the typical firm. Managers of firms strive to earn economic profits by reducing costs. But in a perfectly competitive market, other firms can quickly copy ways of reducing costs, so that in the long run consumers, not producers, benefit from cost reductions.

Allocative efficiency is a state of the economy in which production represents consumer preferences. In particular, every good or service is produced up to the point where the last unit provides a marginal benefit to consumers equal to the marginal cost of producing it. Entrepreneurs in a perfectly competitive market efficiently allocate resources to best satisfy consumer wants.

📖 Study Hint
Critics of the perfectly competitive model complain that few industries feature sellers of identical products who are all price takers. These critics fail to understand either what an economic model is or how economists use these models. Although not many markets are perfectly competitive, many markets are very competitive and experience entry and exit in response to short-run profits and losses. The markets for televisions, calculators, personal computers, and even automobiles have changed over time as firms earned short-run profits or new technologies forced firms to adapt. The steel and coal industries experienced exit by firms in response to short-run losses, just as the model of perfect competition predicts. The model also provides policymakers and analysts with a standard against which to judge the efficiency of real markets. When the price of a product is greater or less than marginal cost, one can argue that too little or too much of the product has been produced, a deviation from allocative efficiency.

Key Terms

Allocative efficiency A state of the economy in which production represents consumer preferences; in particular, every good or service is produced up to the point where the last unit provides a marginal benefit to consumers equal to the marginal cost of producing it.

Average revenue (*AR*) Total revenue divided by the quantity of the product sold.

Economic loss The situation in which a firm's total revenue is less than its total cost, including all implicit costs.

Economic profit A firm's revenues minus all its costs, implicit and explicit.

Long-run competitive equilibrium The situation in which the entry and exit of firms has resulted in the typical firm breaking even.

Long-run supply curve A curve that shows the relationship in the long run between market price and the quantity supplied.

Marginal revenue (*MR*) The change in total revenue from selling one more unit of a product.

Perfectly competitive market A market that meets the conditions of (1) many buyers and sellers, (2) all firms selling identical products, and (3) no barriers to new firms entering the market.

Price taker A buyer or seller that is unable to affect the market price.

Productive efficiency The situation in which a good or service is produced at the lowest possible cost.

Profit Total revenue minus total cost.

Shutdown point The minimum point on a firm's average variable cost curve; if the price falls below this point, the firm shuts down production in the short run.

Sunk cost A cost that has already been paid and that cannot be recovered.

Self-Test

(Answers are provided at the end of the Self-Test.)

Multiple-Choice Questions

1. Which of the following are characteristics of a perfectly competitive industry?
   a. firms are unable to control the prices of the products they sell
   b. firms are unable to earn an economic profit in the long run
   c. firms sell identical products
   d. all of the above

2. Which of the following conditions must exist in order to have a perfectly competitive market?
   a. There must be many buyers and many sellers, all of whom are small relative to the market.
   b. The products sold by firms in the market must be different from each other.
   c. There must be some barriers to entry in order to protect perfect competition.
   d. all of the above

3. A buyer or seller that is unable to affect the market price is called?
   a. a price maker
   b. a price taker
   c. an independent producer
   d. a monopoly

4. Refer to the graph below of the demand curve facing a firm in the perfectly competitive market for wheat. The fact that the demand curve is horizontal implies which of the following?

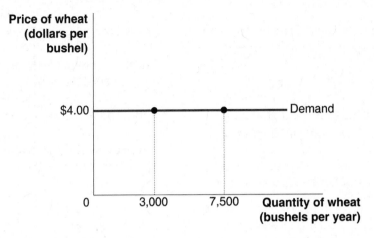

a. The firm must lower the price of wheat to increase the quantity demanded.
b. Increasing production of wheat from 3,000 bushels to 7,500 bushels results in an increase in marginal revenue.
c. The market demand for wheat is identical to the demand for wheat faced by an individual firm.
d. The firm can sell any amount of output as long as it accepts the market price of $4.00.

5. If an individual firm in a perfectly competitive market increases its price, the firm will experience
a. higher revenue.
b. lower average total cost.
c. increased sales.
d. none of the above

6. To maximize profit, which of the following should a firm attempt to do?
a. maximize revenue
b. minimize cost
c. find the largest difference between total revenue and total cost
d. all of the above

7. Refer to the graphs below. The graph on the left depicts demand and supply in the competitive market for wheat. The graph on the right depicts the demand curve facing Farmer Whapple, an individual producer in the market for wheat. The demand curve for Farmer Whapple's wheat is horizontal at the market price of $4.00 because

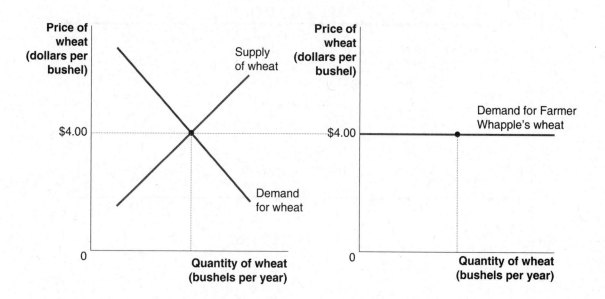

a. Farmer Whapple is the only supplier of wheat in this market.
b. Farmer Whapple is a price taker.
c. Farmer Whapple has control over the price of wheat.
d. Farmer Whapple can choose whether he faces a downward sloping demand curve or a horizontal demand curve.

8. What is the relationship between price, average revenue, and marginal revenue for a firm in a perfectly competitive market?
a. Price is equal to average revenue and greater than marginal revenue.
b. Price is greater than average revenue and equal to marginal revenue.
c. Price is equal to both average revenue and marginal revenue.
d. Price, average revenue, and marginal revenue usually all have different values.

9. Refer to the table below. Based on the numbers in the table, how much should this farmer produce in order to maximize profit?

QUANTITY (BUSHELS) (Q)	TOTAL REVENUE (TR)	TOTAL COSTS (TC)	MARGINAL REVENUE (MR)	MARGINAL COST (MC)
4	16.00	9.50	4.00	2.00
5	20.00	12.00	4.00	2.50
6	24.00	15.00	4.00	3.00
7	28.00	19.50	4.00	4.50
8	32.00	25.50	4.00	6.00
9	36.00	32.50	4.00	7.00
10	40.00	40.50	4.00	8.00

a. 10 bushels
b. 9 bushels
c. 6 bushels
d. 4 bushels

10. Refer to the graph below. Based on the information on the graph, what is true about marginal revenue?

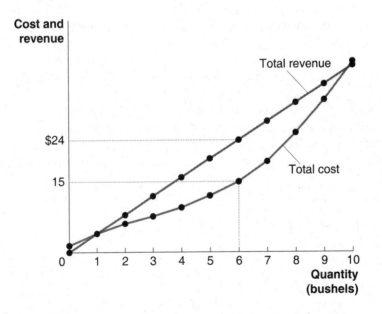

a. marginal revenue increases as the quantity of bushels sold increases
b. marginal revenue decreases as the quantity of bushels sold increases
c. marginal revenue remains constant as the quantity of bushels sold increases
d. marginal revenue is always greater than marginal cost

11. Refer to the graph below which shows the marginal cost and marginal revenue curves for a farmer in the perfectly competitive market for wheat. What is the profit-maximizing level of output if the producer can produce only whole units of output?

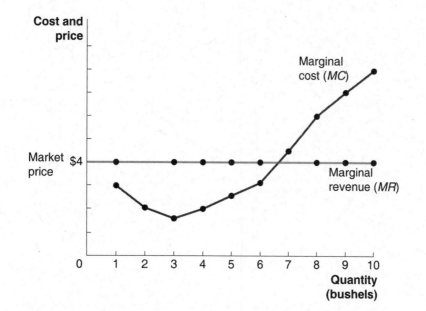

a. 3 bushels
b. 10 bushels
c. 6 bushels
d. 8 bushels

12. Refer to the graph of costs for a perfectly competitive firm below. Which of the following best represents profit per unit?

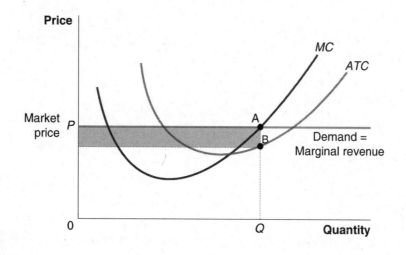

a. the shaded rectangle
b. the distance between points A and B
c. the market price
d. none of the above

13. Refer to the graph below. Which of the curves in the graph is *not* necessary for determining the level of output that maximizes profit for a perfectly competitive firm?

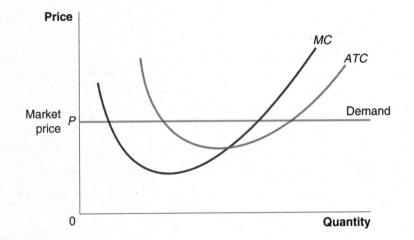

a. the MC curve
b. the demand curve
c. the ATC curve
d. All three curves are needed to determine which level of output maximizes profit.

14. Refer to the graph below. Which of the curves is *not* necessary for determining the level of profit earned by a perfectly competitive firm?

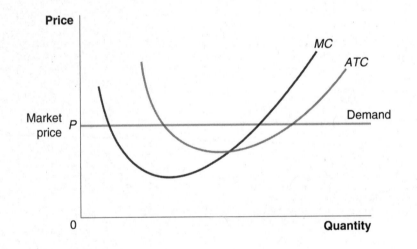

a. the marginal cost curve
b. the demand curve
c. the average total cost curve
d. All three curves are needed to determine the level of profit earned by a perfectly competitive firm.

15. Refer to the graph below. At what level of output does this perfectly competitive firm maximize profit?

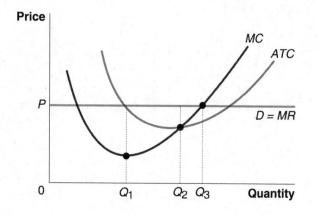

a. Q_1
b. Q_2
c. Q_3
d. 0

16. Refer to the graph below. If a perfectly competitive firm is producing at point A, which of the following is true?

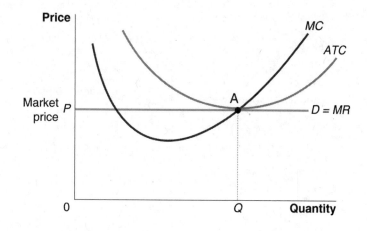

a. The firm earns zero accounting profit.
b. The firm suffers a loss.
c. The firm earns zero economic profit.
d. The firm earns positive economic profit.

17. Refer to the graph below. What does the shaded area in the graph represent for a perfectly competitive firm that produces at output level Q?

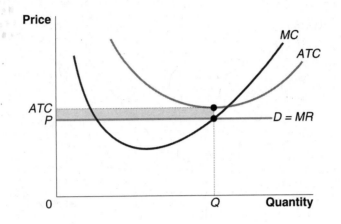

    a.   positive economic profit
    b.   accounting profit
    c.   negative economic profit
    d.   total cost of producing Q

18. Refer to the graph below. At which of the following prices is the perfectly competitive firm earning negative economic profit?

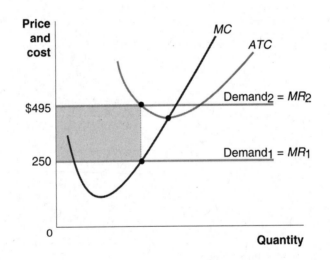

    a. $495
    b. $250
    c.   both $250 and $495
    d.   any price above $495

19. What is the term given to a cost that has already been paid and cannot be recovered?
    a.   unrecoverable cost
    b.   variable cost
    c.   sunk cost
    d.   implicit cost

20. Refer to the graph below. Which demand curve is associated with the shutdown point for this perfectly competitive firm?

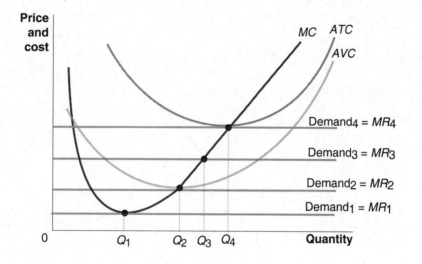

a. Demand₁
b. Demand₂
c. Demand₃
d. Demand₄

21. Refer to the graph below. When the perfectly competitive firm faces demand curve Demand₃, which of the following is true?

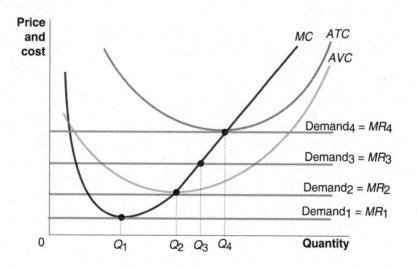

a. The firm is earning positive economic profit.
b. The firm should shut down.
c. The firm will suffer losses, but should continue to operate.
d. The firm should go out of business.

22. Refer to the graph below. What is the value of total fixed cost for this perfectly competitive firm?

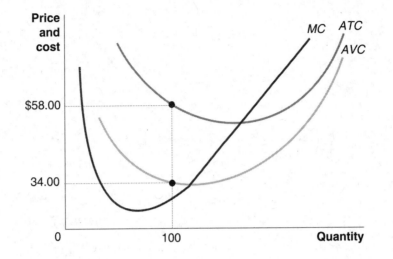

  a. $3,400
  b. $5,800
  c. $2,400
  d. None of the above; there is insufficient information to answer the question.

23. Refer to the graphs below. Suppose the graph on the left represents a typical firm's supply curve in a perfectly competitive industry, and there are 100 identical firms in the industry. Then the graph on the right represents

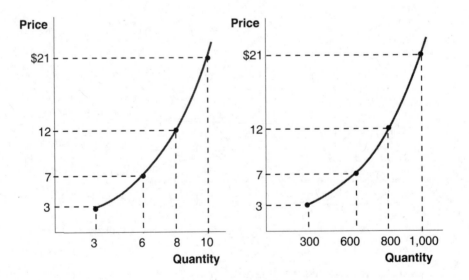

  a. the market supply curve.
  b. the average total cost curve for the industry.
  c. the individual supply curve for each firm in the industry.
  d. the individual demand curve facing each firm in the industry.

24. Which term best describes the minimum amount that a firm needs to earn on a $100,000 investment to be willing to remain in a perfectly competitive industry in the long run?
    a. explicit cost
    b. opportunity cost
    c. economic profit
    d. economic loss

25. Economic loss refers to a situation in which a firm's total revenue is less than its total cost. To calculate the amount of a loss, which of the following costs should be included?
    a. explicit costs only
    b. implicit costs only
    c. both explicit costs and implicit costs
    d. fixed costs only

26. Refer to the graphs below. The perfectly competitive firm represented in the graph on the right is experiencing

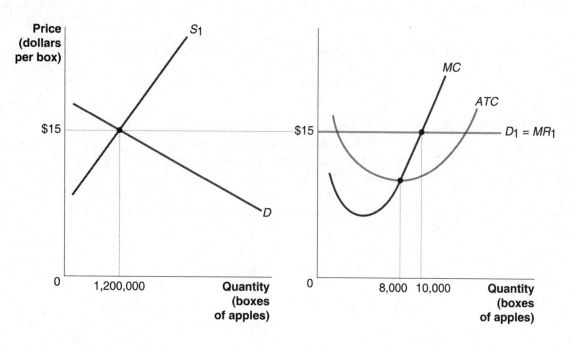

    a. a profit in the short run.
    b. a profit in the long run.
    c. a loss in the short run.
    d. a loss in the long run.

27. Refer to the graphs below. What do you expect to happen in this market as it approaches long-run equilibrium?

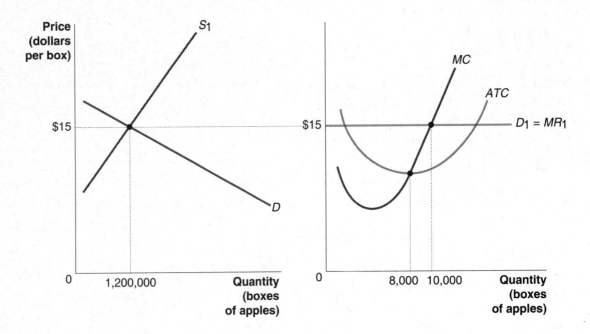

a. a shift to the right of the market demand curve as new firms enter
b. an upward shift of the firm's demand curve as new firms enter
c. a shift to the left of the market demand curve as new firms enter
d. a shift to the right of the market supply curve as new firms enter

28. Refer to the graphs below. What do you expect to happen in this perfectly competitive market as it approaches long-run equilibrium?

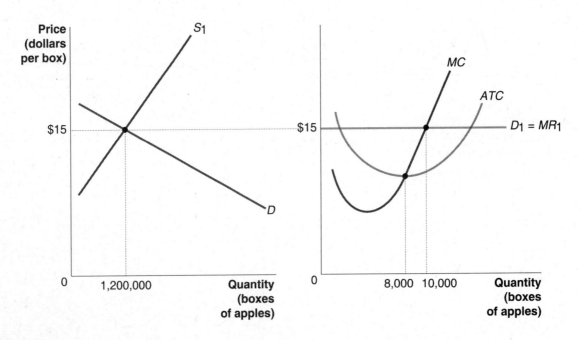

a. The price will increase and profits will become zero.
b. The price will decrease until it is equal to the minimum of average total cost, and profits will increase.
c. The price will decrease until it is equal to the minimum of average total cost, and profits will become zero.
d. Firms will exit because economic profit will become zero.

29. Refer to the graphs below. As market demand shifts to the left, how will the firm's level of output change?

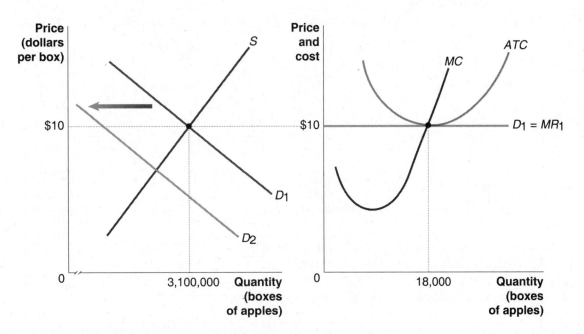

a. The firm will increase its output to increase its profits.
b. The firm will decrease its output and suffer losses.
c. The firm will maintain its output at the current level but suffer losses.
d. The firm will decrease its output and earn higher profit.

30. If market demand shifts to the right, how will a competitive firm's level of output change?
a. The firm will increase its output, and its profits will increase.
b. The firm will need to decrease its output and suffer losses.
c. The firm will keep its output constant, but its profits will increase.
d. The firm will decrease its output, which will increase its profit.

31. Long-run competitive equilibrium is
a. the situation in which the entry and exit of firms have resulted in the typical firm just breaking even.
b. a situation in which market price is at a level equal to the minimum point on the typical firm's marginal cost curve.
c. the end of a process during which firms are prevented from adjusting their production methods.
d. all of the above

32. Refer to the graphs below. After the market demand curve shifts to the left, which of the following would happen in this perfectly competitive market as it adjusts to long-run equilibrium?

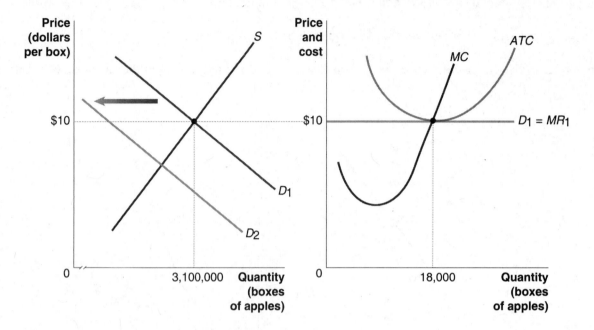

a. The market demand curve will shift back to the right.
b. The market supply curve will shift to the right.
c. The market supply curve will shift to the left.
d. The market demand curve will shift further to the left.

33. If firms in a perfectly competitive industry are earning positive profits, what would you expect to see in the long run?
a. The market demand curve will shift to the left as firms exit the market, prices will rise, and profits will rise.
b. The market supply curve will shift to the right as firms enter the market, prices will fall, and profits will fall.
c. The market supply curve will shift to the left as firms exit the market, prices will rise, and profits will rise.
d. The market demand curve will shift to the right as firms enter the market, prices will rise, and profits will rise.

34. Refer to the graph below. Initially, the market is in long-run equilibrium at point A. If this is a constant-cost industry, after the increase in demand, through which point is the long-run supply curve most likely to cross?

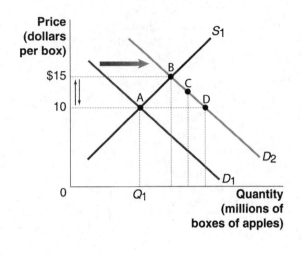

a. B
b. C
c. D
d. none of the above

35. Refer to the graph below. Initially, the market is in long-run equilibrium at point A. Assume this is a constant-cost industry. Immediately after the decrease in demand, which point is likely to be a short-run equilibrium and which point is likely to be the next long-run equilibrium?

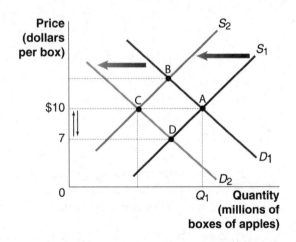

a. Point B is a short-run equilibrium, and point C is the new long-run equilibrium.
b. Point D is a short-run equilibrium, and point C is the new long-run equilibrium.
c. Point C is a short-run equilibrium, and point D is the new long-run equilibrium.
d. Point C is a short-run equilibrium, and point A is the new long-run equilibrium.

36. What determines the position of the long-run supply curve in a perfectly competitive industry?
a. market price
b. the minimum point on the typical firm's marginal cost curve
c. the minimum point on the typical firm's average total cost curve
d. the minimum point on the typical firm's average variable cost curve

37. Refer to the graphs below. Which graph best depicts an industry in which the typical firm's average costs decrease as the industry expands production?

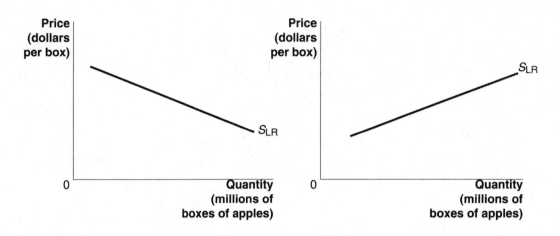

a. the graph on the left
b. the graph on the right
c. either graph could be associated with that industry
d. neither graph

38. Which of the following terms best describes how the result of the forces of competition drives the market price to the minimum average cost of the typical firm?
a. allocative efficiency
b. productive efficiency
c. decreasing-cost industry
d. competitive markdown

39. Which of the following terms best describes a state of the economy in which production reflects consumer preferences?
a. allocative efficiency
b. productive efficiency
c. capitalism
d. consumer equilibrium

40. When the market system allocates inputs efficiently to produce goods and services that best satisfy consumer wants, which of the following is true?
a. The price of a good represents the marginal benefit consumers receive from consuming the last unit of the good sold.
b. Perfectly competitive firms produce up to the point where the price of the good equals the marginal cost of producing the last unit.
c. Firms produce up to the point where the last unit provides a marginal benefit to consumers equal to the marginal cost of producing it.
d. all of the above

Short Answer Questions

1. Entry and exit ensure that perfectly competitive firms will not earn economic profits in the long run. Why would any firm remain in an industry if it cannot earn a profit?

_____

_____

_____

2. Explain why the firm's short-run supply curve is that portion of its marginal cost curve that lies above its average variable cost curve.

_____

_____

_____

_____

3. Why must perfectly competitive firms produce at the lowest point on their average total cost curves when their markets are in long-run equilibrium?

_____

_____

_____

4. When firms suffer short-run losses, the exit of some firms will shift the market supply curve to the left. But some firms will remain in the industry. Which types of firms will leave the market?

_____

_____

_____

5. Explain why a perfectly competitive firm would not advertise its product in order to attract consumers away from rival firms.

_____

_____

_____

_____

True/False Questions

T F 1. Perfectly competitive firms will lower their prices in response to price cuts of rival firms.
T F 2. The slope of the demand curve for a perfectly competitive firm equals zero.
T F 3. The firm's profit equals price minus average total cost.
T F 4. If a firm's price is less than average variable cost in the short run, it will temporarily shut down.
T F 5. The long-run supply curve of a perfectly competitive industry is upward sloping.
T F 6. Allocative efficiency is achieved when a product is produced up to the point where the marginal benefit equals the marginal cost of the last unit sold.
T F 7. In the short run, a perfectly competitive firm will shut down if the total revenue from the quantity of output it sells is less than total cost.
T F 8. When perfectly competitive firms exit a market, the market supply curve shifts to the left.
T F 9. An increase in a firm's fixed costs will raise its price and reduce the quantity of output it sells.
T F 10. When a firm's price equals its average variable cost, it will break even.
T F 11. The market supply curve is derived by adding up the quantity that each firm in a perfectly competitive market is willing to supply at each possible price.
T F 12. The market demand curve for a perfectly competitive market is perfectly elastic.
T F 13. In a constant-cost industry, the market demand curve is a horizontal line.
T F 14. Productive efficiency is achieved when firms produce the level of output that minimizes their variable costs.
T F 15. Allocative efficiency is achieved when a firm produces a good or service up to the point where average total cost of the last unit produced equals price.

Answers to the Self-Test

Multiple-Choice Questions

Question	Answer	Comment
1	d	Firms in a perfectly competitive market are unable to control the prices of the goods they sell, they sell identical products, and the owners are unable to earn economic profits in the long run.
2	a	The three conditions that make a market perfectly competitive are: 1) There must be many buyers and many sellers, all of whom are small relative to the market; 2) The products sold by all firms in the market must be identical; and 3) There must be no barriers to new firms entering the market.
3	b	A buyer or seller that is unable to affect the market price is a price taker.
4	d	When the demand curve is horizontal, the firm can sell as much output as it wants, but it must sell the output for the market price.
5	d	If the firm increases its price, it will not sell any units of the good because consumers will choose to purchase the good from competitors who charge a lower price.
6	c	To maximize profits, a perfectly competitive firm should produce that quantity of the good where the difference between the total revenue and total cost is as large as possible.
7	b	In a perfectly competitive market, firms have no control over the market price and must accept the market price determined by the intersection of market demand and market supply.

8	c	For a firm in a perfectly competitive market, price is equal to both average revenue and marginal revenue.
9	c	To maximize profit, the farmer should produce as long as marginal revenue is at least as great as marginal cost. Marginal revenue is greater than marginal cost for bushels 4, 5, and 6, but not for output greater than 6, so the farmer maximizes profit by producing 6 bushels of wheat.
10	c	When total revenue is linear, marginal revenue is constant.
11	c	A producer maximizes profit where marginal revenue equals marginal cost. In this case, marginal revenue is greater than marginal cost for the first 6 bushels. For the 7th bushel and higher levels of output, the marginal cost is greater than the marginal revenue. The closest the farmer can come to equalizing marginal revenue and marginal cost is by producing 6 bushels of wheat.
12	b	Profit per unit is the difference between price and average total cost. This is the distance between points A and B on the graph.
13	c	Only marginal revenue and marginal cost are needed in order to determine the level of output that maximizes profit.
14	d	Profit is equal to the quantity of output produced multiplied by the difference between price and average total cost. The quantity of output produced is determined where marginal cost crosses the demand curve.
15	c	Profit is maximized at the level of output where marginal revenue equals marginal cost.
16	c	The firm is producing where price is equal to average total cost, so economic profit is equal to zero.
17	c	Because average total cost is greater than price, the area represents losses or a negative economic profit.
18	b	Average total cost is greater than price at a price of $250, and the shaded area represents the loss earned by the firm.
19	c	See page 380 in the textbook.
20	b	The shutdown point is the point where price is equal to the minimum of average variable cost. This occurs when the firm's demand curve is Demand$_2$.
21	c	When demand is Demand$_3$, the firm can cover all of its variable costs but only part of its fixed cost. The firm earns negative economic profit, but is better off producing than shutting down.
22	c	Total fixed cost is equal to the difference between total costs and total variable costs ($TFC = TC - TVC$). In this case, $TC = \$58.00 \times 100 = \$5,800$, $TVC = \$34.00 \times 100 = \$3,400$, so total fixed cost is $\$5,800 - \$3,400 = \$2,400$.
23	a	The market supply curve is found by adding the quantity each firm produces at a given price.
24	b	A firm will remain in the industry as long as it can cover its opportunity costs of production.
25	c	Economic loss is a situation in which a firm's total revenue is less than its total cost, which includes all explicit and implicit costs.
26	a	Because price is greater than average total cost, there is economic profit to be made in the short run.
27	d	Because price is greater than average total cost, there are economic profits to be made and firms will enter the market. As firms enter, the market supply curve shifts to the right.
28	c	As firms enter the market, the market price will decrease until it reaches the minimum of the ATC curve and profit will be eliminated.
29	b	The lower equilibrium market price will cause the firm to reduce its output to maintain the condition where price (marginal revenue) and marginal cost are equal.

30	a	The higher equilibrium market price from an increase in demand would entice the profit-maximizing firm to increase its output so that price (marginal revenue) and marginal cost remain equal. The higher price will also increase profits for the firm.
31	a	In long-run competitive equilibrium, entry and exit have resulted in the typical firm just breaking even. The long-run equilibrium market price is at a level equal to the minimum point on the typical firm's average total cost curve.
32	c	Lower market demand results in losses that cause some firms to exit the industry, thereby shifting the market supply curve to the left.
33	b	Positive economic profit causes some firms to enter the industry, thereby shifting the market supply curve to the right. The increase in supply reduces the market price and reduces profit.
34	d	An increase in demand for apples will lead to a temporary increase in price from $10 to $15 per box, as the market demand curve shifts to the right from D_1 to D_2. The entry of new firms shifts the market supply curve to the right, which in the case of the constant-cost industry will cause the price to fall to its long-run level of $10.
35	b	A decrease in demand will lead to a temporary decrease in price from $10 to $7 per box, as the market demand curve shifts to the left from D_1 to D_2. The exit of firms shifts the market supply curve to the left from S_1 to S_2, which causes the price to rise to its long-run level of $10.
36	c	The position of the long-run supply curve is determined by the minimum point on the typical firm's average total cost curve. Anything that raises or lowers the costs of the typical firm in the long run will cause the long-run supply curve to rotate up or down.
37	a	In the long run, competition will force the price of the product to fall to the level of the new lower average cost of the typical firm. In this case, the long-run supply curve will slope downward. Industries with downward-sloping long-run supply curves are called decreasing-cost industries.
38	b	Productive efficiency refers to the situation in which a good or service is produced at the lowest possible cost. As we have seen, perfect competition results in productive efficiency.
39	a	Allocative efficiency is a state of the economy in which production reflects consumer preferences; in particular, every good or service is produced up to the point where the last unit provides a marginal benefit to consumers equal to the marginal cost of producing it.
40	d	When the market system allocates inputs efficiently to produce goods and services that best satisfy consumer wants: 1) the price of a good represents the marginal benefit consumers receive from consuming the last unit of the good sold; 2) perfectly competitive firms produce up to the point where the price of the good equals the marginal cost of producing the last unit; and 3) firms produce up to the point where the last unit provides a marginal benefit to consumers equal to the marginal cost of producing it.

Short Answer Responses

1. Remember that zero economic profit is not the same as zero accounting profit. The return that a perfectly competitive firm earns in the long run is equal to the value of the owner's opportunity cost. An economic profit is a return greater than this. In competitive markets, economic profits are possible only in the short run.

2. A supply curve shows the relationship between the price of a product and the quantity of the product supplied. The firm's marginal cost curve traces out the quantity the firm will supply at various prices. But for prices less than average variable cost, the firm will shut down temporarily and produce zero units of output. If price falls below average variable cost, the firm is not making enough revenue to cover all of its variables or any of its fixed costs.

3. Because the demand curve for a perfectly competitive firm is horizontal, it has a zero slope. In long-run equilibrium, the firm will earn zero economic profit. For this to be true, price must equal average total cost. This can happen only when the demand curve is tangent to the firm's long-run average total cost curve, and this tangency can only be where both the demand curve and the average total cost curve have slopes equal to zero.

4. Owners of firms are in different locations and have different opportunity costs. Some will be more optimistic about the future of their markets than others. Owners who are less optimistic about the future prospects for profit are more likely to leave. Some firms are also likely to have greater financial resources than others. The firms with lower financial resources are more likely to leave the market when they experience losses.

5. Successful advertising allows firms to gain sales at the expense of other firms and/or to raise the prices of the products they advertise. In perfectly competitive markets, firms can sell all the output they wish to sell at the market price. Advertising would only add to cost and reduce profits.

True/False Answers

1. F Perfectly competitive firms are price takers and will charge the same price other firms in that industry are charging.
2. T The slope of the demand curve—the change in price divided by the change in quantity—is zero.
3. F This defines profit per unit, not total profit.
4. T Because $P < AVC$, the firm cannot cover all the losses.
5. F The statement describes an increasing-cost industry. A perfectly competitive market can have constant, increasing, or decreasing long-run costs.
6. T See the definition of allocative efficiency on page 391 in the textbook.
7. F The firm will continue to produce if total revenue exceeds total *variable* costs.
8. T A decrease in the number of firms in the market will cause the market supply curve to shift left.
9. F Changes in fixed costs will affect a firm's profit but not its output because this does not affect marginal cost. Changes in price result from changes in market demand and supply.
10. F Breaking even occurs when all costs are covered and there is no additional revenue left over, that is, when P = minimum of the ATC curve.
11. T See Figure 11-7 on page 382 in the textbook.
12. F The firm's, not the market's, demand curve is perfectly elastic.
13. F In a constant-cost industry, the long-run market supply curve is a horizontal line.
14. F Productive efficiency occurs when a firm produces the quantity that minimizes average total cost.
15. F Allocative efficiency is achieved when a firm produces up to the point where the marginal benefit of the last unit equals the marginal cost of producing it.

Chapter Summary and Learning Objectives

12.1 Demand and Marginal Revenue for a Firm in a Monopolistically Competitive Market (pages 402–404)

Explain why a monopolistically competitive firm has downward-sloping demand and marginal revenue curves. A firm competing in a **monopolistically competitive** market sells a differentiated product. Therefore, unlike a firm in a perfectly competitive market, it faces a downward-sloping demand curve. When a monopolistically competitive firm cuts the price of its product, it sells more units but must accept a lower price on the units it could have sold at the higher price. As a result, its marginal revenue curve is downward sloping. Every firm that has the ability to affect the price of the good or service it sells will have a marginal revenue curve that is below its demand curve.

12.2 How a Monopolistically Competitive Firm Maximizes Profit in the Short Run (pages 404–407)

Explain how a monopolistically competitive firm maximizes profit in the short run. A monopolistically competitive firm maximizes profits at the level of output where marginal revenue equals marginal cost. Price equals marginal revenue for a perfectly competitive firm, but price is greater than marginal revenue for a monopolistically competitive firm. Therefore, unlike a perfectly competitive firm, which produces where $P = MC$, a monopolistically competitive firm produces where $P > MC$.

12.3 What Happens to Profits in the Long Run? (pages 407–412)

Analyze the situation of a monopolistically competitive firm in the long run. If a monopolistically competitive firm is earning economic profits in the short run, entry of new firms will eliminate those profits in the long run. If a monopolistically competitive firm is suffering economic losses in the short run, exit of existing firms will eliminate those losses in the long run. Monopolistically competitive firms continually struggle to find new ways of differentiating their products as they try to stay one step ahead of other firms that are attempting to copy their success.

12.4 Comparing Perfect Competition and Monopolistic Competition (pages 412–414)

Compare the efficiency of monopolistic competition and perfect competition. Perfectly competitive firms produce where price equals marginal cost and at minimum average total cost. Perfectly competitive firms achieve both allocative and productive efficiency. Monopolistically competitive firms produce where price is greater than marginal cost and above minimum average total cost. Monopolistically competitive firms do not achieve either allocative or productive efficiency. Consumers face a trade-off when buying the product of a monopolistically competitive firm: They are paying a price that is greater than marginal cost, and the product is not being produced at minimum average cost, but they benefit from being able to purchase a product that is differentiated and more closely suited to their tastes.

12.5 How Marketing Differentiates Products (pages 414–416)

Define marketing and explain how firms use it to differentiate their products. **Marketing** refers to all the activities necessary for a firm to sell a product to a consumer. Firms use two marketing tools to differentiate their products: brand management and advertising. **Brand management** refers to the actions of a firm intended to maintain the differentiation of a product over time. When a firm has established a successful brand name, it has a strong incentive to defend it. A firm can apply for a *trademark*, which grants legal protection against other firms using its product's name.

12.6   What Makes a Firm Successful? (pages 416–418)
Identify the key factors that determine a firm's success. A firm's owners and managers control some of the factors that determine the profitability of the firm. Other factors affect all the firms in the market or are the result of chance, so they are not under the control of the firm's owners. The interactions between factors the firm controls and factors it does not control determine its profitability.

Chapter Review

Chapter Opener: Starbucks: The Limits to Growth through Product Differentiation (page 401)

Since the first Starbucks coffee shop opened in 1971, the firm has grown into a worldwide company. But the growth has been in the number of shops, rather than the size of the shops themselves. Neighborhoods often have three or more coffeehouses, so Starbucks faces competition from other firms. The coffeehouse market is monopolistically competitive because there are many firms selling differentiated products, and there are no barriers to new firms entering the industry. In 2008 and 2009, Starbucks closed approximately 900 stores as competition and a weak economy reduced sales.

12.1 Demand and Marginal Revenue for a Firm in a Monopolistically Competitive Market (pages 402–404)
Learning Objective: Explain why a monopolistically competitive firm has downward-sloping demand and marginal revenue curves.

Monopolistic competition is a market structure in which barriers to entry are low and many firms compete by selling similar, but not identical, products. Because their products are differentiated, monopolistically competitive firms can raise their prices without losing *all* their customers. A price increase will, however, cause *some* customers to switch to another similar product, so a monopolistically competitive firm faces downward-sloping demand and marginal revenue curves. Monopolistically competitive firms have only limited control over their prices because they face competition from many firms selling similar products.

📖 Study Hint
Spend some time studying Figure 12-3 on page 404 in the textbook to aid in your understanding of the downward-sloping demand and marginal revenue curves that a monopolistically competitive firm faces. For a monopolistically competitive firm, there is no guarantee lower prices will increase quantity demanded enough to raise revenue. When a decrease in price raises revenue, marginal revenue is positive. This is where the marginal revenue curve lies above the x-axis. When a decrease in price reduces revenue, marginal revenue is negative. This is where the marginal revenue curve falls below the x-axis.

Extra Solved Problem 12-1

Supports Learning Objective 12.1: Explain why a monopolistically competitive firm has downward-sloping demand and marginal revenue curves.

Suppose that the following table represents the demand for pizza at Luigi's Italian Restaurant. Use this table to answer the questions below.

Price	Quantity
$26	30
24	60
22	90
20	120
18	150
16	180
14	210
12	240
11	255

a. What is Luigi's marginal revenue?

b. Is Luigi's a perfectly competitive firm or a monopolistically competitive firm? Explain.

SOLVING THE PROBLEM

Step 1:   Review the chapter material.

This problem is about demand and marginal revenue, so you may want to review the section "Demand and Marginal Revenue for a Firm in a Monopolistically Competitive Market," which begins on page 402 in the textbook.

Step 2:   Answer question (a) by calculating Luigi's marginal revenue.

To calculate marginal revenue, first find total revenue by multiplying the price by the quantity demanded at that price. Then calculate the marginal revenue by dividing the change in total revenue by the change in quantity. For example, at a price of $22, total revenue is: $22 × 90 = $1,980. If Luigi cuts his price from $22 to $20, then his marginal revenue equals: ($2,400 − $1,980)/(120 − 90) = $14.

Price	Quantity	Total Revenue	Marginal Revenue
$26	30	$ 780	-
24	60	1,440	$22
22	90	1,980	18
20	120	2,400	14
18	150	2,700	10
16	180	2,880	6
14	210	2,940	2
12	240	2,880	−2
10	270	2,700	−6

Step 3: **Answer question (b) by determining whether this is a monopolistically or perfectly competitive firm.**

To determine whether Luigi's is a perfect competitor or a monopolistic competitor, consider its marginal revenue. A perfectly competitive firm faces a horizontal demand curve that is also its marginal revenue curve, while a monopolistically competitive firm faces downward-sloping demand and marginal revenue curves. The marginal revenue in the table above decreases as the quantity increases, so Luigi's is a monopolistically competitive firm.

12.2 How a Monopolistically Competitive Firm Maximizes Profit in the Short Run (pages 405–407)

Learning Objective: Explain how a monopolistically competitive firm maximizes profit in the short run.

As with firms in other markets, a monopolistically competitive firm will maximize profits by producing the level of output where marginal revenue (MR) is equal to marginal cost (MC). Because the MR curve lies below the firm's demand curve, the firm will maximize profits where price (P) exceeds MC:

$$P > MC$$

Like firms in perfectly competitive industries, profit is calculated as total revenue minus total cost. When measuring profit on a graph,

$$\text{Profit} = (P - ATC) \times Q$$

As with competitive markets, if the price is greater than average total cost, profit is positive. When price is less than average total cost, profit is negative.

 Study Hint
Review the table and graphs in Figure 12-4 on page 405 in the textbook for an example of a monopolistically competitive firm that makes a profit in the short run. Notice that the profit-maximizing quantity is where MR = MC, but the price the firm charges is determined by the demand curve. This implies that, unlike a perfectly competitive firm, a monopolistically competitive firm produces where price is greater than marginal cost.

12.3 What Happens to Profits in the Long Run? (pages 407–412)

Learning Objective: Analyze the situation of a monopolistically competitive firm in the long run.

When firms in a market are earning economic profits, entrepreneurs have an incentive to enter the market and establish new firms. As a result of this entry of new firms, the demand curve of an established firm shifts to the left and becomes more elastic. Entry will continue until the typical firm's demand curve is tangent to its ATC curve. In the long run, the typical firm's price will equal its average total cost and the firm will break even.

Economic losses will lead some firms to exit the market. As a result, the demand curve for a firm remaining in the market shifts to the right and becomes less elastic. The exit of firms continues until the typical firm can charge a price equal to its average total cost. In the long run, firms that remain in the industry will experience zero economic profit.

📖 Study Hint

See Figure 12-5 on page 408 in the textbook for an illustration of how the entry of competing firms eliminates positive profits in the long run. In perfectly competitive markets, positive profits encourage entry and market supply shifts to the right as a result. In monopolistically competitive markets, positive profits still encourage firms to enter the market, but entry affects each firm's demand curve by shifting demand to the left and making demand more elastic (flatter).

12.4 Comparing Perfect Competition and Monopolistic Competition (pages 412–414)

Learning Objective: Compare the efficiency of monopolistic competition and perfect competition.

There are two important differences between the long-run equilibrium in a perfectly competitive industry and in a monopolistically competitive industry. Unlike perfectly competitive firms, monopolistically competitive firms charge a price greater than marginal cost, and they do not produce at minimum average total cost. Because price is greater than marginal cost, allocative efficiency is not achieved; and because price is greater than minimum average total cost, productive efficiency is not achieved. Monopolistically competitive firms also have excess capacity because they could produce at a lower average cost by increasing output. Despite these apparent inefficiencies, consumers benefit from purchasing products that are differentiated.

Extra Solved Problem 12-4

Supports Learning Objective 12.4: Compare the efficiency of monopolistic competition and perfect competition.

Luigi's Italian Restaurant has the demand and revenue schedules below from Extra Solved Problem 12-1. Assume that the marginal costs for Luigi's are as given in the last column of the table.

Price	Quantity	Total Revenue	Marginal Revenue	Marginal Cost
$26	30	$ 780	-	-
24	60	1,440	$22	$5
22	90	1,980	18	4
20	120	2,400	14	6
18	150	2,700	10	10
16	180	2,880	6	16
14	210	2,940	2	23
12	240	2,880	−2	31
10	270	2,700	−6	40

a.   Compare Luigi's profit-maximizing condition with that of the perfectly competitive firm's profit-maximizing condition. Explain the inefficiency caused by Luigi's being a monopolistically competitive firm.

b.   What do customers gain by participating in industries that are monopolistically competitive?

SOLVING THE PROBLEM

Step 1:   **Review the chapter material.**

This problem is about perfect competition versus monopolistic competition, so you may want to review the section "Comparing Perfect Competition and Monopolistic Competition," which begins on page 412 in the textbook.

Step 2:   **Determine the profit-maximizing quantity for Luigi's and the profit-maximizing quantity if Luigi's was a perfectly competitive firm.**

Luigi's will maximize profit where marginal revenue equals marginal cost. Marginal revenue and marginal cost equal $10 per pizza when 150 pizzas are produced and sold. Note that at the quantity of 150 pizzas, a price of $18 will be charged, which is greater than the marginal revenue and marginal cost of $10. A perfectly competitive firm will produce where marginal cost equals price. Price and marginal cost both equal $16 per pizza when 180 pizzas will be produced.

Step 3:   **Compare the profit-maximization condition for Luigi's and the perfectly competitive firm, while being sure to note the inefficiency that arises due to monopolistic competition.**

As a monopolistic competitor, Luigi's charges a price of $18 per pizza, which is higher than the perfectly competitive price of $16. Luigi's also produces only 150 pizzas, while a perfectly competitive firm that was producing where price equals marginal cost would produce 180 pizzas. We can conclude that Luigi's, as a monopolistically competitive firm, has excess capacity and charges a price greater than its marginal cost.

Step 4:   **Discuss the gains to consumers that buy from monopolistically competitive firms.**

Although consumers pay a higher price and cannot purchase as many units of the good when it is produced in a monopolistically competitive industry, they get to choose from a variety of products when making their consumption choices. The willingness of consumers to pay higher prices for differentiated goods indicates that consumers value these goods enough to be willing to pay the higher prices.

12.5	**How Marketing Differentiates Products (pages 414–416)**

Learning Objective: Define marketing and explain how firms use it to differentiate their products.

Firms can differentiate their products through marketing. **Marketing** refers to all the activities necessary for a firm to sell a product to a consumer. Firms use two marketing tools to differentiate their products:

1.   **Brand management** refers to the actions of a firm intended to maintain the differentiation of a product over time. Economic profits are earned when a firm introduces a new product, but this leads to the entry of firms producing similar products and the profits are eliminated. Firms use brand management to delay the time when they will no longer be able to earn profits.

2.   Advertising shifts the demand curve for a product to the right and makes the demand curve more inelastic. Successful advertising allows the firm to sell more at every price. Advertising also increases costs. If the increase in revenue from advertising exceeds the costs, profits will rise.

Once a firm, such as Coca-Cola or Apple, has established a brand name, it has an incentive to defend it. Firms can apply for a trademark. A trademark grants legal protection against other firms using a product's name. If firms do not prevent the unauthorized use of their trademarks, they may no longer be entitled to legal protection. Firms will spend substantial amounts to ensure that they do not lose legal protection for their trademarks.

Extra Solved Problem 12-5
We Came. We Marketed. We Sold.
Supports Learning Objective 12.5: Define marketing and explain how firms use it to differentiate their products.

The 3Com Corporation was incorporated in 1979 and specializes in providing computer network devices such as routers and network switches. Among 3Com's clients are businesses that want to improve the communication and security capabilities of their computer systems. 3Com is not a household name in the manner of McDonald's or Microsoft, but marketing is an important part of the company's success. It faces stiff competition from other computer service providers, such as Cisco Systems, and uses advertising and trademarks to influence its customers. 3Com's advertising efforts are aimed primarily at computer network managers; for example, an advertising agency developed a two-page ad for 3Com titled, "We Came. We Saw. We Routed." Ads such as these are placed in publications most likely to be seen by the target audience. It would be less effective for 3Com to place ads in *People* or *Time* magazines, as few of their readers are computer network managers, than it would be to advertise in business publications. The importance of establishing and maintaining 3Com's trademarks is indicated by the guidelines the firm's legal experts issue to employees. The following is a sample of these guidelines for over 40 company and product trademarks:

Always Use a Trademark as an Adjective, Followed by the Appropriate Description(s)
If not, the trademark could become generic…make sure that 3Com and the ® symbol (3Com®) precedes a trademark mention of the product or service.

Correct: The 3Com® NBX® business telephone has powerful call-processing features.
Incorrect: NBX® has powerful call-processing features.

Sources: http://www.3com.com/corpinfo/en_US/legal/trademark/prop_usage_tmb.html#1
http://www.langstaffcommunications.com/Portfolio/Advertising/advertising.html

a.   Define marketing and explain the importance of marketing to firms.

b.   Explain how 3Com Corporation uses marketing to differentiate its products.

SOLVING THE PROBLEM:
Step 1:   Review the chapter material.
This problem is about how firms differentiate products, so you may want to review the section "How Marketing Differentiates Products," which begins on page 414 in the textbook.

Step 2: **Define marketing and explain the importance of marketing to firms.**

Marketing refers to all the activities necessary for a firm to sell a product to a consumer. To earn profits, monopolistically competitive firms must differentiate their products. These firms use two marketing tools to do this: brand management and advertising.

Step 3: **Explain how 3Com Corporation uses marketing to differentiate its products.**

3Com Corporation uses brand management, including extensive use of trademarks and advertising, to differentiate its products. 3Com Corporation focuses its marketing strategies on its customers; for example, computer network managers.

12.6 What Makes a Firm Successful? (pages 416–418)

Learning Objective: Identify the key factors that determine a firm's success.

A firm can control some of the factors that allow it to make economic profits, while other factors are uncontrollable. Controllable factors include the ability of a firm to differentiate its product and produce it at a lower average total cost than competing firms. Factors that the firm cannot control include input prices, changes in consumer tastes, and random chance.

Extra Solved Problem 12-6

The Marketing Power of Oprah (or at least her best friend, Gayle)

Supports Learning Objective 12.6: Identify the key factors that determine a firm's success

In August 2009, Oprah Winfrey and her best friend, Gayle King, attended the funeral service of Eunice Shriver in Hyannis, Massachusetts. While in town, Oprah and Gayle sampled a chicken pot pie that had been delivered to Oprah at her hotel. The following week, Gayle spent several minutes on her XM satellite radio show singing the praises of the pie that had been produced by the Centerville Pie Company in Centerville, Massachusetts. Within days of Gayle's endorsement, sales of pies from the Centerville Pie Company rose from 30 per day to over 100 per day. While additional orders came in from all over the country, the Centerville Pie Company had no system for sending pies through the mail, and the company was even unable to accept credit card payments. For a company that opened its doors only five months earlier, the growth in demand, while welcome, presented additional challenges. Despite 12-hour workdays for the company's owners and employees, the company stated on its Web site in September 2009 that there was a 10-day wait for their pot pies, and pies were still only available for pickup directly from the store. As the owner of the Centerville Pie Company, Laurie Bowen, stated, "Bigger isn't always better . . . I just don't want the quality to suffer because of the quantity."

Source: http://www.capecodonline.com/apps/pbcs.dll/article?AID=/20090913/BIZ/909130301/-1/NEWS; www.centervillepies.com

a. What factors have contributed to the success of the Centerville Pie Company?

b. Which of these factors was under the company's control and which were not?

SOLVING THE PROBLEM

Step 1: **Review the chapter material.**

This problem is about the factors that make a firm successful, so you may want to review the section "What Makes a Firm Successful" that begins on page 416 in the textbook.

Step 2:   **Answer part (a) by determining what affected the profitability of the Centerville Pie Company.**

According to its owner, The Centerville Pie Company focuses on making quality pies. The quality of its pies differentiates its product from competing products. Although this focus on quality may increase the average cost of production relative to competing firms, the higher quality helps to keep customer demand high. The focus on quality coupled with the public endorsement from Oprah's best friend increased the demand for pies at the Centerville Pie Company. Whether the company is ultimately "successful" depends on its ability to respond to the sudden increase in demand without losing the quality that differentiates its product from the products of its competitors.

Step 3:   **Answer part (b) by considering what factors the Centerville Pie Company can control and what factors are outside of its control.**

The Centerville Pie company can control its own costs and the quality of the pies it produces. However, it cannot control the words of Gayle King on her radio show. Gayle's endorsement of Centerville Pie Company pies created value relative to competitors that the company itself did not directly control.

Key Terms

Brand management The actions of a firm intended to maintain the differentiation of a product over time.

Marketing All the activities necessary for a firm to sell a product to a consumer.

Monopolistic competition A market structure in which barriers to entry are low and many firms compete by selling similar, but not identical, products.

Self-Test

(Answers are provided at the end of the Self-Test.)

Multiple-Choice Questions

1. Which of the following are characteristics of monopolistic competition?
    a.   high barriers to entry
    b.   few firms compete
    c.   firms sell similar, but not identical, products
    d.   all of the above

2. Why does a monopolistically competitive firm have a downward-sloping demand curve?
    a.   because its customers only buy goods that are being discounted from their original prices
    b.   because changing the price will affect the quantity sold
    c.   because the firm is a price taker, like a wheat farmer
    d.   because the firm's level of output produced depends on its cost structure

3. Refer to the graph below. According to this graph, what will happen if Starbucks increases the price of caffè lattes?

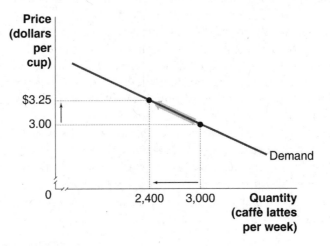

a. It will not lose any customers.
b. It will lose all of its customers.
c. It will lose some, but not all, of its customers.
d. It will gain customers.

4. For what type of market structure is demand curve the same as marginal revenue?
a. monopolistic competition
b. perfect competition
c. both monopolistic and perfect competition
d. neither monopolistic nor perfect competition

5. If marginal revenue slopes downward, which of the following is true?
a. The firm must decrease its price to sell a larger quantity.
b. The firm must increase its price to sell a larger quantity.
c. The firm must decrease its price if it wants to continue selling the same quantity.
d. The firm is unable to adjust price when the quantity sold changes.

6. Which of the following measures is conceptually the same as price?
a. marginal revenue
b. total revenue
c. average revenue
d. none of the above

7. Which of the following terms best describes the additional revenue associated with selling an additional unit of output?
a. price
b. average revenue
c. marginal revenue
d. total revenue

8. When a monopolistically competitive firm decreases price, good and bad things happen. Which of the following is considered a good thing for the firm?
   a. the price effect
   b. the output effect
   c. the revenue effect
   d. all of the above

9. When a monopolistically competitive firm decreases price, good and bad things happen. Which of the following is considered a bad thing for the firm?
   a. the price effect
   b. the output effect
   c. the revenue effect
   d. all of the above

10. Refer to the table below. What is the average revenue associated with the sixth unit of output produced and sold?

Caffé Lattes Sold per Week (Q)	Price (P)	Total Revenue (TR=P x Q)	Average Revenue	Marginal Revenue
4	$4.00	$16.00		
5	3.50	17.50		
6	3.00	18.00		

   a. $3.00
   b. $2.00
   c. $0.50
   d. None of the above; there is insufficient information to answer the question.

11. Refer to the table below. What is the marginal revenue associated with the sixth unit of output produced and sold?

Caffé Lattes Sold per Week (Q)	Price (P)	Total Revenue (TR=P x Q)	Average Revenue	Marginal Revenue
4	$4.00	$16.00		
5	3.50	17.50		
6	3.00	18.00		

   a. $3.00
   b. $2.00
   c. $0.50
   d. none of the above

12. Refer to the graph below. A decrease in price from $3.50 to $3.00 per cup results in a gain and a loss of revenue. Which area represents the loss of revenue?

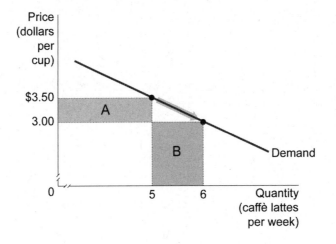

   a.   area A
   b.   area B
   c.   Areas A and B both represent revenue losses.
   d.   an area not shown

13. Refer to the graph below. A decrease in price from $3.50 to $3.00 per cup results in a gain and a loss of revenue. Which area represents the revenue gain?

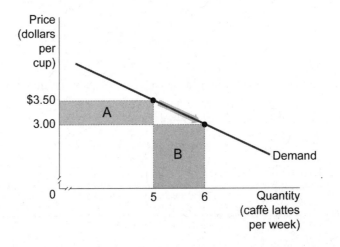

   a.   area A
   b.   area B
   c.   Both shaded areas represent revenue gains.
   d.   an area not shown

14. If a firm has the ability to affect the price of the good or service it sells, what is the relationship between its marginal revenue curve and its demand curve?
   a.   The firm will have a marginal revenue curve that is above its demand curve.
   b.   The firm will have a marginal revenue curve that is below its demand curve.
   c.   The firm will have a marginal revenue curve that is the same as its demand curve.
   d.   The firm will have an upward-sloping marginal revenue curve and a downward-sloping demand curve.

15. Refer to the graph below. The loss in revenue from decreasing price is greater than the gain in revenue from increasing price whenever

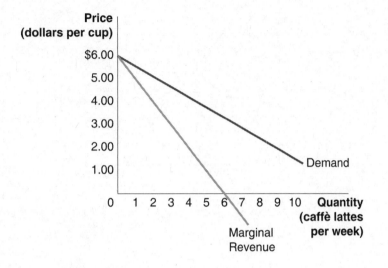

a. marginal revenue is positive.
b. marginal revenue is negative.
c. marginal revenue equals demand.
d. demand has a negative slope.

16. Which of the following types of firms use the marginal revenue equals marginal cost approach to maximize profits?
a. perfectly competitive firms
b. monopolistically competitive firms
c. both perfectly competitive and monopolistically competitive firms
d. neither perfectly competitive nor monopolistically competitive firms

17. What is marginal cost?
a. the cost per unit of output produced
b. the increase in total cost resulting from producing one more unit of output
c. the impact of additional output on total fixed cost
d. the cost of production that is independent of the level of output produced

18. Refer to the graph below. In order to maximize profit, what price should the firm charge?

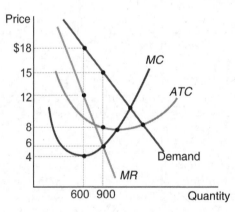

 a. $18
 b. $15
 c. $8
 d. $4

19. Refer to the graph below. Assume that the firm is producing 600 units. What should the firm do in order to maximize profit?

 a. The firm should increase output, because at 600 units, price is above marginal cost.
 b. The firm should maintain output at 600 units, because at this output level, marginal revenue is greater than marginal cost, marginal cost is minimized, and price is the highest.
 c. The firm should increase the level of output, because at 600 units, marginal revenue is greater than marginal cost.
 d. The firm should increase the level of output until it reaches the minimum average total cost.

20. Refer to the graphs below. Assuming both firms are producing 5 cups per week, which firm is maximizing profits?

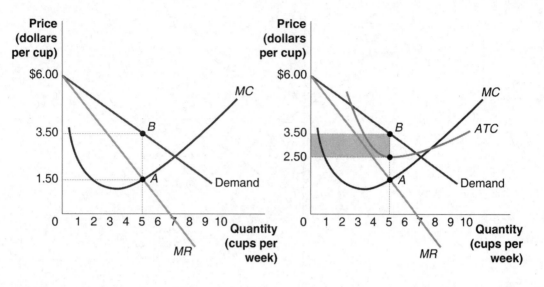

a.   the firm on the left
b.   the firm on the right
c.   both firms
d.   neither firm

21. Refer to the graph below. Assume that the firm represented by the cost and demand curves below is maximizing profit. Which area represents the formula: $(P - ATC) \times Q$?

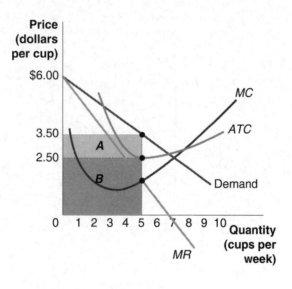

a.   area A
b.   area B
c.   area A + area B
d.   area B − area A

22. Refer to the graph below. Assume that the firm represented by the cost and demand curves below is maximizing profit. The value of profits is

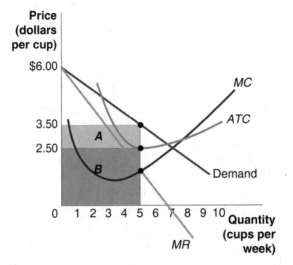

a. $17.50.
b. $12.50.
c. $5.00.
d. None of the above; that information cannot be obtained from this graph.

23. Refer to the table below. When is average total cost minimized?

Cups Sold per Week (Q)	Price (P)	Total Revenue (TR)	Marginal Revenue (MR)	Total Cost (TC)	Marginal Cost (MC)	Average Total Cost (ATC)	Profit
0	$6.00	$0.00	-	$5.00	-		
1	5.50	5.50	$5.50	8.00	$3.00		
2	5.00	10.00	4.50	9.50	1.50		
3	4.50	13.50	3.50	10.00	0.50		
4	4.00	16.00	2.50	11.00	1.00		
5	3.50	17.50	1.50	12.50	1.50		
6	3.00	18.00	0.50	14.50	2.00		
7	2.50	17.50	-0.50	17.00	2.50		
8	2.00	16.00	-1.50	20.00	3.00		
9	1.50	13.50	-2.50	23.50	3.50		
10	1.00	10.00	-3.50	27.50	4.00		

a. at 1 unit of output
b. at 5 units of output
c. at 6 units of output
d. at 10 units of output

24. Refer to the table below. What level of output should be produced in order to maximize profit?

Cups Sold per Week (Q)	Price (P)	Total Revenue (TR)	Marginal Revenue (MR)	Total Cost (TC)	Marginal Cost (MC)	Average Total Cost (ATC)	Profit
0	$6.00	$0.00	-	$5.00	-		
1	5.50	5.50	$5.50	8.00	$3.00		
2	5.00	10.00	4.50	9.50	1.50		
3	4.50	13.50	3.50	10.00	0.50		
4	4.00	16.00	2.50	11.00	1.00		
5	3.50	17.50	1.50	12.50	1.50		
6	3.00	18.00	0.50	14.50	2.00		
7	2.50	17.50	-0.50	17.00	2.50		
8	2.00	16.00	-1.50	20.00	3.00		
9	1.50	13.50	-2.50	23.50	3.50		
10	1.00	10.00	-3.50	27.50	4.00		

a. 1 unit of output
b. 5 units of output
c. 6 units of output
d. 10 units of output

25. Refer to the graphs below. Which firm is a monopolistic competitor operating in the long run?

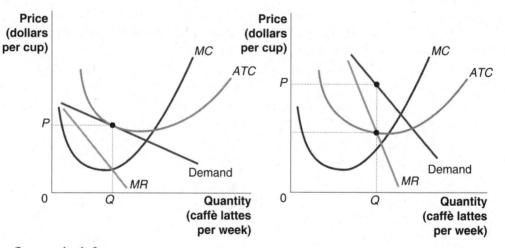

a. the firm on the left
b. the firm on the right
c. both firms
d. neither firm

26. How does the entry of new coffeehouses affect the profits of existing coffeehouses?
a. Entry will increase the profits of existing coffeehouses by shifting the market demand curve for coffee to the right.
b. Entry will increase the profits of existing coffeehouses by shifting each of their individual demand curves to the right.
c. Entry will decrease the profits of existing coffeehouses by shifting each of their individual demand curves to the left and making the demand curves more elastic.
d. Entry will not affect the profits of existing coffeehouses.

27. Suppose you invest $200,000 in a business. The return you could earn each year on a similar investment using that money is 10 percent, or $20,000. In an economic sense, the $20,000 is
    a. an economic cost.
    b. economic profit.
    c. an accounting cost.
    d. both economic profit and accounting profit.

28. Refer to the graphs below. Which graph depicts a situation in which some firms will exit the industry?

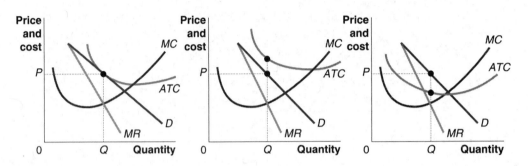

    a. the graph on the left
    b. the graph in the middle
    c. the graph on the right
    d. none of the above

29. Refer to the graphs below. Which graph best depicts the relationship between price and average total cost in the long run for a monopolistically competitive firm?

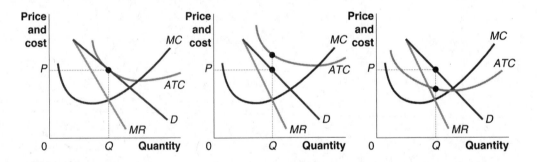

    a. the graph on the left
    b. the graph in the middle
    c. the graph on the right
    d. none of the above

30. Refer to the graphs below. Which graph best depicts the profit or loss situation for a monopolistically competitive firm in the long run?

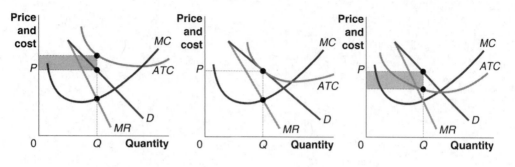

   a.   the graph on the left
   b.   the graph in the middle
   c.   the graph on the right
   d.   none of the above

31. Refer to the graphs below. Which graph best depicts a firm in a monopolistically competitive industry that has an incentive to exit the industry in the long run?

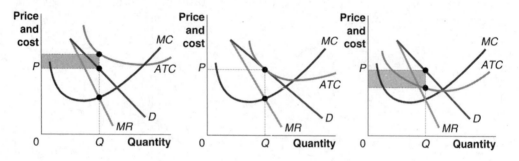

   a.   the graph on the left
   b.   the graph in the middle
   c.   the graph on the right
   d.   none of the above

32. Refer to the graphs below, which represent the situations facing typical firms in three different monopolistically competitive industries. Which graph best represents the situation where new firms are likely to enter the industry?

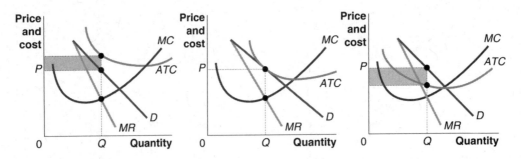

a. the graph on the left
b. the graph in the middle
c. the graph on the right
d. none of the above

33. Refer to the graph below. Assuming the computer industry is monopolistically competitive, which set of demand and marginal revenue curves for a typical firm is more consistent with long-run equilibrium in the computer industry?

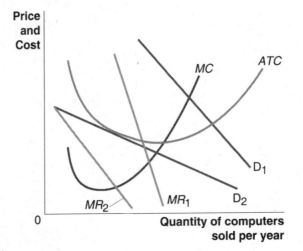

a. D_1 and MR_1
b. D_2 and MR_2
c. D_1 and MR_2
d. D_2 and MR_1

34. Is zero economic profit inevitable in the long run for a monopolistically competitive firm?
    a. Yes; there is nothing the firm can do to avoid zero economic profit in the long run.
    b. No; a firm could try to continue making a profit in the long run by producing a product identical to those of competing firms.
    c. No; a firm could try to continue making a profit in the long run by reducing production costs and improving its products.
    d. No; a firm could try to continue making a profit in the long run by simply offering goods that are cheaper to produce, even if they have less value than those offered by competing firms.

35. Refer to the graphs below. Which points on the graph coincide with productive efficiency?

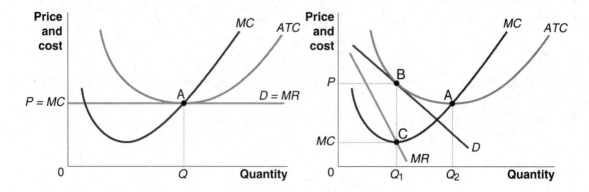

a. point A on both graphs
b. point B on the graph on the right
c. point C on the graph on the right
d. points A, B, and C on the graph on the right

36. Refer to the graph below. Which level of output indicates excess capacity?

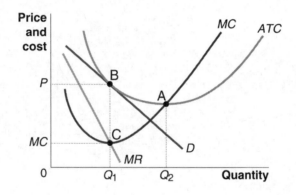

a. Q_1
b. Q_2
c. both Q_1 and Q_2
d. neither Q_1 nor Q_2

37. Which type of efficiency is achieved by a monopolistically competitive firm in the long run?
a. allocative efficiency
b. productive efficiency
c. both allocative and productive efficiency
d. neither allocative nor productive efficiency

38. What trade-offs do consumers face when buying a product from a monopolistically competitive firm?
a. Consumers pay a lower price but also have fewer choices.
b. Consumers pay a price greater than marginal cost but also have choices more suited to their tastes.
c. Consumers pay a higher price but are happy knowing that the industry is highly efficient.
d. Consumers pay a price as low as the competitive price but have difficulty finding and buying the product.

39. What is the term given to all the activities necessary for a firm to sell a product to a consumer?
    a. brand management
    b. advertising
    c. marketing
    d. product differentiation

40. What is the term given to the actions of a firm intended to maintain the differentiation of a product over time?
    a. brand management
    b. advertising
    c. marketing
    d. campaigning

41. Which of the following statements is correct?
    a. Brand names can be easily protected, especially as time goes by.
    b. Legally enforcing trademarks can be difficult.
    c. Establishing franchises is the best strategy to protect a firm's brand name.
    d. all of the above

42. Refer to the figure below. Which of the following terms is missing in the box on the right?

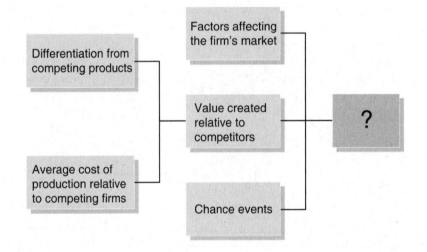

    a. brand management
    b. marketing
    c. profitability
    d. demand

Short Answer Questions

1. Describe how Starbucks has used brand management to differentiate its products.

_____

_____

_____

_____

2. What is the most important characteristic that perfectly competitive and monopolistically competitive firms have in common?

_____

_____

_____

3. Why is it not possible for a monopolistically competitive firm to produce at minimum average total cost in long-run equilibrium?

_____

_____

_____

4. How do consumers benefit from monopolistic competition?

_____

_____

_____

5. The job of some of Coca-Cola's employees is to visit restaurants and bars and order mixed drinks. What motivation would Coca-Cola have to encourage their employees to "drink on the job?"

_____

_____

_____

_____

True/False Questions

T F 1.   The marginal revenue curve lies below the demand curve for any firm that has the ability to affect the price of the product it sells.

T F 2.   A firm's profit equals the total quantity sold times the difference between the price of the product and total cost.

T F 3.   Monopolistically competitive firms charge a price greater than marginal cost in both the short run and the long run.

T F 4.   The market for coffeehouses, such as Starbucks, has many firms and the barriers to entering the market are low.

T F 5.   Unlike perfectly competitive firms, monopolistically competitive firms earn long-run profits.

T F 6.   When some firms exit a monopolistically competitive market, the demand curves of firms that remain become less elastic.

T F 7.   Among the factors that make a firm successful but are not under its control is the ability to differentiate its product.

T F 8.   The word "thermos" was originally a brand name that become so widely used that it is no longer subject to legal protection.

T F 9.   Brand management refers to all activities necessary for a firm to sell a product to a consumer.

T F 10. Because consumers pay a price above marginal cost in a monopolistically competitive market, they are better off than they would be in a competitive market.

T F 11. Unlike perfectly competitive firms, monopolistically competitive firms have excess capacity.

T F 12. Because a monopolistically competitive firm has a downward-sloping demand curve, marginal revenue will always be lower than price.

T F 13. Monopolistically competitive firms will earn higher profit in the long run than perfectly competitive firms.

T F 14. Firms use brand management to postpone the time when they will no longer be able to earn economic profits.

T F 15. One motive for advertising is to make the demand for a product more elastic so that when price is lowered, there will be a greater increase in quantity demanded.

Answers to the Self-Test

Multiple-Choice Questions

Question	Answer	Comment
1	c	Monopolistic competition is a market structure in which barriers to entry are low, and many firms compete by selling similar, but not identical, products.
2	b	Because changing the price affects the quantity sold, a monopolistically competitive firm will face a downward-sloping demand curve, rather than the horizontal demand curve faced by a competitive firm.
3	c	If Starbucks increases the price of cafè lattes, quantity demanded falls from 3,000 to 2,400 but quantity demanded does not fall to zero.
4	b	A perfectly competitive firm faces a horizontal demand curve and does not have to cut its price in order to sell a larger quantity. A monopolistically competitive firm, however, must cut its price to sell more, so its marginal revenue curve will slope downward and will be below its demand curve.

5	a	A monopolistically competitive firm must decrease its price to sell more. Therefore, its marginal revenue curve and demand curve are both downward sloping.
6	c	Price is revenue per unit, or average revenue. Average revenue is equal to total revenue divided by quantity. Because total revenue equals price multiplied by quantity, dividing by quantity leaves just price. Therefore, average revenue is always equal to price. This will be true for firms in any of the four market structures.
7	c	The firm's marginal revenue is the change in total revenue when it sells one more unit of output.
8	b	When the firm decreases its price, one good thing and one bad thing happen. The good thing: It sells more units of the good; this is the *output effect*. The bad thing is that it receives less for each unit that it could have sold at the higher price; this is the *price effect*.
9	a	When the firm decreases its price, one good thing and one bad thing happen. The good thing: It sells more units of the good; this is the *output effect*. The bad thing is that it receives less for each unit that it could have sold at the higher price; this is the *price effect*.
10	a	Average revenue equals price, which is $3.00 when six units are sold. Or, average revenue equals total revenue divided by output ($18.00/6 = $3.00).
11	c	Marginal revenue equals the change in total revenue divided by the change in output. As output increases from 5 to 6 units, the change in total revenue is $18.00 – $17.50 = $0.50, and the change in output is 6 – 5 = 1. Therefore, marginal revenue equals: $0.50/1 = $0.50.
12	a	Area A shows the loss of revenue from a price decrease. The firm is losing $0.50 for each of the caffè lattes that it used to sell for $3.50.
13	b	Area B shows the gain in revenue from the price cut = $3.00 × 1 = $3.00.
14	b	Every firm that has the ability to affect the price of the good or service it sells will have a marginal revenue curve that is below its demand curve. Only firms in perfectly competitive markets, which can sell as many units as they want at the market price, have marginal revenue curves that are the same as their demand curves.
15	b	Marginal revenue from the seventh through the tenth caffè latte is negative. This is because the additional revenue received from selling one more caffè latte is smaller than the revenue lost from receiving a lower price on the caffè lattes that could have been sold at the original price.
16	c	All firms use the same approach to maximize profits: Produce where marginal revenue is equal to marginal cost.
17	b	A firm's marginal cost is the increase in total cost resulting from producing one more unit of output.
18	b	Marginal cost equals marginal revenue when 900 units of output are produced and sold. The price charged by the firm is determined by the demand curve, and consumers are willing to pay $15 for 900 units.
19	c	At 600 units of output, marginal revenue is $12 and marginal cost is $4. As long as $MR > MC$, the firm should continue to expand production.
20	c	Profit is maximized at the quantity where $MR = MC$. In both cases, the output level is set where marginal revenue equals marginal cost.
21	a	Profit $= (P - ATC) \times Q$, so area A represents profit.
22	c	Profit $= (P - ATC) \times Q = ($3.50$/cup - 2.50/cup$) \times 5$ cups $= 5.00.
23	c	When $Q = 6$, $ATC = $14.50/6 = 2.42.
24	b	Profit is maximized where $MR = MC$. This occurs where $MR = MC = 1.50 and an output level of 5 cups.

25	a	In the long run, when the demand curve is tangent to the average total cost curve, price is equal to average total cost, the firm is breaking even, and it no longer earns an economic profit.
26	c	As new coffeehouses open, the firm's demand curve will shift to the left. The demand curve will shift because the existing firms will sell fewer cups of coffee at each price now that there are additional coffeehouses in the area selling similar drinks. The demand curve will also become more elastic because consumers in the area now have additional coffeehouses from which to buy coffee, so existing firms will lose more customers if they raise their prices.
27	a	The annual opportunity cost of investing the funds in your own business is 10 percent of $200,000 or $20,000. This $20,000 is part of your profit in the accounting sense, and you would have to pay taxes on it. But in an economic sense, the $20,000 is a cost.
28	b	Because price is less than average total cost in the graph in the middle, the firm is suffering losses. Firm losses will lead to the exit of some firms in the industry. In the graph on the left, the firm is making zero profit; and, in the graph on the right, the firm is making positive profit.
29	a	In the long run, $P = ATC$ and the firm earns zero economic profit.
30	b	In the long run, a monopolistically competitive firm earns zero economic profit, or $P = ATC$.
31	a	The graph on the left shows a monopolistically competitive firm suffering losses, so there is an incentive for firms to exit.
32	c	The graph on the right shows a monopolistically competitive firm earning profits, so there is an incentive for firms to enter.
33	b	If the computer industry is monopolistically competitive, then in the long run the typical firm's demand curve will be tangent to its average cost curve and economic profit will equal zero.
34	c	Firms try to continue earning profits by reducing the cost of producing their products, by improving their products, or by convincing consumers that their products are different from what competitors offer. To stay one step ahead of its competitors, a firm must offer consumers goods or services that they perceive to have greater value than those offered by competing firms.
35	a	At point A on both graphs, the firms produce where average total cost is at a minimum. When this happens, the firms are productively efficient.
36	a	The monopolistically competitive firm has excess capacity equal to the difference between its profit-maximizing level of output and the productively efficient level of output.
37	d	In a perfectly competitive market, both productive efficiency and allocative efficiency are achieved, but in a monopolistically competitive market, neither is achieved.
38	b	Consumers face a trade-off when buying the product of a monopolistically competitive firm: They are paying a price that is greater than marginal cost and the product is not being produced at minimum average cost, but they benefit from being able to purchase a product that is differentiated and more closely suited to their tastes.
39	c	Firms can differentiate their products through marketing. Marketing refers to all the activities necessary for a firm to sell a product to a consumer.
40	a	The actions of a firm intended to maintain the differentiation of a product over time are called brand management.
41	b	Legally enforcing trademarks can be difficult. Estimates are that each year U.S. companies lose hundreds of billions of dollars of sales worldwide as a result of

unauthorized use of their trademarked brand names. U.S. companies have often found it difficult to enforce their trademarks in the courts of some foreign countries.

42   c   The factors under a firm's control—the ability to differentiate its product and the ability to produce it at lower cost—combine with the factors beyond its control to determine the firm's profitability.

Short Answer Responses

1. On page 401, the textbook explains that Starbucks offers consumers a coffeehouse where they can sit, relax, read, chat, and drink higher-quality coffee than is typically served in diners or donut shops. Company-owned coffeehouses (rather than franchise businesses) enable Starbucks to have greater control of the products sold and how they are marketed. Despite the success it has enjoyed, low entry barriers have enabled other firms to copy much of what Starbucks has done.

2. Low entry barriers are common to both market structures, so firms can easily enter and exit the industry. Ease of entry and exit ensures that firms earn zero economic profits in the long run.

3. The entry and exit of firms ensures that monopolistically competitive firms will earn zero economic profits in the long run. For this to be true, price must equal average total cost. This, in turn, requires a firm's demand curve to be tangent to its average total cost curve. Because the firm's demand curve is downward-sloping, this tangency must be to the left of the minimum point on the average total cost curve.

4. Although consumers pay a price that is greater than the marginal cost of production, they benefit from being able to purchase a product that is differentiated and more closely suited to their tastes.

5. Coca-Cola is very careful to protect its trademarked name. Some employees visit bars and restaurants to order "rum and Coke." If they are served another cola, they will inform their legal department. The offending bar or restaurant will be contacted and warned to either serve Coca-Cola or to inform customers that they do not serve "rum and Coke." Although such actions may seem petty, they serve the important purpose of protecting a valuable trademark. Firms that have not taken positive steps to protect their trademarks have lost legal protection of their brand names.

True/False Answers

1. T   See the section "Marginal Revenue for a Firm with a Downward-Sloping Demand Curve" on page 402.
2. F   A firm's profit equals the total quantity sold times the difference between the price of the product and *average* total cost.
3. T   The firm has downward-sloping demand and marginal revenue curves, and the marginal revenue curve lies below the demand curve. The firm will choose to produce where the marginal revenue intersects the marginal cost and then choose the price to charge by going up to the demand curve and charging the consumers' willingness to pay at that quantity.
4. T   See the Chapter Opener on page 401 in the textbook.
5. F   Low barriers to entry mean firms will enter and exit until economic profit equals zero.
6. T   When firms exit, the demand curves for remaining firms shift to the right and become less elastic.
7. F   The ability to differentiate its product is under the firm's control.
8. T   See "Defending a Brand Name" beginning on page 416 in the textbook.

9. F This is the definition of marketing. See page 414 in the textbook.

10. F Production in monopolistically competitive markets is inefficient, but consumers may be better off because monopolistic competition offers a variety of differentiated products.

11. T Because the quantity a monopolistically competitive firm produces is less than the quantity at the minimum average total cost, the firm has excess capacity.

12. T See the section "Marginal Revenue for a Firm with a Downward-Sloping Demand Curve" on page 402 in the textbook.

13. F In the long run, both monopolistically competitive firms and perfectly competitive firms will earn zero economic profit.

14. T Product differentiation and brand management help firms maintain economic profit.

15. F One motive for advertising is to make the demand for a product *less* elastic so that if price is raised, quantity demanded will not fall as much as it would without advertising.

Chapter Summary and Learning Objectives

13.1 Oligopoly and Barriers to Entry (pages 432–435)

Show how barriers to entry explain the existence of oligopolies. An **oligopoly** is a market structure in which a small number of interdependent firms compete. **Barriers to entry** keep new firms from entering an industry. The three most important barriers to entry are economies of scale, ownership of a key input, and government barriers. Economies of scale are the most important barrier to entry. **Economies of scale** exist when a firm's long-run average costs fall as it increases output. Government barriers include patents, licensing, and barriers to international trade. A **patent** is the exclusive right to a product for a period of 20 years from the date the product is invented.

13.2 Using Game Theory to Analyze Oligopoly (pages 435–443)

Use game theory to analyze the strategies of oligopolistic firms. Because an oligopoly has only a few firms, interactions among those firms are particularly important. **Game theory** is the study of how people make decisions in situations in which attaining their goals depends on their interactions with others; in economics, it is the study of the decisions of firms in industries where the profits of each firm depend on its interactions with other firms. A **business strategy** refers to actions taken by a firm to achieve a goal, such as maximizing profits. Oligopoly games can be illustrated with a **payoff matrix**, which is a table that shows the payoffs that each firm earns from every combination of strategies by the firms. One possible outcome in oligopoly is **collusion**, which is an agreement among firms to charge the same price or otherwise not to compete. A **cartel** is a group of firms that collude by agreeing to restrict output to increase prices and profits. In a **cooperative equilibrium**, firms cooperate to increase their mutual payoff. In a **noncooperative equilibrium**, firms do not cooperate but pursue their own self-interest. A **dominant strategy** is a strategy that is the best for a firm, no matter what strategies other firms use. A **Nash equilibrium** is a situation in which each firm chooses the best strategy, given the strategies chosen by other firms. A situation in which pursuing dominant strategies results in noncooperation that leaves everyone worse off is called a **prisoner's dilemma**. Because many business situations are repeated games, firms may end up implicitly colluding to keep prices high. With **price leadership**, one firm takes the lead in announcing a price change, which is then matched by the other firms in the industry.

13.3 Sequential Games and Business Strategy (pages 443–446)

Use sequential games to analyze business strategies. Recent work in game theory has focused on actions firms can take to deter the entry of new firms into an industry. Deterring entry can be analyzed using a sequential game, where first one firm makes a decision and then another firm reacts to that decision. Sequential games can be illustrated using decision trees.

13.4 The Five Competitive Forces Model (pages 446–449)

Use the five competitive forces model to analyze competition in an industry. Michael Porter of Harvard Business School argues that the state of competition in an industry is determined by five competitive forces: the degree of competition among existing firms, the threat from new entrants, competition from substitute goods or services, the bargaining power of buyers, and the bargaining power of suppliers.

Chapter Review

Chapter Opener: Competition in the Computer Market (page 431)

Firms like Wal-Mart and Apple operate in an oligopoly, where there are a small number of competing firms and a firm's profitability depends on its interactions with other firms in the industry. Firms in an oligopoly must decide not just what price to charge and how many units to produce but also how much to advertise, which new technologies to adopt, how to manage relations with suppliers, and which new markets to enter.

13.1 Oligopoly and Barriers to Entry (pages 432–435)
Learning Objective: Show how barriers to entry explain the existence of oligopolies.

An **oligopoly** is a market structure in which a small number of interdependent firms compete. Economists use concentration ratios to measure the fraction of sales accounted for by the largest firms in an industry. Most economists believe that a four-firm concentration ratio of 40 percent or more indicates an industry is an oligopoly. Concentration ratios have flaws. As usually calculated, the ratios do not include sales in the United States by foreign firms and concentration ratios are calculated for the national market even though competition in some markets is local.

An important reason why oligopolies exist is the presence of barriers to entry. A **barrier to entry** is anything that keeps new firms from entering an industry in which firms are earning economic profits. The most important barrier to entry is **economies of scale**, which exist when a firm's long-run average costs fall as it increases output. A second entry barrier is ownership of a key input. An example of this type of barrier is Ocean Spray's control of most of the supply of cranberries. A third type of barrier to entry is a government-imposed barrier. A patent is an entry barrier. A **patent** is the exclusive right to a product for a period of 20 years from the date the product was invented.

Extra Solved Problem 13-1
Government-Sanctioned Oligopoly
Supports Learning Objective 13.1: Show how barriers to entry explain the existence of oligopolies.

The European Union continues to experience growing pains as the economies of many countries are melded into a single economy. Regulation of the electricity and natural gas industries across countries continues to be one point of contention. One article on the subject contains the following observations:

> Oligopoly is the best structure for a European Union gas and power market, a senior advisor to EU competition commissioner, Neelie Kroes, told an industry seminar in Brussels on May 11.

> "A market which requires such investment and is so technical is not effective if you have thousands of small operators," said Olivier Guersent, deputy head of Kroes' policy advisory team.

Source: "EU Commissioner: Oligopoly is Best Structure for European Union's Power and Gas Markets," *Global Power Report*, May 18, 2006.

Which barriers to entry discussed in the textbook are most relevant to this discussion?

SOLVING THE PROBLEM
Step 1: **Review the chapter material.**
This problem is about barriers to entry, so you may want to review the section "Oligopoly and Barriers to Entry," which begins on page 432 in the textbook.

Step 2: **Discuss barriers to entry that apply to the European Union's gas and power market.**
The barrier to entry that is most relevant to this discussion is economies of scale. The advisors to the EU competition commissioner suggest that there are significant fixed costs in the form of physical capital and intellectual capital. Due to these fixed costs, it is likely that if power and gas were supplied by many small firms, each firm's average cost would be quite high. As a result, consumers would have to pay high prices to cover these high average costs. An oligopolistic market structure would allow the industry to take advantage of economies of scale and offer power and gas at a lower price to consumers than it would otherwise.

13.2 **Using Game Theory to Analyze Oligopoly (pages 435–443)**
Learning Objective: Use game theory to analyze the strategies of oligopolistic firms.

Game theory is the study of how people make decisions in situations in which attaining their goals depends on their interactions with others. Economists use game theory to study the decisions of firms in industries where the profits of each firm depend on its interactions with other firms. Games share three characteristics:

1. *rules* that determine what actions are allowable,
2. *strategies* that players employ to attain their objectives in the game, and
3. *payoffs* that are the result of the interaction among the players' strategies.

A **business strategy** represents actions taken by a firm to achieve a goal, such as maximizing profits. A **payoff matrix** is a table that shows the payoffs that each firm earns from every combination of strategies by the firms. **Collusion** is an agreement among firms to charge the same price, or otherwise not to compete.

A **dominant strategy** is a strategy that is the best for a firm, no matter what strategies other firms use. A situation in which each firm chooses the best strategy, given the strategies chosen by other firms, is called a **Nash equilibrium**.

Some games result in a **cooperative equilibrium**, an equilibrium in which players cooperate to increase their mutual payoff. An equilibrium in a game where players choose not to cooperate is a **noncooperative equilibrium** in which players pursue their own self-interest. An example of a noncooperative equilibrium is a **prisoner's dilemma**, a game in which pursuing dominant strategies results in noncooperation that leaves everyone worse off. Cooperation does not necessarily have to break down. If the business situation will recur, the business owners will be more likely to cooperate to avoid retaliation in future situations. When a situation recurs, it is a repeated game.

A form of implicit collusion in which one firm in an oligopoly announces a price change and the other firms in the industry match the change is called **price leadership**. A **cartel** is a group of firms that colludes by agreeing to restrict output to increase prices and profits. The Organization of the Petroleum

Exporting Countries (OPEC) is a cartel whose members meet periodically to agree on the quantities of oil each will produce. OPEC's production quotas are intended to reduce oil production below the competitive level and to increase the profits of member countries. Until recently, OPEC had difficulty sustaining member quotas and oil prices over time because when prices are high, each member has had an incentive to stop cooperating and increase output beyond its quota. In recent years, however, surging worldwide demand for oil has made it easier for OPEC to sustain high oil prices.

 Study Hint

Don't assume that every equilibrium involving dominant strategies chosen by each firm is also a prisoner's dilemma. It's possible that when each firm has a dominant strategy that both firms are actually better off. It is true that every prisoner's dilemma involves firms choosing their dominant strategies, but the reverse is not necessarily true.

13.3 | **Sequential Games and Business Strategy (pages 443–446)**

Learning Objective: Use sequential games to analyze business strategies.

In many business situations, one firm will make a decision and other firms will respond. These situations can be analyzed by using sequential games. For example, sequential games can be used to analyze strategies designed to deter entry by new firms or to analyze bargaining between firms. A decision tree, as in Figure 13-6 on page 444 in the textbook, can be used to illustrate a sequential game.

 Study Hint

To understand how a sequential game works, review *Solved Problem 13-3* on page 444 in the textbook. This problem explains that deterring the entry of other firms is not always the best idea. A firm should attempt to deter entry of other firms into their industry only if the cost of deterrence is less than the benefits they would receive by deterring entry.

13.4 | **The Five Competitive Forces Model (pages 446–449)**

Learning Objective: Use the five competitive forces model to analyze competition in an industry.

Michael Porter of the Harvard Business School has developed a model to analyze the competitiveness of an industry using five competitive forces. The forces are (1) competition from existing firms, (2) the threat from new entrants, (3) competition from substitute goods or services, (4) the bargaining power of buyers, and (5) the bargaining power of suppliers.

Extra Solved Problem 13-4
Analyzing Competition in the Music Industry Using the Five Forces Model
Supports Learning Objective 13.4: Use the five competitive forces model to analyze competition in an industry.

Until 2004, the music industry was dominated by five major record companies, which accounted for about 75 percent of a $25 billion market in CDs and related products. A merger in 2004 between Sony Music Entertainment and BMG Entertainment reduced the "Big Five" to the "Big Four": EMI, Sony-BMG, Warner Music Group, and Universal Music Group. Together, these four companies control approximately 80% of the music market in the United States. The following is a competitive analysis of the music industry prior to the late 1990s, before consumers began to download music on a wide scale over the Internet. The competitive analysis follows Michael Porter's five forces model, which is designed to assess the degree of competition in an industry.

1. **Competition from existing firms**. Significant competition among the largest firms but little between the Big Five and smaller firms. Little change over time in the market share of the Big Five firms.

2. **The threat from new entrants.** Barriers to entry made the potential threat from new entrants negligible. The financial resources required to establish a recording artist or group were substantial. Sound and video recordings had to be made and distributed, and contacts had to be made with venues where the artists would perform. It was difficult for a new firm to become established.

3. **Substitute goods or services**. Music was essentially available and playable in one format, the CD, and from one source, the music company that owned the rights to an artist's recordings. Few substitutes were available.

4. **Bargaining power of buyers**. Buyers' options were limited. They could obtain music in only one format, and the Big Five had considerable control over the prices of CDs.

5. **Bargaining power of suppliers**. Because recording artists were compelled to work with one of the Big Five, they had little negotiating power. Terms included in record contracts for new performers were very standardized.

Changes in the degree of competition in the industry have come about since the late 1990s primarily due to new technology. Widespread access to personal computers, MP3 encoding, and the Internet have made it possible for consumers to copy and distribute music at low cost.

Source: Google Answers: April 5, 2004. http://answers.google.com/answers/threadview?id=325373

Analyze the competitiveness of the music industry in the early twenty-first century using Porter's model.

SOLVING THE PROBLEM
Step 1: **Review the chapter material.**

This problem is about Michael Porter's model, so you may want to review the section "The Five Competitive Forces Model," which begins on page 446 in the textbook.

Step 2: **Discuss the extent of competition from existing firms.**

New music technology has reduced the start-up costs for new artists. High-quality recordings can be made, copied, and marketed directly through the Internet. Some artists have even established their own companies, bypassing the Big Four. Competition is likely to erode the market share of the Big Four in the future.

Step 3: **Discuss the threat from new entrants.**

Entry barriers have been lowered by the new technologies. New artists are less dependent on the traditional marketing network. Music can be advertised and sold directly from the artists' Web sites. The threat from entrants has increased.

Step 4: **Discuss competition from substitute goods or services.**

More substitutes are available for consumers. If the format used by record companies is not what consumers want, or if music is sold at high prices, consumers can easily download it through the Internet. Consumers who want only two or three songs from a CD with 10 or more songs can download only those they want.

Step 5: **Discuss the bargaining power of buyers.**

As the availability of substitutes has grown, so has the bargaining power of consumers. Because consumers can download songs at little cost beyond their time, the Big Four companies have had to offer consumers lower prices and different formats.

Step 6: **Discuss the bargaining power of suppliers.**

As noted in the previous steps, musicians and consumers can use the Internet to bypass the traditional distribution networks and are less dependent on established companies, in particular the Big Four. The bargaining power of suppliers has increased, because musicians can credibly threaten to sell their music directly to consumers if the Big Four are unwilling to offer the musicians favorable contracts.

Key Terms

Barrier to entry Anything that keeps new firms from entering an industry in which firms are earning economic profits.

Business strategy Actions taken by a firm to achieve a goal, such as maximizing profits.

Cartel A group of firms that collude by agreeing to restrict output to increase prices and profits.

Collusion An agreement among firms to charge the same price or otherwise not to compete.

Cooperative equilibrium An equilibrium in a game in which players cooperate to increase their mutual payoff.

Dominant strategy A strategy that is the best for a firm, no matter what strategies other firms use.

Economies of scale The situation when a firm's long-run average costs fall as it increases output.

Game theory The study of how people make decisions in situations in which attaining their goals depends on their interactions with others; in economics, the study of the decisions of firms in industries where the profits of each firm depend on its interactions with other firms.

Nash equilibrium A situation in which each firm chooses the best strategy, given the strategies chosen by other firms.

Noncooperative equilibrium An equilibrium in a game in which players do not cooperate but pursue their own self-interest.

Oligopoly A market structure in which a small number of interdependent firms compete.

Patent The exclusive right to a product for a period of 20 years from the date the product is invented.

Payoff matrix A table that shows the payoffs that each firm earns from every combination of strategies by the firms.

Price leadership A form of implicit collusion in which one firm in an oligopoly announces a price change and the other firms in the industry match the change.

Prisoner's dilemma A game in which pursuing dominant strategies results in noncooperation that leaves everyone worse off.

Self-Test

(Answers are provided at the end of the Self-Test.)

Multiple-Choice Questions

1. Which of the terms below is defined as "A market structure in which a small number of interdependent firms compete?"
   a. game theory
   b. barriers to entry
   c. oligopoly
   d. economies of scale

2. Which of the terms below is defined as "Anything that keeps new firms from entering an industry in which firms are earning economic profits?"
   a. game theory
   b. barriers to entry
   c. oligopoly
   d. economies of scale

3. According to the textbook, which of the following industries in the retail trade had the highest concentration ratios in the United States?
   a. hobby, toy, and game stores; radio, television, and other electronic stores
   b. college bookstores and athletic footwear stores
   c. warehouse clubs and supercenters; discount department stores
   d. pharmacies and drugstores

4. According to the textbook, which of the following industries in manufacturing had the highest concentration ratios in the United States?
   a. aircraft and breakfast cereal
   b. automobiles and dog and cat food
   c. cigarettes and beer
   d. computers

5. Economies of scale help determine the extent of
   a. market failure in an industry.
   b. competition in an industry.
   c. product differentiation in an industry.
   d. product innovation in an industry.

6. Economies of scale exist when a firm's _____ average costs fall as it _____ output.
    a. short-run; increases
    b. short-run; decreases
    c. long-run; increases
    d. long-run; decreases

7. Refer to the graph below. Which quantity is more likely to be the quantity produced by the typical firm in an oligopoly?

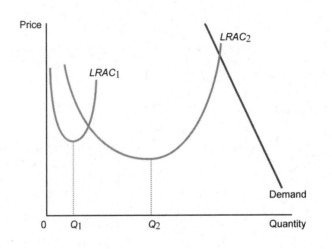

    a. Q_1
    b. Q_2
    c. the sum of Q_1 and Q_2
    d. the difference between Q_2 and Q_1

8. Refer to the graph below. Fill in the blanks. When the level of output produced is Q_1, economies of scale in the industry are relatively _____ and the industry will have a _____ number of firms.

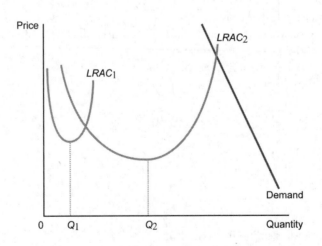

    a. important; small
    b. important; large
    c. unimportant; small
    d. unimportant; large

9. Which of the following is a barrier to entry?
   a. economies of scale
   b. ownership of a key input
   c. patents
   d. all of the above

10. A patent typically gives the holder exclusive rights to a product for a period of
    a. 10 years.
    b. 20 years.
    c. 30 years.
    d. 40 years.

11. In the broadest sense, game theory studies the decisions of firms in industries where the profits of each firm depend on
    a. the ability of a firm to set up barriers to entry.
    b. the firm's interactions with other firms.
    c. agreements among firms to charge the same price.
    d. the ability to achieve a dominant position in the industry.

12. Every game has these characteristics:
    a. winners, losers, and payoffs.
    b. rules, an intermediary, and payouts.
    c. rules, strategies, and payoffs.
    d. strategies and defeats.

13. Which of the following is the definition of business strategy?
    a. A business strategy refers to the rules that determine what actions are allowable.
    b. A business strategy refers to actions taken by firms to attain their objectives.
    c. A business strategy is a study of how people make decisions.
    d. A business strategy is an agreement among firms to charge the same price.

14. Match the following definition with one of the terms below: "A situation where each firm chooses the best strategy, given the strategies chosen by other firms."
    a. payoff matrix
    b. collusion
    c. dominant strategy
    d. Nash equilibrium

15. An agreement among firms to charge the same price or to otherwise not compete is
    a. a payoff matrix.
    b. collusion.
    c. a dominant strategy.
    d. a Nash equilibrium.

16. A strategy that is the best for a firm, no matter what strategies other firms use is
    a. a payoff matrix.
    b. collusion.
    c. a dominant strategy.
    d. a Nash equilibrium.

17. Refer to the payoff matrix below. Suppose that Wal-Mart and Target are selling Sony flat-screen computer monitors for a price of either $150 or $200 each. Based on the information on the payoff matrix, what is the dominant strategy?

   a.   Both firms will charge $150.
   b.   Both firms will charge $200.
   c.   Wal-Mart will charge $150, and Target will charge $200.
   d.   Wal-Mart will charge $200, and Target will charge $150.

18. Refer to the payoff matrix below. Suppose that Wal-Mart and Target are selling Sony flat-screen computer monitors for a price of either $150 or $200 each. Based on the information on the payoff matrix, does a Nash equilibrium exist?

   a.   yes
   b.   no
   c.   yes, but only for Wal-Mart.
   d.   yes, but only for Target.

19. An equilibrium in a game in which players cooperate to increase their mutual payoff is called
   a.   a cooperative equilibrium.
   b.   a noncooperative equilibrium.
   c.   a prisoner's dilemma.
   d.   a dominant strategy.

20. A game where pursuing dominant strategies results in noncooperation that leaves everyone worse off is called
   a.   a cooperative equilibrium.
   b.   a noncooperative equilibrium.
   c.   a prisoner's dilemma.
   d.   a dominant strategy.

21. Price leadership is a form of _____ in which one firm in an oligopoly announces a price change and the other firms in the industry match the change.
    a. auction strategy
    b. implicit collusion
    c. explicit collusion
    d. retaliation strategy

22. What type of auction is used in eBay?
    a. a first-price auction
    b. a second-price auction
    c. a zero sum game auction
    d. None; eBay does not conduct auctions.

23. What is the dominant strategy of eBay auction participants?
    a. to place a bid well below the subjective value you place on the item
    b. to place a bid equal to the maximum value you place on the item
    c. to place a bid well above the subjective value you place on the item
    d. There is no dominant strategy on eBay auctions.

24. Fill in the blank. In a repeated game, the losses associated with not cooperating are _____ the losses of cooperating.
    a. greater than
    b. less than
    c. equal to
    d. either greater than or less than, depending on the circumstances

25. How does the prisoner's dilemma compare to the outcome of a repeated game?
    a. The equilibrium in both cases is identical.
    b. In a repeated game, two firms are more likely to charge a low price, even though they would be better off if they charged a high price.
    c. In a repeated game, two firms are more likely to charge the high price and receive high profits.
    d. There are no comparisons to be made between the two.

26. A group of firms that colludes by agreeing to restrict output to increase prices and profits is called
    a. a duopoly.
    b. an oligopoly.
    c. a cartel.
    d. a conglomerate.

27. Fill in the blanks with the word and phrase that best describe the history of OPEC: Sustaining high prices has been _____ because members often _____ their output quotas.
    a. easy; produce less than
    b. easy; produce more than
    c. difficult; produce less than
    d. difficult; produce more than

28. If individual countries that are members of OPEC exceed their production quotas, the amount of oil supplied to the world _____, and the price of oil _____.
    a. increases; decreases
    b. increases; increases
    c. decreases; increases
    d. decreases; decreases

29. Refer to the payoff matrix below. The payoff matrix describes the payoffs to two members of the OPEC cartel. The Nash equilibrium of this game will occur with Saudi Arabia producing a _____ output and Nigeria producing a _____ output.

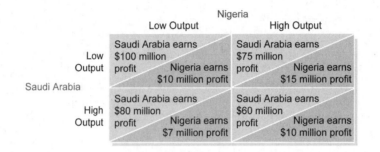

    a. low; low
    b. high; high
    c. low; high
    d. high; low

30. A game theory analysis of deterring entry concludes that
    a. deterring entry is always a good idea.
    b. deterring entry is always a bad idea.
    c. deterring entry may be a good or a bad idea, depending on the circumstances.
    d. it is difficult to predict whether deterring entry is a good or a bad idea.

31. Refer to the table below. Given the decision tree for an entry game, Wal-Mart will

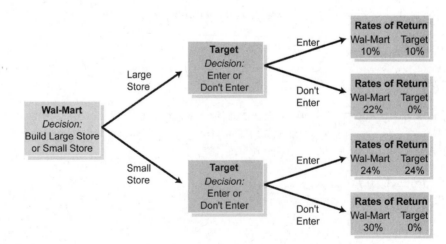

    a. build a large store.
    b. build a small store.
    c. be indifferent between building a large store or a small store.
    d. do whatever it takes to prevent Target from entering.

32. In Michael Porter's Competitive Forces Model, which term describes the threat of competition from firms that might enter the market?
    a. bargaining power of buyers
    b. bargaining power of suppliers
    c. competition from existing firms
    d. threat from new entrants

33. During the 1940s, the Hollywood movie studios' interaction with the Technicolor Company can best be described as
    a. competition from a substitute good.
    b. a threat from a new entrant.
    c. a reduction in profits caused by the bargaining power of a buyer.
    d. a reduction in profits caused by the bargaining power of a supplier.

34. If automobile companies have significant bargaining power when buying tires, you would expect that
    a. tire prices will be low.
    b. tire prices will be high.
    c. the profitability of tire manufacturers is unlimited.
    d. tire suppliers also have significant bargaining power.

35. Fill in the blanks. Suppliers have more bargaining power when _____ firms can supply the input and the input _____ specialized.
    a. many; is
    b. many; is not
    c. few; is
    d. few; is not

36. Fill in the blanks. If an input is specialized and only a few firms can provide it, the profits of the firms that supply that input will be _____, and the firms will have _____ bargaining power with buyers.
    a. high; more
    b. low; less
    c. high; less
    d. low; more

37. Refer to the figure below. The figure shows the Competitive Forces Model. What is the name of the box in the center?

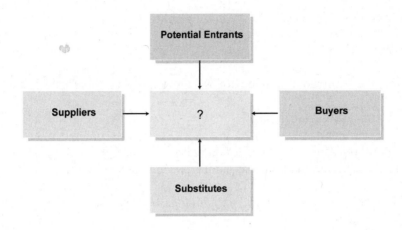

   a. Industry Competitors
   b. Bargaining Power
   c. Industry Threats
   d. Extent of Competition

38. Refer to the figure below. The figure shows the Competitive Forces Model. How many competitive forces are identified in this model?

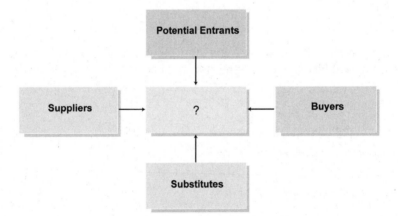

   a. three
   b. four
   c. five
   d. six

Short Answer Questions

1. Assume that industry A and industry B each have a four-firm concentration ratio of 80 percent. Both industries sell their products in national markets and firms in both industries face no competition from foreign firms. Can you conclude from this that the level of competition in both industries is similar?

_____

_____

_____

_____

2. The Organization of the Petroleum Exporting Countries (OPEC) operates as a cartel. Representatives of OPEC countries meet periodically to agree on quotas, the quantities of oil each will produce. Why does OPEC have difficulty maintaining high oil prices over the long run?

_____

_____

_____

_____

3. Occupational licensing laws in the United States require medical doctors and other practitioners to obtain licenses in order to operate legally. These laws are designed to protect the public—no one wants to be operated on by an unqualified surgeon—but critics point out that licensing restricts the number of people who enter the licensed professions. Is it necessary to have licensing laws to protect the public from using the services of unqualified medical doctors?

_____

_____

_____

4. In a famous 1945 antitrust case, the Aluminum Company of America (Alcoa) was declared a monopoly because the company controlled nearly all of the world's known supplies of bauxite, an essential input in the production of aluminum. Could Alcoa have argued that it faced competition despite its control of the bauxite market?

_____

_____

_____

5. Making the Connection, "American Airlines and Northwest Airlines Fail to Cooperate on a Price Increase," on page 440 in the textbook described the difficulty American Airlines had in raising ticket prices for business travelers in 2002. American subsequently lowered prices on some of its other routes in order to punish airlines for not matching its price increases. Why didn't American Airlines officials discuss their plans with other airline executives before prices were raised to find out if their strategy would be successful?

_____

_____

True/False Questions

T F 1.   The Herfindahl-Hirschman Index is an alternative to concentration ratios as a measure of competition in an industry.

T F 2.   In game theory, a Nash equilibrium is an equilibrium position where each firm chooses the best strategy, given the strategies chosen by other firms.

T F 3.   The most important barrier to entry is ownership of a key resource.

T F 4.   A prisoner's dilemma is a game that results in a cooperative equilibrium that leaves all parties better off.

T F 5.   A duopoly is an oligopoly with two firms.

T F 6.   John Nash won the Nobel Prize in economics for developing game theory in the 1940s.

T F 7.   OPEC is a cartel that consists of 12 Arab countries that own about 75 percent of the world's proven oil reserves.

T F 8.   Because the prisoner's dilemma assumes that a game will be played once, it does not describe most business situations.

T F 9.   In a second-price auction, the winning bidder pays the price of the second-highest bidder.

T F 10. An oligopoly that results from ownership of a key input will result in a government-imposed barrier to entry.

T F 11. In repeated games, a retaliation strategy increases the chances of cooperative behavior.

T F 12. A patent grants exclusive rights to a product for a period of 15 years.

T F 13. Because the four-firm concentration ratio for college bookstores is greater than the four-firm concentration ratio for pharmacies and drugstores, competition is greater among pharmacies and drugstores.

T F 14. Competition from complement goods or services is one of the Five Competitive Forces defined by Michael Porter.

T F 15. Most business situations are repeated games.

Answers to the Self-Test

Multiple-Choice Questions

Question	Answer	Comment
1	c	An oligopoly is a market structure in which a small number of interdependent firms compete.
2	b	Barriers to entry refer to anything that keeps new firms from entering an industry in which firms are earning economic profits.

3	c	The concentration ratios for these retail industries were 92 percent and 95 percent respectively according to Table 13-1 on page 433 in the textbook.
4	c	The concentration ratios for these manufacturing industries were 95 percent and 91 percent respectively according to Table 13-1 on page 433 in the textbook.
5	b	Economies of scale help determine the extent of competition in an industry.
6	c	Economies of scale exist when a firm's long-run average costs fall as it increases output.
7	b	In this case, the minimum point on the long-run average cost curve is at a level of output that is a large fraction of industry sales (closer to market demand); thus, the industry is an oligopoly.
8	d	Q_1 is a smaller fraction of total industry output than is Q_2. This means that economies of scale are relatively unimportant and allow a large number of firms to survive in the industry.
9	d	Economies of scale, ownership of a key input, and patents are all barriers to entry.
10	b	A patent typically gives the holder exclusive rights to a product for a period of 20 years.
11	b	Profits depend on strategy, or how a firm reacts to the moves made by other firms.
12	c	Rules determine what actions are allowable; strategies are used by players to attain their objectives in the game; payoffs are the results of the interaction among the players' strategies.
13	b	Strategies are actions taken by a business firm to achieve a goal, such as maximizing profits.
14	d	Nash equilibrium is a situation where each firm chooses the best strategy, given the strategies chosen by other firms.
15	b	Collusion is an agreement among firms to charge the same price or to otherwise not compete.
16	c	A dominant strategy is a strategy that is the best for a firm, no matter what strategies other firms use.
17	a	The dominant strategy of each firm is to charge $150.
18	a	Given the strategy of the other firm, each firm maximizes profit by charging a price of $150.
19	a	Equilibrium in a game in which players cooperate to increase their mutual payoff is called a cooperative equilibrium.
20	c	The prisoner's dilemma is a game where pursuing dominant strategies results in noncooperation that leaves everyone worse off.
21	b	See page 440 in the textbook.
22	b	The winning bidder pays the price of the second-highest bidder. See Making the Connection, "Is There a Dominant Strategy for Bidding on eBay?" on page 438 in the textbook.
23	b	A strategy of bidding the maximum value you place on an item dominates any other bidding strategy.
24	a	The possibility of retaliation for failing to cooperate increases the cost of failing to cooperate in a repeated game.
25	c	When the prisoner's dilemma is repeated, the firms are more likely to charge a high price and receive high profits.
26	c	A cartel is a group of firms that collude by agreeing to restrict output to increase prices and profits.
27	d	Sustaining high prices has been difficult because members often exceed their output quotas in order to increase their own profits.

28	a	When OPEC countries produce more than their quota, the supply of oil increases, and the world price of oil decreases.
29	c	The equilibrium of this game will occur with Saudi Arabia producing a low output and Nigeria producing a high output. Nigeria will choose a high volume of output because it will make it better off regardless of Saudi Arabia's production. Likewise, Saudi Arabia will choose a low volume of output because its profits will be higher regardless of Nigeria's output.
30	c	Deterrence is worth pursuing only if the costs of deterring entry are less than the benefits derived from deterrence.
31	b	In this case, Wal-Mart will build a small store because it can make a greater rate of return, and Target will enter.
32	d	Potential entrants refer to the threat of competition from new entrants.
33	d	In the 1940s, the movie studios could produce color movies only by using the cameras supplied by Technicolor. Technicolor took advantage of this situation to charge high prices, which reduced the profits of the movie studios.
34	a	See page 448 in the textbook.
35	c	If few firms can supply an input and the input is specialized, the suppliers are likely to have the bargaining power to limit a firm's profits.
36	a	If many firms can supply an input and the input is not specialized, the suppliers are unlikely to have the bargaining power to limit a firm's profits.
37	a	This box is labeled "Industry Competitors." See Figure 13-8 on page 447 in the textbook.
38	c	See page 447 in the textbook.

Short Answer Responses

1. Not necessarily. A concentration ratio is the share of the market of the largest firms (usually the four largest) in an industry, not the distribution of market shares of among the largest firms. For example, the market shares of the four largest firms in industry A could be 20 percent each, while the market share of the largest firm in industry B could be 76 percent, with the other firms each having only a 1 percent share. In addition, concentration ratios do account for competitive forces included in Michael Porter's model. These include competition from existing firms, the threat from new entrants, competition from substitute goods, and the bargaining power of buyers and sellers.

2. OPEC quotas are designed to reduce oil production below the competitive level. This forces the price of oil up and increases the profits of OPEC members. But individual countries can gain market share and profits at the expense of other countries if they exceed their quotas and reduce the price they charge for oil. Because all countries have the same incentive, when one country exceeds its quota, other countries are likely to do the same. As a result, oil prices and profits fall.

3. Even without licensing there would be a demand on the part of the public for information about the qualifications of medical doctors. Patients would likely make greater use of the Internet and other sources of information about how many operations a surgeon has performed, how many times a doctor or hospital has been sued for malpractice, etc.

4. One could argue that the company faced competition from substitute goods, one of the elements of Michael Porter's Five Competitive Forces Model. Steel and other materials are possible substitutes for aluminum in the construction of some products (automobiles and machinery, for example), and

wax paper and plastic wrap are substitutes for aluminum foil. In fact, company officials made these arguments, albeit unsuccessfully.

5. Openly discussing pricing strategies is illegal in the United States. Airline officials would subject themselves and their companies to fines and possibly jail terms if they were found guilty of fixing prices.

True/False Answers

1. T See page 433 in the textbook.
2. T This is the definition of Nash equilibrium.
3. F The most important barrier to entry is economies of scale.
4. F A prisoner's dilemma results in noncooperation that leaves everyone worse off.
5. T See the section "A Duopoly Game: Price Competition between Two Firms" beginning on page 435 in the textbook.
6. F Although Nash was a pioneer in the field, game theory was initially developed in the 1940s by John von Neumann and Oskar Morgenstern.
7. F Four members of OPEC are non-Arab countries.
8. T Most business situations involve repeated games; the prisoner's dilemma is not a repeated game.
9. T See Making the Connection, "Is There a Dominant Strategy for Bidding on eBay?" on page 438 in the textbook.
10. F Oligopolies may exist due to ownership of key inputs, but the government need not be involved in the market for this barrier to entry to exist.
11. T If firms fear retaliation, they are less likely to cheat on a collusion agreement.
12. F Patent protection is granted for 20 years.
13. F The concentration ratio is a flawed measure of competition because it does not include foreign competition, and it includes only national competition, not local competition.
14. F Competition from substitute goods or services is one of the Five Competitive Forces defined by Michael Porter.
15. T See the section "Can Firms Escape the Prisoner's Dilemma?" beginning on page 439 in the textbook.

CHAPTER 14 | Monopoly and Antitrust Policy

Chapter Summary and Learning Objectives

14.1 Is Any Firm Ever Really a Monopoly? (pages 462–463)
Define monopoly. A **monopoly** exists only in the rare situation in which a firm is producing a good or service for which there are no close substitutes. A narrow definition of monopoly that some economists use is that a firm has a monopoly if it can ignore the actions of all other firms. Many economists favor a broader definition of monopoly. Under the broader definition, a firm has a monopoly if no other firms are selling a substitute close enough that the firm's economic profits are competed away in the long run.

14.2 Where Do Monopolies Come From? (pages 463–469)
Explain the four main reasons monopolies arise. To have a monopoly, barriers to entering the market must be so high that no other firms can enter. Barriers to entry may be high enough to keep out competing firms for four main reasons: (1) A government blocks the entry of more than one firm into a market by issuing a **patent**, which is the exclusive right to a product for 20 years, or a **copyright**, which is the exclusive right to produce and sell a creation, or giving a firm a **public franchise**, which is the right to be the only legal provider of a good or service; (2) one firm has control of a key raw material necessary to produce a good; (3) there are important *network externalities* in supplying the good or service; or (4) economies of scale are so large that one firm has a *natural monopoly*. **Network externalities** refer to the situation where the usefulness of a product increases with the number of consumers who use it. A **natural monopoly** is a situation in which economies of scale are so large that one firm can supply the entire market at a lower average cost than can two or more firms.

14.3 How Does a Monopoly Choose Price and Output? (pages 469–473)
Explain how a monopoly chooses price and output. Monopolists face downward-sloping demand and marginal revenue curves and, like all other firms, maximize profit by producing where marginal revenue equals marginal cost. Unlike a perfect competitor, a monopolist that earns economic profits does not face the entry of new firms into the market. Therefore, a monopolist can earn economic profits even in the long run.

14.4 Does Monopoly Reduce Economic Efficiency? (pages 473–476)
Use a graph to illustrate how a monopoly affects economic efficiency. Compared with a perfectly competitive industry, a monopoly charges a higher price and produces less, which reduces consumer surplus and economic efficiency. Some loss of economic efficiency will occur whenever firms have **market power** and can charge a price greater than marginal cost. The total loss of economic efficiency in the U.S. economy due to market power is small, however, because true monopolies are very rare. In most industries, competition will keep price much closer to marginal cost than would be the case in a monopoly.

14.5 Government Policy toward Monopoly (pages 476–482)
Discuss government policies toward monopoly. Because monopolies reduce consumer surplus and economic efficiency, most governments regulate monopolies. Firms that are not monopolies have an incentive to avoid competition by **colluding**, or agreeing to charge the same price or otherwise not to compete. In the United States, **antitrust laws** are aimed at deterring monopoly, eliminating collusion, and promoting competition among firms. The Antitrust Division of the U.S. Department of Justice and the

Federal Trade Commission share responsibility for enforcing the antitrust laws, including regulating mergers between firms. A **horizontal merger** is a merger between firms in the same industry. A **vertical merger** is a merger between firms at different stages of production of a good. Local governments regulate the prices charged by natural monopolies.

Chapter Review

Chapter Opener: Is Cable Television a Monopoly? (page 461)

Time Warner Cable, a division of the Time Warner Company, operates cable television systems in the United States. As the only provider of cable television in Manhattan, it has a monopoly in this market. There are few monopoly firms in the United States because when a firm earns economic profits, other firms have an incentive to enter the market.

14.1 Is Any Firm Ever Really a Monopoly? (pages 462–463)
Learning Objective: Define monopoly.

A **monopoly** is a firm that is the only seller of a good or service that does not have a close substitute. A narrow definition of monopoly is that a firm is a monopoly if it can ignore the actions of other firms. Broadly defined, a firm is a monopoly if it can retain economic profits in the long run.

📖 Study Hint

Reading through *Making the Connection* "Is Xbox 360 a Close Substitute for the PlayStation 3?" may help you determine whether a given company is truly a monopoly. Understanding the meaning of the term "close substitute" is the key. Although the Xbox and the PS3 are not identical in terms of production, consumers consider the two products substitutes. The ability of the PS3 to play Blu-ray discs made it more expensive to produce, but Microsoft was able to charge $200 less for the Xbox than Sony charged for the PS3. The lower price of the Xbox encouraged some consumers to purchase the Xbox instead of the PS3. While Microsoft is the only producer of the Xbox, and Sony is the only producer of the PS3, neither is considered to have a monopoly in video game consoles because there are close substitutes for their products.

Extra Solved Problem 14-1
Is the Cable Television Monopoly Over?
Supports Learning Objective 14.1: Define monopoly.

Comcast is the largest cable provider in the United States, with 24 million subscribers. Throughout the second half of the twentieth century, municipalities often contracted with a single cable provider, and residents had to choose whether to buy cable from that cable company or simply go without access to cable television. In the late 1990s, changes in legislation and the development of new technologies opened the door for companies to provide services that could compete with traditional cable companies. With the emergence of Dish Network, DirecTV, fiber optic cable, Internet cable, and Web sites like YouTube and Hulu that offer full-length movies and television shows for free, the monopoly position Comcast once held began to erode.

Source: http://biz.yahoo.com/ic/13/13034.html

a.   What is the definition of monopoly?

b.   Are cable television companies such as Comcast monopolies?

SOLVING THE PROBLEM
Step 1:   **Review the chapter material.**

This problem is about the definition of monopoly, so you may want to review the section "Is Any Firm Ever Really a Monopoly?" which begins on page 462 in the textbook.

Step 2:   **Answer question (a) by defining monopoly.**

A monopoly is the only seller of a good or service that does not have a close substitute.

Step 3:   **Answer question (b) by explaining whether Comcast is a monopoly.**

The key to identifying a firm as a monopoly is determining whether the good or service it offers has close substitutes. Applying a narrow definition of monopoly, Comcast is a monopoly if one can demonstrate Comcast can ignore other firms' prices. Although this was true at one time, Comcast cannot ignore the prices competitors charge now that they can offer customers comparable services.   A broader definition of monopoly would consider Comcast to be a monopoly, even if there are substitutes for its service, if it can earn long-run economic profits.   Using this definition, it is too early to state that Comcast and other cable television companies have lost their monopoly status.   But it will be increasingly difficult for cable companies to earn economic profits as more firms offer similar services in the future.

14.2   Where Do Monopolies Come From? (pages 463–469)
Learning Objective: Explain the four main reasons monopolies arise.

A monopoly requires that barriers to entry into the market must be so high that no other firms can enter. There are four reasons entry barriers may be high enough to keep out competing firms:

1.   Government can block the entry of more than one firm into a market by granting a patent or copyright or by granting a firm a public franchise. A **patent** is the exclusive right to a product for a period of 20 years from the date the product was invented. U.S. laws grant copyright protection to creators of books, films, and music. State and local governments in the United States have granted **public franchises**—the legal right to be the sole provider of a good or service—to providers of electricity, natural gas, cable television, and water.

2.   A firm can become a monopoly by controlling a key resource. Examples of this entry barrier include the Aluminum Company of America (until the 1940s), the International Nickel Company of Canada, and major professional sports teams.

3.   **Network externalities** exist in the consumption of a product if the usefulness of the product increases with the number of consumers who are using it. Some economists argue that network externalities are a barrier to entry, but other economists believe dominant positions by firms reflect their efficiency in satisfying consumer preferences.

4.   Economies of scale are so large that one firm has a natural monopoly. A **natural monopoly** is a situation in which one firm can supply the entire market at a lower average total cost than can two or more firms.

14.3 How Does a Monopoly Choose Price and Output? (pages 469–473)

Learning Objective: Explain how a monopoly chooses price and output.

A monopoly maximizes profit by producing where marginal revenue equals marginal cost. The monopoly's demand curve is the same as the market demand curve for the product. The monopolist is a price maker and has a downward-sloping demand curve. The monopoly's marginal revenue curve lies below its demand curve, so at any level of output its marginal revenue is less than its price. If the monopolist earns an economic profit, then new firms will not be able to enter the market. Therefore, long-run economic profits can be earned.

📖 Study Hint

It is a common misconception that monopolies can charge any price they want. Remember that a monopoly can only charge prices that consumers are willing to pay. In other words, monopolies are constrained by consumer demand. It is true that a monopoly will charge a price that is above marginal cost, but if a monopoly attempts to charge a price that is higher than consumers' willingness to pay, the monopoly will be unable to sell that output.

14.4 Does Monopoly Reduce Economic Efficiency? (pages 473–476)

Learning Objective: Use a graph to illustrate how a monopoly affects economic efficiency.

Compared to equilibrium in a perfectly competitive market, which results in the maximum amount of economic surplus, a monopoly will produce less output and charge a higher price. This results in a reduction of economic surplus and a deadweight loss. Many firms that are not monopolies have some market power. **Market power** is the ability of a firm to charge a price greater than marginal cost. The loss of economic efficiency due to market power in the United States is small, probably less than 1 percent of total production. Some economists claim that the economy may benefit from firms having market power.

Firms with market power are more likely than competitive firms to earn profits that can be used to conduct research and develop new products. The argument that economic progress depends on technological change in the form of new products and that new technology pushes out old technology is closely associated with Joseph Schumpeter. For example, the computer you use replaced the typewriter your parents and grandparents used. However, many economists disagree with Schumpeter and argue that firms that started small, such as Apple and Google, have produced many new products.

📖 Study Hint

Review Figures 14-4 and 14.5, which compare economic efficiency under conditions of monopoly and perfect competition. Although small firms are one source of invention and innovation, firms with market power are better able to afford product development. Product development involves taking a new product or process, perhaps one developed by a small firm, and making it commercially successful. The failure rate for product development can be very high, over 50 percent in some industries, and it may take several years for new products to become profitable.

Extra Solved Problem 14-4

Comcast Cable

Supports Learning Objective 14.4: Use a graph to illustrate how a monopoly affects economic efficiency.

The following table is reproduced from *Solved Problem 14-3* in the textbook and represents the demand and costs that Comcast faces in the provision of cable television.

Price	Quantity	Total Revenue	Marginal Revenue	Total Cost	Marginal Cost
$17	3	$51	--	$56	--
16	4	64	$13	63	$7
15	5	75	11	71	8
14	6	84	9	80	9
13	7	91	7	90	10
12	8	96	5	101	11

a. Use a graph to show the profit-maximizing quantity and price that Comcast will produce and charge.

b. Use this graph to calculate the deadweight loss associated with this cable monopoly.

SOLVING THE PROBLEM

Step 1:   Review the chapter material.

This problem is an extension of *Solved Problem 14-3*, so you may want to review this problem beginning on page 472 in the textbook. This problem also requires an understanding of the section "Does Monopoly Reduce Economic Efficiency?" which begins on page 473 in the textbook.

Step 2:   Answer question (a) by drawing a graph representing the demand, marginal revenue, and marginal cost curves of the firm and indicate the profit maximizing quantity and price.

Comcast produces where marginal revenue equals marginal cost and charges the price that consumers are willing to pay for that quantity.

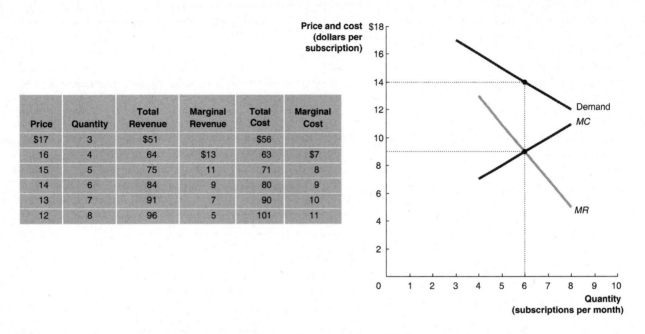

Price	Quantity	Total Revenue	Marginal Revenue	Total Cost	Marginal Cost
$17	3	$51		$56	
16	4	64	$13	63	$7
15	5	75	11	71	8
14	6	84	9	80	9
13	7	91	7	90	10
12	8	96	5	101	11

Step 3: **Answer question (b) by showing the deadweight loss on your graph and use your graph to calculate the deadweight loss to society of the cable monopoly.**

To calculate the deadweight loss associated with monopoly, we must first find what price and quantity would be in this market if the industry was perfectly competitive. The perfectly competitive quantity will be where price equals marginal cost, which occurs where the demand curve and the marginal cost curve intersect. Given the numbers in the table in **Step 2**, this would occur at a quantity of 8.5 where price is $11.50 and marginal cost is $11.50. Shade in the area between the monopoly's profit maximizing quantity and the perfectly competitive equilibrium and between the marginal cost and demand curves. See the graph below. To calculate this area, we calculate the area of a triangle:

½ × base × height =
½ × ($14/ subscription − $9/subscription) × (8.5 subscriptions − 6 subscriptions)
= $6.25 per month.

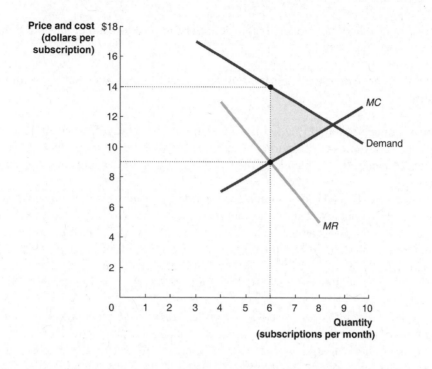

14.5 Government Policy toward Monopoly (pages 476–482)
Learning Objective: Discuss government policies toward monopoly.

Because monopolies reduce consumer welfare and efficiency, most governments regulate their behavior. **Collusion** refers to an agreement among firms to charge the same price or otherwise not to compete. **Antitrust laws** are laws aimed at eliminating collusion and promoting competition among firms. The passage of the first antitrust law was spurred by the formation of various "trusts" in the 1870s and 1880s. Trusts are combinations of firms in several industries that operate independently but are controlled by a common board of trustees.

The Sherman Act of 1890 was the first important law regulating monopolies in the United States. This Act prohibited price fixing, collusion, and monopolization. The Clayton Act of 1914 made a merger illegal if its effect was to lessen competition or if the merger tended to create a monopoly.

The federal government regulates business mergers because mergers can result in firms gaining market power. **Horizontal mergers** are mergers between firms in the same industry. **Vertical mergers** are mergers between firms at different stages of production of a good.

It is important to define the appropriate market when evaluating a proposed merger. The newly merged firm may be more efficient than the merging firms were individually. Merging firms must substantiate efficiency claims that would result from their proposed merger.

The Department of Justice and the Federal Trade Commission developed merger guidelines in 1982. The merger guidelines have three main parts:

1. Market definition. A market consists of all firms making products that consumers view as close substitutes.

2. Measure of concentration. A market is concentrated if a relatively small number of firms have a large share of total sales in the market. The guidelines use the *Herfindahl-Hirschman Index (HHI)* to measure concentration, which adds the squares of the market shares of each firm in an industry.

3. Merger standards. The HHI calculation for a market is used to evaluate proposed mergers. If the post-merger HHI is below 1,000, the merger will not be challenged because the market is not concentrated. If the post-merger HHI is between 1,000 and 1,800, this indicates the market is moderately concentrated. Depending on how much the HHI will be increased, the merger may be challenged. If the post-merger HHI is above 1,800, the market is highly concentrated. Mergers in this market may be challenged based on how much the merger will increase the HHI.

Local or state regulatory commissions usually set prices for natural monopolies. To achieve economic efficiency, regulators should require that the monopoly charge a price equal to marginal cost. Often, though, a natural monopoly's marginal cost will be less than its average total cost. In this case, most regulators will allow the monopoly to charge a price equal to its average total cost so that the owners of the monopoly can earn a normal return on their investment.

📖 Study Hint

Chapter 13 introduced one measure of concentration in a market called the concentration ratio. In calculating the four-firm concentration ratio, you simply add together the market shares of the top four firms in the industry. When calculating the Herfindahl-Hirschman Index (HHI), remember to add together the *squared* market shares of *all* firms in the industry, not just the top four. Also, make sure you square the market shares first and then add them together. Otherwise, you'll find an index equal to 10,000 every time; and the HHI will only truly be 10,000 if there is only one firm in the industry with a market share of 100%.

Extra Solved Problem 14-5

Does Microsoft Stifle Innovation?
Supports Learning Objective 14.5: Discuss government policies toward monopoly.

In 2004, the European Commission found that Microsoft was using its market power to impede innovation and competition in the information technology market. Microsoft was fined 497 million euros, or $675 million U.S. dollars. Microsoft appealed this ruling to the European Union's Court of First Instance and lost the appeal, so the original ruling that Microsoft was impeding competition was upheld.

Sources: "Always Look On the Bright Side of Innovation" by Alan Burnside and Lars Liebeler, *Financial Times*, September 5, 2007. "Protect Innovators from Microsoft's Stifling Monopoly," by Maurits Dolmans and Thomas Graf, *Financial Times*, September 13, 2007.

Explain why the European Commission and the European Union's Court of First Instance would be concerned with Microsoft's actions that impeded competition.

SOLVING THE PROBLEM
Step 1: **Review the chapter material.**

European countries and the European Union have laws to increase and protect competition like those in the United States. To help understand why the European Union agents found Microsoft guilty of impeding competition, review the section "Government Policy toward Monopoly," which begins on page 476 in the textbook.

Step 2: **Answer the question by discussing why the European Union's court system was concerned with Microsoft's actions that impeded competition.**

As in the United States, European governments have a strong desire to maintain a significant amount of competition in their markets to maximize the economic surplus in these markets. When a firm, in this case Microsoft, has market power, the firm has the ability to determine the price and quantity of a good that will be sold in the market. It may also mean that the firm has created artificial barriers to entry to keep other firms from competing against it in the market. The European Commission and the Court of First Instance are charged with maintaining competition in European markets. Therefore, if Microsoft has, in fact, been impeding competition, the European Commission will be obliged to take action.

Key Terms

Antitrust laws Laws aimed at eliminating collusion and promoting competition among firms.

Collusion An agreement among firms to charge the same price or otherwise not to compete.

Copyright A government-granted exclusive right to produce and sell a creation.

Horizontal merger A merger between firms in the same industry.

Market power The ability of a firm to charge a price greater than marginal cost.

Monopoly A firm that is the only seller of a good or service that does not have a close substitute.

Natural monopoly A situation in which economies of scale are so large that one firm can supply the entire market at a lower average total cost than can two or more firms.

Network externalities A situation in which the usefulness of a product increases with the number of consumers who use it.

Patent The exclusive right to a product for a period of 20 years from the date the product is invented.

Public franchise A government designation that a firm is the only legal provider of a good or service.

Vertical merger A merger between firms at different stages of production of a good.

Self-Test

(Answers are provided at the end of the Self-Test.)

Multiple-Choice Questions

1. In which of the following situations can a firm be considered a monopoly?
   a. when a firm is surrounded by other firms that produce close substitutes
   b. when a firm can ignore the actions of all other firms
   c. when a firm uses other firms' prices in order to price its products
   d. when barriers to entry are eliminated

2. Using the broader definition of monopoly, in which of the following cases could we argue that Microsoft has a monopoly in computer operating systems?
   a. if Macintosh and Linux were not considered close substitutes for Windows
   b. if Microsoft charged prices similar to those that Macintosh and Linux charge for their operating systems in order to compete
   c. if Macintosh and Linux started to produce operating systems similar to Windows
   d. if there are no barriers to entry in the market for computer operating systems

3. Which type of barrier to entry is the granting of a patent or copyright to an individual or firm considered?
   a. entry blocked by government action
   b. entry blocked by externalities
   c. entry blocked by economies of scale
   d. entry blocked by natural or technical constraints

4. Which of the following rights is given to the holder of a patent?
   a. the exclusive right to a new product
   b. control over a key resource used in production of a good or service
   c. the right to earn profits from creation of the product indefinitely
   d. a public franchise

5. The more cell phones in use, the more valuable they become to consumers. This is an example of
   a. what happens when a firm is granted a patent.
   b. network externalities.
   c. what happens when a firm has control of a key resource.
   d. natural monopoly.

6. What is the name given to the situation where economies of scale are so large that one firm can supply the entire market at a lower average total cost than two or more firms?
   a. network externalities
   b. productive efficiency
   c. natural monopoly
   d. market power

7. Refer to the graph below. Which point corresponds to a natural monopoly serving this market and breaking even?

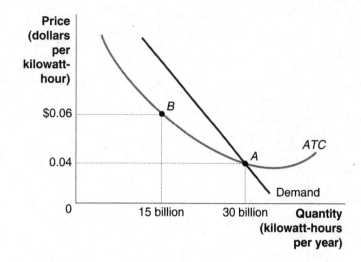

a. point *A*
b. point *B*
c. Both point *A* and point *B* are associated with a natural monopoly breaking even.
d. Neither point *A* nor point *B* is associated with a natural monopoly breaking even.

8. Refer to the graph below. If 30 billion kilowatt-hours of electricity are supplied by two firms who supply 15 billion kilowatt-hours of electricity each instead of by one firm, the average total cost of electricity

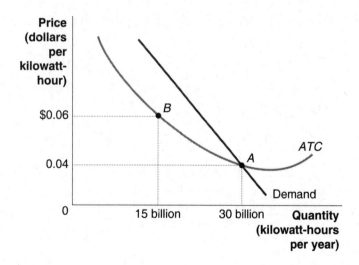

a. rises from $0.04 to $0.12.
b. rises from $0.04 to $0.06.
c. rises from $0.02 to $0.03.
d. falls from $0.06 to $0.02.

9. Which of the following statements regarding natural monopoly is true?
   a. One firm can supply twice as much output as two smaller firms at the same average total cost.
   b. One firm can supply the entire market at a lower fixed cost than two or more firms.
   c. The source of monopoly power is the control of a key natural resource.
   d. Natural monopoly is most likely to occur in markets where fixed costs are very large relative to variable costs.

10. If increased competition leads to higher costs and higher prices in an industry, how should that market be characterized?
    a. as a perfectly competitive market
    b. as a monopolistically competitive market
    c. as an oligopoly
    d. as a natural monopoly

11. Which of the following types of firms use the marginal revenue equals marginal cost approach to maximize profits?
    a. perfectly competitive firms
    b. monopolistically competitive firms
    c. monopolies
    d. all of the above

12. In which of the following market structures is the firm's demand curve the same as the market demand for the product?
    a. perfect competition
    b. monopolistic competition
    c. monopoly
    d. all of the above

13. Which firms face a downward-sloping demand curve and a downward-sloping marginal revenue curve?
    a. all price takers
    b. all price makers
    c. monopolies only
    d. monopolistically competitive firms only

14. When a firm's demand curve slopes downward and the firm decides to cut price, which of the following happens?
    a. It sells more units and receives higher revenue per unit.
    b. It sells more units but receives lower revenue per unit.
    c. It sells fewer units and receives lower revenue per unit.
    d. It sells fewer units but receives higher revenue per unit.

15. Refer to the table below. How much is the average revenue associated with serving five subscribers per month?

Subscribers per Month (Q)	Price (P)	Total Revenue (TR = P x Q)	Average Revenue (AR = TR/Q)	Marginal Revenue (MR = ΔTR/ΔQ)
0	$60	$0		
1	57	57		
2	54	108		
3	51	153		
4	48	192		
5	45	225		
6	42	252		
7	39	273		
8	36	288		
9	33	297		
10	30	300		

   a. $33
   b. $45
   c. $5
   d. none of the above

16. Refer to the table below. How much is the marginal revenue associated with serving seven subscribers per month?

Subscribers per Month (Q)	Price (P)	Total Revenue (TR = P x Q)	Average Revenue (AR = TR/Q)	Marginal Revenue (MR = ΔTR/ΔQ)
0	$60	$0		
1	57	57		
2	54	108		
3	51	153		
4	48	192		
5	45	225		
6	42	252		
7	39	273		
8	36	288		
9	33	297		
10	30	300		

   a. $39
   b. $45
   c. $21
   d. None of the above

17. Refer to the graph below. In this graph, which curve is conceptually the same as average revenue?

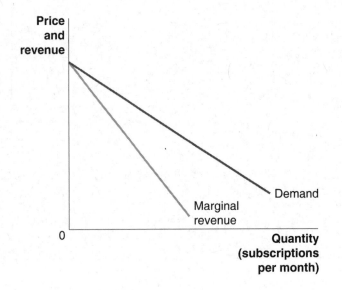

a. the demand curve
b. the marginal revenue curve
c. both curves
d. neither curve

18. Refer to the graph of monopoly below. What is profit when the firm sells six subscriptions per month?

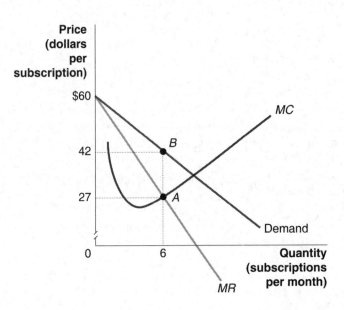

a. $90
b. $42
c. $27
d. None of the above; there is insufficient information to answer the question.

19. Refer to the graph below. What is firm's profit when it sells six subscriptions per month?

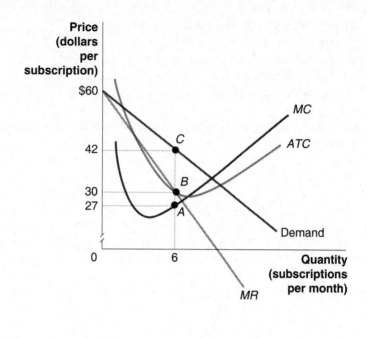

a. $90
b. $72
c. $42
d. $18

20. Refer to the graph of monopoly below. What point represents the price and output level that a monopoly will choose?

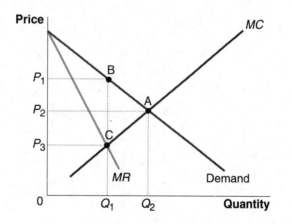

a. point A
b. point B
c. point C
d. none of the above

21. Assume that an industry that began as a perfectly competitive industry becomes a monopoly. Which of the following describes a change in the market as a result of becoming a monopoly? Compared to when the industry was perfectly competitive, the monopolist will
    a.   charge a higher price and produce less output.
    b.   charge a higher price and increase consumer surplus.
    c.   produce less output and decrease producer surplus.
    d.   produce more output and increase producer surplus.

22. Refer to the graph below. What point represents the price and quantity that will prevail when the industry is perfectly competitive?

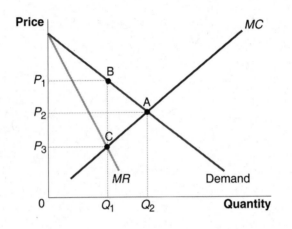

    a.   point A
    b.   point B
    c.   point C
    d.   none of the above

23. Refer to the graph below. Which area shows the reduction in consumer surplus that results from this industry being a monopoly rather than perfectly competitive?

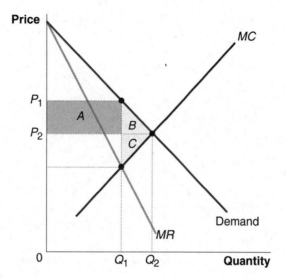

    a.   area A
    b.   area B + area C
    c.   area A + area B
    d.   none of the areas indicated on the graph

24. Refer to the graph below. Which area shows a reduction in consumer surplus that is transferred to producers as a result of this industry being a monopoly rather than being perfectly competitive?

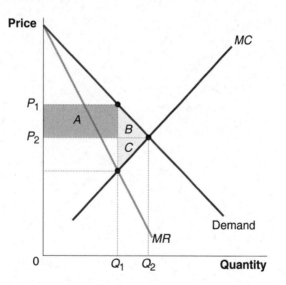

    a.   area A
    b.   area B + area C
    c.   area A + area B
    d.   none of the areas indicated on the graph

25. Refer to the graph below. Which area is considered a reduction in economic surplus as a result of this industry being a monopoly rather than being perfectly competitive?

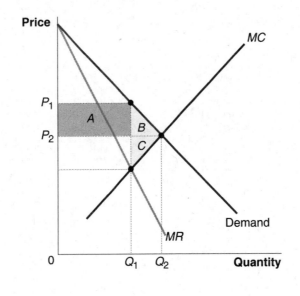

a. area A
b. area B
c. area C
d. area B + area C

26. Refer to the graph below. If the industry changes from being perfectly competitive to being a monopoly, what happens to producer surplus?

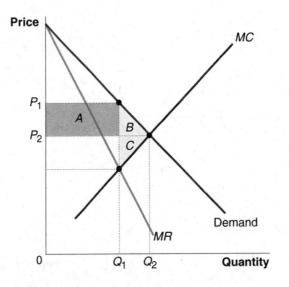

a. It increases by area A and decreases by area B.
b. It increases by area A and decreases by area C.
c. It increases by area B + C.
d. It increases by area A and decreases by area B + C.

27. Which of the following are effects of monopoly?
    a. Monopoly causes a reduction in consumer surplus.
    b. Monopoly causes an increase in producer surplus.
    c. Monopoly causes a reduction in economic efficiency.
    d. all of the above

28. What is the definition of market power?
    a. Market power is the same as inefficiency as measured by the amount of deadweight loss from a monopoly.
    b. Market power is the ability of a firm to eliminate competition.
    c. Market power is the ability of one firm to control other firms in the market.
    d. Market power is the ability of a firm to charge a price greater than marginal cost.

29. Refer to the graph below. How can the loss of economic efficiency resulting from this market being a monopoly rather than being perfectly competitive be estimated?

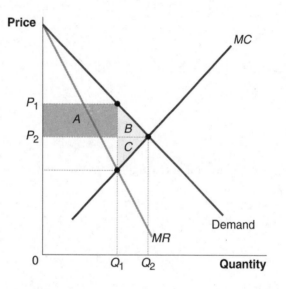

    a. by estimating the size of the triangle $B + C$
    b. by estimating the size of the rectangle A
    c. by estimating the size of the area $A + B + C$
    d. None of the above; the loss of economic efficiency cannot be estimated using this graph.

30. According to Joseph Schumpeter, what does economic progress depend on?
    a. competition, especially price competition
    b. technological change in the form of new products
    c. government protection of competition
    d. the initial endowment of economic resources, such as the amount of labor and capital available

31. What does the term collusion refer to?
    a. Collusion refers to an agreement among firms to charge the same price or otherwise not to compete.
    b. Collusion refers to an agreement among existing firms to prevent potential competitors from entering an industry.
    c. Collusion refers to laws aimed at promoting competition among firms.
    d. Collusion refers to a price war among competing firms.

32. What are laws aimed at promoting competition among firms called?
    a.   collusion
    b.   antitrust laws
    c.   laws of comparative advantage
    d.   merger legislation

33. Which of the following laws outlawed monopolization?
    a.   the Sherman Act
    b.   the Clayton Act
    c.   the Robinson-Patman Act
    d.   the Cellar-Kefauver Act

34. Which of the following laws prohibited charging buyers different prices if the result would reduce competition?
    a.   the Sherman Act
    b.   the Clayton Act
    c.   the Robinson-Patman Act
    d.   the Cellar-Kefauver Act

35. What is a merger between firms in the same industry called?
    a.   a horizontal merger
    b.   a vertical merger
    c.   a conglomerate
    d.   a divestiture

36. Which of the following is most likely to increase market power?
    a.   horizontal mergers
    b.   vertical mergers
    c.   stricter enforcement of antitrust laws
    d.   divestitures

37. Refer to the graph below. Suppose that two firms each produce with a marginal cost of MC_1 and that when the two firms merge, marginal cost falls to MC_2. As a result of the merger, the price consumers pay _____, and the quantity produced _____.

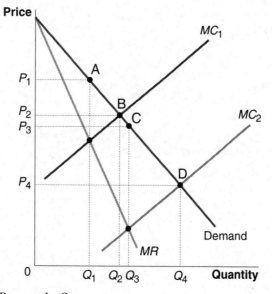

   a. decreases from P_1 to P_2; equals Q_4
   b. decreases from P_2 to P_4; equals Q_3
   c. decreases from P_3 to P_4; equals Q_4
   d. increases from P_2 to P_1; equals Q_1

38. Which of the following is among the guidelines used by economists and attorneys to understand whether the government is likely to allow a merger or to oppose it?
   a. market definition
   b. measure of concentration
   c. merger standards
   d. all of the above

39. What is the value of the Herfindahl-Hirschman Index (HHI) when there are four firms in an industry with each firm having an equal market share?
   a. 4
   b. 625
   c. 2,500
   d. 4,000

40. Refer to the graph of natural monopoly below. If regulators want to achieve economic efficiency, what price would regulators require?

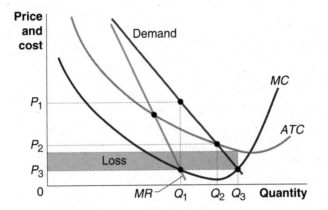

a. P_1
b. P_2
c. P_3
d. none of the above

41. Refer to the graph of natural monopoly below. What price will ensure that the owners of the monopoly are able to earn a normal rate of return on their investment?

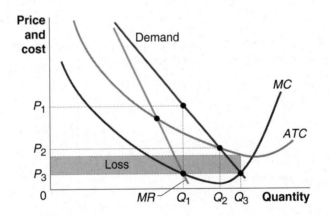

a. P_1
b. P_2
c. P_3
d. none of the above

Short Answer Questions

1. There are four firms in Industry A with the following market shares: 75 percent, 12 percent, 10 percent, and 3 percent. Industry B also has four firms, but each firm has a 25 percent market share. Compare the four-firm concentration ratio and the Herfindahl-Hirschman Index (HHI) of concentration for both of these industries.

_____

_____

_____

2. In the United States, regulatory commissions usually set prices for natural monopolies, such as firms selling natural gas. To achieve economic efficiency, commissions should require the firms they regulate to charge a price equal to marginal cost. Explain why regulators do not generally require that price be equal to marginal cost.

_____

_____

_____

_____

3. Some economists argue that small, competitive firms have developed new products and technologies. Competition spurs firms to continually develop new products in order to stay ahead of competing firms. As a result, smaller firms are more effective at developing new products than larger firms. How might Joseph Schumpeter counter that argument?

_____

_____

_____

_____

4. In the Making the Connection "The End of the Christmas Plant Monopoly," on page 464 in the textbook, the story of the Ecke family's development of a new variety of poinsettia plants was described. The Ecke family was able to maintain a monopoly on its poinsettias by keeping secret the technique they used to develop the plants. But the monopoly ended when a researcher discovered and published the technique. Did the Ecke family err in not obtaining a patent on the technique it used to develop its poinsettias?

_____

_____

_____

_____

5. In 2007, the Federal Trade Commission attempted to block a merger between an organic grocery store, Whole Foods Market, and Wild Oats Markets, a competitor of Whole Foods. It wasn't until 2009 that Whole Foods and the FTC reached a settlement where Whole Foods agreed to sell the majority of the Wild Oats stores they had acquired. Why did the FTC object to a merger between Whole Foods and Wild Oats?

_____

_____

_____

_____

_____

_____

_____

True/False Questions

T F 1.   A broad definition considers a firm a monopoly if it can earn economic profits in the long run.

T F 2.   A public franchise grants a firm an exclusive right to sell a good or service for 20 years.

T F 3.   A merger between two firms in an industry with a Herfindahl-Hirschman Index value below 1,000 will not be challenged by the federal government.

T F 4.   The Clayton Act (1890) prohibited price fixing and collusion.

T F 5.   Joseph Schumpeter argued that small competitive firms are responsible for the development of most of the technological change that occurs over time.

T F 6.   John D. Rockefeller organized the Standard Oil Trust.

T F 7.   A monopolist will charge the highest price possible in order to make the most profit.

T F 8.   A monopolist's demand curve is the same as the market demand curve for the product it sells.

T F 9.   A professional sports team's long-term stadium lease is an example of a barrier to entry.

T F 10. A broad definition of monopoly is that a monopolist can ignore the actions of all other firms.

T F 11. A public franchise is granted by the government to give one firm an exclusive right to provide a good or service.

T F 12. A "generic drug" refers to a drug that is no longer protected by a patent.

T F 13. A merger between two soft drink manufacturers is an example of a vertical merger.

T F 14. Department of Justice and Federal Trade Commission guidelines for evaluating proposed mergers use the Herfindahl-Hirschman Index to measure market concentration.

T F 15. The Justice Department requires that the Xbox 360 and the PS3 be sold for the same price.

Answers to the Self-Test

Multiple-Choice Questions

Question	Answer	Comment
1	b	A narrow definition of monopoly used by some economists is that a firm has a monopoly if it can ignore the actions of all other firms. In other words, other firms must not be producing close substitutes if the monopolist can ignore other firms' prices.
2	a	For most computer users, Linux and the Macintosh system are not close substitutes for Windows. So, using the broader definition, we can say that Microsoft has a monopoly in the market for computer operating systems.
3	a	Governments ordinarily try to promote competition in markets, but sometimes governments take action to block the entry of more than one firm into a market. In the United States, there are two main ways government blocks entry. One way is to grant a patent or copyright to an individual or firm, which gives it the exclusive right to produce a product. The second way is to grant a firm a public franchise, which makes it the exclusive legal provider of a good or service.
4	a	In the United States, a patent gives a firm the exclusive right to produce a product.
5	b	There are network externalities in the consumption of a product if the usefulness of the product increases with the number of people who are using it. The more cell phones that are in use, the more useful they become to consumers.
6	c	A natural monopoly is a situation where economies of scale are so large that one firm can supply the entire market at a lower average total cost than two or more firms.
7	a	With a natural monopoly, the average total cost curve is still falling when it crosses the demand curve (point A). If there is only one firm producing electric power in the market and it produces where average cost intersects the demand curve, average total cost will equal $0.04 per kilowatt-hour of electricity produced.
8	b	If the market for electricity is divided between two firms, each producing 15 billion kilowatt-hours, then the average cost of producing electricity rises to $0.06 per kilowatt-hour (point B).
9	d	Natural monopoly occurs when firms must make a substantial investment in fixed costs (for example, machinery and equipment) in order to produce any output. As output increases, the increase in variable cost (marginal cost) is relatively small and average fixed cost falls. The net result is that average total cost falls continually until the entire market is supplied.
10	d	In certain markets, cost conditions are such that competition is likely to lead to higher costs and higher prices. These markets are natural monopolies that are well served by one firm.

11	d	Like every other firm, a monopoly maximizes profit by producing where marginal revenue equals marginal cost.
12	c	A monopoly differs from other firms in that a monopoly's demand curve is the same as the demand curve for the product. The textbook emphasizes in Chapter 11 that the market demand curve for wheat was very different from the demand curve for the wheat produced by any one farmer. But if that farmer had a monopoly on wheat production, then the two demand curves would be the same.
13	b	Firms in perfectly competitive markets—such as a farmer in the wheat market—face horizontal demand curves. They are *price takers*. All other firms, including monopolies, are *price makers*. If they raise their price, they will lose some, but not all, of their customers. Therefore, they face a downward-sloping demand curve and a downward-sloping marginal revenue curve as well.
14	b	When a firm cuts the price of a product, one good thing and one bad thing happen. The good thing: It sells more units of the product. The bad thing: It receives less revenue from each unit than it would have received at the higher price.
15	b	Average revenue (*AR*) equals total revenue (*TR*) divided by output (*Q*). For five subscribers, $AR = 225/5 = P = \$45$.
16	c	The marginal revenue of the seventh subscription is $\$273 - \$252 = \$21$.
17	a	Demand is conceptually the same as average revenue. Total revenue is equal to the number of subscriptions sold per month times the price. Average revenue—or revenue per subscription sold—is equal to total revenue divided by the number of subscriptions sold.
18	d	Profit equals $(P - ATC) \times Q$. When six units are produced and sold, this amount equals $(\$42 - ATC) \times 6$. The average cost curve must be shown in order to estimate the amount of profit.
19	b	Profit equals $(P - ATC) \times Q$. When six units are produced and sold, this amount equals $(\$42 - \$30) \times 6 = \$72$.
20	b	A monopoly will produce the quantity that maximizes profit—that is, the quantity where marginal revenue equals marginal cost. The monopolist will charge the price that consumers are willing to pay as represented by the demand curve.
21	a	Price will be higher and there will be less output under monopoly. Because of this, there will be a decrease in consumer surplus and an increase in producer surplus.
22	a	If the industry is perfectly competitive, price and quantity are determined by the intersection of the supply (*MC*) and demand curves.
23	c	The higher price reduces consumer surplus by the area equal to the rectangle *A* plus the triangle *B*. Area *A* is a transfer of consumer surplus to producers, and area *B* is part of the deadweight loss of monopoly.
24	a	Area *A* represents a transfer of consumer surplus to the monopoly.
25	d	Economic surplus is equal to the sum of consumer surplus plus producer surplus. By increasing price and reducing the quantity produced, the monopolist has reduced economic surplus by an amount equal to the areas of the triangles *B* and *C* (see Figure 14-5 in the textbook). This reduction in economic surplus is called deadweight loss and represents the loss of economic efficiency due to monopoly.
26	b	We measure producer surplus as the area above the supply curve and below the market price. The increase in price due to monopoly increases producer surplus by an amount equal to rectangle *A*, and reduces it by an amount equal to triangle *C*. Because rectangle *A* is larger than triangle *C*, we know that a monopoly increases producer surplus.

27	d	We can summarize the effects of monopoly as follows: 1. Monopoly causes a reduction in consumer surplus. 2. Monopoly causes an increase in producer surplus. 3. Monopoly causes a reduction in economic efficiency, measured by the deadweight loss.
28	d	The only firms that do not have market power are firms in perfectly competitive markets who must charge a price equal to marginal cost.
29	a	It is possible to put a dollar value on the loss of economic efficiency by estimating the size of the deadweight loss triangle—as in Figure 14-5 on page 474 in the textbook.
30	b	Schumpeter argued that economic progress depended on technological change in the form of new products. Schumpeter was unconcerned that firms with market power would charge higher prices than perfectly competitive firms.
31	a	Collusion refers to an agreement among firms to charge the same price or otherwise not to compete.
32	b	Antitrust laws are laws aimed at eliminating collusion and promoting competition among firms.
33	a	The Sherman Act prohibited "restraint of trade," including price fixing and collusion, and it outlawed monopolization.
34	c	The Robinson-Patman Act prohibited charging buyers different prices if the result would reduce competition.
35	a	Horizontal mergers are mergers between firms in the same industry. Vertical mergers are mergers between firms at different stages of production of a good.
36	a	The government is most concerned with horizontal mergers, or mergers between firms in the same industry, because horizontal mergers are more likely to increase market power than vertical mergers.
37	b	When the merger realizes efficiency gains, marginal cost shifts to MC_2 and the profit maximizing level of output becomes Q_3 with a price of P_3.
38	d	One of the fruits of this economic expertise was the joint development by the Department of Justice and FTC of merger guidelines in 1982. The guidelines made it possible for economists and attorneys employed by firms considering a merger to understand whether the government was likely to allow the merger or to oppose it. The guidelines have three main parts: 1. Market definition 2. Measure of concentration 3. Merger standards
39	c	In this case, the Herfindahl-Hirschman Index (HHI) is calculated as follows: $25^2 + 25^2 + 25^2 + 25^2 = 2,500$.
40	c	To achieve economic efficiency, regulators should require that the monopoly charge a price equal to its marginal cost.
41	b	The price P_2 corresponds to the level required to cover average total cost, which includes a normal rate of return.

Short Answer Responses

1. The four-firm concentration ratios for both Industry A and Industry B are 100 percent. The HHI for Industry A $= 75^2 + 12^2 + 10^2 + 3^2 = 5,878$. The HHI for industry B $= 25^2 + 25^2 + 25^2 + 25^2 = 2,500$. The HHI index indicates a higher level of concentration in Industry A than in Industry B because it accounts for the distribution of market shares among the largest firms in the industries. Concentration ratios do not account for the distribution of market shares among firms.

2. Natural monopolies are characterized by economies of scale so that average costs fall as output rises. If the regulated price was equal to marginal cost, it would be less than average total cost, and the firm would suffer an economic loss. Investors would demand an interest premium for any funds lent to the firm, and the firm's credit rating would suffer. If the firm was publicly owned, stockholders would sell their shares and buy shares of firms that offered a higher return. In the long run, the firm would go out of business. This may well leave consumers worse off than if they had to pay a price higher than marginal cost.

3. Joseph Schumpeter argued that the positive economic profits monopolies earn can be used to finance research and development that lead to the production of new products and new technologies. Larger companies may also be effective at developing new products then as well.

4. A patent would have preserved the family's monopoly position but only for a limited time. The textbook explains that "…because the Ecke family kept the technique secret for decades, it was able to maintain a monopoly on the commercial development of the plants." Because the family was able to earn monopoly profits for decades, the absence of a patent probably had little impact on the firm's profits. If they had a patent, their monopoly control over the technique would have lasted, at most, only 20 years (2 decades).

5. Whole Foods and Wild Oats competed in the same market, so a merger between the two companies was a horizontal merger that resulted in an increase in market power for Whole Foods. With an increase in market power, output is likely to fall and prices are likely to rise. Concern about the impact of the merger on consumers caused the FTC to object to the merger.

True/False Answers

1. T See the section "Is Any Firm Ever Really a Monopoly?" beginning on page 462 in the textbook.
2. F A patent grants an inventor exclusive rights to a product for 20 years.
3. T See page 480 in the textbook.
4. F The Sherman Act (1890) contained provisions prohibiting price fixing and collusion.
5. F Joseph Schumpeter argues that large firms are more readily able to have funds available to use for research and development.
6. T See page 477 in the textbook.
7. F Charging the "highest price possible" means charging the price at the very top of the demand curve and (presumably) selling only one unit. That is rarely the profit-maximizing price.
8. T The monopolist faces the entire market demand curve as it is the only firm providing the good.
9. T The control of a key resource, in this case the stadium, is a barrier to entry.
10. F See page 462 in the textbook.
11. T This is the definition of a public franchise.
12. T Generic drugs are drugs that are no longer protected by patents and are produced by a number of pharmaceutical companies.
13. F A merger between firms that produce the same product is a horizontal merger.
14. T See the section "The Department of Justice and FTC Merger Guidelines" beginning on page 479 in the textbook.
15. F Microsoft and Sony find they must charge similar prices because consumers view them as substitutes, not because the government requires it.

Chapter Summary and Learning Objectives

15.1 Pricing Strategy, The Law of One Price, and Arbitrage (pages 494–496)

Define the law of one price and explain the role of arbitrage. According to the *law of one price*, identical products should sell for the same price everywhere. If a product sells for different prices, it will be possible to make a profit through *arbitrage*: buying a product at a low price and reselling it at a high price. The law of one price will hold as long as arbitrage is possible. Arbitrage is sometimes blocked by high **transactions costs**, which are the costs in time and other resources incurred to carry out an exchange or because the product cannot be resold. Another apparent exception to the law of one price occurs when companies offset the higher price they charge for a product by providing superior or more reliable service to customers.

15.2 Price Discrimination: Charging Different Prices for the Same Product (pages 496–505)

Explain how a firm can increase its profits through price discrimination. **Price discrimination** occurs if a firm charges different prices for the same product when the price differences are not due to differences in cost. Three requirements must be met for a firm to successfully practice price discrimination: (1) A firm must possess market power; (2) some consumers must have a greater willingness to pay for the product than other consumers, and firms must be able to know what customers are willing to pay; and (3) firms must be able to divide up—or segment—the market for the product so that consumers who buy the product at a low price cannot resell it a high price. In the case of *perfect price discrimination*, each consumer pays a price equal to the consumer's willingness to pay.

15.3 Other Pricing Strategies (pages 505–510)

Explain how some firms increase their profits through the use of odd pricing, cost-plus pricing, and two-part tariffs. In addition to price discrimination, firms also use odd pricing, cost-plus pricing, and two-part tariffs as pricing strategies. Firms use *odd pricing*—for example, charging $1.99 rather than $2.00—because consumers tend to buy more at odd prices than would be predicted from estimated demand curves. With *cost-plus pricing*, firms set the price for a product by adding a percentage markup to average cost. Using cost-plus pricing may be a good way to come close to the profit-maximizing price when marginal revenue or marginal cost is difficult to measure. Some firms can require consumers to pay an initial fee for the right to buy their product and an additional fee for each unit of the product purchased. Economists refer to this situation as a **two-part tariff**. Sam's Club, cell phone companies, and many golf and tennis clubs use two-part tariffs in pricing their products.

Chapter Review

Chapter Opener: Getting into Walt Disney World: One Price Does Not Fit All (page 493)

Walt Disney World charges different consumers different prices for admission based on their willingness to pay. When Disneyland opened in 1955, Disney charged different prices for admission into the park *and* had a separate charge for rides. Today, there is a high price for admission to Disneyland and Walt Disney World but once a customer is in the park the rides are free. This change in strategy was designed to increase profits.

15.1   Pricing Strategy, The Law of One Price, and Arbitrage (pages 494–496)

Learning Objective: Define the law of one price and explain the role of arbitrage.

Firms sometimes increase their profits by practicing *price discrimination*, charging different prices to different consumers for the same product when the price differences are not due to differences in cost. The development of information technology has made it possible for firms to gather information on consumers' preferences and their responsiveness to price changes. This practice, called *yield management*, is particularly important to airlines and hotels. To practice price discrimination, firms must prevent arbitrage. Arbitrage is the process of buying a product in one market at a low price and reselling it in another market at a higher price. Arbitrage explains the *law of one price*: Identical products should sell for the same price everywhere.

The law of one price holds only if transactions costs are zero. **Transactions costs** are costs in time and other resources that parties incur in the process of agreeing to and carrying out an exchange of goods or services.

15.2   Price Discrimination: Charging Different Prices for the Same Product (pages 496–505)

Learning Objective: Explain how a firm can increase its profits through price discrimination.

Charging different prices to different consumers for the same product when the price differences are not due to differences in cost is called **price discrimination**. Successful price discrimination has three requirements.

1. A firm must possess market power.
2. Some consumers must have a greater willingness to pay for the product than others, and the firm must know the prices consumers are willing to pay.
3. The firm must be able to segment the market so consumers who buy the product at a low price cannot resell it at a high price. Firms will charge a higher price to consumers whose demand is less elastic than other consumers.

Airlines have a strong incentive to use price discrimination to manage their prices because airline seats are a perishable product, and the marginal cost of flying one additional passenger is low. Airlines divide their customers into two main categories: business travelers who are not very sensitive to changes in price, and leisure passengers who are sensitive to changes in price. Airlines use yield management to make frequent price adjustments in response to fluctuations in demand.

Firms sometimes engage in price discrimination over time. These firms charge a higher price for a product when it is first introduced and a lower price later. This pattern was followed by firms that sold products such as HD-DVD players and digital cameras. Book publishers routinely use price discrimination over time to increase their profits. Hardcover editions of novels have much higher prices and are published months before paperback editions.

The Robinson-Patman Act of 1936 outlawed price discrimination *if* its effect is to reduce competition in an industry. In recent years, the courts have interpreted Robinson-Patman to allow firms to use common types of price discrimination.

15.3   **Other Pricing Strategies (pages 505–510)**

Learning Objective: Explain how some firms increase their profits through the use of odd pricing, cost-plus pricing, and two-part tariffs.

In addition to price discrimination, firms can use the strategy of *odd pricing*. Odd pricing refers to charging prices just less than even dollar amounts—for example, $3.98 instead of $4.00—to give the appearance that the price is less than it really is. Some evidence supports the effectiveness of odd pricing in increasing profits, but this evidence is not conclusive.

Another pricing strategy is *cost-plus pricing*. Cost-plus pricing involves adding a percentage markup to average cost to determine prices. This technique may be a good way to approximate the profit-maximizing price when marginal cost or marginal revenue are difficult to estimate. A **two-part tariff** is another pricing strategy. This is a situation in which consumers pay one price (or tariff) for the right to buy as much of a related good as they want at a second price. An amusement park that charges an admission fee and also separate fees for rides is using a two-part tariff.

Extra Solved Problem 15-3

Tennis Anyone?

Supports Learning Objective 15.3: Explain how some firms increase their profits through the use of odd pricing, cost-plus pricing, and two-part tariffs.

The Topeka (Kansas) Racquet Club charges club members a monthly membership fee as well as an hourly fee to use its indoor tennis courts. The following graph illustrates the Racquet Club's demand, marginal revenue and marginal cost curves. Because marginal cost is constant, it is also equal to average cost ($2). The graph shows that if the Club charges a fee of $11 per hour, Club members will use the tennis courts a total of 9,000 hours in a month. This is the quantity where marginal revenue equals marginal cost. The Club's profit from its court fees for one month is equal to area *A* in the diagram ($11 − $2) × 9,000 = $81,000.

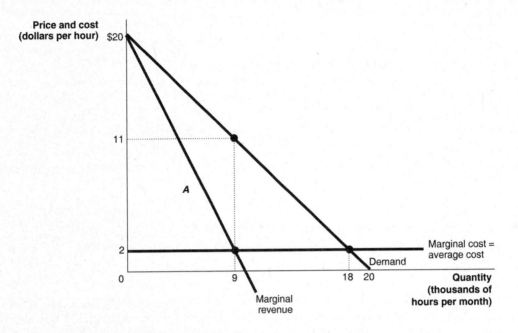

a. What is the maximum amount the Club can charge as a monthly fee if it charges an $11 per hour court fee?

b. Is it possible for the Club to charge a different hourly court fee and increase its profit?

SOLVING THE PROBLEM

Step 1: **Review the chapter material.**

This problem is about pricing strategies, so you may want to review the section "Other Pricing Strategies" which begins on page 505 in the textbook.

Step 2: **Answer question (a) by calculating the maximum monthly fee the Club can charge.**

When the Club charges an $11 hourly fee, members receive a total consumer surplus of [½ × ($20 − $11) × 9,000 = $40,500]. Assuming that Club members are interested in joining the Club only to play tennis and the club is able to perfectly price discriminate in setting the monthly fee, total revenue from monthly fees can be as much as $40,500. If the Club has no other costs, then the maximum total profit it would receive would be $81,000 + $40,500 = $121,500.

Step 3: **Answer question (b) by explaining whether the Club can increase its profits by changing its court fee from $11 per hour.**

Club members would receive the maximum amount of consumer surplus if there were no hourly court fee. Consumer surplus would equal the areas under the demand curve: ½ × $20 × 20,000 = $200,000. This is the maximum total revenue the Club could receive from monthly membership fees. If members used the courts 20,000 hours, the Club's total cost would be $2 × 20,000 = $40,000. Assuming the Club received the maximum amount of revenue in the form of monthly fees, the Club's profit would be: $200,000 − $40,000 = $160,000. More profit would result if the club charged a $2 per hour court fee (this would cover all of its costs) and received the value of the consumer surplus (½ × 18 × 18,000 = $162,000).

Key Terms

Price discrimination Charging different prices to different customers for the same product when the price differences are not due to differences in cost.

Transactions costs The costs in time and other resources that parties incur in the process of agreeing to and carrying out an exchange of goods or services.

Two-part tariff A situation in which consumers pay one price (or tariff) for the right to buy as much of a related good as they want at a second price.

Self-Test

(Answers are provided at the end of the Self-Test.)

Multiple-Choice Questions

1. Which of the following is the main purpose of pricing strategies?
   a. to increase economic profit
   b. to gain market share
   c. to find information about consumers
   d. to stay ahead of the competition

2. What name is given to the practice of gathering information on consumers' preferences and using it to rapidly adjust prices?
   a. price discrimination
   b. arbitrage
   c. yield management
   d. odd pricing

3. According to the law of one price, which of the following must be true?
   a. Identical products should sell for the same price everywhere.
   b. Perfectly competitive firms must end up charging the same price for their products.
   c. In a homogeneous economy, all goods should be sold for the same price.
   d. Market forces ensure that the price in a market is always a single price.

4. What name is given to the practice of buying a product in one market at a low price and almost simultaneously reselling it in another market at a high price?
   a. price discrimination
   b. speculation
   c. arbitrage
   d. cost-plus pricing

5. What name is given to the costs in time and other resources that parties incur in the process of agreeing to and carrying out an exchange of goods and services?
   a. shoe-leather costs
   b. arbitrage profits
   c. shipping costs
   d. transactions costs

6. When does the law of one price hold exactly?
   a. when transactions costs are zero
   b. when transactions costs are minimized
   c. when transactions costs are maximized
   d. when it is impossible to resell a product

7. When will firms be able to price discriminate?
   a. when the law of one price does not hold and it is impossible to resell a product
   b. when the law of one price holds and it is possible to resell a product
   c. when the law of one price does not hold but it is possible to resell a product
   d. when the law of one price holds but it is not possible to resell a product

8. According to economists, does the practice of selling and reselling goods on eBay have a useful economic purpose?
   a. No; selling and reselling does not add any value to the goods exchanged.
   b. Yes; if people are willing to participate, they must be made better off.
   c. Yes, but the value added is difficult to measure.
   d. No; participants usually end up paying more on eBay than they would have paid elsewhere.

9. Table 15-1 in the textbook is reproduced below. How is the difference in prices explained in the textbook?

   PRODUCT: DAN BROWN'S *THE LOST SYMBOL*

	PRICE
Amazon.com	$14.83
BarnesandNoble.com	14.83
WaitForeverForYourOrder.com	13.50
JustStartedinBusinessLastWednesday.com	13.25

   a. The law of one price appears to be violated in this case.
   b. Booksellers must not be offering identical products.
   c. Competitors must be competing strictly on the basis of price.
   d. all of the above

10. When is charging different prices to different buyers *not* considered price discrimination?
    a. if the difference in price is due to differences in cost
    b. if the difference in price is due to differences in demand
    c. if the difference in price is due to differences in consumer preferences
    d. if the difference in price is due to differences in elasticity

11. Which of the following is a requirement for successful price discrimination?
    a. A firm must possess market power.
    b. Some consumers must have a greater willingness to pay for the product than other consumers, and the firm must be able to know what prices customers are willing to pay.
    c. The firm must be able to divide up—or segment—the market.
    d. all of the above

12. Which of the following is true if arbitrage is possible?
    a. Price discrimination will work.
    b. Price discrimination will not work.
    c. Price discrimination will work but only under specific conditions.
    d. The market cannot be segmented.

13. If products cannot be resold, which of the following is true?
    a. Firms can practice price discrimination.
    b. The law of one price is contradicted.
    c. Firms can charge only the market price.
    d. Firms must be perfectly competitive.

14. Refer to the graphs below. Which strategy will maximize profit?

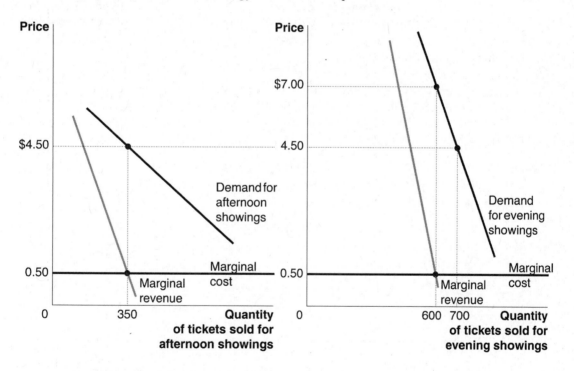

    a. charging $4.50 to all customers
    b. setting marginal revenue equal to marginal cost in the market shown on the left
    c. charging $7.00 to all customers
    d. none of the above

15. Refer to the graphs below. Which demand curve is relatively more elastic?

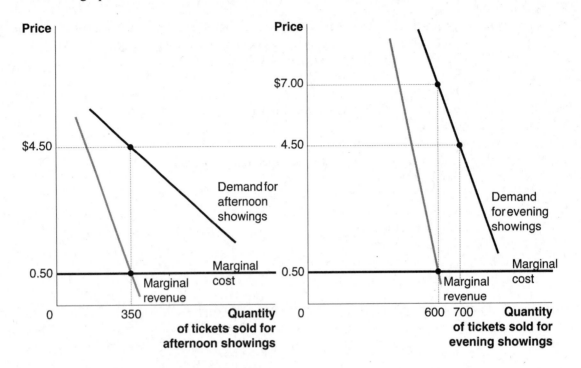

a. the demand curve for afternoon showings
b. the demand curve for evening showings
c. Both demand curves have the same elasticity value.
d. Neither demand curve is elastic; they are both relatively inelastic.

16. Refer to the graphs below. Which customers have a lower price elasticity of demand?

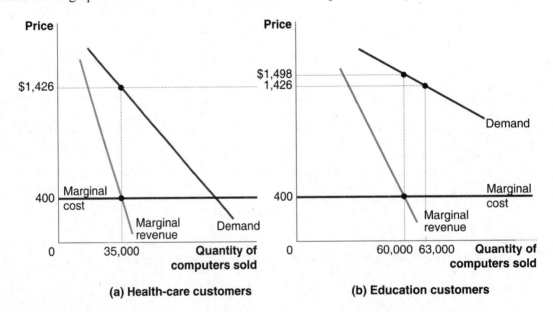

(a) Health-care customers   (b) Education customers

a. the health care customers
b. the education customers
c. Both customers have the same elasticity of demand.
d. Education customers have a higher elasticity but only when charged the higher price.

17. Refer to the graphs below. How can a price-discriminating firm maximize profit?

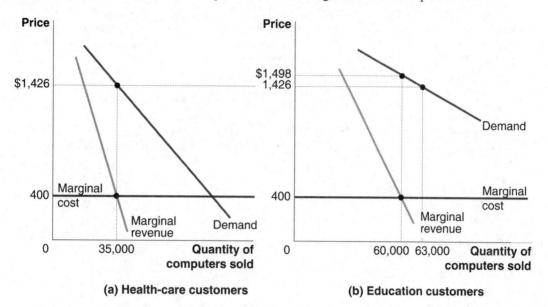

(a) Health-care customers   **(b) Education customers**

a. by setting marginal revenue equal to marginal cost in the health care segment and charging all customers the corresponding price
b. by setting price in each segment according to the price elasticity of demand and charging each segment the corresponding price
c. by charging a higher price to education customers because they have a higher price elasticity of demand
d. by charging the highest prices to consumers with the greatest incomes

18. Which of the following industries uses sophisticated methods to calculate the price of each unit sold each day?
a. college education
b. airlines
c. wheat producers
d. all of the above

19. Which of the following is known as first-degree price discrimination?
a. perfect price discrimination
b. imperfect price discrimination
c. zero price discrimination
d. exponential price discrimination

20. Which of the following is a result of perfect price discrimination?
a. maximum consumer surplus
b. price is greater than marginal cost
c. zero consumer surplus
d. infinite consumer surplus

21. Refer to the graphs below. Which monopolist is practicing perfect price discrimination?

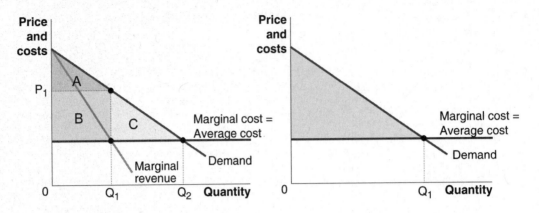

    a.   the monopolist on the left
    b.   the monopolist on the right
    c.   both monopolies
    d.   neither monopoly

22. Refer to the graphs below. In which case does the existence of a monopoly result in a larger amount of consumer surplus?

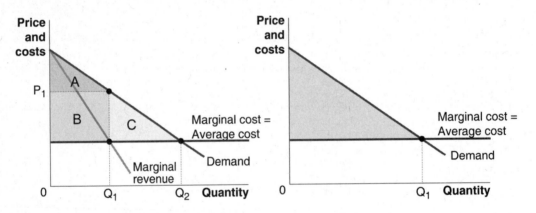

    a.   in the case of the monopolist on the left
    b.   in the case of the monopolist on the right
    c.   in both cases
    d.   in neither case

23. Refer to the graphs below. In which case does the existence of a monopoly result in a larger deadweight loss?

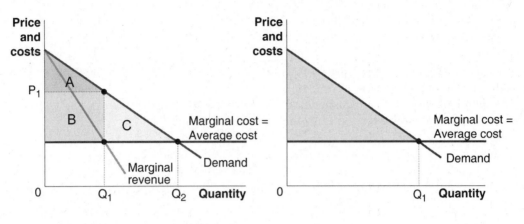

    a.   in the case of the monopolist on the left
    b.   in the case of the monopolist on the right
    c.   in both cases
    d.   in neither case

24. Refer to the graphs below. With which monopolist is economic efficiency greater?

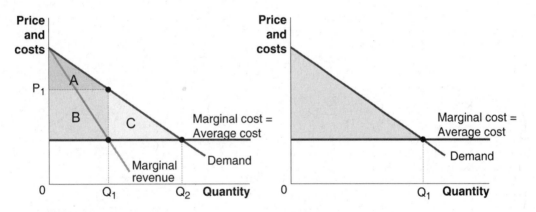

    a.   the monopolist on the left
    b.   the monopolist on the right
    c.   both monopolists
    d.   neither monopolist

25. Which of the following statements is true about price discrimination?
    a.   Under certain circumstances, price discrimination could improve economic efficiency.
    b.   In some cases, except for perfect price discrimination, other types of price discrimination could reduce economic efficiency.
    c.   No general conclusion can be drawn about the effects of price discrimination on economic efficiency.
    d.   All of the above.

26. Which of the following are key results of price discrimination?
    a.   profits increase and consumer surplus increases
    b.   profits increase and consumer surplus decreases
    c.   profits decrease and consumer surplus decreases
    d.   profits decrease and consumer surplus increases

27. The price discrimination across time routinely practiced by book publishers appears to be attributed primarily to what event?
    a.   substantial differences in the cost of hardcover versus paperback copies
    b.   early adoption of hardcover copies by the most devoted book fans
    c.   unexpected taxation
    d.   an increase in the general level of prices over time in the economy

28. Refer to the graphs below, which refer to the demand curves for a book written by a popular author. Which readers have a relatively more elastic demand?

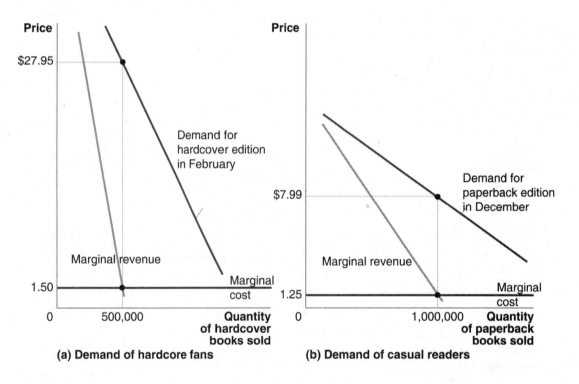

(a) Demand of hardcore fans   (b) Demand of casual readers

    a.   casual readers
    b.   hardcore fans
    c.   Both groups of fans have very elastic demands.
    d.   Neither casual readers nor hardcore fans have elastic demands; they both have inelastic demands.

29. Which of the following price-discriminating strategies used by insurance companies has been accepted by the courts?
    a.   charging women lower prices than men for automobile insurance
    b.   charging blacks higher life insurance prices than whites (who have longer life spans)
    c.   discriminating on the basis of arbitrary characteristics
    d.   all of the above

30. Which of the following facts related to odd pricing was found in surveys of consumers about their willingness to purchase a product?
    a. People connect odd prices with high-quality goods.
    b. The quantity demanded of goods with odd prices was greater than predicted using an estimated demand curve.
    c. Odd prices prevent employee theft.
    d. all of the above

31. In cost-plus pricing, a percentage markup is added to which of the following measures?
    a. average cost
    b. marginal cost
    c. total cost
    d. implicit cost

32. In a firm selling multiple products, what is the intent of cost-plus pricing?
    a. to segment the market
    b. to cover all costs, including those that are difficult to assign
    c. to increase economic profit
    d. to obtain a better idea of the demand curve

33. What are the views of economists about cost-plus pricing?
    a. Cost-plus pricing is simply a mistake that firms should avoid.
    b. Cost-plus pricing ignores demand.
    c. Cost-plus pricing does not appear to maximize profits because it ignores marginal cost.
    d. all of the above

34. According to economists, which of the following is a condition under which cost-plus pricing could be the best way to determine the optimal price?
    a. when marginal cost differs substantially from average cost
    b. when the firm has difficulty estimating its demand curve
    c. both of the above
    d. none of the above

35. Fill in the blanks: In general, companies that take demand into account will charge _____ markups on products that are _____ price elastic.
    a. higher; more
    b. lower; more
    c. zero; less
    d. zero; relatively

36. Which of the following are pricing schemes associated with a two-part tariff?
    a. annual memberships and hourly court rental fees at tennis clubs
    b. monthly fees for cellular phone subscriptions
    c. fees for shopping privileges at a certain store
    d. all of the above

37. Refer to the graphs below. Which graph shows a higher profit obtained from the sale of ride tickets at Disney World?

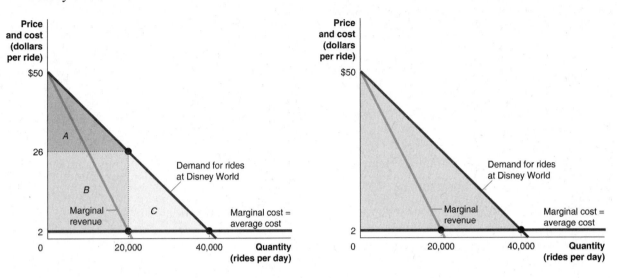

a. the graph on the left
b. the graph on the right
c. The amount of profit is the same in both graphs.
d. None of the above; neither graph shows any profit associated with the sale of ride tickets.

38. Refer to the graphs below. Which graph shows a larger deadweight loss from the sale of ride tickets at Disney World?

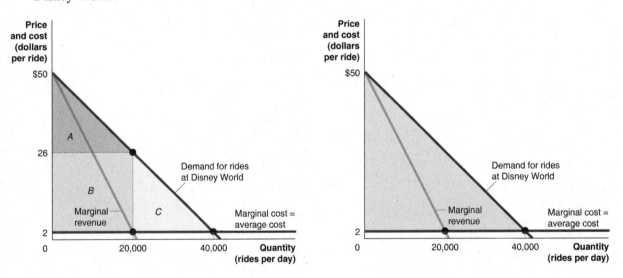

a. the graph on the left
b. the graph on the right
c. The amount of profit is the same in both graphs.
d. None of the above; neither graph shows any profit associated with the sale of ride tickets.

39. Refer to the graphs below. Which outcome is economically efficient in the market of ride tickets at Disney World?

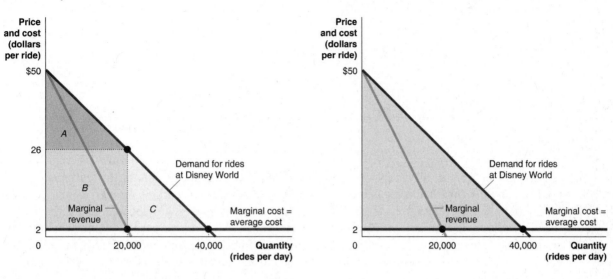

a. the outcome shown in the graph on the left
b. the outcome shown in the graph on the right
c. Both outcomes are economically efficient.
d. Neither outcome is economically efficient.

Short Answer Questions

1. Stockbrokers know that the key to earning profits is to "buy low and sell high." Are the profits earned from buying stocks when their prices are low and selling stocks when their prices are high due to arbitrage?

_____

_____

_____

_____

2. The Web site of Priceline.com featured the following advertisement: "Last-Minute Cruises—Sail within 30 days and Save!" Why do cruise lines offer discount fares on Priceline.com?

_____

_____

_____

_____

3. Referring to a study of the impact on quantity demanded due to odd pricing, the textbook says: "The study was not conclusive because it relied on surveys rather than on observing purchasing behavior…" Why would consumers not respond accurately to surveys designed to determine their responses to price changes?

_____

_____

_____

_____

4. An economist from a university in California noted that the parking lots on his campus offer a good example of price discrimination. There are "faculty only" parking spaces in lots located close to university classrooms and offices while student spaces are located in more remote locations. Price discrimination requires a firm (in this case, the university) to segment its market so that consumers with a greater willingness to pay than other consumers can be identified. How can the university identify those students who have the greatest willingness to pay for parking spaces located close to classroom buildings?

_____

_____

_____

_____

_____

5. The Making the Connection feature on page 501 in the textbook describes the yield management techniques colleges and universities use to maximize tuition revenue and improve the quality of students they enroll. Because students are charged different prices (tuition minus financial aid) for the same service, yield management results in price discrimination. Is this form of price discrimination legal?

_____

_____

_____

_____

_____

True/False Questions

T F 1. The profits received from engaging in arbitrage are referred to as *transactions profits*.
T F 2. Yield management refers to the gathering of information on consumer preferences and consumers' responsiveness to price changes in order to adjust prices rapidly.
T F 3. There is no evidence that odd-pricing is an effective pricing strategy.
T F 4. The Sherman Act (1890) made price discrimination illegal if its effect is to reduce competition in an industry.
T F 5. *Early adopters* are consumers who are willing to pay a high price to be among the first to own a product.
T F 6. Price discrimination causes consumer surplus to decrease.
T F 7. Perfect price discrimination results in no consumer surplus.
T F 8. Two-part tariffs result in a reduction in economic efficiency because consumers pay higher prices than they would if they paid only one price.
T F 9. Cost-plus pricing is the best way to determine the optimal price when the marginal cost of production is much lower than the average cost of production.
T F 10. Book publishers often engage in price discrimination over time.
T F 11. Perfect price discrimination is often used by natural monopolies because of their high barriers to entry.
T F 12. Colleges that use yield management techniques typically offer less generous financial aid packages (other things being equal) to students who apply for early admission.
T F 13. Perfect price discrimination can convert a deadweight loss and consumer surplus into profit.
T F 14. Price discrimination occurs only in monopoly and oligopoly markets.
T F 15. Transactions costs are incurred in the process of carrying out an exchange of goods or services.

Answers to the Self-Test

Multiple-Choice Questions

Question	Answer	Comment
1	a	Pricing strategies are one way firms attempt to increase their economic profits.
2	c	The practice of gathering information on consumers' preferences and the responsiveness of consumers to changes in prices, and using it to rapidly adjust prices is called yield management.
3	a	According to the law of one price, identical products should sell for the same price everywhere.
4	c	Buying a product in one market at a low price and reselling it in another market at a high price is referred to as arbitrage.
5	d	The costs of carrying out a transaction—by, for example, listing items on eBay and shipping them across the country—are called transactions costs.
6	a	The law of one price holds exactly only if transactions costs are zero.
7	a	In cases where it is impossible to resell a product, the law of one price will not hold and firms will be able to price discriminate.
8	b	Both the person who sold and the person who bought an item from eBay must have been made better off by the deals, or they would not have made them.
9	b	The difference in the prices of products offered on Web sites does not violate the

law of one price. A book offered for sale by Amazon.com is not the same product as a book offered for sale by JustStartedinBusinessLastWednesday.com.

| 10 | a | Charging different prices to different customers for the same product, when the price differences are not due to differences in cost, is called price discrimination. |

| 11 | d | There are three requirements for a successful strategy of price discrimination:
1. A firm must possess market power.
2. Some consumers must have a greater willingness to pay for the product than other consumers, and the firm must be able to know what prices customers are willing to pay.
3. The firm must be able to divide up—or segment—the market. |

| 12 | b | The firm must be able to divide up—or segment—the market for the product so that consumers who buy the product at a low price are not able to resell it a high price. In other words, price discrimination will not work if arbitrage is possible. |

| 13 | a | Only firms that can keep consumers from reselling a product are able to practice price discrimination. Because the product cannot be resold, the law of one price is not contradicted. |

| 14 | d | To maximize profits, the theater should charge $4.50 for afternoon showings and $7.00 for evening showings. |

| 15 | a | Because demand for afternoon showings is more elastic, these customers will pay a lower price than customers in the evening who have less elastic demands. |

| 16 | b | Because education customers are being charged the higher price, they must have a lower price elasticity of demand than health care customers. |

| 17 | b | The firm maximizes its profits by charging education customers a higher price than health care customers. |

| 18 | b | Airlines have a strong incentive to manage prices so that as many seats as possible are filled on each flight. |

| 19 | a | If a firm knew every consumer's willingness to pay—and could keep consumers who bought at a low price from reselling the product—it could charge every consumer a different price. This is the case of perfect price discrimination—also known as first-degree price discrimination. |

| 20 | c | In this case of perfect price discrimination—also known as first-degree price discrimination—each consumer would have to pay a price equal to his willingness to pay and, therefore, would receive no consumer surplus. |

| 21 | b | The monopolist on the right is able to perfectly price discriminate by charging a different price to each consumer. |

| 22 | a | The monopolist on the left leaves some consumer surplus, while the monopolist on the right turns all consumer surplus into profit. |

| 23 | a | In this case, there is a deadweight loss equal to area C, while in the case of the monopolist on the right, there is no deadweight loss. |

| 24 | b | This monopolist on the right produces the same amount of output as a perfectly competitive industry would, at Q_1. |

| 25 | d | Less than perfect price discrimination often will improve economic efficiency. But under certain circumstances, it may actually reduce economic efficiency, so we can't draw a general conclusion. |

| 26 | b | The two key results of price discrimination are that profits increase and consumer surplus decreases. |

| 27 | b | The difference in price between the hardcover and paperback is driven primarily by differences in demand. The author's most devoted fans want to read his next book at the earliest possible moment and are not too sensitive to price. Many casual readers are also interested in this author's books, but will read something else if the price is too high. |

28	a	In panel (b), the more elastic demand of casual readers and the slightly lower marginal cost result in a profit-maximizing output of 1,000,000 for the paperback edition, sold at a price of $7.99.
29	a	The courts have ruled that this is not illegal discrimination under the civil rights laws because women, on average, have better driving records than men. Because the costs of insuring men are higher than the costs of insuring women, insurance companies are allowed to charge men higher prices.
30	b	Researchers surveyed consumers about their willingness to purchase different products at a series of prices. Ten of the prices were either odd cent prices—99 cents or 95 cents—or odd dollar prices—$95 or $99. For 9 of these 10 odd prices there was an odd price effect, with the quantity demanded being greater than predicted using the estimated demand curve.
31	a	Many firms use cost-plus pricing, which involves adding a percentage markup to average cost. With this pricing strategy, the firm first calculates average cost at a particular level of production, usually equal to the firm's expected sales.
32	b	In a firm selling multiple products, the markup is intended to cover all costs, including those that the firm cannot assign to any particular product. Many firms have costs that are difficult to assign to one particular product.
33	d	Economists have two views of cost-plus pricing. One is that cost-plus pricing is simply a mistake that firms should avoid. The other view is that cost-plus pricing is a good way to at least come close to the profit-maximizing price when marginal revenue or marginal cost is difficult to calculate. The most obvious problems with cost-plus pricing are that it ignores demand and focuses on average cost, rather than marginal cost.
34	b	Economists conclude that cost-plus pricing may be the best way to determine the optimal price when: 1. Marginal cost and average cost are roughly equal. 2. The firm has difficulty estimating its demand curve.
35	b	In general, companies that take demand into account will charge lower markups on products that are more price elastic and higher markups on products that are less price elastic.
36	d	A two-part tariff is a situation where consumers pay one price (or tariff) for the right to buy as much of a related good as they want at a second price.
37	a	In the graph on the left, Disney charges the monopoly price of $26 per ride ticket, and sells 20,000 ride tickets. Its profit from ride tickets is shown by the area of triangle B, $480,000. In the graph on the right, the profit from ride tickets equals zero.
38	a	In this case, Disney charges the monopoly price of $26 per ride ticket, and sells 20,000 ride tickets. The deadweight loss equals area C. In the graph on the right, there is no deadweight loss.
39	b	Because price equals marginal cost at the level of output supplied, the outcome is economically efficient.

Short Answer Responses

1. No. Arbitrage refers to buying a product in a market where the price is low and selling it in a market where the price is high *at the same time*. Although arbitrage transactions do take place in stock markets, most buying occurs with the expectation that stocks can be sold at a higher price at some time in the future. Traders profit from selling stocks when the prices they sell at are higher than the prices at which they bought the stocks at some earlier period of time.

2. Both airlines and cruise ships have high fixed costs but very low marginal costs from adding passengers to what would otherwise be a partially full cruise. Even at prices drastically lower than prices paid by other passengers who booked their travel well ahead of the cruise, almost all of the discount fares will add to profits.

3. Survey responses may be inaccurate even when responses are truthful. This is especially true when consumers are asked for their responses to price changes for items they do not buy on a regular basis. It is difficult for respondents to determine what a "high" or "low" price is for an item they have not recently purchased. What someone says she will do can differ from what she actually will do. This does not mean she has lied. Inevitably, survey responses are less accurate than actual purchasing behavior.

4. To restrict access to the faculty parking lots, the university fines students who park in faculty-designated spaces. University officials can identify these students by their license plate numbers or the numbers on their parking stickers. Those students with the most fines over a given period of time have the greatest willingness to pay. (The economist who made this observation also noted that the university's decision to locate faculty parking spaces in the most desirable locations differs from the practice used by retail stores. These stores usually require employees to park in remote locations to accommodate their customers.)

5. The Robinson-Patman Act (1936) outlawed price discrimination that reduced competition. One can argue that yield management increases competition among schools so that this type of price discrimination is legal. However, the Department of Justice investigated Ivy League schools and MIT for possible violations of the Sherman Antitrust Act because of their practice of collectively adopting a financial aid policy. Collusion, rather than price discrimination, was the focus of the investigation. School officials would meet each spring to jointly determine a student's contribution to tuition if the student was admitted to more than one of the schools. A settlement was reached in 1993 that allowed school officials to meet, but placed restrictions on the policies they used to award financial aid.

True/False Answers

1. F   They are referred to as arbitrage profits.
2. T   See page 494 in the textbook.
3. F   Some evidence based on consumer surveys supports the effectiveness of this strategy but the evidence is not conclusive. See the section "Odd Pricing: Why Is the Price $2.99 Instead of $3.00?" that begins on page 505 in the textbook.
4. F   The Robinson-Patman Act (1936) made price discrimination illegal if its effect is to reduce competition in an industry.
5. T   See the section "Price Discrimination across Time" on page 503 in the textbook.
6. T   See the section "Perfect Price Discrimination" that begins on page 501 in the textbook.
7. T   See the section "Perfect Price Discrimination" that begins on page 501 in the textbook.
8. F   When the price (tariff) is set equal to marginal cost, the outcome is economically efficient.
9. F   Cost-plus pricing may be the best way to determine the optimal price if marginal and average costs are about equal or when the firm has difficulty estimating its demand curve.
10. T   See "Price Discrimination across Time" on page 503 in the textbook.
11. F   It is unlikely that any firm would know each consumer's willingness to pay and could prevent consumers who buy a product at a low price from reselling it to consumers willing to pay a higher price. Perfect price discrimination requires both of these conditions.
12. T   See Making the Connection, "How Colleges Use Yield Management," on page 501 in the textbook.

13. T See the section "Perfect Price Discrimination" that begins on page 501 in the textbook.
14. F Price discrimination may be practiced by any firm that possesses market power. Perfectly competitive firms cannot practice price discrimination but firms in other types of market structures may be able to do so.
15. T See the section "Arbitrage" on page 494 in the textbook.

CHAPTER 16 | The Markets for Labor and Other Factors of Production

Chapter Summary and Learning Objectives

16.1 The Demand for Labor (pages 522–526)

Explain how firms choose the profit-maximizing quantity of labor to employ. The demand for labor is a **derived demand** because it depends on the demand consumers have for goods and services. The additional output produced by a firm as a result of hiring another worker is called the **marginal product of labor**. The amount by which the firm's revenue will increase as a result of hiring one more worker is called the **marginal revenue product of labor (MRP)**. A firm's marginal revenue product of labor curve is its demand curve for labor. Firms maximize profit by hiring workers up to the point where the wage is equal to the marginal revenue product of labor. The market demand curve for labor is determined by adding up the quantity of labor demanded by each firm at each wage, holding constant all other variables that might affect the willingness of firms to hire workers. The most important variables that shift the labor demand curve are changes in human capital, technology, the price of the product, the quantity of other inputs, and the number of firms in the market. **Human capital** is the accumulated training and skills that workers possess.

16.2 The Supply of Labor (pages 526–528)

Explain how people choose the quantity of labor to supply. As the wage increases, the opportunity cost of leisure increases, causing individuals to supply a greater quantity of labor. Normally, the labor supply curve is upward sloping, but it is possible that at very high wage levels, the supply curve might be backward bending. This outcome occurs when someone with a high income is willing to accept a somewhat lower income in exchange for more leisure. The market labor supply curve is determined by adding up the quantity of labor supplied by each worker at each wage, holding constant all other variables that might affect the willingness of workers to supply labor. The most important variables that shift the labor supply curve are increases in population, changing demographics, and changing alternatives.

16.3 Equilibrium in the Labor Market (pages 528–531)

Explain how equilibrium wages are determined in labor markets. The intersection between labor supply and labor demand determines the equilibrium wage and the equilibrium level of employment. If labor supply is unchanged, an increase in labor demand will increase both the equilibrium wage and the number of workers employed. If labor demand is unchanged, an increase in labor supply will lower the equilibrium wage and increase the number of workers employed.

16.4 Explaining Differences in Wages (pages 532–541)

Use demand and supply analysis to explain how compensating differentials, discrimination, and labor unions cause wages to differ. The equilibrium wage is determined by the intersection of the labor demand and labor supply curves. Some differences in wages are explained by **compensating differentials**, which are higher wages that compensate workers for unpleasant aspects of a job. Wages can also differ because of **economic discrimination**, which involves paying a person a lower wage or excluding a person from an occupation on the basis of irrelevant characteristics, such as race or gender. **Labor unions** are organizations of employees that have the legal right to bargain with employers about wages and working conditions. Being in a union increases a worker's wages about 10 percent, holding constant other factors, such as the industry in question.

16.5 Personnel Economics (pages 542–544)
Discuss the role personnel economics can play in helping firms deal with human resources issues.
Personnel economics is the application of economic analysis to human resources issues. One insight of personnel economics is that the productivity of workers can often be increased if firms move from straight-time pay to commission or piece-rate pay.

16.6 The Markets for Capital and Natural Resources (pages 544–547)
Show how equilibrium prices are determined in the markets for capital and natural resources. The approach used to analyze the market for labor can also be used to analyze the markets for other factors of production. In equilibrium, the price of capital is equal to the marginal revenue product of capital, and the price of natural resources is equal to the marginal revenue product of natural resources. The price received by a factor that is in fixed supply is called an **economic rent**, or a **pure rent**. A **monopsony** is the sole buyer of a factor of production. According to the **marginal productivity theory of income distribution**, the distribution of income is determined by the marginal productivity of the factors of production individuals own.

Chapter Review

Chapter Opener: Why Are the New York Yankees Paying CC Sabathia $161 million? (page 521)

If you are a baseball fan, you are aware of the high salaries many players earn and you may wonder why players such as CC Sabathia can earn millions of dollars annually for playing a game for the New York Yankees. Wages and salaries for professional athletes are determined in the labor market by the demand and supply of labor, just as the price of any good is determined by its demand and supply. But unlike the markets for goods and services, concepts of fairness arise more frequently in labor markets.

The Demand for Labor (pages 522–526)

Learning Objective: Explain how firms choose the profit-maximizing quantity of labor to employ.

A **derived demand** is the demand for a factor of production; it depends on the demand for the good the factor produces. The demand for labor is dependent on the amount of output produced and the additional revenue received from selling that output. The **marginal product of labor (*MRP*)** is the additional output a firm produces as a result of hiring one more worker. Because of the law of diminishing returns, the marginal product of labor declines as a firm hires more workers. To decide how many workers to hire, a firm must compare the additional revenue it earns from hiring another worker to the increase in costs from paying the worker.

The marginal revenue product of labor (*MRP*) curve is the demand curve for labor. In constructing the demand curve for labor, all variables, except the wage rate, that affect the willingness of firms to demand labor are held constant. A change in the wage rate causes a change in the quantity of labor demanded. If any of the non-wage variables change, the demand curve will shift.

There are four important non-wage factors that affect the demand for labor:

1. Increases in human capital. Human capital represents the accumulated training and skills that workers possess.

2. Changes in technology. As new and better machinery is developed, workers become more productive and the labor demand curve shifts to the right.
3. Changes in the price of the product. Higher prices increase the marginal revenue product of labor and the labor demand curve shifts to the right.
4. Changes in the quantity of other inputs. Workers are able to produce more if they have more machinery and other inputs to work with.

16.2 The Supply of Labor (pages 526–528)
Learning Objective: Explain how people choose the quantity of labor to supply.

The opportunity cost of leisure is the wage. The higher the wage you can earn from working, the higher the opportunity cost of leisure. Normally the labor supply curve is upward sloping, but it is possible for the curve to be backward bending at high wages. An increase in the wage raises the opportunity cost of leisure and causes a worker to devote more time to working. This is the substitution effect from a wage change. Because leisure is a normal good, as the wage rises, the income effect of a wage change causes a worker to devote less time to working and more time to leisure. Whether a worker supplies more or less labor following a wage increase depends on whether the substitution effect is greater than the income effect.

The supply curve of labor is constructed holding constant all variables other than the wage. If any of the nonwage variables change, the supply curve will shift. The most important nonwage variables are:

1. Increases in population
2. Changing demographics
3. Changing alternatives in other labor markets

 Study Hint
Make sure you do not confuse the supply of *labor* with the supply of *jobs*. You are used to viewing yourself as a consumer rather than as a producer. When you search for a job, you represent the supply side of the labor market, while employers represent the demand side.

Extra Solved Problem 16-2
Dear Adam: I'm Confused. Help!
Supports Learning Objective 16.2: Explain how people choose the quantity of labor to supply.

The following letter was written to an advice column titled "Dear Adam." The column provides online advice to college economics students who have difficulty understanding economics concepts.

> Dear Adam:
> I am a college microeconomics student from Santa Fe. My hometown passed a law in 2003 that raised the minimum wage for all businesses in the city with 25 or more workers. In 2009, the minimum wage was raised to $9.92. My friends have expressed different opinions about the minimum wage law, but what I am confused about is the effect it has had on the market for jobs. An owner of a Sante Fe coffeehouse claims that the current minimum wage is "too high for the kind of work involved" in his business. If this is true, it means that the higher wage

will reduce the quantity supplied of jobs. But we learned in my microeconomics class that the labor supply curve is upward sloping!

After the New Mexico state court upheld the minimum wage ordinance, a lawyer who supported the law claimed that it will "benefit the low-wage workers of Sante Fe." This statement implies that the quantity demanded of jobs will rise as the minimum wage rises; I thought the demand curve for labor was downward sloping!

I have an exam in two weeks on the labor market. Help!

Yours truly,

Hopeless in Sante Fe

Sources: "Court Upholds Sante Fe Wage Ordinance," Brennan Center for Justice, June 25, 2004. Bob Quick, "City gives workers a boost." www.santafenewmexican.com. November 21, 2008.

Write a reply to Hopeless in Sante Fe explaining:

a. The market supply curve for labor.

b. The impact of an increase in the minimum wage on Sante Fe workers.

SOLVING THE PROBLEM:

Step 1: **Review the chapter material.**

This problem is about labor supply, so you may want to review the section "The Supply of Labor," which begins on page 526 in the textbook.

Step 2: **(a) Dear Hopeless:**

You made a common mistake in believing the market for labor was a market for jobs. The labor supply curve is the relationship between the quantity supplied of labor—not jobs—and the price of labor, or the wage rate. Understand, too, that the demand for labor refers to business firms' demand for workers, not jobs. It should make sense to you that the owner of the coffeehouse you referred to believed that an increase in the wage firms must pay to workers would reduce the quantity demanded (of workers, not jobs!).

Step 3: **(b) P.S.**

The increase in the minimum wage will increase the quantity supplied of workers because the opportunity cost of one hour of work is an hour spent doing something else. Let's call this "something else" leisure because the opportunity cost of working will be different for different people. At $5.15, fewer people would choose to work, or would work fewer hours, than at a wage rate of $9.92. But this does not mean all who are willing to work will be able to find jobs. I am sure you learned in your course that a worker will be hired only if the marginal revenue product he or she produces per hour is greater than the wage rate. Good luck on your exam!

Yours truly,

Adam

Equilibrium in the Labor Market (pages 528–531)
Learning Objective 3: Explain how equilibrium wages are determined in labor markets.

Demand and supply determine equilibrium in the labor market. Changes in demand and supply cause changes in the equilibrium wage and the level of employment. Increases in labor productivity cause increases in the demand for labor, which lead to increases in the equilibrium wage and in the number of workers employed. An increase in the labor supply, if the labor demand is unchanged, will decrease the equilibrium wage and increase the number of workers employed.

Extra Solved Problem 16-3
Survey Results Show Wide Variation in Average Salaries
Supports Learning Objective 16.3: Explain how equilibrium wages are determined in labor markets.

A survey conducted by the American Federation of Teachers found that the average salary of K-12 (kindergarten through 12th grade) teachers in 2007 in the United States was $51,009. The same survey reported that the average annual salary for workers in 23 occupations requiring education (a bachelor's degree) similar to that of a K-12 teacher was $72,678. Some of these occupations and their reported annual salaries appear in the following table.

Average 2007 Salaries for Selected Occupations	
Occupation	**Average Salary**
Accountants and auditors	$63,180
Athletic trainers	40,720
Child, family, and school social workers	41,920
Computer software engineers, systems software	90,780
Financial managers	106,200

a. Why would someone want to earn a bachelor's degree to be hired as an athletic trainer or a school social worker when she could earn more than twice as much as a financial manager, a position that also requires a bachelor's degree?

b. Assume that in response to recent financial scandals, Congress passes a law that significantly increases the financial reporting and auditing requirements of U.S. corporations. The new law causes a large increase in the demand for accountants and auditors. Draw a graph that illustrates the impact this has on the market for K-12 teachers.

Source: "Survey and Analysis of Teacher Salary Trends 2007," American Federation of Teachers. http://www.aft.org/salary/

SOLVING THE PROBLEM:
Step 1: **Review the chapter material.**
This problem is about equilibrium in labor markets, so you may want to review the section "Equilibrium in the Labor Market," which begins on page 528 in the textbook.
Step 2: **Why would someone want to earn a bachelor's degree to be hired as an athletic trainer or a school social worker when she could earn more than twice as much as a financial manager, a position that also requires a bachelor's degree?**

Many factors influence someone's choice of career. Although expected salary is important, so are working conditions—required work hours, location, opportunity for advancement etc. Perhaps the most important consideration is to choose a career that is best suited to your preferences and abilities. Those who are committed to doing social work will be willing to accept a relatively low salary to do work they like and for which their talents are well-suited. Also, there is a great deal of variation in the types of courses required to get bachelor's degrees in different subjects. A high future salary may not be enough incentive to induce a student to take courses in advanced calculus or biology.

Step 3: **Assume that a law is passed that causes a large increase in the demand for accountants and auditors. Draw a graph that illustrates the impact this has on the market for K-12 teachers.**

The increase in the demand for accountants and auditors will result in a higher equilibrium annual wage for these positions. The higher annual wage will result in an increase in the quantity supplied of accountants and, in turn, in the number of college students who choose to major in accounting. Assuming that some of these students would have otherwise chosen to major in education, the supply of education majors will decrease, as will the supply of K-12 teachers. The impact of these changes will be spread over a number of years. The graph shows a decrease in the supply of K-12 teachers from S_1 to S_2. The equilibrium quantity of K-12 teachers will decrease from L_1 to L_2, and the equilibrium annual wage will rise from W_1 to W_2.

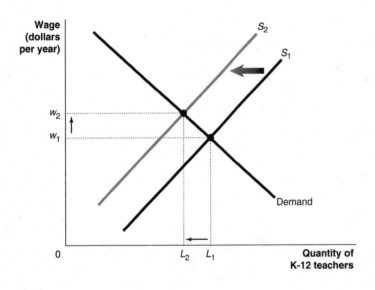

16.4	**Explaining Differences in Wages (pages 532–541)**

Learning Objective: Use demand and supply analysis to explain how compensating differentials, discrimination, and labor unions cause wages to differ.

Differences in marginal revenue product are the most important factor in explaining differences in wages. The more productive a worker is and the higher the price the worker's output can be sold for, the higher the wage the worker will receive. Compensating differentials can also explain wage differences. **Compensating differentials** are higher wages that compensate workers for unpleasant aspects of a job.

In the United States, white males, on average, earn more than other groups. One possible explanation for this difference is economic discrimination. **Economic discrimination** refers to paying a person a lower wage or excluding a person from an occupation on the basis of an irrelevant characteristic such as race or gender. Excluding groups from certain jobs or paying one group more than another is illegal in the United States, but some employers may ignore the law.

Most economists believe that only a small amount of the gap between the wages of white males and other groups is due to discrimination. Most of the gap in wages is due to differences in education, differences in experience, and differing preferences for jobs. Many economists argue that economic discrimination is no longer a major factor in labor markets in the United States because employers pay an economic penalty if they engage in economic discrimination.

Workers' wages can differ depending on whether they are members of labor unions. A **labor union** is an organization of employees that has the legal right to bargain with employers about wages and working conditions. A smaller fraction of the U.S. labor force is unionized than in most other industrial countries. In the United States, union workers receive higher wages than workers who are not in unions.

 Personnel Economics (pages 542–544)
Learning Objective: Discuss the role personnel economics can play in helping firms deal with human resources issues.

Personnel economics is the application of economic analysis to human resources issues. Personnel economics analyzes the link between differences in jobs and differences in the way workers are paid. Firms need to design compensation policies that take into account differences in the skill requirements of jobs, working environments, and the extent of interaction among workers.

One compensation policy firms consider is whether workers will receive a certain wage or salary per week or month or be paid a commission or piece-rate pay. Although a commission or piece-rate system of compensation can be more profitable than a salary system for some firms, other firms have good reasons to choose a salary system. Firms choose a salary system when there is difficulty in measuring output and attributing output to a particular worker, or when firms have concerns about output quality. Many workers dislike the risk inherent in a piece-rate or commission compensation system.

Extra Solved Problem 16-5
Dumping Piece-Rate Compensation Leads to Disaster at Levi Strauss
Supports Learning Objective 16.5: Discuss the role personnel economics can play in helping firms deal with human resources issues.

Making the Connection on page 543 in the textbook describes a study of Safelite AutoGlass by Edward Lazear. Worker productivity and profits both increased when the firm abandoned a straight-time pay system in favor of a piece-rate system. Lazear found different results for Levi Strauss & Co. when the clothing company changed its compensation scheme in the opposite direction.

> Levi's is a worker-oriented company. It had good intentions when the piecework system was abandoned in 1992. Under that system, individual workers performed single, specialized tasks and were paid according to the work they completed. Under the new system, groups of 10-35 workers shared tasks and were paid according to the work they completed...instead of motivating workers...it damaged morale and triggered corrosive infighting. Skilled workers were pitted

against slower colleagues. Threats and insults became common…the quantity of pants produced per hour plunged in 1993 to 77 percent of pre-team levels…labor and overhead costs raced up 25 percent. It was a disaster.

But Lazear found that a team incentive approach worked very well for British Petrol and Exploration (BPE). A team incentive approach rewards workers based on the output produced by a group of workers. BPE has an oil field in Prudhoe Bay, Alaska, with about 300 workers. Six months after introducing its team bonus approach, productivity increased more than 12 percent.

Source: Edward P. Lazear. "Personnel Economics and Economic Approaches to Incentives." *The Hong Kong Centre for Economic Research Letters,* vol. 61. September/October 2000.

a. Why did the team incentive approach fail at Levi Strauss & Co. but prove successful at BPE?

b. Under what circumstances are piece-rate systems and team incentive approaches likely to be successful?

SOLVING THE PROBLEM:

Step 1:   Review the chapter material.
This problem is about personnel economics, so you may want to review the section "Personnel Economics," which begins on page 542 in the textbook.

Step 2:   Why did the team incentive approach fail at Levi Strauss & Co. but prove successful at BPE?
The team incentive approach failed at Levi Strauss & Co. because producing jeans does not require teamwork. As was true with production at Safelite AutoGlass, each task is easily performed by individual workers and can be monitored. When the team incentive approach was used by Levi Strauss & Co., there was a tendency for some workers to be "free riders"— to not work very hard, and to let others do most of the work but still get paid the same. At BPE's Prudhoe Bay field, output could not be produced by one worker. Teamwork at BPE was necessary to produce oil; team-based pay was effective because production was truly a team effort.

Step 3:   Under what circumstances are piecework systems and team incentive approaches likely to be successful?
In summarizing the lessons learned from the experience of Levi Strauss & Co. and BPE, Lazear wrote: "For production workers, pay [based] on output is very effective. However, many firms are reluctant to tie compensation to tangible measures of output…It is easier to simply pay everybody the same…Team-based pay is only effective when production is truly a team effort. Often times, team incentives are weak and may cause resentment."

 ### The Markets for Capital and Natural Resources (pages 544–547)
Learning Objective: Show how equilibrium prices are determined in the markets for capital and natural resources.

The markets for other factors of production are analyzed in much the same way as the market for labor. The demand for capital is a derived demand. Physical capital includes machinery, equipment, and buildings. The marginal revenue product of capital curve is the demand curve for capital. The supply curve for capital goods is upward sloping because the firms that produce capital goods face increasing marginal costs.

The marginal revenue product curve for natural resources is the demand curve for natural resources. The supply curve for natural resources is usually upward sloping. In some cases, the quantity of a natural resource is fixed and will not change as price changes. **Economic rent** (or **pure rent**) is the price of a factor of production that is in fixed supply.

Monopsony refers to a firm that is the sole buyer of a factor of production. A lumber mill in a small town is an example. A monopsony firm restricts the quantity of a factor demanded to force down the price of the factor and increase the firm's profits. A firm with a monopsony in a labor market will hire fewer workers and pay lower wages than a perfectly competitive firm would.

The **marginal productivity theory of income distribution** is the theory that the distribution of income is determined by the marginal productivity of the factors of production that individuals own. The more factors of production an individual owns, and the more productive those factors are, the higher the individual's income will be.

📖 **Study Hint**

Be careful when deciding whether the quantity of a natural resource is fixed. For example, many people believe the supply curve for oil is vertical because "there's a limited amount of oil in the earth's crust." These people have confused the stock of oil with the flow of newly produced oil. Quantity supplied is the flow of newly pumped oil. As the price of oil rises, it becomes economical to reopen closed oil wells and pump oil from fields where extraction is costly, increasing the flow supply. So the supply curve for oil is not vertical after all. Review textbook Figures 16-11 and 16-12, which illustrate equilibrium in the market for capital and natural resources.

Extra Solved Problem 16-6

Falling Natural Gas Prices and Recession Hammer the Market for Coal
Supports Learning Objective 16.6: Show how equilibrium prices are determined in the markets for capital and natural resources.

Increased domestic supplies of natural gas and a recession sent gas prices falling in 2009. Although this was good news for consumers, it was bad news for producers of alternative energy sources, including wind farms, solar power, and coal. But the market for coal is much greater than the market for these alternative supplies of energy. Lower natural gas prices threaten coal's biggest advantage as a fuel for electricity: low cost. Coal still costs about one-half as much as natural gas, but gas is less expensive to transport, and power plants can burn gas more efficiently than coal. An additional selling point for gas is its impact on the environment because gas has only about one-half of the greenhouse emissions as coal. Planned legislation that would tax carbon emissions would make coal even less attractive and natural gas more so.

The slump in coal prices has caused supplies to pile up and buyers to reduce orders. Michael Morris, chief executive of American Electric Power (AEP) Company stated that "we're renegotiating terms." AEP is the largest user of coal in the United States, with operations in 11 states. AEP delayed 2009 shipments of coal into 2010 when, it hopes, the demand for electricity—and coal that is used to produce it—increases.

Sources: "Gas Attack: Coal (And Clean Energy) Under Assault from Cheap Natural Gas," *Wall Street Journal*, June 15, 2009. Rebecca Smith and Kris Maher, "Once-Hot Coal Piles Up as Demand Cools," *Wall Street Journal*, July 30, 2009.

Draw a graph that illustrates the impact of lower natural gas prices on the market for coal.

SOLVING THE PROBLEM:

Step 1:   Review the chapter material.

This problem is about natural resources, so you may want to review the section "The Markets for Capital and Natural Resources," which begins on page 544 in the textbook.

Step 2:   Draw a graph that illustrates the impact of lower natural gas prices on the market for coal.

The graph shows the market for coal in equilibrium initially where the demand curve (Coal demand$_1$) intersects the supply curve (Coal supply). The decline in the price of natural gas— a substitute for coal—results in a decrease in the demand for coal to Coal demand$_2$. The equilibrium price and quantity decline from P_1 to P_2 and Q_1 to Q_2.

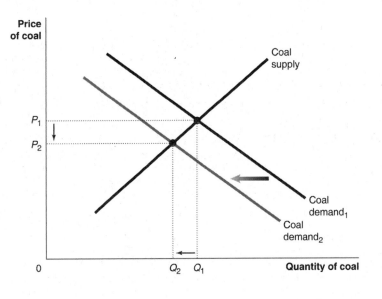

Key Terms

Compensating differentials Higher wages that compensate workers for unpleasant aspects of a job.

Derived demand The demand for a factor of production; it depends on the demand for the good the factor produces.

Economic discrimination Paying a person a lower wage or excluding a person from an occupation on the basis of an irrelevant characteristic such as race or gender.

Economic rent (or **pure rent**) The price of a factor of production that is in fixed supply.

Factors of production Labor, capital, natural resources, and other inputs used to produce goods and services.

Human capital The accumulated training and skills that workers possess.

Labor union An organization of employees that has the legal right to bargain with employers about wages and working conditions.

Marginal product of labor The additional output a firm produces as a result of hiring one more worker.

Marginal productivity theory of income distribution The theory that the distribution of income is determined by the marginal productivity of the factors of production that individuals own.

Marginal revenue product of labor (*MRP*) The change in a firm's revenue as a result of hiring one more worker.

Monopsony The sole buyer of a factor of production.

Personnel economics The application of economic analysis to human resources issues.

Self-Test

(Answers are provided at the end of the Self-Test.)

Multiple-Choice Questions

1. Which of the following is a factor of production?
   a. labor
   b. natural resources
   c. capital
   d. all of the above

2. Why do economists say that labor demand is a derived demand?
   a. because in order to derive labor demand, we must derive labor supply first
   b. because the demand for labor is derived from the demand for the products produced by workers
   c. because the demand for labor depends on the amount of capital available; without capital there is no need for labor
   d. because the demand for labor depends entirely on the willingness of firms to hire workers

3. Link one of the terms below to the following definition: "_____ is the additional output a firm produces as a result of hiring one more worker."
   a. Marginal cost
   b. Marginal revenue
   c. The marginal product of labor
   d. The marginal revenue product of labor

4. Link one of the terms below to the following definition: "_____ is the change in the firm's revenue as a result of hiring one additional worker."
   a. Marginal cost
   b. Marginal revenue
   c. The marginal product of labor
   d. The marginal revenue product of labor

5. Which of the following formulas is correct?
   a. product price = marginal product of labor × marginal revenue product
   b. marginal product of labor = product price × marginal revenue product
   c. marginal revenue product = product price × marginal product of labor
   d. none of the above

6. What happens as the number of workers increases?
    a. The marginal product of labor decreases, and the marginal revenue product of labor increases.
    b. The marginal product of labor increases, and the marginal revenue product of labor decreases.
    c. Both the marginal product and the marginal revenue product of labor increase.
    d. Both the marginal product and the marginal revenue product of labor decrease.

7. Let *MRP* equal the marginal revenue product of labor and *W* equal the wage rate. When should a firm hire more workers to increase profit?
    a. when *MRP* > *W*
    b. when *MRP* < *W*
    c. when *MRP* = *W*
    d. when *MRP* = 0

8. Which of the following is the equivalent of the demand curve for labor?
    a. the marginal revenue product curve
    b. the marginal product of labor curve
    c. the demand curve for the firm's product
    d. the firm's total revenue curve

9. Refer to the table below. Which two columns must a firm compare to determine the profit-maximizing quantity of workers to hire?

Number of Workers	Output of Televisions per Week	Marginal Product of Labor (television sets per week)	Product Price	Total Revenue	Marginal Revenue Product of Labor (dollars per week)	Wage (dollars per week)	Additional Profit from Hiring One More Worker (dollars per week)
(1)	(2)	(3)	(4)	(5)	(6)	(7)	(8)
0	0	–	$200		–	$500	–
1	6	6	180			500	
2	11	5	160			500	
3	15	4	140			500	
4	18	3	120			500	
5	20	2	100			500	
6	21	1	80			500	

    a. columns 4 and 6
    b. columns 6 and 7
    c. columns 5 and 6
    d. columns 3 and 4

10. Refer to the table below. How many workers should the firm hire to maximize profit?

Number of Workers	Output of Televisions per Week	Marginal Product of Labor (television sets per week)	Product Price	Total Revenue	Marginal Revenue Product of Labor (dollars per week)	Wage (dollars per week)	Additional Profit from Hiring One More Worker (dollars per week)
(1)	(2)	(3)	(4)	(5)	(6)	(7)	(8)
0	0	–	$200		–	$500	–
1	6	6	180			500	
2	11	5	160			500	
3	15	4	140			500	
4	18	3	120			500	
5	20	2	100			500	
6	21	1	80			500	

    a. 2
    b. 3
    c. 4
    d. 5

11. What name is given to the accumulated training and skills that workers possess?
    a. the marginal product of labor
    b. human capital
    c. physical capital
    d. productivity

12. Which of the factors listed below does *not* cause the demand curve for labor to shift?
    a. a change in the wage
    b. a change in human capital
    c. a change in technology
    d. a change in the price of the product

13. Which of the following shifts the demand curve for labor to the right?
    a. a decrease in the wage
    b. an increase in the wage
    c. an increase in the price of the product
    d. a decrease in the quantity of inputs other than labor

14. According to the substitution effect, what is the impact of an increase in the wage?
    a. an increase in the opportunity cost of leisure
    b. an increase in the opportunity cost of work
    c. a decrease in the opportunity cost of leisure
    d. an increase in purchasing power

15. Which of the following best describes the change in consumer purchasing power as a result of a price change?
    a. the substitution effect
    b. the income effect
    c. the opportunity cost of leisure
    d. a shift of the labor supply curve

16. Along a backward-bending supply curve, which effect is larger at low wage levels?
    a.   The substitution effect is larger than the income effect.
    b.   The income effect is larger than the substitution effect.
    c.   The tax effect is larger than the income effect.
    d.   The work effect is larger than the leisure effect.

17. Which of the following factors shifts the labor supply curve?
    a.   a change in demographics
    b.   a change in alternatives available in other labor markets
    c.   a change in population
    d.   all of the above

18. A change in which of the following factors would cause a movement along the labor supply curve rather than a shift of the curve?
    a.   a change in demographics
    b.   a change in alternatives available in other labor markets
    c.   a change in population
    d.   a change in the wage

19. Refer to the graph below. Which of the following could have caused the shift in the labor demand curve?

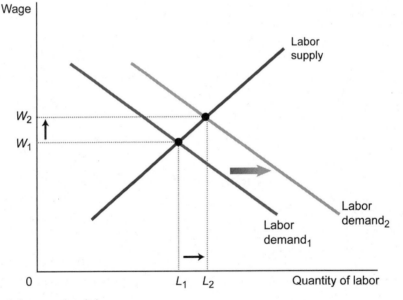

    a.   a change in labor productivity
    b.   a change in the substitution effect
    c.   a change in the income effect
    d.   all of the above

20. According to the signaling hypothesis, what signal does a college education send to prospective employers about a college graduate?
    a. College graduates require higher wages without necessarily being more productive than non-college graduates.
    b. College graduates possess certain desirable characteristics such as self-discipline and the ability to meet deadlines.
    c. A college graduate has knowledge that is worth paying for.
    d. A college graduate deserves a job because she has made an investment in education.

21. Refer to the graphs below. Which of the graphs best depicts the impact of an increase in population on the labor market?

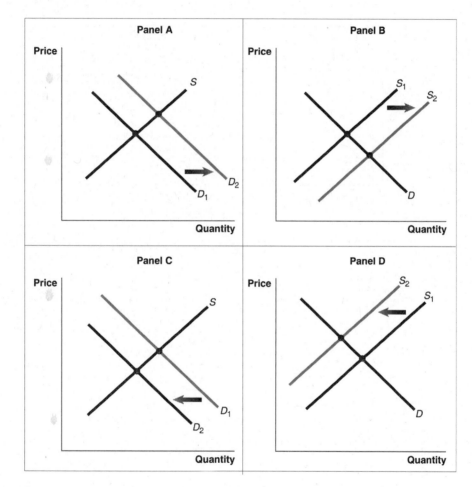

    a. Panel A
    b. Panel B
    c. Panel C
    d. Panel D

22. Refer to the graphs below. Judging by the relative position of supply and demand in each of these labor markets, which occupation appears to offer more desirable working conditions, holding everything else constant?

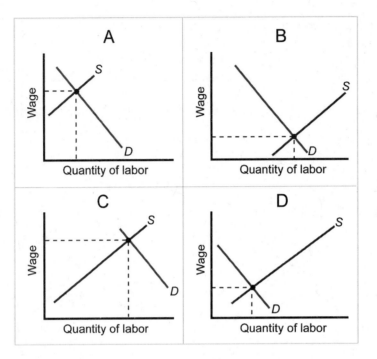

a. A
b. B
c. C
d. D

23. Refer to the graph below. According to the graph, who has a higher marginal revenue product of labor?

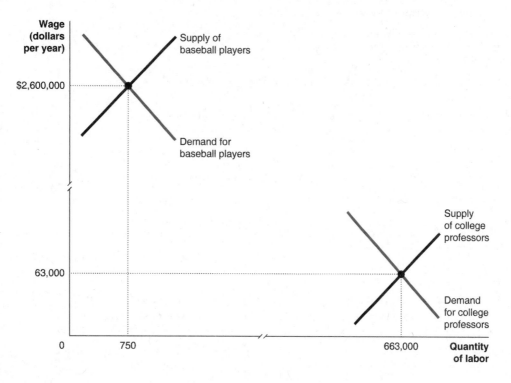

    a. a college professor
    b. a baseball player
    c. There is insufficient information to answer the question.
    d. College professors and baseball players appear to have the same marginal revenue product of labor.

24. Which of the following is more relevant in determining the wages of baseball players?
    a. the total value of the baseball games
    b. the marginal value of baseball games
    c. Both the total value and the marginal value are equally important.
    d. the educational level of baseball players

25. When an employer pays higher wages to compensate workers for unpleasant aspects of their jobs, which of the following is the employer offering?
    a. a discriminating wage
    b. a labor union wage
    c. a compensating differential
    d. a risk premium

26. What does the term cognitive dissonance refer to?
    a. the tendency for workers to ignore the going wage rate in a labor market
    b. a distortion to the free labor market created by compensating differentials
    c. the tendency for workers to underestimate the true risks of their jobs
    d. the willingness of some workers to accept low wages for jobs involving low risk

27. Which of the following is true about economic discrimination?
    a. Economic discrimination is illegal and, therefore, impossible.
    b. Economic discrimination is both legal and possible.
    c. Economic discrimination is illegal, but it is possible that employers ignore the law.
    d. Economic discrimination is legal, but few if any employers would actually practice it.

28. Which of the following groups earns the lowest annual earnings?
    a. Hispanic males
    b. Hispanic females
    c. black females
    d. black males

29. Which of the following is least likely to be the cause of differences between the wages of white males and those of other groups?
    a. economic discrimination
    b. differences in education
    c. differences in experience
    d. differing preferences for jobs

30. Which of the following is true about men's jobs versus women's jobs?
    a. Men are overrepresented in jobs where average weekly earnings are relatively low.
    b. Women are overrepresented in jobs where average weekly earnings are relatively low.
    c. There appears to be no preference between men and women in choosing particular jobs.
    d. Women tend to take jobs where work experience is very important.

31. Which of the following is a textbook argument about employer discrimination of workers?
    a. Employers who discriminate pay an economic penalty because very few workers are willing to work for a discriminating employer.
    b. Employers who discriminate pay an economic penalty imposed by the market system and by competition.
    c. Employers who discriminate receive an economic reward by keeping only the most productive workers.
    d. Employers who discriminate are rewarded by authorities who usually ignore their criminal behavior.

32. If discrimination makes it difficult for a member of a group to find employment in a particular occupation, his or her incentive to be trained to enter that occupation is reduced. Which of the terms below is most closely associated with this condition?
    a. worker discrimination
    b. customer discrimination
    c. negative feedback loop
    d. irrational expectations

33. In which of the following countries is the percentage of the labor force that belongs to unions the lowest?
    a. Sweden
    b. Canada
    c. Germany
    d. The United States

34. In the United States, how do the average weekly earnings of union workers compare with the earnings of nonunion workers?
    a. The earnings of union workers are higher than the earnings of nonunion workers.
    b. The earnings of union workers are lower than the earnings of nonunion workers.
    c. The earnings of union workers are almost identical to the earnings of nonunion workers.
    d. There is no way to compare the two.

35. What is the term given to the application of economic analysis to human resources issues?
    a. labor economics
    b. personnel economics
    c. human resource management
    d. occupational economics

36. Refer to the graph below. According to the textbook analysis of compensation, which line represents the compensation of a salesperson based on commission?

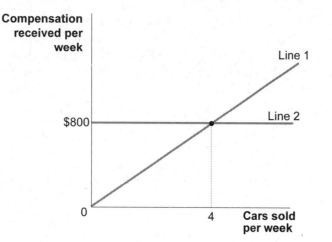

    a. Line 1
    b. Line 2
    c. both lines
    d. neither line

37. Which of the following is a reason for choosing a salary system rather than the more profitable commission, or piece-rate system, of compensation?
    a. difficulty in measuring output
    b. concerns about quality
    c. worker dislike of risk
    d. all of the above

38. What is the definition of economic rent?
    a. the price of a resource when that price is strictly determined by supply
    b. the marginal revenue product of natural resources
    c. the price received by a factor of production that is in fixed supply
    d. the earnings of a landlord

39. Which of the following is caused by the existence of a firm with a monopsony in the labor market?
    a. More workers will be hired at higher wages.
    b. More workers will be hired at lower wages.
    c. Fewer workers will be hired at higher wages.
    d. Fewer workers will be hired at lower wages.

40. Which of the statements below best describes the premise of the marginal productivity theory of income distribution?
    a. Workers become productive and receive income only at the margin.
    b. Income is distributed in such a way as to encourage workers to increase their productivity.
    c. The distribution of income is determined by the marginal productivity of the factors of production that individuals own.
    d. Income and productivity necessarily increase with additional hours spent at work.

Short Answer Questions

1. A professor in the Department of Foreign Languages at a Midwestern college complained that his salary is much less than an accounting professor at the same college. Both professors have Ph.D. degrees, 20 years of teaching experience, and similar research records. Is this difference in salary due to a compensating differential, economic discrimination, or some other factor?

_____

_____

_____

_____

_____

_____

_____

2. Between 2005 and 2010, members of the "baby boom" generation began to reach retirement age (over 62 years). How does this affect the labor market in the United States?

_____

_____

_____

3. Clergymen and clergywomen (ministers, rabbis, priests, etc.) work long hours and provide services to people at times of personal stress such as illness, death, and marriage problems. Economic reasoning would suggest that to attract people to these professions, a compensating differential would be needed. But economist Daniel Hamermesh estimated that male clergy in the United States earn less than 60 percent of the income earned by otherwise identical workers. How can this be explained?

_____

_____

_____

_____

4. Left-handed pitchers in Major League Baseball earn higher average salaries than right-handed pitchers of similar ability. Some lefty pitchers have found employment with Major League teams despite being over 40 years old. Aaron Jerslid, a scout for the Toronto Blue Jays, commented on the difference in teams' desire for right-handed and left-handed pitchers: "Veteran scouts tell me 'A lefty should give you a reason not to like him. A right-hander has to show you something.'" (It's important to note that the demand for left-handed pitchers is strongly influenced by the fact that left-handed pitchers are more successful against left-handed batters.)

Source: "When it comes to pitching, left-handers get extra benefits," by Mel Antonen. June 6, 2006. www.usatoday.com

Why do teams pay a premium for left-handed pitchers?

_____

_____

_____

_____

_____

5. Table 16-2 on page 536 in the textbook lists annual earnings for different racial and gender groups. The annual earnings of black males ($36,233) exceed the annual earnings of Hispanic males ($30,151). Is this difference due to discrimination?

_____

_____

_____

True/False Questions

T   F   1.   The price received by a factor of production that has a perfectly *inelastic* supply curve is called an economic rent.

T   F   2.   Hazard pay is the term used by economists to refer to the wage premium paid to those who work in dangerous or unpleasant jobs.

T   F   3.   If the price of iPods increases, then the demand for iPod workers will shift to the right.

T   F   4.   Leisure is a normal good. Therefore, as wages increase, the substitution effect will cause a worker to devote less time to work and more time to leisure.

T   F   5.   Research has shown that increases in the number of science and mathematics courses that students take in college (*ceteris paribus*) increase their future earnings.

T   F   6.   Salaries paid to movie stars today are greater than salaries paid to movie stars of the 1930s and 1940s mainly because of advances in technology.

T   F   7.   The differences between the salaries of white males and black males are due mostly to racial discrimination.

T   F   8.   An increase in the wage rate causes an increase in the demand for labor.

T   F   9.   Pure rent is another name for economic rent.

T   F   10. An increase in unemployment benefits from the government has been found to be an effective way to reduce the unemployment rate.

T   F   11. Compensating differentials explain why college graduates receive incomes higher than incomes of other workers who are 25 years of age and older.

T   F   12. If the demand for labor is unchanged, an increase in the supply of labor will decrease the equilibrium wage rate and increase the number of employed workers.

T   F   13. Although the labor force participation of women increased from 1950 to over 60 percent in 1970, the rate has fallen to less than 50 percent today as more women have left the labor market and become full-time undergraduate and graduate students.

T   F   14. The fraction of the labor force that is unionized is higher in the United States than in most other high-income countries, such as Japan, Germany, and Sweden.

T   F   15. Increases in human capital will cause workers to have more skills and be more productive. This will shift the supply curve of labor.

Answers to the Self-Test

Multiple-Choice Questions

Questions	Answers	Comment
1	d	Firms use factors of production—the most important of which are labor, capital, and natural resources—to produce goods and services.
2	b	Economists say that labor demand is a derived demand—that is, derived from the demand for the products produced by workers.
3	c	The marginal product of labor is the change in a firm's output from having one additional worker.
4	d	The marginal revenue product of labor (*MRP*) is how much a firm's revenue will rise when it sells the additional output it can produce by hiring one more worker. We can calculate this amount by multiplying the additional output produced by the product price.
5	c	The marginal revenue product of labor (*MRP*) is defined as the extra revenue generated by one additional worker.

6	d	Because of diminishing returns, the marginal product of labor (the change in output from one additional worker) decreases as the number of workers increases. Because the marginal product drops as the number of workers increases, the *MRP* curve is negatively sloped.
7	a	When *MRP* > *W*, the value of an additional worker to the firm exceeds the cost of hiring that worker. The difference is additional profit. Therefore the firm will hire the additional worker.
8	a	The *MRP* curve is also the firm's demand curve for labor.
9	b	To determine the profit-maximizing quantity of workers to hire, a firm needs to compare the marginal revenue product of labor with the wage. Column 8 does this by subtracting the wage (column 7) from the marginal revenue product (column 6). As long as the values in column 8 are positive, the firm should continue to hire workers.
10	a	The marginal revenue product of the second worker is $680 and her wage is $500, so column 7 shows that hiring her will add $180 to the firm's profits. The marginal revenue product of the third worker is $340 and his wage is $500, so hiring him would reduce the firm's profits by $160. Therefore, the firm will maximize profits by hiring 2 workers.
11	b	Human capital refers to the accumulated training and skills that workers possess.
12	a	An increase or decrease in the wage causes an increase or decrease in the *quantity of labor demanded*, which we show by a movement along the demand curve. If any variable other than the wage changes, the result is an increase or decrease in the *demand for labor*.
13	c	The marginal revenue product of labor depends on the price the firm receives for its output. A higher price increases the marginal revenue product and shifts the labor demand curve to the right. (Decreasing the quantities of other inputs may shift the labor demand curve in either direction depending on whether those other inputs are substitutes for labor or complements to labor in production.)
14	a	As the wage increases, the opportunity cost of leisure increases, causing individuals to supply a greater quantity of labor. Therefore, the labor supply curve is upward sloping. But this occurs only if the substitution effect prevails over the income effect.
15	b	The income effect of a price change refers to the change in the quantity demanded of a good that results from the effect of a change in the good's price on consumer purchasing power.
16	a	The substitution effect of a wage increase causes a worker to supply a larger quantity of labor. The backward-bending labor supply curve shows the typical case of the substitution effect being larger than the income effect at low levels of wages—so the worker supplies a larger quantity of labor as the wage rises.
17	d	These are the main determinants of labor supply other than the wage.
18	d	A change in quantity supplied or quantity demanded is always caused by a change in price. The wage rate is the price of labor.
19	a	Higher productivity will result in an increase in the demand for labor.
20	b	According to the signaling hypothesis, employers see a college education as a signal that workers possess certain desirable characteristics: self-discipline, the ability to meet deadlines, and the ability to make a sustained effort, even if these characteristics are not related to the specifics of a particular job.
21	b	Increases in labor supply will cause the equilibrium wage to fall, but the equilibrium level of employment to rise. As population increases, the labor supply curve shifts to the right; the equilibrium wage falls, and the equilibrium level of employment increases.

22	b	Labor supply is relatively high in this market, meaning that more workers are attracted to it; therefore, labor supply is abundant.
23	b	The marginal revenue product for baseball players is very high, and the supply of people with the ability to play major league baseball is low. The result is that the 750 major league baseball players receive an average wage of $2 million. The marginal revenue product for college professors is much lower, and the supply of people with the ability to be college professors is much higher. The result is that the 663,000 college professors in the United States receive an average wage of $73,000, far below that of baseball players. (Because $MRP = W$ in equilibrium, it's clear from comparing the wage rates of the two groups that baseball players have a higher MRP.)
24	b	Wages—like prices—do not depend on total value, but on marginal value, or the value of the additional baseball games a team expects to win.
25	c	Higher wages that compensate workers for unpleasant aspects of a job are called compensating differentials.
26	c	A psychological principle known as cognitive dissonance might cause workers to underestimate the true risk of their jobs. According to this principle, people prefer to think of themselves as intelligent and rational and tend to reject evidence that seems to contradict this image.
27	c	Economic discrimination is illegal in the United States since the passage of the Equal Pay Act of 1963 and the Civil Rights Act of 1964. Nevertheless, it is possible that employers are ignoring the law and practicing economic discrimination.
28	b	Among the groups listed in Table 16-2 in the textbook, Hispanic females have the lowest annual earnings.
29	a	Most economists believe that only a small amount of the gap between the wages of white males and the wages of other groups is due to discrimination. Instead, most of the gap is explained by three main factors: 1) differences in education; 2) differences in experience; and 3) differing preferences for jobs.
30	b	As Table 16-3 in the textbook shows, women are overrepresented in some jobs where average weekly earnings are less than $600 per week and men are overrepresented in some jobs where weekly earnings are greater than $800 per week.
31	b	Many economists argue that economic discrimination is no longer a major factor in labor markets in the United States. One reason is that employers who discriminate pay an economic penalty in the form of higher wages, as Figure 16-8 in the textbook illustrates.
32	c	In the textbook example, an unfortunate feedback loop occurred when few women prepared to become lawyers because many law firms discriminated against women and non-discriminating law firms were unable to drive discriminating law firms out of business because there were too few women lawyers available.
33	d	As Figure 16-9 in the textbook shows, a smaller fraction of the U.S. labor force is unionized than in most other industrial countries.
34	a	As Table 16-4 in the textbook shows, in the United States workers in unions receive higher wages than workers who are not in unions.
35	b	Personnel economics is the application of economic analysis to human resources issues.
36	a	With a straight salary, the salesperson receives $800 per week, no matter how many cars he sells. This outcome is shown by the horizontal line in the figure. If the salesperson receives a commission of, say, $200 per car, then his compensation will increase with every car he sells. This outcome is shown by the

upward-sloping line in the figure.

37	d	All of the above are reasons why companies choose a salary system rather than the more profitable commission, or piece-rate system, of compensation.
38	c	The price received by a factor of production that is in fixed supply is called an economic rent, or a pure rent.
39	d	A firm with a monopsony in a labor market will hire fewer workers and pay lower wages than would be the case in a competitive market.
40	c	Individuals will receive income equal to the marginal contributions to production from the factors of production they own, including their labor. The more factors of production an individual owns, and the more productive those factors are, the higher the individual's income will be. This approach to explaining the distribution of income is called the marginal productivity theory of income distribution.

Short Answer Responses

1. It is highly doubtful that the accounting professor's higher salary was due to a compensating differential. Although the professional responsibilities of professors vary by department, the accounting professor's job is not more dangerous or unpleasant enough to warrant a compensating differential. Economic discrimination would explain this difference only if it could be demonstrated that the accounting professor was paid more on the basis of race, gender, or some other irrelevant characteristic. A more plausible explanation is that there are more people who want to be foreign language professors, relative to the demand for these positions, and relatively fewer people who want to be accounting professors, relative to the demand for these positions. There is a greater demand for accountants than foreign language specialists by private firms. The Midwestern college competes with private firms as well as with other colleges and universities for the services of their accounting professors.

2. As baby boomers retire, there will be an increase in the demand for labor to replace those who retire. Holding everything else constant, this will increase the wages and salaries of the replacement workers because of the greater number of retired baby boomers compared to the number of new entrants into the labor force.

3. It seems clear that many clergy members choose their professions for reasons other than the salary and benefits offered. A large number of these people must enjoy helping other people (they may be said to receive "psychic income" from their work) and believe they are responding to a spiritual, rather than a monetary, calling. However, the number of people choosing this profession has declined over time in several religious denominations. This has led some to suggest other ways to attract clergy, including advertising, loosening restrictions on personal behavior (for example, allowing Catholic priests to marry), and permitting non-clergy to perform some religious tasks. Not all of these suggestions have been adopted, but if recent trends continue, religious leaders will be forced to consider alternative means of recruiting clergy and providing services.

4. Because of the angles from which pitches are thrown, many right-handed batters hit more effectively against left-handed pitchers and many left-handed batters have greater success against right-handed pitchers. Many batters, even those who throw right-handed, learn to bat left-handed to take advantage of the greater number of right-handed pitchers. Using data for 2005, about 31 percent of Major League hitters batted left-handed, 56 percent batted right-handed, and 12 percent were switch-hitters. (Switch-hitters usually bat right-handed against left-handed pitchers and left-handed against right-handed pitchers.) Only about 10 percent of the general population is left-handed. The supply of left-handed pitchers is relatively inelastic. This means that salaries can increase substantially without a large increase in quantity supplied. It is common for Major League teams to hire left-handed pitchers to pitch

to only one or two left-handed hitters per game. The premium paid to left-handed pitchers compared to right-handed pitchers of similar ability reflects their relative scarcity.

5. It is impossible to rule out discrimination as one factor responsible for the earnings gaps among groups divided by gender or race. But it is likely that this earnings gap can be explained by other factors as well, including differences in education, experience, and preferences for jobs.

True/False Answers

1.   T   Economic rent or pure rent refers to the price of a factor of production that is in fixed supply. The supply curve of this factor is vertical, or perfectly inelastic.
2.   F   Compensating differential is the term economists use to describe this wage premium.
3.   T   The demand curve for labor is the same as the marginal revenue product of labor curve. The marginal revenue product of iPods equals the product price multiplied by the additional output produced by iPod workers. Therefore, if the price of iPods rises, then the demand for iPod workers will shift to the right.
4.   F   The income effect of a wage change has this effect. See the section "The Supply of Labor" beginning on page 526 in the textbook.
5.   T   Research by Daniel Hamermesh and Stephen Donald found this to be true. See Making the Connection on pages 530–531 in the textbook.
6.   T   DVDs, Internet streaming video, and other technologies developed since the 1930s and 1940s have resulted in large increases in revenue earned by popular movies and, in turn, large increases in salaries paid to those who star in these movies. See Making the Connection on pages 533–534 in the textbook.
7.   F   Most, but not all, of this difference is explained by differences in education, experience and preferences for jobs.
8.   F   An increase in the real wage caused by a shift of the supply curve causes the quantity demanded of labor to decrease. If the increase in the real wage was caused by a shift in the demand for labor, then the causality would run in the opposite direction.
9.   T   See the explanation for answer number 1 above.
10. F   An increase in unemployment benefits reduces the pressure for unemployed workers to find another job. Many economists believe generous unemployment benefits help explain the higher unemployment rates in some European countries than in the United States. See the section "Factors That Shift the Market Supply Curve of Labor" on page 528 in the textbook.
11. F   Compensating differentials explain the higher wages workers receive for dangerous or unpleasant jobs.
12. T   See the section "The Effect on Equilibrium Wages of a Shift in Labor Supply" on page 531 in the textbook.
13. F   The current labor force participation rate for women is still about 60 percent.
14. F   As Figure 16-9 in the textbook shows, the percentage of the labor force that is unionized in the United States is about 10 percent, lower than the percentage of the labor force that is unionized in most other high-income countries.
15. F   Increases in human capital will shift the *demand curve* for labor.

CHAPTER 17 | The Economics of Information

Chapter Summary and Learning Objectives

17.1 Asymmetric Information (pages 560–564)

Define asymmetric information and distinguish between adverse selection and moral hazard. **Asymmetric information** is a situation in which one party to an economic transaction has less information than the other party. Asymmetric information can lead to **adverse selection**, which occurs when one party to a transaction takes advantage of knowing more than the other party to the transaction. An example is the "lemons" problem, where adverse selection may lead to only unreliable used cars being offered for sale. Asymmetric information can also lead to **moral hazard**, which refers to actions people take after they have entered into a transaction that make the other party to the transaction worse off. For example, a firm that has taken out a fire insurance policy on a warehouse may be less careful in the future about avoiding fire hazards. Information problems result in the equilibrium quantity in markets being smaller than it would be if these problems did not exist. Therefore, there is a reduction in economic efficiency.

17.2 Adverse Selection and Moral Hazard in Financial Markets (pages 564–566)

Apply the concepts of adverse selection and moral hazard to financial markets. Adverse selection and moral hazard are serious problems in financial markets. When firms sell stocks and bonds, they know much more about their true financial condition than do potential investors. Investors are reluctant to buy stocks and bonds issued by small and medium-sized firms because they lack sufficient information about these firms. Investors also worry about the moral hazard problem of firms misusing the funds they raise through the sale of stocks and bonds. The Securities and Exchange Commission (SEC) has the authority to regulate the stock and bond markets and attempts to reduce adverse selection and moral hazard problems. The failure of financial firms and the financial frauds of the late 2000s indicate that information problems persist in financial markets.

17.3 Adverse Selection and Moral Hazard in Labor Markets (pages 566–568)

Apply the concepts of adverse selection and moral hazard to labor markets. The potential for a **principal–agent problem** exists between employers and workers. This problem is caused by agents—workers—pursuing their own interests rather than the interests of the principals who hired them. When workers are not monitored, they may have no incentive to work hard. Employers try to avoid this moral hazard problem by increasing the value to a worker of the worker's current job. Three ways to increase the value of a worker's job are offering efficiency wages, using a seniority system, and offering profit sharing.

17.4 The Winner's Curse: When Is It Bad to Win an Auction? (pages 568–571)

Explain the winner's curse and why it occurs. In auctions where bidders do not know the true value of what is being auctioned, the winner, by overestimating the value of what is being bid for, can end up worse off than the losers. This is known as the **winner's curse**, and it occurs in auctions of common-value assets that would be given the same value by all bidders if they had perfect information.

Chapter Review

Chapter Opener: Why Does State Farm Charge Young Men So Much More Than Young Women for Auto Insurance? (page 559)

State Farm Insurance charges different prices for automobile insurance based on a driver's gender, age, and other factors. State Farm and other insurance companies attempt to match the prices they charge with the costs they are likely to incur on each policy. Many insurance companies use sophisticated computer models to predict the chance that a driver will have an accident. As a result, in recent years there has been an increase in the variety of prices insurance companies charge drivers.

17.1 Asymmetric Information (pages 560–564)

Learning Objective: Define asymmetric information and distinguish between adverse selection and moral hazard.

The difficulty in correctly pricing insurance policies arises from asymmetric information. **Asymmetric information** is a situation in which one party to an economic transaction has less information than the other party. For example, if someone drinks, smokes, doesn't sleep well, and has heart disease in his or her family, a health insurance company does not necessarily have that information when pricing a policy. Guarding against the effects of asymmetric information is a major objective of sellers in the insurance market and of buyers in financial markets.

The study of asymmetric information began with the study of used car markets or the market for "lemons." Sellers of used cars have more information about the cars they sell than do buyers. Most used cars offered for sale will be lemons. This is due to adverse selection. **Adverse selection** is a situation in which one party to a transaction (for example, a used car dealer) takes advantage of knowing more than the other party to the transaction (for example, the car buyer). Used car dealers can take steps to assure buyers they are not selling lemons by offering warranties that guarantee repair or replacement over a certain time period. Sellers can also build a reputation for selling reliable cars.

Buyers of insurance will always know more than insurance companies about the likelihood of the event being insured against happening. For example, people with bad health habits and histories of health problems will have a better idea of the probability that they will suffer a heart attack or other health problem than will insurance companies. Insurance companies cover their costs only if they set the prices (premiums) of their policies at levels that represent how many payment claims the people they have insured are likely to submit. The adverse selection problem can be reduced if people are automatically covered by insurance. For example, state governments require drivers to have automobile insurance. Adverse selection problems can also be reduced by offering group coverage to large companies and other organizations.

The insurance market is also subject to moral hazard. **Moral hazard** is the tendency of people who have insurance to change their actions because of the insurance or, more broadly, actions taken by one party to a transaction that are different from what the other party expected at the time of the transaction. An example of moral hazard is a firm that has taken out fire insurance may be less careful about avoiding fire hazards. Insurance companies use deductibles and co-payments to reduce moral hazard.

> 📖 **Study Hint**
> ***Don't Let This Happen to YOU!*** on page 564 in the textbook explains how you can understand the difference between adverse selection and moral hazard:
> - Adverse selection happens at the time you enter into the transaction. Example: You sell your roommate a computer that crashes on you every three or four weeks.
> - Moral hazard refers to what happens after you enter into the transaction. Example: You get insurance for your apartment and are less careful about locking the door when you leave in the morning.
>
> Work through related end-of-chapter problems 1.10, 1.13, and 3.3 to increase your understanding of these two concepts.

Extra Solved Problem 17-1

The Consequences of Asymmetric Information in the Insurance Market
Supports Learning Objective 17.1: Define asymmetric information and distinguish between adverse selection and moral hazard.

Although most people with health and life insurance are honest, some policy holders take advantage of having asymmetric information—having more information than the companies that insure them—which can lead to adverse selection: some people change their behavior as a result of having insurance. Among the most conspicuous examples of behavioral change are those involving people who lie about their circumstances or take deliberate actions that endanger their health. There are reported cases of self-mutilation in order to collect on disability insurance. Perhaps the most bizarre story concerns a town in Florida that acquired the macabre nickname of "Nub City" in the 1970s.

Over 50 people in the town have suffered "accidents" involving the loss of various organs and appendages, and claims of up to $300,000 have been paid out by insurers. Their investigators are positive the maimings are self-inflicted; many witnesses to the "accidents" are prior claimants or relatives of the victims, and one investigator notes that "somehow they always shoot off parts they seem to need least."

Another type of moral hazard involves staging automobile accidents. The following is a brief description of how this is done.

> *How do I get started?* For a "paper accident," try inflicting "controlled damage" on a couple of cars with a sledgehammer in a dark parking lot. Insert passengers. Summon a witness. Gather broken glass in bags for re-use.

> *That was easy, what next?* "Staged" accidents: Buy rustbuckets, insure one and run it into another one full of recruited claimants-to-be ("cows"). If you're nice, give them pillows.

> *How do I keep from getting caught?* Vary your fact patterns. Don't stamp a doctor's name on medical reports months after he's died. Don't lose your ledger—needed to keep hundreds of accidents straight—or your scripts and tip sheets.

Sources: "Moral Hazard and Adverse Selection." http://ingrimayne.saintjoe.edu/econ/RiskExclusion/Risk.html
Walter Olsen, "New Trends in Highway Robbery," *Wall Street Journal*, December 20, 1996.

a. Use the passage in this problem to describe asymmetric information.

b. Use the passage to distinguish adverse selection and moral hazard.

SOLVING THE PROBLEM:

Step 1: **Review the chapter material.**

This problem is about asymmetric information, so you may want to review the section "Asymmetric Information," which begins on page 560 in the textbook.

Step 2: **Use the passage in this problem to describe asymmetric information.**

Asymmetric information is the situation in which one party to an economic transaction has less information than the other party. Those who are insured obviously have more knowledge of their circumstances than the companies that insure them. But not all insured parties demonstrate moral hazard.

Step 3: **Use the passage to distinguish adverse selection and moral hazard.**

Adverse selection occurs when someone who has entered into a transaction tries to take advantage of knowing more about his circumstances than the other party to the transaction. Those who are alleged to commit insurance fraud are demonstrating adverse selection. This problem also illustrates moral hazard, which is the actions people take after entering into a transaction, in this case buying insurance, that make the other party to the transaction, in this case the insurance company, worse off. The possibility of collecting on an insurance policy is the motivation for self-mutilation and staging phony automobile accidents.

17.2	**Adverse Selection and Moral Hazard in Financial Markets (pages 564–566)**

Learning Objective: Apply the concepts of adverse selection and moral hazard to financial markets.

Adverse selection and moral hazard pose problems for the managers of firms and for their owners. Because firms know more about their financial situations than stockholders, the firm can use the funds in ways that reduce profits. For example, a firm that has no debt on its balance sheet may suddenly issue a large quantity of bonds. This increases the risk to current owners of their stock.

Congress created the Securities and Exchange Commission (SEC) in 1934 to regulate the stock and bond markets. The SEC requires firms to register stocks and bonds they wish to sell, increasing the amount of information available to investors.

Extra Solved Problem 17-2

Do Financial Economists Know How to Limit Risks Due to Moral Hazard?

Supports Learning Objective 17.2: Apply the concepts of adverse selection and moral hazard to financial markets.

The financial crisis that led to the recession in 2007–2009 caused financial economists to question widely held theories regarding why markets become illiquid and how to manage the risk of moral hazard—the likelihood that government regulation will encourage financial market participants to take bigger risks than they otherwise would. One theory called into question is the so-called "efficient-market hypothesis" (EMH), which states that the price of a financial asset reflects all available information regarding its market value. Deviations from equilibrium prices, according to the EMH, do not last long. If, for example, the price of an asset was lower than its equilibrium value, then well-informed investors would buy it and sell it later for a profit. If the price of an asset was too high, then it would be sold, and the price would return to a level that would reflect its underlying value. Andrei Shleifer of Harvard University offers one explanation for the apparent failure of the EMH during the financial crisis. If "informed" traders who knew the true value of stocks and bonds traded against less informed traders (so-called "noise traders"), then it is possible that noise traders could push prices so far away from their true value that "it could be too costly for informed traders to borrow enough to bet against the noise traders."

Another explanation for the shortcomings of the EMH is offered by behavioral economists who apply psychology to explain how people make choices. They argue that people are often too confident in their own abilities and extrapolate past trends into the future; for example, if housing prices have soared in recent years, then people believe they will continue to rise in the future. One result of this is that traders can contribute to excessive price increases that lead to equally excessive price declines when their trading errors are realized. Richard Thaler, a leading behavioral economist from the University of Chicago, claims that those who believed that prices could never get out of line "look foolish." But Thaler also concedes that part of the EMH hypothesis has been vindicated by the events of recent years. He explains that the EMH has two parts: "the no-free-lunch part and the price-is-right part, and if anything the first part has been strengthened as we have learned that some investment strategies are riskier than they look and it is really difficult to beat the market." The "price is right" is the part of the EMH that has taken a beating.

Economist Andrew Lo of the Massachusetts Institute of Technology sees value in both the EMH hypothesis and the behavioral approach. He argues that humans are neither completely rational nor psychologically unstable. Lo believes traders make best guesses regarding their investments strategies; if one strategy works, they will continue to use it, but they will reject strategies that are proven to be wrong. He makes a suggestion that he believes could reduce the risk of moral hazard in the future. Lo's suggestion is that the equivalent of the National Transportation Safety Board be formed that would examine financial failures to determine their causes and suggest measures that will lessen the chance of future failures.

a. Which group of economists—advocates of the EMH or behavioral economists—would be more likely to recommend increased federal government regulation to reduce the likelihood of future financial crises?

b. Richard Thaler claims that the financial crisis that began in 2007 illustrated the shortcomings of what he referred to as "the price is right" part of the efficient markets hypothesis. Explain what Richard Thaler meant by the "price is right" part of the efficient markets hypothesis.

Source: "Efficiency and beyond," www.economist.com July 16, 2009.

SOLVING THE PROBLEM:
Step 1: **Review the chapter material.**
This problem is about adverse selection and moral hazard, so you may want to review the section "Adverse Selection and Moral Hazard in Financial Markets," which begins on page 564 in the textbook.

Step 2: **Which group of economists—advocates of the EMH or behavioral economists—would be more likely to recommend increased federal government regulation to reduce the likelihood of future financial crises?**
Advocates of the efficient markets hypothesis believe markets are self-regulating; prices adjust to shortages and surpluses without need of government intervention. Behavioral economists believe that traders are sometimes too confident in their own abilities and they

may cause excessive price increases for assets that are later reversed. Behavioral economists are more likely to recommend that government regulation may be needed to prevent fluctuations in asset prices from causing future crises.

Step 3:   Explain what Richard Thaler meant by the "price is right" part of the efficient markets hypothesis.

Thaler meant that the part of the efficient markets hypothesis that assumed asset prices would return to their equilibrium level without excessive fluctuations—fluctuations that could lead to a financial crisis—was shown to have shortcomings by the financial crisis that began in 2007.

Adverse Selection and Moral Hazard in Labor Markets (pages 566–568)

Learning Objective: Apply the concepts of adverse selection and moral hazard to labor markets.

Economists refer to the conflict between the interests of shareholders and the interests of top management as a principal–agent problem. The **principal–agent problem** is caused by an agent pursuing his own interests rather than the interests of the principal who hired him. In labor markets, this problem arises because workers may shirk their obligations and not work hard.

Firms may reduce shirking through close monitoring of workers or by making a worker's job seem more valuable. Firms may pay *efficiency wages*, which are higher-than-equilibrium wages used to give workers an incentive to work harder.

A *seniority system* that rewards workers who have been with the firm longer with higher pay and other benefits may also reduce shirking. *Profit sharing* provides workers with a share of the firm's profits; the harder the employee works, the more profit the firm earns and the higher the employee's income. But this may not work well in large firms where there is only a slight connection between an individual worker's effort and the firm's profitability.

The Winner's Curse: When Is It Bad to Win an Auction? (pages 568–571)

Learning Objective: Explain the winner's curse and why it occurs.

In some auctions, neither the bidder nor the seller has complete information about what is being auctioned. The **winner's curse** is the idea that the winner in certain auctions may overestimate the value of the good, thus ending up worse off than the losers. When there is uncertainty regarding the value of the item auctioned, the average competitive bid is likely to be close to the true value. The winning bid in an auction will be the one that is most optimistic and, therefore, greater than the true value. The winner's curse applies to auctions of common-value assets that would be given the same value by bidders if they had perfect information. The winner's curse does not apply to auctions of private-value assets when the value to each bidder depends on the bidder's own preferences.

> 📖 **Study Hint**
> You've probably heard statistics that over 40 percent of marriages end in divorce. *Making the Connection* on page 569 in the textbook suggests that the winner's curse can explain why marriages often end in divorce: Some people overestimate another person's value as a spouse. *Making the Connection* on pages 570–571 in the textbook describes another example of the winner's curse through a classroom experiment. *Solved Problem 17-4* further explores the winner's curse using an auction of Alaskan oil fields. Working through related end-of-chapter problems 4.5, 4.7, and 4.10 will increase your understanding of this material.

Key Terms

Adverse selection The situation in which one party to a transaction takes advantage of knowing more than the other party to the transaction.

Asymmetric information A situation in which one party to an economic transaction has less information than the other party.

Moral hazard The actions people take after they have entered into a transaction that make the other party to the transaction worse off.

Principal–agent problem A problem caused by agents pursuing their own interests rather than the interests of the principals who hired them.

Winner's curse The idea that the winner in certain auctions may have overestimated the value of the good, thus ending up worse off than the losers.

Self-Test

(Answers are provided at the end of the Self-Test.)

Multiple-Choice Questions

1. What is the reason for the existence of asymmetric information?
   a. Asymmetric information exists when people who have insurance change their actions because of the insurance.
   b. Asymmetric information exists when one party to an economic transaction has less information than the other party.
   c. Asymmetric information exists when parties to an economic transaction must pay different prices to obtain the same information.
   d. Asymmetric information exists when adverse selection leads to moral hazard.

2. Fill in the blanks: Guarding against the effects of asymmetric information is a major objective of _____ in the insurance market and _____ in financial markets.
   a. buyers; sellers
   b. sellers; buyers
   c. buyers; buyers
   d. sellers; sellers

3. If potential buyers have difficulty separating lemons from good used cars, what will they do?
   a. They will take this into account in the prices they are willing to pay.
   b. They will not take this into account in the prices they are willing to pay.
   c. They will be absolutely indifferent between cars, and will pay the same price for either type of car.
   d. They will pay a price for a car that is always too high.

4. When adverse selection exists in the used car market, which of the following will prevail?
   a. Buyers will generally offer a very high price, closer to the price of a good car.
   b. Buyers will generally offer a very low price, closer to the price of a lemon.
   c. Buyers will generally offer a price somewhere between the price they would be willing to pay for a good car and the price they would be willing to pay for a lemon.
   d. All buyers will end up buying a car.

5. Suppose that half of used cars offered for sale are reliable and half are unreliable. If potential buyers are willing to pay $5,000 for a reliable car, but only $2,500 for an unreliable one, how much will buyers offer for a car?
   a. $2,500
   b. $3,750
   c. $5,000
   d. $4,999

6. When uninformed buyers of used cars are willing to pay a price that is the average of the value of a lemon and the value of a good used car, which of the following will occur?
   a. Most used cars offered for sale will be lemons.
   b. Most used cars offered for sale will not be lemons.
   c. The quantity supplied of lemons will be identical to the quantity supplied of good used cars.
   d. Only good used cars will be offered for sale.

7. What is the impact of adverse selection on economic efficiency in a market?
   a. Adverse selection will increase economic efficiency.
   b. Adverse selection will reduce economic efficiency.
   c. Adverse selection does not have any impact on economic efficiency in a market.
   d. Consumer wants will shift toward the goods left in the market.

8. Which of the following is a way to reduce adverse selection in the car market?
   a. providing manufacturer warranties
   b. providing dealer warranties
   c. building a good reputation
   d. all of the above

9. Which of the following is true about lemon laws?
   a. Lemon laws require a full refund if a new car needs several major repairs within the first two years.
   b. Car manufacturers have actually supported lemon laws.
   c. Most states today have enacted lemon laws and strictly enforce them.
   d. all of the above

10. Asymmetric information problems are particularly severe in the market for insurance. This is true because
    a. insurance companies will always know more about the likelihood of an event happening than will buyers of insurance.
    b. buyers of insurance will always know more about the likelihood of an event happening than will insurance companies.
    c. insurance companies and buyers of insurance cannot distinguish between good and bad information.
    d. insurance companies are non-depository financial institutions.

11. Which of the following groups tends to worsen the problem of adverse selection?
    a. good drivers
    b. sick people
    c. people living in houses made entirely of rock
    d. all of the above

12. Which of the following makes the adverse selection problem in the health insurance market worse?
    a. charging high premiums for insurance coverage
    b. refusing to offer insurance policies to certain people
    c. requesting a medical examination for new applicants
    d. all of the above

13. How can insurance companies reduce adverse selection?
    a. by offering policies mostly to individuals rather than groups of people
    b. by offering group coverage rather than individual coverage
    c. by *not* requiring that every patient buy health insurance
    d. by increasing the price of participation in the health insurance program

14. When is it easier for insurance companies to estimate the average number of claims likely to be filed?
    a. when policies are offered to individuals, not groups
    b. when companies offer group coverage rather than individual coverage
    c. when companies insure small groups rather than large groups
    d. when companies reduce the number of participants so as to deal with a small rather than large number of customers

15. Insurance companies can reduce the problems that arise from adverse selection by offering group coverage to large firms. Group coverage is an example of
    a. risk abatement.
    b. risk aversion.
    c. risk pooling.
    d. hazard reduction.

16. Which of the following is a consequence of the adverse selection problems that health insurance companies face?
    a. Health insurance companies charge less for young, healthy people than old, less healthy people.
    b. Health insurance companies sometimes refuse to offer health insurance to people with chronic illnesses.
    c. Health insurance companies sometimes refuse to offer group insurance to large companies because there are too many insured people to accurately price this insurance.
    d. The equilibrium quantity of health insurance is greater than it would be in the absence of adverse selection.

17. Which of the following is true about adverse selection and moral hazard?
    a. Adverse selection is a consequence of asymmetric information; asymmetric information is a consequence of moral hazard.
    b. Insurance companies can eliminate adverse selection by charging deductibles and co-insurance, but charging deductibles and co-insurance increases the risk of moral hazard.
    c. Adverse selection affects only the market for automobile insurance; moral hazard affects only the markets for health and life insurance.
    d. Adverse selection refers to what happens at the time of entering into a transaction; moral hazard refers to what happens after entering into a transaction.

18. Match one of the terms below to the following definition: Actions taken by one party to a transaction that are different from what the other party expected at the time of the transaction.
    a. adverse selection
    b. moral hazard
    c. the Coase theorem
    d. the winner's curse

19. Which of the following actions is an attempt by a fire insurance company to reduce moral hazard?
    a. requiring a warehouse to install a sprinkler system
    b. reserving the right to inspect the warehouse for fire hazards
    c. establishing a system of deductibles and co-payments
    d. all of the above

20. Which of the following refers to a system in which an insurance company pays only a percentage of any claim, not a certain dollar amount?
    a. a deductible
    b. a co-payment
    c. both deductibles and co-payments
    d. neither deductibles nor co-payments

21. Fill in the blanks: There are two consequences of asymmetric information. _____ refers to what happens *at the time* a transaction is made, while _____ refers to what happens *after* entering into the transaction.
    a. Adverse selection; moral hazard
    b. Moral hazard; adverse selection
    c. Imperfect information; economic inefficiency
    d. Voluntary exchange; involuntary participation

22. If your medical insurance policy has a $100 deductible and a 10 percent co-payment, how much will you pay on a medical bill of $1,000?
    a. $100
    b. $900
    c. $110
    d. $190

23. What is the effect of adopting deductibles and co-payments for all holders of insurance policies?
    a. Holders will have an incentive to file more claims.
    b. Holders will have an incentive to avoid filing claims.
    c. The moral hazard problem in the insurance market will be greater.
    d. The adverse selection problem in the insurance market will be greater.

24. When will potential investors be reluctant to buy the stocks and bonds of particular companies?
    a. when the firm knows more about its financial situation than does the potential investor
    b. when a great deal of public information is available about the firm
    c. when asymmetric information is absent
    d. all of the above

25. Which firms have an easier time selling stocks and bonds to potential investors?
    a. firms that are studied closely by investment analysts
    b. small corporations rather than large corporations
    c. firms for which little public information is made available
    d. all of the above

26. If the managers of a corporation use funds in ways that actually reduce profits, which of the following problems is present?
    a. diminishing returns to labor
    b. moral hazard
    c. adverse selection
    d. the winner's curse

27. Fill in the blanks: The _____ the firm is and the more carefully investment analysts follow its activities, the _____ likely moral hazard is to be a problem.
    a. larger; more
    b. smaller; less
    c. larger; less
    d. smaller; more

28. Which agency was established by Congress in 1934 to regulate the stock and bond markets?
    a. the Federal Reserve System
    b. the Federal Trade Commission
    c. the Commerce Department
    d. the Securities and Exchange Commission

29. What did the creation of the Securities and Exchange Commission do for financial markets?
    a. It made the problems of adverse selection and moral hazard worse, and reduced the number of firms that could raise funds by selling stocks and bonds.
    b. It helped reduce adverse selection and moral hazard and increased the number of firms that could raise funds by selling stocks and bonds.
    c. It helped reduce adverse selection and moral hazard, but decreased the number of firms that could raise funds by selling stocks and bonds.
    d. It increased adverse selection and moral hazard but also increased the number of firms that could raise funds by selling stocks and bonds.

30. Which of the following financial reports does the Securities and Exchange Commission require any firm that registers stocks or bonds to provide to potential investors?
    a. a balance sheet
    b. an income statement
    c. a prospectus
    d. an audit

31. Bernie Madoff's Ponzi scheme is an example of which of the following?
    a. adverse selection
    b. moral hazard
    c. the winner's curse
    d. profit sharing

32. Which of the following best describes a Ponzi scheme?
    a. An investment firm uses funds from new investors to pay returns to existing investors instead of investing the funds.
    b. An investment firm buys stocks with risks higher than its investors can tolerate.
    c. An investment firm claims to make losses even though it has made substantial profits.
    d. An investment firm buys mortgage-backed securities instead of making mortgages directly to borrowers.

33. Which of the following is the main reason for Bernie Madoff's ability to successfully carry out a Ponzi scheme?
    a. Madoff knew less about his own finances than investors in his funds did.
    b. Madoff knew more about his own finances than investors in his funds did.
    c. Madoff was more aggressive in investing his funds than investors in his funds expected.
    d. Madoff was less aggressive in investing his funds than investors in his funds expected.

34. What is the term given to the problem caused by an agent pursuing his own interests rather than the interests of the principal who hired him?
    a. the principal–agent problem
    b. adverse selection
    c. the capture theory of regulation
    d. organizational misbehavior

35. Which of the following is most closely associated with the term "shirking"?
    a. making an effort to report accurate information on financial statements
    b. the possibility that a worker may be hired at a wage that is higher than the equilibrium wage in a given labor market
    c. the possibility that workers, once hired, may not work as hard as anticipated
    d. actions by managers and workers designed to reduce the risk of being fired

36. What is an efficiency wage?
    a. a wage designed to give workers an incentive to work harder
    b. any minimum wage is an efficiency wage
    c. a wage below the equilibrium wage
    d. all of the above

37. Which of the following compensation schemes would reduce moral hazard among salespeople?
    a. compensation based on a straight salary without commission
    b. compensation that depends on how much workers sell, such as straight commission
    c. compensation based on a set fee for services rendered rather than an hourly salary or commission
    d. none of the above

38. What is the idea behind the winner's curse?
   a. The act of winning a good in a certain auction may cause the bidder to build too much confidence and end up overbidding in subsequent auctions.
   b. In certain auctions, the winner may overestimate the value of the good that is auctioned and end up worse off than the losers.
   c. In certain auctions, the winner may underestimate the value of the good that is auctioned and end up far better off than the losers.
   d. Bad luck usually strikes those who win an auction.

39. When a common-value asset is auctioned, if there are seven bids (in millions) of $32, $18, $11, $8, $6, $4, and $3, what is the most likely value of the asset?
   a. close to $32 million
   b. close to $3 million
   c. close to $12 million
   d. None of the above; there is insufficient information to answer the question.

40. In which of the following auctions is the winner's curse most applicable?
   a. in auctions of private-value assets
   b. in auctions where the value to each bidder depends on the bidder's own preferences
   c. in auctions of common-value assets, such as oil fields
   d. in auctions where bidders place different bids even when they have perfect information

Short Answer Questions

1. Most colleges and universities have a tenure system for their faculty. After faculty members have been granted tenure, they receive a degree of employment security rare among other professions. One reason for the tenure system is that it promotes academic freedom. With tenure, a faculty member need not worry about being dismissed for stating controversial beliefs in his or her classroom. Could the tenure system also result in moral hazard? Explain your answer.

_____

_____

_____

_____

2. Making the Connection on page 569 in the textbook noted that over 40 percent of marriages in the United States end in divorce. The high rate of divorce may be evidence of a winner's curse in the so-called *marriage market*. If divorce were banned in the United States, would this result in a lower percentage of people who are dissatisfied with their marriages?

_____

_____

_____

_____

3. In 2007, the baseball that Barry Bonds hit for his record-breaking 756th home run was auctioned. The winning bid was over $750,000. Does the winner's curse explain why the auction resulted in such a high winning bid for this baseball?

_____

_____

_____

_____

4. Many fast-food restaurants pay their workers no more than the national minimum wage ($7.25 per hour in 2009), but some pay *more* than the minimum wage. Are these above-minimum wages also efficiency wages? Explain your answer.

_____

_____

_____

_____

_____

_____

5. Each academic term, a large number of students decide to take principles of economics courses. Most universities offer several sections of these courses. Explain how asymmetric information can influence a student's decision about which principles of economics section to enroll in.

_____

_____

_____

_____

True/False Questions

T F 1. Adverse selection causes many used cars offered for sale to be "lemons" and reduces the total quantity of used cars sold.

T F 2. The "lemon laws" passed by most states include a provision that car manufacturers must indicate whether a used car they offer for sale was repurchased from the original owner as a lemon.

T F 3. Michael Spence began the study of asymmetric information with an analysis of the market for used cars.

T F 4. The Securities and Exchange Commission requires firms to take actions that reduce the problems associated with adverse selection and moral hazard in financial markets.

T F 5. Equilibrium wages paid to workers that reflect their marginal revenue products are called efficiency wages.

T F 6. The Ponzi scheme carried out by Bernie Madoff is an example of moral hazard.

T F 7. Insurance companies can reduce problems caused by adverse selection by offering group coverage to large firms.

T F 8. A warehouse owner who purchases a fire insurance policy may become less careful about reducing potential fire hazards in his warehouse. This is an example of adverse selection.

T F 9. The engineers of the Atlantic Richfield oil company used economic reasoning and knowledge of the winner's curse to successfully bid on licenses that allowed the firm to drill on the North Slope of Alaska and in the Gulf of Mexico.

T F 10. A firm can use a seniority system for its workers to reduce the incidence of moral hazard.

T F 11. A *co-payment* requires the holder of an insurance policy to pay a certain dollar amount of a claim.

T F 12. The main reason for Bernie Madoff's initial success in his financial fraud was that he was exempt from providing a prospectus to his investors.

T F 13. Profit-sharing typically does not overcome the risk of moral hazard on the part of employees because profits are affected by many factors that are unrelated to how hard a particular employee works.

T F 14. The winner's curse applies only to auctions of private-value assets.

T F 15. Lemon laws apply to both new and used car markets.

Answers to the Self-Test

Multiple-Choice Questions

Question	Response	Comment
1	b	Asymmetric information is a situation where one party to an economic transaction has less information than the other party.
2	b	Guarding against the effects of asymmetric information is a major objective of sellers in the insurance market, and of buyers in financial markets. But it was in the market for used automobiles that economists first began to carefully study the problem of asymmetric information.
3	a	If potential buyers of used cars know that they will have difficulty separating the good used cars from the bad used cars, or "lemons," they will take this into account in the prices they are willing to pay.

4	c	When adverse selection in the used car market exists, buyers will generally offer a price somewhere between the price they would be willing to pay for a good car and the price they would be willing to pay for a lemon.
5	b	This price is halfway between the price they would pay if they knew for certain the car was a good one and the price they would pay if they knew it was a lemon.
6	a	To sellers of lemons, an offer of the average price is above the true value of the car and they will be quite happy to sell. As sellers of lemons take advantage of knowing more about the cars they are selling than buyers do, the used car market will fall victim to adverse selection: most used cars offered for sale will be lemons.
7	b	Adverse selection reduces the total quantity of used cars bought and sold in the market because few good cars are offered for sale. As a result, we can conclude that information problems reduce economic efficiency in a market.
8	d	All of these are suggested ways of reducing adverse selection in the car market.
9	a	Most lemon laws have two main provisions. One is that new cars that need several major repairs during the first year or two after the date of original purchase may be returned to the manufacturer for a full refund. The other is that car manufacturers must indicate whether a used car they are offering for sale was repurchased from the original owner as a lemon. Although popular with consumers, opposition from manufacturers has resulted in lemon laws being enacted in fewer than 20 states. Enforcement has also been spotty.
10	b	Asymmetric information problems are particularly severe in the market for insurance. Buyers of insurance policies will always know more about the likelihood of the event being insured against happening than will insurance companies.
11	b	The adverse selection problem arises because sick people are more likely to want medical insurance than healthy people, reckless drivers are more likely to want automobile insurance than careful drivers, and people living in homes that are fire hazards are more likely to want fire insurance than people living in safe homes.
12	a	Insurance companies are reluctant to charge higher premiums because it increases the likelihood that only people who are almost certain to make a claim will purchase a policy.
13	b	Insurance companies can reduce adverse selection problems by offering group coverage. Everyone employed by a firm with group coverage is insured. If the group is large enough, coverage is likely to represent the proportions of healthy and unhealthy people in the general population.
14	b	As long as the group is large enough, it is likely to represent the proportions of healthy and unhealthy people found in the general population. That makes it easier for insurance companies to estimate the average number of claims likely to be filed under a group medical insurance or life insurance policy, than it would be to predict the number of claims likely to be filed under an individual policy.
15	c	See the section "Reducing Adverse Selection in the Insurance Market" beginning on page 561 of the textbook.
16	b	See Making the Connection on pages 562–563 in the textbook.
17	d	See Don't Let This Happen to YOU! on page 564 in the textbook.
18	b	Moral hazard is the tendency of people who have insurance to change their actions because of the insurance, or, more broadly, actions people take after they have entered into a transaction that make the other party to the transaction worse off.
19	d	Insurance companies can take steps to reduce moral hazard problems. For example, a fire insurance company may insist that a firm install a sprinkler system in a warehouse in order to offset any increased carelessness once the policy is in place. It may also reserve the right to inspect the warehouse periodically to check for fire

hazards. Insurance companies also use deductibles and co-payments to reduce moral hazard.

20   b   A deductible requires the holder of the insurance policy to pay a certain dollar amount of a claim. With a co-payment, the insurance company pays only a percentage of any claim.

21   a   Adverse selection refers to what happens at the time the transaction is entered into. Moral hazard refers to what happens after the transaction has been entered into.

22   d   If you have a medical insurance policy with a $100 deductible and a 10 percent co-payment and you have a medical bill of $1,000, then you must pay the first $100 of the bill and 10 percent of the other $900, or $100 + $90 = $190.

23   b   Deductibles and co-payments give the holders of the insurance policy an incentive to avoid filing claims.

24   a   Asymmetric information is a key reason why only large corporations are able to raise funds by selling stocks and bonds. Every firm knows more about its financial situation than does any potential investor. Because investors have trouble distinguishing between well-run firms and poorly-run firms, they are reluctant to buy the stocks and bonds of companies unless there is a great deal of public information available about these companies.

25   a   Because investors have trouble distinguishing between well-run firms and poorly-run firms, they are reluctant to buy the stocks and bonds of companies unless there is a great deal of public information available about these companies. In practice, this means that unless firms are studied closely by investment analysts working for brokerage firms and investment companies, firms will have difficulty selling stocks and bonds to investors.

26   b   Investors are worried about moral hazard. Once a firm has sold stocks and bonds, the possibility exists that the company will use the funds in ways that reduce profits.

27   c   The larger the firm is and the more carefully investment analysts follow its activities, the less likely moral hazard is to be a problem. This is a reason why investors will be willing to buy the stocks and bonds of large firms, but not of small firms.

28   d   When firms failed to provide investors with clear information about their true financial positions, Congress responded by establishing the Securities and Exchange Commission (SEC) in 1934 to regulate the stock and bond markets.

29   b   The SEC succeeded in increasing the amount of information available to potential investors. This helped reduce the adverse selection and moral hazard problems in financial markets and increased the number of firms that have been able to raise funds by selling stocks and bonds.

30   c   A prospectus is a document that a firm must provide potential investors for its stocks or bonds. This document contains all relevant financial information on the firm.

31   b   The news about Bernie Madoff's "Ponzi" scheme illustrates the difficulty that moral hazard poses for investors. Madoff knew far more about his firm's finances than any outside investor could.

32   a   Ponzi schemes are named after Charles Ponzi, who earned millions from investors during the 1920s by telling them he would invest their money in a way that would earn a 50 percent return in just a few months, when in fact he intended to spend their money rather than invest it.

33	b	Asymmetric information exists because Bernie Madoff knew more about his own finances than investors in his funds did. Moral hazard was the result of this asymmetric information.
34	a	The principal–agent problem is caused by an agent pursuing his own interests rather than the interests of the principal who hired him.
35	c	The moral hazard behind the principal–agent problem between the managers of a firm and its workers is that once hired, workers may shirk their obligations and not work hard.
36	a	An efficiency wage is a higher than equilibrium wage used by firms to give workers an incentive to work harder.
37	b	Compensation that depends on how much workers sell reduces the risk associated with moral hazard because workers will not get paid for shirking.
38	b	In an auction for a common-value asset, the winning bidder may overestimate the value of the good, and so end up worse off than the losing bidders.
39	c	Mistakes of sometimes being too high would tend to offset the mistakes of sometimes being too low, so the average estimate would be close to the asset's value. In this case, it is likely that the true value of the asset in the auction is about $11.7 million, or the average of the seven bids.
40	c	The winner's curse applies only to auctions of *common-value assets*—such as oil fields—that would be given the same value by all bidders if they had perfect information. The winner's curse does not apply to auctions of *private-value assets* where the value to each bidder depends on the bidder's own preferences.

Short Answer Responses

1. Some critics of the tenure system argue that moral hazard may be a by-product of granting tenure to members of a college's faculty. Prior to receiving tenure, faculty have strong incentives to demonstrate excellence in teaching and research, two criteria used to evaluate faculty performance. After tenure is granted, some faculty will not work as hard on their teaching and research unless they have other incentives to do so. (Most universities have an additional promotion step to full professor that gives tenured associate professors some additional incentive to demonstrate continued excellence in teaching and research.)

2. It is possible that some people would take longer to select a marriage partner—and may choose not to marry at all—if divorce were made illegal in the United States. But keep in mind that people often make mistakes when they make decisions (recall from Chapter 9 that one common mistake is that consumers are overly optimistic about their future behavior), so it is highly unlikely that banning divorce would lead to a large increase in the number of successful marriages. The law would make it more likely that people would remain in unhappy marriages (not necessarily a better outcome) and would certainly lead some people to seek divorces in other countries where the practice was legal. Such a law might also encourage extra-legal solutions to the problem of unhappy marriages.

3. Many people believe that paying such a high price for a baseball must leave the buyer worse off, but the winner's curse applies only to common-value assets that would be given the same value by all bidders if they had perfect information. This is not the case with the Barry Bonds baseball, assuming that the winning bid reflected the buyer's true preferences. The buyer had full and complete information about the product being sold. The exchange was voluntary. Therefore, no "winner's curse" resulted from this auction.

4. It is possible that an above-minimum wage is an equilibrium wage. An equilibrium wage is one that equates the quantity demanded with the quantity supplied in a given market. Some fast-food restaurants pay wages that exceed the minimum wage because they face competition from other employers who also pay more than the minimum wage. Other firms pay more than the minimum wage because local economic conditions make it impossible to hire enough workers for the minimum wage. This does not mean that some fast-food restaurants do not pay efficiency wages. The motive for doing so is not only to provide an incentive for workers to work harder and not shirk (as the textbook explains), but to reduce worker turnover. Many service firms have difficulty retaining workers. Retaining experienced workers reduces training costs and may result in better customer service.

5. Most colleges and universities offer a number of sections of principles of microeconomics and macroeconomics each academic term. Freshmen and transfer students as well as non-majors often have little information about the teaching styles and course requirements of the course instructors. Students who have taken other courses from these instructors, and the instructors themselves, provide some of this information through conversation, course syllabi and (increasingly) through Web sites that summarize course content and students' opinions of the instructors whose courses they have taken.

True/False Answers

1. T   See the section "Asymmetric Information" beginning on page 560 in the textbook.
2. T   Another provision included in the laws is that new cars that need several major repairs during the first year or two after the original purchase date may be returned for a full refund.
3. F   George Akerlof was the author of the study of asymmetric information in the market for used cars.
4. T   See the section "Adverse Selection and Moral Hazard in Financial Markets" beginning on page 564 in the textbook. By requiring firms to register the stocks and bonds they wish to sell with the SEC and requiring each firm to provide potential investors with a prospectus, the problems associated with adverse selection and moral hazard are reduced.
5. F   An efficiency wage is a greater-than-equilibrium wage paid to encourage workers to work harder.
6. T   See Making the Connection beginning on page 565 in the textbook.
7. T   See the section "Asymmetric Information" beginning on page 560 in the textbook.
8. F   This is an example of moral hazard, because the warehouse owner changed his actions as a result of obtaining fire insurance.
9. F   The engineers of the Atlantic Richfield oil company used the economic reasoning of the winner's curse to explain why the winning bidders in government auctions of the oil fields were disappointed with their profits. See the section "The Winner's Curse: When Is It Bad to Win an Auction?" on page 568 in the textbook.
10. T   A seniority system grants higher pay and other benefits to workers who have served with a firm for a long time.
11. F   A *deductible* requires the holder of an insurance policy to pay a certain dollar amount of a claim.
12. F   All firms that issue stocks or bonds to the public are required to provide a prospectus to investors. The main reason for Bernie Madoff's fraud was his ability to hide his Ponzi scheme. See Making the Connection beginning on page 565 in the textbook.
13. T   See the section "Adverse Selection and Moral Hazard in Labor Markets" beginning on page 566 in the textbook.
14. F   The winner's curse applies only to auctions of common-value assets, not private-value assets.
15. T   See the section "Asymmetric Information" beginning on page 560 in the textbook.

Chapter Summary and Learning Objectives

18.1 Public Choice (pages 580–584)

Describe the public choice model and explain how it is used to analyze government decision making. The **public choice model** applies economic analysis to government decision making. The observation that majority voting may not always result in consistent choices is called the **voting paradox**. The **Arrow impossibility theorem** states that no system of voting can be devised so that it will consistently represent the underlying preferences of voters. The **median voter theorem** states that the outcome of a majority vote is likely to represent the preferences of the voter who is in the political middle. Individuals and firms sometimes engage in **rent seeking**, which is the use of government action to make themselves better off at the expense of others. Although government intervention can sometimes improve economic efficiency, public choice analysis indicates that *government failure* can also occur, reducing economic efficiency.

18.2 The Tax System (pages 584–592)

Understand the tax system in the United States, including the principles that governments use to create tax policy. Governments raise the funds they need through taxes. The most widely used taxes are income taxes, social insurance taxes, sales taxes, property taxes, and excise taxes. Governments take into account several important objectives when deciding which taxes to use: efficiency, ability to pay, horizontal equity, benefits received, and attaining social objectives. A **regressive tax** is a tax for which people with lower incomes pay a higher percentage of their incomes in tax than do people with higher incomes. A **progressive tax** is a tax for which people with lower incomes pay a lower percentage of their incomes in tax than do people with higher incomes. The **marginal tax rate** is the fraction of each additional dollar of income that must be paid in taxes. The **average tax rate** is the total tax paid divided by total income. When analyzing the impact of taxes on how much people are willing to work or save or invest, economists focus on the marginal tax rate rather than the average tax rate. The **excess burden** of a tax is the efficiency loss to the economy that results from a tax having reduced the quantity of a good produced.

18.3 Tax Incidence Revisited: The Effect of Price Elasticity (pages 592–595)

Understand the effect of price elasticity on tax incidence. **Tax incidence** is the actual division of the burden of a tax. In most cases, buyers and sellers share the burden of a tax levied on a good or service. When the elasticity of demand for a product is smaller than the elasticity of supply, consumers pay the majority of the tax on the product. When the elasticity of demand for a product is larger than the elasticity of supply, sellers pay the majority of the tax on the product.

18.4 Income Distribution and Poverty (pages 595–602)

Discuss the distribution of income in the United States and understand the extent of income mobility. No dramatic changes in the distribution of income have occurred over the past 70 years, although there was some decline in inequality between 1936 and 1980, as well as some increase in inequality between 1980 and today. A **Lorenz curve** shows the distribution of income by arraying incomes from lowest to highest on the horizontal axis and indicating the cumulative fraction of income earned by each fraction of households on the vertical axis. About 12 percent of Americans are below the **poverty line**, which is defined as the annual income equal to three times the amount necessary to purchase the minimum quantity of food required for adequate nutrition. Over time, there has been significant income mobility in the United States. The United States has a more unequal distribution of income than do other high-income countries. The **poverty rate**—the percentage of the population that is poor—has been declining in most countries around the world, with the important exception of Africa. The *marginal productivity theory of income distribution* states that in equilibrium, each factor of production receives a payment equal to its marginal revenue product. The more factors of production an individual owns and the more productive those factors are, the higher the individual's income will be.

Chapter Review

Chapter Opener: Should the Government Use the Tax System to Reduce Inequality? (page 579)

Tax laws affect economic incentives and can also affect perceptions of fairness. The debate over the tax system was an important part of the 2008 presidential campaign. When Barack Obama became president in January 2009, he proposed a number of changes to the tax system. The design of the tax system and the criteria to use in evaluating it are important questions.

18.1 Public Choice (pages 580–584)

Learning Objective: Define the public choice model and explain how it is used to analyze government decision making.

The **public choice model** applies economic analysis to government decision making. The model assumes that policymakers are likely to pursue their own self-interest, even if this conflicts with the public interest. We expect public officials to take actions that are likely to result in their re-election.

The **voting paradox**, which is the failure of majority voting to always result in consistent choices, demonstrates that politicians do not simply represent the views of voters. According to the **Arrow impossibility theorem**, no system of voting can be devised that will consistently represent the underlying preferences of voters. The **median voter theorem** is the proposition that the outcome of a majority vote is likely to represent the preferences of the voter who is in the political middle.

The public choice model assumes policymakers behave in their own self-interest. There are three reasons for this behavior:

1. *Rent seeking* refers to attempts by individuals and firms to use government actions to make themselves better off at the expense of others. Because firms can benefit from government intervention in the economy, they are willing to make campaign contributions to politicians who vote for special interest legislation the firms will benefit from.

2. *Logrolling* refers to the situation where a member of Congress votes to approve a bill in exchange for favorable votes from other members on other bills.

3. *Rational ignorance* means that voters often lack an economic incentive to become informed about legislation because the cost of the time and effort required to do so exceeds the benefit.

The government sometimes intervenes in the economy by establishing a regulatory agency or commission with authority over a particular industry or product. When this happens, the affected firms have an incentive to try to influence the agency's actions. In extreme cases, this may lead to the agency making decisions that benefit the regulated firms, even if these actions are not in the public interest. In these cases, the agency is said to be subject to *regulatory capture*.

Public choice analysis indicates that government failure can occur where government intervention reduces economic efficiency rather than increases it.

Extra Solved Problem 18-1
The Public Choice Model
Supports Learning Objective 18.1: Define the public choice model and explain how it is used to analyze government decision making.

Traditional political theory holds that government agents (elected politicians, appointed bureaucrats, and other government employees) put aside their private interests and attempt to achieve goals that are in the general public's interest. Alternatively, public choice theory applies the same assumption that economists make about people's actions in private markets to collective, or government, decision making; namely, people are motivated mainly by self-interest. Self-interest is also assumed to motivate voters, who are largely ignorant with regard to political issues, including those that require tax revenue to support. This ignorance is rational because the impact of a well-informed vote on an election is essentially nil. Even if the voter's preferred candidate is elected, he or she cannot bring about policy changes without the support of other elected officials. Elected officials make decisions to use other people's resources to promote the "public interest." Although politicians may intend to do so, efficient decisions will not save their own money nor reward them with any portion of the taxpayers' money they save. But interest groups that benefit from government programs have strong incentives to provide politicians who agree with, and vote for, these programs with campaign funds and other support. As a result, public officials often support special interest programs that are costly for taxpayers. Public choice economists point to "logrolling," or vote trading, as an important example of political self-interest that can result in inefficient legislation. Logrolling refers to politicians voting for special interest legislation that favors another jurisdiction in order to win the votes of politicians for their own special interest legislation. Public choice economists recognize that government regulation or provision of services is necessary in some cases. If government action is required, they prefer that it take place at the local level whenever possible. This provides an opportunity for competition and experimentation among local governments. Citizens can move to areas that provide superior public services, and governments have incentives to provide services efficiently.

Source: Jane S. Shaw, "Public Choice Theory," *The Concise Encyclopedia of Economics*, http://www.econlib.org/Library/Enc/PublicChoiceTheory.html

Citizens Against Government Waste (CAGW) is a private non-profit organization founded in 1984 to "eliminate waste, fraud, abuse and mismanagement in the federal government." Each year CAGW publishes the *Congressional Pig Book*, which lists federal government spending projects the organization believes are of questionable value to taxpayers. The 2009 *Pig Book* revealed 10,160 Congressional projects CAGW labeled as pork barrel spending. Total spending on these projects was $19.6 billion. CAGW highlights some of the more colorful projects by naming them recipients of "oinker awards." Some of the oinker awards for 2009 are:

- $1.9 million for the Pleasure Beach water taxi service in Connecticut
- $1.8 million for swine odor and manure management research in Iowa
- $413,000 for tri-state joint peanut research

a. How would the public choice model explain the large amount of pork barrel spending in the federal government's budget?

b. Which political party—Republican or Democrat—does the public choice model predict would be responsible for the greater number of pork barrel projects?

Source: Citizens Against Government Waste. http://www.cagw.org/site/PageServer

SOLVING THE PROBLEM:

Step 1: **Review the chapter material.**

This problem is about public choice, so you may want to review the section "Public Choice," which begins on page 580 in the textbook.

Step 2: **How would the public choice model explain the large amount of pork spending in the federal government's budget?**

The public choice model would claim that pork spending is a result of (1) the self-interest of voters; because each taxpayer pays a small fraction of any program, he or she has little incentive to become well-informed or to vote for or against a candidate who supports these programs; (2) a bias in favor of special interest projects; the money spent for government projects is concentrated so that the recipients have a strong incentive to lobby and provide financial support for politicians who vote in favor of their projects.

Step 3: **Which political party does the public choice model predict would be responsible for the greater number of pork barrel projects?**

The public choice model assumes that elected politicians, regardless of their party affiliation, are motivated by self-interest even if their self-interest conflicts with the public interest. However, if one party has a majority in both the House of Representatives and the Senate, and the president is affiliated with that same party, it is more likely that spending projects will reflect the preferences of that party.

 The Tax System (pages 584–592)

Learning Objective: Understand the tax system in the United States, including the principles that governments use to create tax policy.

Taxes are necessary to raise the funds required to provide public goods and various government activities at the federal, state, and local levels. Taxes are also used to discourage what society views as undesirable behavior. In the United States, the federal government, most state governments, and some local governments tax the incomes of households and the profits of firms. This individual income tax is the largest source of revenue for the federal government. The federal government taxes wages and salaries to raise revenue for the Social Security and Medicare programs. The federal and state governments also tax wages and salaries to fund unemployment insurance programs.

Most state and local governments tax retail sales of most products. Most local governments use property taxes—taxes on homes, offices, and factories and the land they are built on—to fund public schools. Excise taxes are levied by the federal government and some state governments on the sale of specific goods. The federal government raises more than 80 percent of its revenue through individual income and social insurance taxes. Over the past 40 years, federal revenues as a share of gross domestic product have ranged between 17 and 23 percent.

Economists categorize taxes based on how much people with different levels of income pay relative to their incomes. A **regressive tax** is a tax for which people with lower incomes pay a higher percentage of their income in tax than do people with higher incomes. A **progressive tax** is a tax for which people with lower incomes pay a lower percentage of their income in tax than do people with higher incomes. The federal income tax is a progressive tax. Every taxpayer is allowed to exclude from taxation a certain amount of income, called the personal exemption. Deductions are used to reduce the amount of income subject to tax.

The fraction of each additional dollar of income that must be paid in taxes is the **marginal tax rate**. The **average tax rate** is the total tax paid divided by total income. When a tax is progressive, the marginal and average tax rates will differ. Economists focus on the marginal tax rate when considering a change in tax policy. The marginal tax rate tells economists how a tax change will affect people's willingness to work, save, and invest.

The federal government taxes the profits earned by corporations with the corporate income tax. Some economists argue that if the purpose of the tax is to tax the owners of corporations, then it would be better to do this directly by taxing owners' incomes rather than indirectly through the corporate income tax.

In selecting which taxes to use, governments take into account several goals and principles:

- The goal of economic efficiency
- The ability-to-pay principle
- The horizontal-equity principle
- The benefits-received principle
- The goal of attaining social objectives

The **excess burden** of a tax is the efficiency loss to the economy that results from a tax causing a reduction in the quantity of a good produced. This is also known as the deadweight loss from a tax. A tax is efficient if it imposes a small excess burden relative to the revenue it raises. Taxation can have substantial effects on economic efficiency by altering the incentives to work, save, and invest.

Although tax simplification would reduce the administrative burden and deadweight loss from taxation, complicated tax loopholes benefit certain taxpayers who would oppose simplification. Taxes are sometimes used to attain social objectives, such as to discourage smoking or drinking alcohol.

> 📖 **Study Hint**
>
> *Making the Connection* on page 587 in the textbook provides statistics on which income groups pay the most in federal taxes. Review the table on that page and notice that the 20 percent of taxpayers with the highest incomes pay 64 percent of federal income taxes. *Making the Connection* on page 590 discusses a proposed shift from an income tax to a consumption tax. Some economists oppose this shift because they believe a consumption tax will be more regressive than an income tax and would impose a burden on people with very low incomes.
>
> Work through related end-of-chapter problems 2.9 and 2.11 to test your understanding of the concepts in these features.

Extra Solved Problem 18-2

The Evolution of the Income Tax System

Supports Learning Objective 18.2: Understand the tax system in the United States, including the principles that governments use to create tax policy.

The United States did not have an income tax prior to the Civil War. Government revenue had come from such sources as excise taxes, customs duties, and the sale of public lands. The demands placed on government because of the war forced Congress to pass a law in 1862 that raised excise taxes, imposed a

3 percent tax on incomes up to $10,000 and taxed higher incomes at 5 percent. As the war ended, the government's revenue needs waned. The income tax was abolished in 1872, and from 1868 to 1913 the federal government derived most of its revenue from excise taxes and tariffs. By the early 1900s, the nation was becoming increasingly aware that tariffs and excise taxes were neither efficient nor fair as they fell disproportionately on lower income citizens. Proposals for a new income tax were championed by Congressmen from agricultural states who feared the possibility of a tax on land. By 1913, 36 states had ratified the 16th Amendment to the Constitution which allowed Congress to institute a new income tax. In October, Congress passed a law that levied a tax of 1 percent on those with low incomes. The tax rose to 7 percent for those with incomes exceeding $500,000. But less than 1 percent of the population paid the tax.

The entry of the United States into World War I increased the revenue needed by the federal government. The Revenue Act of 1916 raised the lowest tax rate to 2 percent and the top rate to 15 percent for incomes in excess of $1.5 million. Other revenue acts followed. Still, in 1918 only 5 percent of the population paid income taxes. As the economy boomed in the 1920s, Congress cut income tax rates five times. But after the economy plunged into the Great Depression, tax receipts fell. Congress passed the Tax Act of 1932, which raised tax rates. Another tax hike followed in 1936. The lowest tax rate was 4 percent and the top rate reached 79 percent. Individual and corporate taxes were raised in 1940 and 1941. Once again, wartime spending led to greater tax demands. By the end of the war, taxpayers with taxable incomes of only $500 were subject to a tax rate of 23 percent, while taxpayers with incomes over $1 million faced a top rate of 94 percent. Federal taxes as a share of national income rose from 7.6 percent in 1941 to 20.4 percent in 1945.

Source: Fact Sheets: Taxes. History of the U.S. Tax System. United States Treasury.
http://www.treas.gov/education/fact-sheets/taxes/ustax.shtml

a. Why did the United States first institute an income tax system?

b. Select one goal or principle that was associated with the decision to pass the 16th Amendment to the U.S. Constitution.

SOLVING THE PROBLEM:
Step 1: Review the chapter material.
This problem is about the tax system, so you may want to review the section "The Tax System," which begins on page 584 in the textbook.

Step 2: Why did the United States first institute an income tax system?
Prior to the Civil War, federal government spending was a relatively small percentage of national income. The government's revenue needs could be met through excise taxes, tariffs, and sales of public land. Many people paid little or no taxes. But wartime spending required much more revenue. The government needed a broader tax base; that is, a tax or taxes that would affect many more people.

Step 3: Select one goal or principle that was associated with the decision to pass the 16th Amendment to the U.S. Constitution.
Even before the 16th Amendment was passed, income taxes were progressive; people with lower incomes paid a lower percentage of the income tax than people with higher incomes. Since the amendment was passed, progressive tax rates have always been a characteristic of the income tax system. This is a response to the ability-to-pay principle. One could also argue that an income tax scores higher on the benefits-received principle than the alternatives of a land tax, excise tax, or tariff. As government spending grew, especially during times of war, the benefits of government programs and services were broadly spread across the population. Therefore, a tax with a broader base was justified.

18.3 **Tax Incidence Revisited: The Effect of Price Elasticity (pages 592–595)**
Learning Objective: Understand the effect of price elasticity on tax incidence.

Tax incidence is the actual division of the burden of a tax between buyers and sellers in a market. When a tax is imposed on the sale of a product, consumers pay the majority of the tax when the price elasticity of demand is smaller than the price elasticity of supply. When the elasticity of demand for a product is larger than the elasticity of supply, firms pay the majority of the tax.

📖 **Study Hint**

Don't Let This Happen to YOU! cautions you not to confuse the burden of tax with who pays it. Although your receipt for a product tells you the amount of sales tax you paid, the seller also shares the burden of that tax. Review Figure 18-4 on page 593 in the textbook and the figure caption in the margin to understand this point.

  Solved Problem 18-3 examines how the burden of a tax is dependent on the elasticities of demand and supply of the good that is taxed. Complete related end-of-chapter problems 3.5, 3.6, 3.7, and 3.9 to improve your understanding of these topics.

18.4 **Income Distribution and Poverty (pages 595–602)**
Learning Objective: Discuss the distribution of income in the United States and understand the extent of income mobility.

The distribution of income in the United States is unequal, and there have been no dramatic changes in the distribution of income over time. According to the federal government's definition, a family is poor if it is below the poverty line. The **poverty line** is a level of annual income equal to three times the amount of income necessary to purchase the minimum quantity of food required for adequate nutrition. The **poverty rate** is the percentage of the population that is poor according to the federal government's definition. Between 1960 and 1973, the poverty rate declined from 22 percent to 11 percent, but since 1973, the poverty rate has shown little change. Figure 18-5 on page 596 in the textbook shows the poverty rate over time.

For most people, the most important factor of production they own is their labor. The income they earn depends on how productive they are and on the prices of the goods and services their labor helps to produce. Therefore, the distribution of income is related to the productivity of labor and ownership of other productive resources.

Income inequality has increased in the United States over the past 25 years. Rapid technological change contributed to this trend as computers and other machines were substituted for labor. Another contributing factor has been the expansion of international trade, which has put more U.S. workers in competition with foreign workers. As a result, the wages of unskilled workers have been reduced relative to the wages of other workers.

A **Lorenz curve** is a curve that shows the distribution of income by arraying incomes from lowest to highest on the horizontal axis and indicating the cumulative fraction of income earned by each fraction of households on the vertical axis. The *Gini coefficient* is a way to summarize the information provided by the Lorenz curve. If the income distribution were completely equal, the Gini coefficient would equal 0. If the income distribution were completely unequal, the Gini coefficient would equal 1.

Measures of poverty and the distribution of income are misleading. These measures do not account for income mobility. For example, a family below the poverty line one year may be above the line the next year. One study showed that only 50.5 percent of people who were in poverty in 1996 remained in poverty in 1999. Also, measures of poverty and income distribution ignore the effect of government programs meant to reduce poverty. Conventional statistics do not include transfer payments such as Social Security payments and noncash benefits, such as food stamps. Because the income tax system is progressive, income after taxes is more equally distributed than is income before taxes.

Although poverty remains a problem in high-income countries such as Australia, Canada, and Japan, it is a much larger problem in poor countries. The percentage of the population in poverty in countries in Sub-Saharan Africa was over 35 percent in 1970 and has risen since. Poverty reduction occurred in Asia and Latin America between 1970 and 2000 due to relatively rapid rates of economic growth.

Key Terms

Arrow impossibility theorem A mathematical theorem that holds that no system of voting can be devised that will consistently represent the underlying preferences of voters.

Average tax rate Total tax paid divided by total income.

Excess burden A measure of the efficiency loss to the economy that results from a tax having reduced the quantity of a good produced; also known as the deadweight loss.

Lorenz curve A curve that shows the distribution of income by arraying incomes from lowest to highest on the horizontal axis and indicating the cumulative fraction of income earned by each fraction of households on the vertical axis.

Marginal tax rate The fraction of each additional dollar of income that must be paid in taxes.

Median voter theorem The proposition that the outcome of a majority vote is likely to represent the preferences of the voter who is in the political middle.

Poverty line A level of annual income equal to three times the amount of money necessary to purchase the minimum quantity of food required for adequate nutrition.

Poverty rate The percentage of the population that is poor according to the federal government's definition.

Progressive tax A tax for which people with lower incomes pay a lower percentage of their income in tax than do people with higher incomes.

Public choice model A model that applies economic analysis to government decision making.

Regressive tax A tax for which people with lower incomes pay a higher percentage of their income in tax than do people with higher incomes.

Rent seeking Attempts by individuals and firms to use government action to make themselves better off at the expense of others.

Tax incidence The actual division of the burden of a tax between buyers and sellers in a market.

Voting paradox The failure of majority voting to always result in consistent choices.

Self-Test

(Answers are provided at the end of the Self-Test.)

Multiple-Choice Questions

1. A key insight of the public choice model is that
   a. most politicians are dishonest.
   b. majority voting will fail to result in policies that represent the median voter.
   c. majority voting may result in inconsistent policy choices.
   d. votes in the U.S. Senate will result in more consistent policy choices than votes taken in the House of Representatives because the Senate has fewer voting members.

2. The voting paradox refers to the proposition that the outcome of a majority vote
   a. will not represent the preferences of the voter who is in the political middle.
   b. will result in consistent choices, but the choices will not be transitive.
   c. will result in rent seeking behavior.
   d. will fail to always result in consistent choices.

3. Kenneth Arrow developed a theorem stating that no system of voting can be devised that will consistently represent the underlying preferences of voters. This is called the Arrow
   a. voting paradox.
   b. median voter theorem.
   c. inconsistency theorem.
   d. impossibility theorem.

4. One way in which the government intervenes in the economy is by establishing a regulatory agency or commission that has authority over a particular industry or product. Because the firms that are regulated have an incentive to influence those actions, regulation may lead to
   a. logrolling, where regulators will support legislation that increases the power of the agency or commission.
   b. rational ignorance, where voters do not have an incentive to become informed about how the agency or commission reaches its regulatory decisions.
   c. the voting paradox.
   d. regulatory capture.

5. Which of the following is an example of logrolling?
   a. Congressman Hacker votes for an increase in the defense budget even though he knows that a majority of other representatives will vote against the increase. Hacker's vote demonstrates to his constituents that he supports national defense.
   b. Congressman Hacker votes in favor of funding for a national park in Congresswoman Sleet's district because Sleet has promised to vote in favor of funding for a new highway in Hacker's district.
   c. Congressman Hacker supports funding in his district for a bridge despite several analyses that show the cost of the bridge is far in excess of the benefits the bridge will provide.
   d. Congressman Hacker votes in favor of a government subsidy program that will benefit farmers because of a strong lobbying effort by farmers in his district.

6. Which of the following statements is correct about the U.S. tax system?
   a. Most taxes are intended to discourage behavior rather than to raise revenue.
   b. The largest source of revenue for the federal government is the corporate income tax.
   c. "Payroll taxes" include Social Security and Medicare taxes.
   d. The sales tax is the largest source of funds for public schools.

7. Refer to the figure below. The figure shows the sources of government revenue. Which segments correspond to corporate income taxes on these pies?

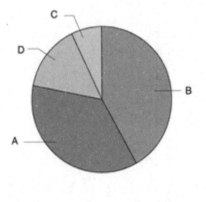 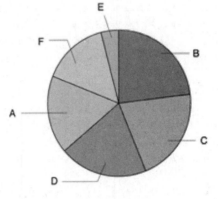

(a) Sources of federal govenment revenue, 2008   (b) Sources of state and local government revenue, 2008

   a. A on the left and B on the right
   b. C on the left and C on the right
   c. D on the left and E on the right
   d. B on the left and D on the right

8. Refer to the figure below. Which letter corresponds to the segment of a pie chart that shows sales taxes?

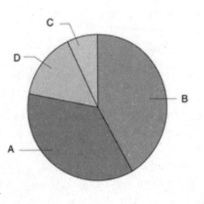

(a) Sources of federal govenment revenue, 2008   (b) Sources of state and local government revenue, 2008

   a. A on the right
   b. B on the right
   c. E on the right
   d. D on the left and E on the right

9. Refer to the figure below. Which letter corresponds to the segment of a pie chart that shows social insurance taxes?

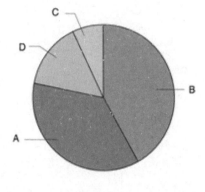

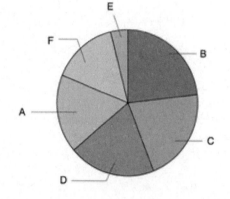

(a) Sources of federal govenment revenue, 2008   (b) Sources of state and local government revenue, 2008

   a. A on the left
   b. C on the right
   c. D on the left
   d. E on the right

10. Which of the following statements about U.S. government revenues is correct?
    a. In 2008, federal revenues amounted to about $2.6 trillion, or $8,300 per person.
    b. Federal revenues as a share of Gross Domestic Product have ranged between 17 and 23 percent for a long time.
    c. The largest source of revenue for state and local government is grants from the federal government intended to pay for federal mandates.
    d. all of the above

11. When is a tax regressive?
    a. when people with lower incomes pay a higher percentage of their income in tax than do people with higher incomes
    b. when people with lower incomes pay a lower percentage of their income in tax than do people with higher incomes
    c. when people with lower incomes pay the same percentage of their income in tax as do people with higher incomes
    d. when people who are poorer pay lower taxes and people who are richer pay higher taxes

12. When is a tax progressive?
    a. when people with lower incomes pay a higher percentage of their income in tax than do people with higher incomes
    b. when people with lower incomes pay a lower percentage of their income in tax than do people with higher incomes
    c. when people with lower incomes pay the same percentage of their income in tax as do people with higher incomes
    d. when people who are poorer pay lower taxes and people who are richer pay higher taxes

13. Which of the following types of tax is the federal income tax?
    a. a progressive tax
    b. a regressive tax
    c. a proportional tax
    d. none of the above

14. Which of the following does a tax rate refer to?
    a. a percentage of income
    b. a range of income
    c. an income group
    d. the portion of income earned that is exempt from taxes

15. As presented in the text, how is the federal income tax structured?
    a. All taxpayers pay the same tax rate. The dollar amount of the tax is equal to this tax rate times their taxable income.
    b. The rate at which income is taxed increases as income increases. Additional amounts of income are taxed at ever greater rates.
    c. The rate at which income is taxed decreases as income increases. Additional amounts of income are taxed at ever lower rates.
    d. Most taxpayers pay taxes only on a portion of their incomes, not on their entire incomes.

16. Refer to the table below. Based on the information in the table, how much in federal income taxes will someone owe who earns $150,000?

INCOME	TAX RATE
$0–$7,825	10%
$7,826–$31,850	15
$31,851–$77,100	25
$77,101–$160,850	28
$160,851–$349,700	33
Over $349,70	35

    a. $36,111
    b. $42,000
    c. $49,500
    d. $14,653

17. Which of the following groups pays the most in federal taxes?
    a. the lowest 20 percent of income earners
    b. the third highest 20 percent of income earners
    c. the fourth highest 20 percent of income earners
    d. the top 20 percent of income earners

18. Which of the following groups bears a greater share of all the federal taxes paid?
    a. the 40 percent of taxpayers with the lowest incomes
    b. the 20 percent of taxpayers with the lowest incomes
    c. the 20 percent of taxpayers with the highest incomes
    d. None of the above; in the United States, everyone pays the same portion of the total taxes paid.

19. Which of the following is the average tax rate?
    a. the fraction of each additional dollar of income that must be paid in taxes
    b. the total tax paid divided by total income
    c. the income range within which a tax rate applies
    d. the tax rate paid by the average taxpayer

20. If the last dollar of income earned by individuals with the highest incomes is taxed at a rate that is less than the average tax rate, which of the following is correct?
    a. The marginal tax rate is equal to the average tax rate.
    b. The income tax is a progressive income tax.
    c. The income tax is a regressive income tax.
    d. The individuals with the highest incomes will pay less in taxes than those with the lowest incomes.

21. Which of the following tax rates is a better indicator of people's willingness to work, save, and invest?
    a. the average tax rate
    b. the marginal tax rate
    c. The average and the marginal tax rates are equally good indicators.
    d. Neither the average tax rate nor the marginal tax rate affects those decisions.

22. Which of the following statements is correct?
    a. The individual income tax is progressive but the corporate income tax is regressive.
    b. Most corporations are taxed at the highest tax rate of 35 percent.
    c. The corporate income tax eliminates the double taxation of dividends.
    d. all of the above

23. Refer to the graph below. Which of the following represents the government's revenue from a tax?

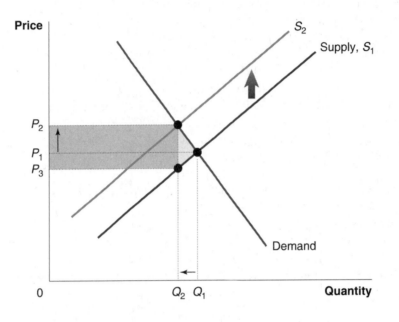

    a.   the triangular area to the right of the shaded rectangle
    b.   the shaded rectangle
    c.   the arrow showing an increase in price, from P_1 to P_2
    d.   the arrow showing a decrease in quantity, from Q_1 to Q_2

24. Refer to the graph below. Which of the following represents the excess burden of the tax?

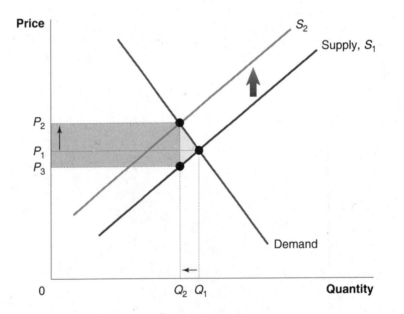

    a.   the triangular area to the right of the shaded rectangle
    b.   the shaded rectangle
    c.   the arrow showing an increase in price, from P_1 to P_2
    d.   the arrow showing a decrease in quantity, from Q_1 to Q_2

25. Which term is given to a tax that imposes a small excess burden relative to the revenue it raises?
    a. fair
    b. efficient
    c. vertically equitable
    d. horizontally equitable

26. Which of the following is a tax associated with a high deadweight loss?
    a. a tax on leisure
    b. a tax on cigarettes
    c. a tax on interest earned from saving
    d. all of the above

27. If a CD offers a 3 percent interest rate and the interest is subject to a tax rate of 33 percent, what is the after-tax return on the investment in the CD?
    a. 1 percent
    b. 2 percent
    c. 4 percent
    d. −30 percent

28. Which of the following is an accurate statement associated with the debate over whether the United States should switch from an income tax to a consumption tax?
    a. Under a consumption tax, present consumption would be taxed more favorably than future consumption.
    b. A better measure of well-being is income rather than consumption.
    c. Individuals whose savings are mainly in IRAs or 401(k) plans are already in effect paying consumption taxes rather than income taxes.
    d. all of the above

29. Which term below is associated with raising more taxes from people with high incomes than from people with low incomes?
    a. horizontal equity
    b. vertical equity
    c. benefits received principle
    d. tax incidence

30. Which of the following represents the horizontal-equity principle of taxation?
    a. People in the same economic situation should be treated equally.
    b. Two people with the same income receive equal utility from consumption.
    c. A greater share of the tax burden should be borne by people who have a greater ability to pay.
    d. People who receive the benefits from a government program should pay the taxes that support that program.

31. Why is a sales tax inconsistent with the ability-to-pay principle?
    a. A sales tax does not treat two people who are in the same economic situation equally.
    b. The revenue from a sales tax is used to benefit people who don't pay the tax.
    c. Poorer people tend to spend a larger fraction of their income than do richer people.
    d. Sales taxes are progressive.

32. Refer to the graph below. When do consumers bear more of the burden of a tax?

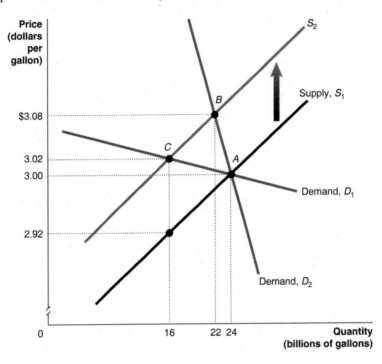

a. when demand is D_1
b. when demand is D_2
c. The tax burden to consumers is identical for both demand curves.
d. when the elasticity of supply is very small

33. What name is given to the actual division of the burden of a tax between buyers and sellers in a market?
a. horizontal equity
b. vertical equity
c. tax incidence
d. the benefits-received principle

34. Refer to the graph below. In which case do firms end up paying the majority of the tax?

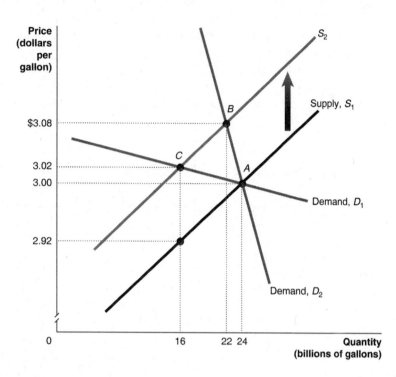

a. when demand is D_1
b. when demand is D_2
c. when supply is S_1
d. when the excess burden is small

35. Which of the following is true about the distribution of income in the United States over time?
    a. Over time, there has been a dramatic decline in income inequality.
    b. Over time, there has been a dramatic increase in income inequality.
    c. Over time, there have been no dramatic changes in the distribution of income.
    d. Over time, the distribution of income has been very volatile, with both large increases and large declines in income equality.

36. What do you call the level of annual income equal to three times the amount necessary to purchase the minimum quantity of food required for adequate nutrition?
    a. the poverty rate
    b. the poverty line
    c. the Lorenz curve
    d. the Gini coefficient

37. Which of the following is a true statement about the poverty rate in the United States?
    a. Over the last 30 years, the poverty rate has fluctuated between 11 and 15 percent of the population.
    b. Over the last 30 years, the poverty rate declined substantially, from 35 percent to 9 percent.
    c. The poverty rate increased, from 16 percent in 1970 to over 23 percent in 2008.
    d. Over the last 30 years, the poverty rate has remained constant at about 4 percent of the population.

38. Which of the following statements about poverty in the United States is correct?
    a. Individuals who are less productive or who help to produce goods and services that can be sold for only a low price will earn lower incomes.
    b. Ownership of capital is more equally distributed than income earned from labor.
    c. Poverty in the United States has increased dramatically in the last 20 years.
    d. all of the above

39. One of the following factors *does not* appear to contribute to income inequality. Which one?
    a. expanding international trade
    b. technological change
    c. changes in tax rates
    d. None of the above; all of the above factors contribute to income inequality.

40. Refer to the graph below. Which of these curves shows a more unequal distribution of income?

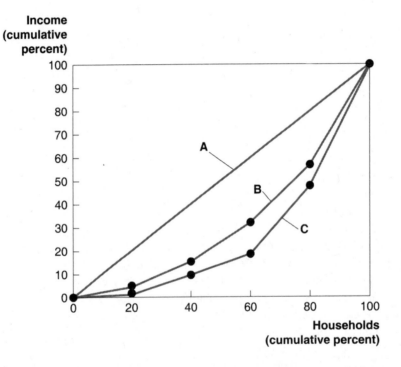

    a. A
    b. B
    c. C
    d. None of the above; the distribution of income is the same along all three curves.

41. Refer to the graph below. When the income distribution is described by the line labeled A, what is the value of the Gini coefficient?

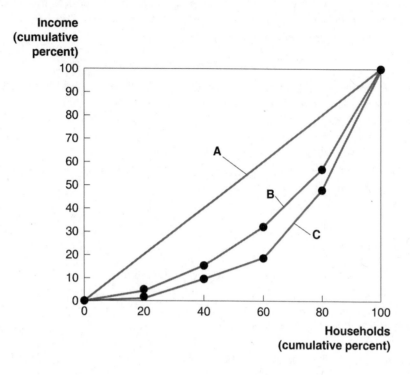

a. zero
b. one
c. a value between zero and one
d. 45

42. What do statistics on income mobility in the United States show?
    a. Over time, there is very little income mobility.
    b. Over time, there is significant income mobility.
    c. Over time, income mobility has varied. Sometimes income mobility is significant and other times it is almost nonexistent.
    d. There are no studies on income mobility because income mobility is impossible to measure.

43. Which of the following statements about poverty in the United States is correct?
    a. The people who fall into poverty in any one year are likely to remain in poverty for many years.
    b. If 10 percent of the population is in poverty in a given year, the same 10 percent is likely to be in poverty in the next ten years.
    c. The number of people who remain in poverty for many years is much smaller than the number who are in poverty during any one year.
    d. none of the above

44. Which of the following statements about the effect of taxes and transfers on income distribution is correct?
    a. The Social Security system has failed to reduce poverty among people older than 65.
    b. The distribution of income worsens when we take transfer payments into account.
    c. Income after taxes is more equally distributed than income before taxes.
    d. all of the above

45. Which of the following statements about the distribution of income around the world is correct?
    a. The distribution of income in the United States is more equal than in some moderate-income countries, such as Brazil and Chile.
    b. The United States has the most unequal distribution of income of any high-income country in the world.
    c. The U.S. distribution of income is significantly less equal than some high-income countries, such as Norway and Japan.
    d. all of the above

Short Answer Questions

1. In the song "Taxman," George Harrison of The Beatles wrote this line:

   Let me tell you how it will be;
   There's one for you, nineteen for me

   What marginal tax rate does this imply? What percentage of George Harrison's total income would be paid in taxes at this tax rate?

   _____

   _____

   _____

   _____

   _____

2. U.S. taxpayers may reduce their federal income tax liability by deducting the amount they pay for mortgage interest and real estate taxes on their homes. If these deductions were eliminated, how would this affect the housing market?

   _____

   _____

   _____

   _____

   _____

   _____

3. Investment in research and capital are important means for less developed countries to increase their rates of economic growth. To encourage saving and investment, should a less developed country use a consumption tax rather than an income tax to raise revenue needed for government expenditures?

_____

_____

_____

_____

4. If the current federal income tax system was replaced by a consumption tax, what impact would this have on the demand for accountants and lawyers and firms who assist taxpayers to complete their tax forms?

_____

_____

_____

5. A 2001 study of the impact of cigarette prices on smoking found that the price elasticity of demand for high school smokers was about −1.0. This compares to an estimated price elasticity of demand for adults of about −0.4. Assume that the overall elasticity is −0.8. Who would bear the greater burden—consumers or producers—of a 10 percent increase in the price of cigarettes as a result of a federal excise tax increase?

Source: H. Ross and F. Chaloupka, "The Effect of Cigarette Prices on Youth Smoking," http://repositories.cdlib.org/tc/reports/YO4.

_____

_____

_____

_____

True/False Questions

T F 1. In the United States, income after taxes is more equally distributed than income before taxes.

T F 2. From 1970 to 2000, the poverty rate in Sub-Saharan Africa and south Asia declined but rose in Latin America.

T F 3. The closer the value of the Gini coefficient is to 1, the more unequal the distribution of income.

T F 4. Reductions in marginal tax rates in the United States from the 1950s to the 1990s have led to an increase in the degree of income inequality.

T F 5. Most economists favor increasing the corporate income tax because it is the most efficient tax imposed by the federal government.

T F 6. A consumption tax imposes the same tax rate on income spent and saved.

T F 7. The ability-to-pay principle states that people who receive benefits from a particular government program should pay for that program.

T F 8. Differences in tax rates on work explain much of the difference in the average annual number of hours worked in Europe and the United States.

T F 9. A progressive income tax system is consistent with the ability-to-pay principle of taxation.

T F 10. An excise tax is a tax imposed on the sale of a specific good.

T F 11. In the United States, sales taxes and excise taxes are the main sources of funds for public schools.

T F 12. Medicaid is a federally funded program that provides medical assistance to the elderly.

T F 13. The public choice model can be used to conclude that Congress should abolish the Food and Drug Administration and the Federal Trade Commission.

T F 14. The Arrow impossibility theorem is used to explain why logrolling and rational ignorance help explain why rent-seeking makes efficient government regulation impossible.

T F 15. In a regressive income tax system, the marginal tax rate rises as income rises.

Answers to the Self-Test

Multiple-Choice Questions

Question	Response	Comment
1	c	This result is known as the voting paradox. See pages 580–581 in the textbook.
2	d	The voting paradox refers to the failure of majority voting to always result in consistent choices.
3	d	See the discussion of the Arrow impossibility theorem on page 581 in the textbook.
4	d	Regulatory capture occurs in extreme cases where the influence of regulated firms leads the agency to make decisions that are not in the public interest. Some economists use the now-abolished Interstate Commerce Commission as an example of regulatory capture.
5	b	Logrolling occurs when a member of Congress votes to approve a bill in exchange for favorable votes from other members of Congress on other bills.
6	c	See the section "The Tax System," which begins on page 584 in the textbook.
7	c	Corporate income taxes amount to 11 percent of federal tax receipts and 2.5 percent of state tax receipts in 2008. Refer to Figure 18-2 in the textbook.
8	b	Sales taxes are collected only by state and local governments. They are the largest source of revenue for state and local governments.
9	a	Social insurance taxes comprised 38 percent of federal government revenue in 2008.
10	d	Over the past 40 years, federal revenues as a share of Gross Domestic Product have remained in a fairly narrow range between 17 and 23 percent. The largest source of revenue for state and local government is grants from the federal government. These grants are intended, in part, to pay for programs that the federal government requires state and local governments to carry out. These programs are often called *federal mandates*.
11	a	A tax is regressive if people with lower incomes pay a higher percentage of their

income in tax than do people with higher incomes.

12   b   A tax is progressive if people with lower incomes pay a lower percentage of their income in tax than do people with higher incomes.

13   a   As income rises, tax rates on additional income also rise.

14   a   A *tax rate* is the percentage of income paid in taxes. A *tax bracket* refers to the income range within which a tax rate applies.

15   b   Federal income taxes are paid according to predetermined tax brackets, or income ranges. The rate at which income is taxed increases as additional income moves taxpayers into higher brackets.

16   a   Her first $7,825 of income is in the 10 percent bracket, so she pays $782.50 on this income. Her next $24,025 of income is in the 15 percent bracket, so she pays $3,603.75 on this income. Her next $45,250 of income is in the 25 percent bracket, so she pays $11,312.50 on this income. Her last $72,900 of income is in the 28 percent bracket, so she pays $20,412, which brings her total federal income tax bill to $36,110.75.

17   d   The highest 20 percent of income earners pay 64 percent of total federal taxes. Refer to Making the Connection, "Which Groups Pay the Most in Federal Taxes?" on page 587 in the textbook.

18   c   The 40 percent of taxpayers with the lowest incomes pay only about 4 percent of all federal taxes, while the 20 percent with the highest incomes pay about two-thirds of all federal taxes.

19   b   The fraction of each additional dollar of income that must be paid in taxes is called the marginal tax rate. The average tax rate is the total tax paid divided by total income.

20   c   In a regressive income tax system, people with lower incomes pay a higher percentage of their income in tax than do people with higher incomes. This means that the last dollar earned by people with the highest incomes will be taxed at a lower rate than the average tax rate.

21   b   When policymakers consider a change in tax policy, they should focus on the marginal tax rate rather than the average tax rate, because the marginal tax rate tells them how a change in a tax will affect people's willingness to work, save, and invest.

22   b   Like the individual income tax, the corporate income tax is progressive, with the lowest tax rate being 15 percent and the highest being 35 percent. Unlike the personal income tax, however, most corporations are in the 35 percent tax bracket. The corporate income tax "double taxes" earnings on individual shareholders' investments in corporations.

23   b   The government collects tax revenue equal to the tax per unit multiplied by the number of units sold. The shaded rectangle in the figure represents the government's tax revenue.

24   a   The deadweight loss from the tax is shown in the figure by the triangular area to the right of the shaded rectangle. The deadweight loss from a tax is referred to as the *excess burden* of the tax.

25   b   A tax is efficient if it imposes a small excess burden relative to the tax revenue it raises.

26   c   Economists argue that the government should reduce its reliance on taxes that have a high deadweight loss relative to the revenue raised. Taxes on income from saving are an example of such a reform because savings often come from income already taxed once.

27   b   The after-tax return is 3 percent $\times (1 - 0.33) = 2$ percent.

28	c	Because the income tax taxes interest and other returns to saving, it taxes *future* consumption more heavily than *present* consumption. Individuals whose savings are mainly in retirement accounts are, in effect, already paying a consumption tax rather than an income tax.
29	b	Raising more taxes from people with high incomes than from people with low incomes is sometimes referred to as *vertical equity*.
30	a	Under the horizontal-equity principle, people in the same economic situation should be treated equally.
31	c	The sales tax is not consistent with the ability-to-pay principle because poorer people tend to spend a larger fraction of their income than richer people. As a result, poorer people will pay a greater fraction of their income in sales taxes than will richer people.
32	b	D_2 is a relatively inelastic demand curve. When the elasticity of demand for a product is smaller than the elasticity of supply, consumers pay the majority of the tax on the product.
33	c	The actual division of the burden of a tax between buyers and sellers in a market is referred to as tax incidence.
34	a	When demand is more elastic, as with demand curve D_1, firms end up paying the majority of the tax. When demand is less elastic, as with demand curve D_2, consumers end up paying the majority of the tax.
35	c	Over time there have not been dramatic changes in distribution of income. There was some decline in inequality from 1936 to 1980, followed by some increase in inequality from 1980 to today.
36	b	The poverty line is the level of annual income equal to three times the amount necessary to purchase the minimal quantity of food required for adequate nutrition. The poverty rate is the percentage of the population that is poor, according to the definition of the poverty line.
37	a	Between 1960 and 1973, the poverty rate declined by half, falling from 22 percent of the population to 11 percent. In the past 30 years, however, the poverty rate has declined very little. Over this time, the poverty rate has fluctuated between 11 percent and 15 percent of the population.
38	a	People who are less productive, or who help to produce goods and services that can be sold only for a low price, will earn lower incomes.
39	c	Tax rates have changed dramatically, but the distribution of income has changed relatively little, so it seems unlikely that changes in tax rates have had a large impact on the distribution of income.
40	c	Because this curve is farthest away from the line of perfect equality (A), it shows a less equally distributed income than lines A or B.
41	a	If the income distribution were perfectly equal, the Lorenz curve would be the same as the line of perfect income equality, area A would be zero, and so would the Gini coefficient. If the income distribution were perfectly unequal, the Gini coefficient would equal one. Therefore, the greater the degree of income inequality, the greater the value of the Gini coefficient.
42	b	The study illustrated in the textbook indicates that there is significant income mobility in the United States over time.
43	c	Poverty remains a problem in the United States, but the number of people who remain in poverty for many years is much smaller than the number that are in poverty during any one year.
44	c	We have seen that at the federal level taxes are progressive, meaning that high income people pay a larger share of their incomes in taxes than do low income people. Therefore, income remaining after taxes is more equally distributed than

income before taxes.

45   d   The distribution of income in the United States is more equal than some moderate-income countries, such as Brazil and Chile, but less equal than other moderate-income countries, such as Thailand. The United States has the most unequal distribution of income of any high-income country in the world.

Short Answer Responses

1. Harrison's song was a reaction to the marginal tax rates that had been levied on taxpayers in the highest tax brackets (those with the highest incomes) in Great Britain in the 1960s. The song implies that the government's marginal tax rate was 95 percent (£19 of each £20 of income was taxed). Although this rate applies to the next, or last, British pound Harrison earned, one cannot determine the percentage of total income he paid in taxes—his average tax rate—because different marginal tax rates apply to different levels of income.

2. The elimination of these deductions would increase the price of home ownership. The quantity demanded of single-family houses would fall as some people who would have purchased a home look for other forms of shelter (for example, an apartment or moving in with relatives). The increase in demand for rental units should raise rents in the short run. In the long run, there will likely be increased construction of rental units and some decline in the construction of new single family homes. Proposals to eliminate these deductions would face strong opposition from home owners and their elected representatives. Those who purchased homes in the past in anticipation of receiving these deductions would argue their elimination would unfairly punish them by increasing their tax liability and reducing the market value of their homes. (Most current proposals for eliminating the mortgage interest deduction include a clause that would allow holders of existing mortgages to continue to deduct the interest.)

3. It is very difficult for people from poor countries to reduce their consumption in order to increase saving. Most of their income is spent on food, clothing, shelter, and other necessities. A consumption tax would be more effective in increasing saving among high income earners in developed countries.

4. There would be a large decrease in the demand for tax lawyers and accountants. H&R Block, the largest tax service firm in the United States, had sales of over $4 billion in 2008. Most of Block's employees, along with thousands of others who provide income tax assistance to individuals, would have to find other work to do. Income tax assistance can be considered a "regrettable necessity." Those made unemployed by the elimination of the income tax would be free to produce other goods and services which would (eventually) result in a net benefit to the U.S. economy.

5. The answer to this question depends on the elasticity of supply of cigarettes. Taking the absolute value of the demand elasticity, if the elasticity of supply is less than 0.8, smokers would bear the greater burden of the price increase. If the elasticity of supply is less than 0.8, smokers would bear the greater burden of the price increase. In response to the price increase, teenage smokers would reduce their consumption of cigarettes more than adults; teenagers are less likely to be addicted to nicotine and have lower average incomes than adults.

True/False Answers

1. T   This is due to the progressivity of the federal income tax and the income received from Social Security payments and other government transfer payments.

2. F   The poverty rate in Asia and Latin America fell, but rose in Sub-Saharan Africa due to differences in rates of economic growth.

3. T   See the section "Income Distribution and Poverty" beginning on page 595 of the textbook.

4. F   The top marginal tax rate declined from 91 percent in the 1950s to 35 percent in 2009, but the distribution of income has changed only slightly.

5. F   The corporate income tax is one of the least efficient federal taxes. Many economists support corporate income tax reform.

6. F   A consumption tax applies only to income spent, not income saved.

7. F   This is a statement of the benefits-received principle.

8. T   This is a conclusion reached by Edward Prescott. See the section "Evaluating Taxes" beginning on page 589 in the textbook.

9. T   See the section "Evaluating Taxes" beginning on page 589 in the textbook.

10. T   See the section "The Tax System" beginning on page 584 in the textbook.

11. F   The property tax is the major source of funds for public schools.

12. F   Medicaid provides health care to poor people. Medicare helps to pay the medical expenses of people over age 65.

13. F   Most economists believe that these agencies can serve a useful purpose, but the public choice model helps us to understand that government regulation imposes costs on consumers as well as provides benefits.

14. F   The Arrow impossibility theorem shows how no system of voting can be devised that will consistently represent the underlying preferences of voters.

15. F   Marginal tax rates rise with income in a progressive income tax system.